Sharks Over China

Also by Carl Molesworth

Wing to Wing: Air Combat in China, 1943–45

Gabby: A Fighter Pilot's Life (with Francis S. Gabreski)

Sharks Over China

The 23rd Fighter Group in World War II

Carl Molesworth

BRASSEY'S
Washington

First paperback edition 1999

Library of Congress Cataloging-in-Publication Data
Molesworth, Carl.
        Sharks over China: the 23rd Fighter Group in World War II / Carl Molesworth.
        p.   cm.
    Includes bibliographical references and index.
    1. United States. Army Air Forces. Fighter Group, 23rd—History. 2. World War, 1939–1945—Aerial operations, American. 3. World War, 1939–1945—Campaigns—China. I. Title.
D790.M563   1994
940.54'4973—dc20   94–1558
                                                                                   CIP

        ISBN 1-57488-225-2 (alk.paper)

Printed in Canada on acid-free paper that meets the American National Standards Institute Z39-48 Standard.

Brassey's
22883 Quicksilver Drive
Dulles, Virginia 20166

10   9   8   7   6   5   4   3   2   1

TO VIRGINIA E. MOLESWORTH
AND CARLTON MOLESWORTH, JR.,
MY MOTHER AND FATHER

Contents

Foreword

The 23rd Fighter Group of the United States Army Air Force was activated in Kunming, China, on the Fourth of July 1942 and went into combat against the Japanese immediately. This was more than unusual; it was unique.

There was no gradual assimilation and shakedown of equipment. Neither was there a period of unit training in the States or anywhere else. The 23rd inherited the planes and other matériel assets of the American Volunteer Group (AVG, or "Flying Tigers") and "hit the ground running."

The 23rd also inherited the most important factor for ensuring early success. The AVG was deactivated the same day as the 23rd's activation, and about twenty key AVG people volunteered for induction in the U.S. military as commissioned and noncommissioned officers and to serve in the group. These were pilots, mechanics, armorers, and communicators—all seasoned combat veterans. Three outstanding former leaders were made squadron commanders. Collectively, these men transcended "invaluable"; they were a godsend.

The positive spirit, hard work, and innovative practices of the Flying Tigers continued undiminished as a hallmark of the new 23rd. These were also godsends, for everything else—fuel, ammunition, transportation, ground handling equipment, medical supplies, communication systems and equipment, navigation aids, and maintenance facilities and supplies—was in short supply.

Two of the shortages, communication systems and navigation aids, deserve special mention. The former was plagued by unreliable equipment and weather degradations. The latter was essentially nonexistent, unless you count landmarks such as rivers and a few railroads and inaccurate maps. One of the most astounding aspects of my experience in China, which has seemed ever more miraculous to me as the years have passed, is that we accomplished what we did without greater losses and fewer successes. We did have a Chinese-manned ground observer net that functioned well for air raid warning purposes, but as a navigation direction-finding system for lost pilots, it was only marginally effective.

The original mission of the 23rd Fighter Group was to defend the eastern terminus of the airlift route into China. This meant principally Kunming and a few outlying airfields and facilities in Yunnan

Province. Fortunately, instructions did not specify how we were supposed to do that. Accordingly, Maj. Gen. Claire Lee Chennault, commander of the China Air Task Force and later of the Fourteenth Air Force, adopted a commensurately simple operations policy. He established a threshold of fuel, ammunition, and in-commission aircraft below which his only initial bomber force (the 11th Bomb Squadron with B-25s) would stand down, and the fighter forces would stand defensive ground alert. It worked well, and the threshold was updated periodically.

Offensive operations were well planned and covered a large area. In the beginning we had four good operating bases besides Kunming, one to the west and three to the east. They constituted an excellent matrix from which we could hit targets with significant force in a wide ring stretching from Hankow in the northeast through the Nanchang rice belt to Canton and Hong Kong in the southeast and on to Haiphong, Indo-China (now Vietnam), in the south, thence to air bases in Burma and traffic along the Burma Road. This base structure, wisely used, was a cardinal asset for doing wide-ranging damage to Japanese forces with our small numbers of limited-range aircraft.

Contrary to much that has been reported over the years, additional circumstances were significantly more favorable (or less unfavorable) than commonly believed. We did not live in Waldorf-Astoria style, but we lived quite well. Housing and food were provided by the Chinese, and it was, respectively, adequate and nourishing with few exceptions. To the best of my knowledge, nobody suffered from hunger or malnutrition, and in some cases cooks took special pains to enhance the palatability of their dishes. There was a cook at Lingling, for instance, who made delicious lemon pies. I do not know how he did it without lemons, but his pies were so good that I stopped there for lunch whenever possible.

Another circumstance that has been exaggerated was the weather. It was not the best in the world but not the worst, either. Thunderstorms, tornadoes, severe icing, and similar phenomena were rare. Conditions in south-central China were predominantly cloudy and rainy and were distinct hazards to navigation without radio aids. But during my seventeen months in the theater I never encountered a thunderstorm or experienced clear wing ice.

The centerpiece of strength, iron will, and unswerving resolve throughout the years of 23rd Fighter Group activity in China was General Chennault. He was a tactical mentor and genius who had the uncanny penchant for predicting what the Japanese were going to do the next day, the next week, and the next month. He understood their tactics and their regimentations in detail, and he knew where their forces were weak and what course of action they would likely take if we dealt a severe blow to particular targets. Accordingly, the commanders of all his combat forces, which began to grow significantly in 1944, were singularly dependent on his leadership and his sources of intelligence. These sources were undoubtedly extensive, but for obvious reasons, some were probably never revealed to any of us. All in all, he was a revered boss.

The group's performance remained high right to the end of World War II. Tactics, methodologies, and targeting changed dramatically as Japanese defeats mounted throughout the Pacific and their air power in China dwindled. But the 23rd's spirit, inherited from its Flying Tiger predecessors, prevailed throughout the long period of combat. It is legendary stuff and a tribute to all who served in the group.

Since deactivation in 1946, the group has been reactivated as the 23rd Fighter Wing three times. These ups and downs were keyed to the roller-coaster budget cycles that we live with. The 23rd's A-10 fighter-bombers did a stellar job in 1991 during Operation Desert Storm under the command of Col. David Sawyer, and although the last deactivation occurred thereafter because of large force reductions, the wing was immediately reactivated at Pope Air Force Base, North Carolina, under Brig. Gen. Bobby Floyd.

So the banner lives on! From the Flying Tigers in Burma to the 23rd Fighter Group in China to the 23rd Wing in the Persian Gulf, the unit has signified exemplary action in the finest traditions of U.S. military air power.

Bruce K. Holloway
General, USAF (Retired)

Acknowledgments

It is difficult for me to say when I started working on *Sharks over China*. It could go back to my earliest memories of my mother telling me stories about her childhood spent in China during the 1920s. Later, the Sundays I spent on the airports and open fields of western Maryland retrieving my father's free-flight model airplanes sparked a lifelong interest in aviation. The first picture I ever saw of a P-40 with a fearsome shark's mouth and eye painted on the nose grabbed my fascination, and it never has let go.

But it was in an office at the National Air and Space Museum nearly fifteen years ago that this project actually began to take form. I had come to the museum to interview its then-assistant director for aeronautics, fighter ace Don Lopez, for a magazine article. This friendly, intelligent man not only answered my questions and spun tales about his experiences flying in China during World War II, but he also encouraged me to look further into the history of the air war in China. In the years since then, Don has been a steady source of material, advice, and inspiration. He provided a key list of addresses I needed to begin research on my first book, *Wing to Wing*, and he graciously wrote a statement for its jacket.

My longtime goal was to write a book about the 23rd Fighter Group, the highest-scoring fighter unit in the China-Burma-India theater during World War II. So when I told Don in 1991 that I was working on a history of his China outfit, Don invited me to a group reunion so I could get to know more of the men who served in the fabled 23rd.

At that reunion I was fortunate to meet nearly all of the surviving top aces and commanders who had served in the 23rd Fighter Group during World War II. Three who stood out and made great contributions to this book were Bruce Holloway, Bob Liles, and Tex Hill.

There are many others who have contributed as well. Some answered my requests for information in great detail. Bill Hawkins sat down in front of a video camera and told his stories. Jack Best, Ed Cassada, Ray Crowell, and Dick Lee sent me long tape recordings. Tex Hill and John Stewart submitted to lengthy phone interviews. Others sent detailed letters and stacks of their precious photographs. Some could send only a short note or a single snapshot.

Several surviving family members sent material, too. I appreciate everyone who answered my letters, even those who could contribute nothing at all. Each of the following contributors made my job a little easier; all I had to do was fit the pieces together.

23rd Fighter Group headquarters: Father Albert J. Buckley, David L. ("Tex") Hill, Bruce K. Holloway, Charles H. Older, Edward F. Rector, and Norbert C. Treacy.

16th Fighter Squadron: George F. Aldridge, George R. Barnes, Jack R. Best, Dale R. Broom, David J. Brown, Edgar H. Cassada, Dallas Clinger, Harvey G. Elling, William B. Evans, Vernon J. Henderson, Richard C. Lee, Robert L. Liles, Ward McMillen, Jack Muller, Robert A. O'Neill, Carter K. Sorenson, Al Sorrentino, Charles T. Urquhart, and Heath H. Wayne.

74th Fighter Squadron: Theodore R. Adams, Robert L. Baillew, Oren Bates, Jack E. Binkerd, Eugene R. Burkett, Henry L. Cohen, John C. Conn, Charles E. Cook Jr., James Crawford, Arthur W. Cruikshank Jr., Phillip A. Dial, Bernard Fudge Jr., Hubert Fyke, John Gannon, Alfred D. Griffy, William B. Hawkins, Charles W. Hoffman, Dan Hough, Craig M. Kift, Luther C. Kissick Jr., Leon Klesman, Nimrod W. E. Long, Clark P. Manning, Fred L. Meyer, Robert L. Milks, John Millonig, William Parker, James R. Pugh, Robert L. Sheldon, Robert T. Smith, Marshall B. Stout, Wade Terry, and John W. Wheeler.

75th Fighter Squadron: Nicholas Afendoulis, John R. Alison, Robert F. Barnes, Christopher S. Barrett, Mervin E. Beard, Hollis Blackstone, Edward J. Bollen, George R. Casey, Morton J. Cohen, Ellsworth Curran, Adrian De Kraker, Oswin H. Elker, Harold J. Freeman, William F. Gaines, Charles R. Glanville, Art Goodworth, Joseph H. Griffin, William Grosvenor Jr., William M. Harris, George Herndon, Donald B. Hyatt, Everett W. Hyatt, H. L. Kirkpatrick, Dennis C. Laws, James L. Lee, Myron D. Levy, Lyndon R. Lewis, Wallace H. Little, Philip C. Loofbourrow, Donald S. Lopez, Forrest F. Parham, Robert S. Peterson, Donald L. Quigley, Elmer W. Richardson, Florentino Rodrigues, John D. Rosenbaum, Joe H. Schmidt, Curtis L. Scoville, Wiltz P. Segura, Clyde B. Slocumb, Donald Stivers, James M. Taylor, Floyd Testa, Donald B. Van Cleve, and Louis W. Weber.

76th Fighter Squadron: Arthur Athanas, Ivan Ball, Fausty Bartolini, Harold A. Bedient, Joel E. Beezley, Glen E. Beneda, Stephen J. Bonner Jr., Richard F. Breder, Charles A. Breingan, Judson D. Bullard Jr., Robert W. Carner, Edward M. Collis, Willard M. Dahlberg, Jerome P. Ellis, Dan Fread, Victor G. Gehlhausen, Byron H. Gilmore, Rex Gouger, Burton Greenberg, Hugh L. Jenkins, William R. Johnston, Eugene King, Vernon J. Kramer, Otis

Law, Edward H. Lawman Jr., Albert J. Lecce, George L. Mackie, Mortimer D. Marks, Lyman F. Martin, Richard M. Perkins, Price J. Perrill, William H. Quimby Jr., Lester A. Reeves Jr., Donald L. Scott, Myron R. Sees, Robert H. Serra, George H. Spencer, John S. Stewart, Edward Tavares, Richard J. Templeton, Benjamin R. Thompson, Arthur E. Waite, William T. Watt, Raymond S. Weiss, and James M. Williams.

118th Tactical Reconnaissance Squadron: Aldo E. Cardelli, Richard P. Chouinard, Normand C. Collette, Raymond A. Crowell, Raymond V. Darby, Henry F. Davis Jr., Glenn J. Geyer, George H. Greene Jr., John F. Grover, Kenneth R. Guy, Wayne G. Johnson, Marvin Lubner, Russell E. Packard, Raymond J. Parenteau, Max L. Parnell, Everson F. Pearsall, Berthold H. Peterson, Ronald M. Phillips, Frederick J. Poats, Ralph C. Schindler, Seymour R. Singer, Jack C. Smith, Richard E. Stutzman, Oran S. Watts, and Henry R. Wilk.

449th Fighter Squadron: Billie M. Beardsley, Sam L. Palmer, Seymour D. Singer, David E. Tribby, and David A. Williams.

Family members: Betty J. Anderson, Mrs. James Bosserman, Robert M. Fay, Lenora (Distefano) Greenland, Bruce R. Griffith, George G. Hazlett, Eleanor A. Lewis, Alene Nislar, Kathleen J. Shapou, Marguerite Simpson, Wanda Steidle, Jane Stoneham, Peggy Vincent, and Calvin Yoh.

Others who assisted: Fred Charlton, Jack Cook, John Foster, Fred Holderith, Steve Muth, Lester Pagliuso, Ed Penick, Dwayne Tabatt, and Dave Warren.

Finally, I would like to thank my wife, Kris, and daughter, Claire, for their help, support, and patience during the long months of research and writing that went into this book.

Carl Molesworth
Mount Vernon, Washington

CHINA 1942-45

⊙ Airbases used by the 23rd Fighter Group

0 ——————— 200
Scale in miles

Peiping

Yellow River

Yellow River

Suchow

Nanking

Shanghai

Kingmen

Yangtze River

Hangchow

Chengtu • Liangshan ⊙

Ichang

Enshih

Chungking

Hankow

Paliuchi ⊙ Kiukiang

Tungting Lake

Poyang Lake

Lishui

Changteh

Yochow

Changsha

Nanchang

Chihkiang

Hengyang

Kienow

Yangtze River

INDIA

Chabua •

Laohwangping ⊙

Lake Tali

Tsingchen ⊙

Lingling ⊙

Suichwan ⊙

Foochow

Myitkyina •

Yunnanyi ⊙ Chanyi ⊙ Tushan

Hsiang River

Kanchow

Changting

Tengchung •

Paoshan

Kunming ⊙ Luliang

Kweilin

Namyung ⊙

Amoy

• Shinchiku

Lungling •

Chengkung ⊙

**FORMOSA
ISLAND**

Lashio •

Mengtze ⊙

Liuchow

Nanning

Tanchuk

West River

Canton

Swatow

• Mandalay

Lao Kay

Pakhoi

Kowloon

Hanoi

Hong Kong

**FRENCH
INDOCHINA**

Haiphong

Mon Kay

Fort Bayard

BURMA

*GULF OF
TONKIN*

HAINAN ISLAND

SOUTH CHINA SEA

1

Desperate Days

It was still dark when a houseboy shook Maj. Edward F. Rector awake in the hostel at Hengyang, China. The twenty-five-year-old fighter pilot rubbed the sleep from his eyes, dressed quickly, and made his way downstairs to the tree-lined courtyard in front of the two-story building, a former girls' school. There he met several other pilots, and they boarded an old bus that would take them to the airfield.

Today, July 4, 1942, was the beginning of a new phase in the air war that had been raging over China for five years. It also marked a new chapter in Rector's life. Yesterday he had been a civilian and a member of Claire L. Chennault's fabled American Volunteer Group (AVG), or as they were better known back home in the States, the "Flying Tigers." Rector, a handsome 1938 graduate of Catawba College in North Carolina, had won his Navy wings of gold in 1940 and served for a year as a dive-bomber pilot on aircraft carriers. When recruiters for Chennault pitched him the idea of joining the AVG in 1941, he resigned his commission and left for the Far East.

Assigned to the AVG's 2nd Pursuit Squadron, Rector shot down his first enemy aircraft on December 20, 1941, near Kunming, China. Now, six and a half months later, he was a seasoned veteran, credited with seven Japanese planes destroyed. It was no wonder that Rector was one of the pilots General Chennault had specifically requested to stay on with him in China after the AVG disbanded.

Ed Rector was not the kind of guy who could walk out on "the Old Man," the pilots' pet name for Chennault. Rector knew the Army fighter group coming in to replace the AVG would be a green outfit. A couple of combat veterans in key leadership positions could make a big difference in the first few months, and they probably would save a few lives. He could not turn Chennault down.

1

So as of today, Rector was a brand new major in the U.S. Army Air Force (USAAF). His job: commanding officer (CO) of the 76th Fighter Squadron, a unit of the fledgling 23rd Fighter Group.

Rector glanced at the *jing bao* pole as soon as he stepped down from the bus. It was a habit people learned in China if they wanted to stay alive. *Jing bao*, loosely translated, is Chinese for "air raid." In the pre-dawn light, he could see one ball—actually a fabric-covered globe—hanging at the top of the pole. This signaled that enemy aircraft had been spotted somewhere in the region. He was not surprised. The Japanese had hit nearby air bases at Lingling and Kweilin during the night, and Rector knew they would probably attack Hengyang soon. It was the worst-kept secret in the Far East that today the AVG was folding and a new American fighter group was being activated. Surely the Japanese would try to wipe out the new American unit quickly, before it had a chance to gain combat experience.

Rector walked into the alert shack, a low building next to the flight line, and learned Japanese aircraft had been spotted flying near Hankow. They were headed this way. Next he checked the operations board and noted he would be flying number 104, a P-40E, this morning. It was parked with the other planes on the gravel taxiway, with its nose pointed in the direction of the runway and ready for a quick takeoff.

Some of the other pilots scheduled to fly this morning were already checking their airplanes, and Rector walked out to join them. He spoke briefly with Capt. Charlie Sawyer, who was looking over his plane. The slim Sawyer was another AVG pilot who had elected to stay in China, and he would serve as Rector's vice commander in the 76th Fighter Squadron. Down the line Rector could see Jim Howard and Van Shapard, too. Deciding not to accept induction into the U.S. Army, they were among the eighteen AVG pilots who nevertheless had agreed to stay on for two weeks after the Army took over and fill in until the new group became combat ready.

Rector checked in with the crew chief on his plane and found it was fully loaded and ready to go. Then he and the other pilots walked back to the alert shack to wait. They tried to relax, but there was no escaping the tension. The Japanese were coming, and it was only a matter of time before these pilots would be taking off to challenge them.

The second ball went up a little before 6:00 A.M. That was what Rector had been waiting for. The enemy formation was about half an hour out to the northeast and definitely heading toward Hengyang. It was time to scramble so they would have the opportunity to gain altitude before the third ball went up on the *jing bao* pole, indicating the enemy raiders were overhead. The pilots trotted from the operations shack to their waiting aircraft and climbed into the cockpits. The early morning quiet was split by successive roars as the Allison engines of the P-40s thundered to life. The pilots carefully taxied their planes to the end of the runway, swinging the long noses back and forth so they could see if the path ahead of them was clear. Then one by one the fighters sped down the runway and lifted off.

Rector searched the horizon carefully as his Curtiss fighter carried him higher into the sky. Fanned out near him, he could see Sawyer in number 132, Howard in 116, and Shapard in 112. Each of the dull olive-colored planes was decorated with the AVG's famous trademark, a leering shark's mouth painted around the air intake in the lower engine cowling. These tired hand-me-downs from the AVG climbed slowly, but the P-40s were never noted for their climb performance under the best of circumstances anyway.

Meanwhile, two AVG pilots had taken off from the field at Lingling, about sixty miles away, and were headed toward Hengyang to give support. Leading was Bob Neale, a squadron leader and the AVG's top-scoring ace. Chennault had chosen Neale to serve as temporary commander of the new fighter group until its permanent headquarters was ready to go. It was the only time in Air Force history that a civilian was allowed to serve in such a position, but then Chennault never hesitated to apply unusual solutions to difficult problems.

Also heading for Hengyang was a formation of twelve Japanese Nakajima Ki-27 Nate fighters of the 54th Air Regiment based at Hankow. The Ki-27 was a lightweight fighter with a radial engine and fixed landing gear. A prewar design, it was highly maneuverable but not particularly fast or well armed, mounting just two 7.7-millimeter machine guns. The 54th Air Regiment, which, like an average U.S. fighter group, consisted of three combat squadrons, boasted combat-seasoned pilots who had been flying the Ki-27 for several years. The AVG pilots had tangled with Ki-27s numerous times and knew what to expect.

The three groups of aircraft converged not far north of Hengyang.[1] Rector's P-40s were highest, at about eighteen thousand feet. As Rector spotted the Japanese fighters a few thousand feet below, he saw them begin to dive down toward Neale and his wingman. Neale also saw the Japanese coming and pushed his P-40 over into a dive to get away. That maneuver was the AVG's standard evasion technique, because the P-40 could dive much faster than the Japanese fighters of the day. If the P-40 was a brick on its way up, it came down like one, too.

Rector pushed his P-40 over into a dive and led his flight down after the Nates. He could see the enemy planes outlined clearly against a white backdrop of clouds several thousand feet below. He pulled in behind a Ki-27 in a slight diving turn and opened fire. The four-second burst from Rector's six .50-caliber machine guns set the Japanese fighter ablaze. With fire streaming back and pieces falling off, it dived into the cloud layer.

Rather than follow his victim down through the clouds and confirm his "kill," Rector turned back toward the Japanese formation and made several more passes at enemy fighters. By this time he was alone, as the other pilots in his flight had separated to chase targets of their own. Then Rector spotted a Ki-27 lining him up for a shot from the rear, so he dived away. As Rector rushed downward, two more Japanese fighters approached him head-on in a climb. He snapped off a shot at them and saw a large burst of smoke blossom from one Ki-27 as he flashed past. Low on ammunition, Rector leveled out and headed back to base.

Neale, meanwhile, had used the speed from his dive to zoom back up toward his Japanese attackers. He took a shot and missed one Ki-27, but then he shot up another one and saw smoke begin to pour out of the fighter as it dropped off in a dive.

When the Japanese pilots began to withdraw, Neale chased them northward. He caught up with one fighter and made a pass from the rear before zooming past and turning for a head-on shot at it. He got good hits on the Ki-27's nose and saw it start to smoke, but then he spotted two more fighters attacking him, so he had to dive out once more. This time he spotted four Nates and followed them north for one hundred miles, but he gave up the chase when he began to run low on gas.

Sawyer, Howard, and Shapard also got into the fight. The final tally gave Rector one confirmed victory and one probable victory, Sawyer got one confirmed victory and one aircraft damaged, Howard and Shapard each got credit for one confirmed victory, and Neale got two probables.[2] All of the P-40s landed safely.

The fighting was over for the first day in the history of the 23rd Fighter Group, U.S. Army Air Force, and it was barely past breakfast time.

★ ★ ★ ★

It is no small distinction that the 23rd Fighter Group was the first U.S. combat group to be formed in a combat zone during World War II. The standard USAAF fighter group of that era consisted of three squadrons, with each assigned about 40 officers and 150 enlisted men, plus group headquarters personnel. The number of aircraft assigned to a group varied greatly but averaged about 20 per squadron.

A fighter group is more than fighter planes and pilots, however. It is a free-standing combat organization. It needs all the equipment, tools, and spare parts that the maintenance and armament crews use keep to airplanes ready for operations. It needs an intelligence section to keep track of the enemy. It needs medical personnel to keep everyone fit. Its list of requirements goes on and on.

In short, to form a fighter group and prepare it for combat are major organizational tasks. It was standard practice for USAAF fighter groups to form in the United States and train for six months or more before they ever reached foreign soil, much less encountered an enemy aircraft. Chennault did it all literally overnight in China and right under the nose of a watchful enemy.

On paper, the 23rd Fighter Group was created as the 23rd Pursuit Group at Langley Field, Virginia, on March 1, 1942. It was part of the massive military buildup that took place in the United States immediately following the Japanese attack on Pearl Harbor December 7, 1941. The group's first commander was Maj. Robert A. Culbertson, a broad-shouldered, gray-haired career officer. Culbertson and a small cadre of experienced military men were given about one hundred recruits drawn from other units at Langley and told to get them ready to ship out overseas. Some of these men had just joined the Army a few days before and had not even experienced the pleasures of basic training.

Within a week, an advance detail under Master Sgt. Clyde Casto went to Charleston, South Carolina, to secure supplies and equipment the group would need to take overseas. A week later, the rest of the group arrived at Charleston's "Overseas Discharge and Replacement Center" on orders to leave for foreign assignment. The unit still was not organized into squadrons, because it had neither pilots nor aircraft.

The men of the 23rd Pursuit Group boarded the converted ocean liner USS *Brazil* late in the evening on March 17, 1942, and the ship left Charleston's harbor at six o'clock the next morning. Its destination was unknown to the 23rd's men, who were but a small number of the sixty-five hundred troops aboard. A B-25 medium bomber patrolled overhead in the cool morning air as the ship made its way on a zigzag course toward San Juan, Puerto Rico.

On board the ship, the men found themselves in cramped quarters. They stood in long chow lines at mealtime and had little to do during the rest of the day. After a quick stop without shore leave at San Juan, the USS *Brazil*, along with an escort cruiser and a small aircraft carrier loaded with scout biplanes, headed out across the Atlantic Ocean. The convoy arrived at Freetown, Sierra Leone, on the western coast of Africa and stopped briefly. Again, the men did not get shore leave, but they found a diversion in counting the nearly two hundred ships in the harbor and watching Royal Air Force (RAF) Spitfire and Hurricane fighters patrolling overhead.

Next the USS *Brazil* landed at Cape Town, South Africa, on April 18, and the men got their first chance to set foot on dry land in a month. From there, the ship went around the Cape of Good Hope to Port Elizabeth, where the men got another short shore leave and found the local people just as friendly as the ones in Cape Town. Back aboard the ship for the final leg of their journey, they went through the Mozambique Straits between Madagascar and Africa before heading up the Indian Ocean to land at Karachi, India (now Pakistan).

The USS *Brazil* anchored in Karachi harbor on the night of May 16, 1942, and docked the next day. An advance detachment made its way past the busy dock area, where war equipment for the Far Eastern fronts was being unloaded around the clock, and out of the city to the New Malir Cantonment on the Sind Desert. There they would prepare sleeping and mess facilities for what was now the 23rd Fighter Group. The group's designation had been changed from "pursuit" to "fighter" in orders dated May 15.

The men made themselves as comfortable as possible under the circumstances. New Malir was a huge air base without much on it but a large hangar that originally had been built for a British dirigible. The 23rd was assigned to "C Area," which consisted of just a few block buildings. It was dusty and unbearably hot. Soon, however, Sgt. Roy Sell had an excellent mess hall operation going, and that improved life quite a bit. Meanwhile, Staff Sgt. Edwin Jones organized baseball, softball, and volleyball teams and games to give the men an opportunity to blow off some steam.

What Malir really needed to bring things to life were some pilots and airplanes, but these still were nowhere to be seen. Nine Army pilots who later would serve in the 23rd had been sent up to China to get some combat experience with the AVG. Other pilots were busy ferrying their P-40Es across Africa toward Karachi. These men already had one adventure behind them, having flown their planes off the deck of the aircraft carrier USS *Ranger* on May 10 to begin their journey. Their successful takeoff was no small feat, because the P-40—a heavy aircraft with a slow rate of climb—had not been designed with the takeoff capabilities needed for carrier operations.

One of those pilots was 1/Lt. (First Lieutenant) Art Waite. He had graduated from flight school at Randolph Field, Texas, in 1940 and gained considerable experience flying fighters, the most recent at Orlando, Florida, where he trained new pilots on the P-40. Waite continued the tale from there.

"In early April three of us were picked for a special mission. We flew to Mitchell Field, N.Y., and practiced short takeoffs for a few days (with other pilots). Then it was off to Quonset Point [Rhode Island], a Navy base, where we and 68 P-40s were loaded on the car-

rier *Ranger* and left for points unknown. After a few weeks at sea
and many U-boat attempts at us, we took off from the carrier and
landed at Accra [Ghana], Africa.

"I remember the Navy was most efficient. My takeoff was one of
the first four or five, so we did not have much room to work with.
The bow of the ship was pointed into the wind and the deck was
about 60 to 70 feet above the water. When we left the ship on takeoff, most of us fell some before we had our flight speed. It was hairy,
but all but one of the 68 planes made it. One, I understand, went in
the water and the pilot was picked up by a destroyer.

"We flew into Accra and from there went to Lagos [Nigeria]. Then
we were escorted by a B-25 to Khartoum [Sudan] and Luxor
[Egypt], where about five of us took a row boat with a guide across
the Nile River at night and went to King Tut's tomb. We then went
on to Cairo, where we took off to meet a German air raid that had
planned to attack. They must not have liked the odds, though, as
they turned back. We flew on to Karachi, and finally 25 of the original 68 got to China. I was in this bunch."[3]

The rest of the pilots were assigned to the 51st Fighter Group,
which also was at Karachi then. Waite went on to fly fifty missions
in the 76th Fighter Squadron, destroying one Japanese fighter and
winning the Distinguished Flying Cross plus two Air Medals. After a
year of combat, he began to suffer spells of blindness and was reassigned as a copilot on C-47s transporting supplies inside China. He
finally went home on December 20, 1943.

Life went on unchanged in Karachi until June 12, when orders
arrived to send an advance detail of nineteen enlisted men to
Kunming, China, the AVG's headquarters. By this time it was known
that the 23rd Fighter Group would be taking over for the AVG but it
was not clear how. To further complicate matters, Major Culbertson
fell ill at New Malir and was hospitalized, while the group's adjutant, Maj. Peter Borre, was reassigned to the air base command at
Karachi. Without planes, pilots, or leadership, the 23rd was nothing
but a paper organization.

The 23rd's advance cadre consisted of technicians from the different sections of the group—intelligence, aircraft maintenance, armament, radio maintenance and operations, and photography. After
stops at Delhi, Allahabad, and Dinjan, India, they flew to Kunming
and arrived on June 15. The last leg of the trip took them over the
"Hump," the popular name for the treacherous stretch of the
Himalaya Mountains that lay between the air base at Dinjan and
those in China's Yunnan Province. Many thousands of men would
follow them over the Hump in the next three years of war.

The men were pleasantly surprised by their new surroundings at
Kunming. After the sweltering heat of India, they greatly appreciat-

ed the cooler climate at Kunming's 6,230-foot altitude. The airfield was near the north end of Tien Chih Lake (also called "Lake Kunming"), with rice paddies all around and the seven-thousand-foot peaks of the Himalaya foothills in the distance. The hillside city of Kunming was three miles north of the field. On their first trip to town, the men were amazed to find Kunming packed with refugees who had fled from Japanese-occupied areas of China.

The air base itself was laid out in a square, six thousand feet on a side. The runway ran northeast to southwest, as did nearly every runway in China, to take advantage of the prevailing winds. It was 6,137 feet long and 375 feet wide and had a gravel surface. Again typical of airfields in China, it had been built entirely by hand, with thousands of Chinese coolies contributing their labors. The runway was flanked by grass fields on both sides, and the north side was stable enough to be used for landings and takeoffs by fighters during dry weather.

The advance detachment of the 23rd went to work immediately. AVG Squadron Leader Arvid Olson instructed them to work with AVG crews in their specialties and to learn their jobs as quickly as possible. More ground personnel arrived in the days that followed.

On June 18, the first Army pilots arrived for training on the AVG P-40s that would be turned over to them in a couple of weeks. The AVG was down to forty-eight fighters by this time,[4] after having started with one hundred early model P-40s in July 1941 and later receiving about thirty-five P-40Es starting in the spring of 1942. The early model P-40s were similar to the P-40B but had been modified for export to the Royal Air Force before being diverted to China. The P-40E was a more advanced design, with heavier armament, improved visibility from the cockpit, and the ability to carry a bomb or drop tank under its fuselage. But the flight performance of the two types was similar. Obviously, the P-40Es had logged fewer hours than the others, but all the aircraft had seen heavy service in the AVG.

With pilots and ground crews reaching China, the 23rd Fighter Group needed a commander, and the ailing Culbertson would not be coming to China. The command structure called for a pilot with the rank of lieutenant colonel or full colonel, and such men were in short supply in India and China at that time. Chennault also wanted an honest-to-goodness fighter pilot who would command the 23rd with all the aggressiveness and imagination that Chennault himself had poured into the AVG. Fortunately, Chennault knew where he could get just such a man.

Colonel Robert L. ("Scotty") Scott Jr. was a thirty-four-year-old West Point graduate who had spent most of his prewar career flying fighters. Scott had arrived in the theater in May as part of an abortive attempt to attack Japan with a squadron of B-17s flying out of China. When that plan was canceled, Scott cooled his heels in the Assam-Burma-China Ferry Command, flying transports across the Hump into China. He pumped the AVG pilots for information wherever he met them, trying to find a way to get himself assigned to their outfit. Finally on one of his trips into Kunming he convinced Chennault to let him borrow an AVG P-40E so he could fly patrols out of Dinjan and over the Hump. Later, he would write in great detail about these experiences in his best-selling book, *God Is My Co-pilot.*

Colonel Scott was at Dinjan on June 20 when he received word of his new assignment as commander of the 23rd Fighter Group. He cleared out of Assam as quickly as possible and flew up to Kunming on June 27 to begin organizing his fighter group headquarters and to get more closely acquainted with his new boss.[5]

★ ★ ★ ★

Brigadier Gen. Claire Lee Chennault was world famous by the summer of 1942, thanks to the tremendous success of his American Volunteer Group. At age forty-nine, he had already lived a full and exciting life, but much more was ahead of him.

Chennault grew up on a cotton farm in Louisiana near the Mississippi River. His family was descended from the French Huguenots, and four of his ancestors fought in the American Revolution. As a boy, Chennault spent many hours hunting and fishing in the rugged swamp country, developing a lifelong love of the outdoors. He attended Louisiana State University for two years, earned his teaching certificate, and then went to work as a public schoolteacher in the fall of 1910. He married the following year and had children quickly after that. Seeking a more lucrative line of work, he moved his family to Ohio in the mid-teens and worked in a Goodyear factory. When the United States declared war against Germany in 1917, he quickly enlisted in the U.S. Army.

Chennault was commissioned a first lieutenant in November 1917, but his repeated requests for flight training met with rejection. The frustrated young officer sneaked instruction rides whenever he could and quickly learned to fly, but he was not accepted for Army flight training until the war in France was nearly over. He completed training in the spring of 1919, but by then the war had ended and the Army had far more pilots than it needed. Chennault was discharged from the Army in April 1920 and took his family back to the family farm in Waterproof, Louisiana. The farm life was not for him, however, and Chennault rejoined the Army with a regular commission that September.

During Chennault's Army career, he served with many of the pioneers of U.S. military aviation. A highly skilled, natural pilot, he gained notoriety in the '20s and '30s for aerobatic routines he performed at air shows and county fairs around the country. He also became a strong advocate of pursuit, or fighter, aviation, conflicting with the conventional wisdom of the era, that heavily armed bombardment aircraft were unstoppable by air defenses. Eventually Chennault put his thoughts together in a treatise titled "The Role of Defensive Pursuit" that explained persuasively how intercepting fighters could mount an effective defense against enemy bombers. Written in 1933, the short manuscript was highly controversial among the brass of the Army Air Corps at the time, but it stands today as a classic of military theory, its tenets proven time after time during the course of World War II.

Constantly at odds with his superiors and suffering from hearing loss (a common problem for aviators then), Chennault accepted retirement from the Army in April 1937. His decision was easier because the Chinese government wanted his services to help build its fledgling air force. This opportunity offered a clean slate, a chance to prove his theories. He left for China the following month.

Chennault's first few years in China were notable for several reasons, not the least of which was the close relationship he developed with the leader of the country, Generalissimo Chiang Kai-shek, and his wife, Madame Chiang (the former Soong Mei-ling). Chiang Kai-shek had spent years trying to unify the 450 million Chinese under his Kuomintang government, with some success. By 1937, nearly all of China's warlords had submitted to his central authority, and the flourishing Communist movement had been bottled up in a remote area of northern China. The Japanese posed another problem for Chiang. Starting in 1931, they had successively encroached on China's territory and eventually forced him to surrender Manchuria, the northeastern region of China. Japan's aggression did not stop, however; thus Chiang needed someone like Chennault to build an air force for him.

When China's war with Japan rekindled in full fury after the Marco Polo Bridge incident, in which ground forces of the two nations clashed briefly near Peiping on July 7, 1937, the weakness of the Chinese Air Force (CAF) quickly became evident. Chennault went right to work on the problem. His efforts to buy modern aircraft and train Chinese pilots to fly them were frustrated, however, by China's rigid class system and the vast corruption in Chiang's government. Over time, Chennault was able to launch several effective interceptions of Japanese raiders, but these amounted to mere skirmishes against a constantly advancing enemy. First Peiping fell, then Shanghai and Nanking. When Chiang's government moved inland to Hankow, the Japanese attacked there, too. In late 1938 when Hankow was captured, the Kuomintang government retreated deep into the interior to the city of Chungking on the Yangtze River.

Finally, the Chinese were able to stop the Japanese advance in May 1939 at Tsaoyang, in the mountainous Hupeh Province. With the battle lines stabilized, the Japanese turned to a strategy of attrition. They blockaded China's coast to prevent supplies from reaching the interior and supplied their own forces with indigenous Chinese resources. Through all of this, Japan continued to bomb the cities of Free China. Millions of Chinese died.

By late 1940, China was in deep trouble. Earlier that year, when France surrendered to Germany, an ally of Japan, Hanoi's port in French Indo-China also was closed to supplies bound for China. The last port of entry left to China was Rangoon in the British colony of Burma (Myanmar). From there, supplies could be shipped north over the newly completed "Burma Road" into China. It was vital that the Burma Road be kept open. Chennault saw that the route would be vulnerable to air attack if Japan and Great Britain should go to war, which appeared increasingly likely. Thus Chennault had the impetus for creating of the American Volunteer Group. Convinced by this time that Chinese airmen would not be capable of defending the Burma Road, Chennault knew that American military pilots flying modern U.S. fighter planes could.

Beginning just a few days after Japan's attack on Pearl Harbor, Chennault's AVG fought throughout the unsuccessful defense of Burma, maintaining air superiority while British and Chinese ground forces retreated into India and China. In doing so, the AVG won worldwide notoriety as one of the only Allied combat units that outfought the Japanese during the first few months of America's involvement in the war. However, Allied ground forces failed to stop the advancing Japanese, who cut the Burma Road link anyway in the spring of 1942. After that, all supplies coming to China had to be flown in from India over the Hump. That slim lifeline was China's only link to the outside world.

When Burma fell, the AVG withdrew to China, where the P-40 pilots provided air defense for the cities and the Hump route. They also supported Chinese ground troops attempting to stop the Japanese from advancing across the Salween River and into China's Yunnan Province. It was a grueling seven months of combat for the AVG personnel, and most of them were anxious to go home for a rest when their contracts with the Chinese government expired. Of the one hundred original AVG pilots, only Rector, Sawyer, and three others agreed to be inducted into the Army in China and stay on with the Old Man. In addition, thirty-three ground personnel accepted induction. These men formed the foundation of combat experience and technical skill on which the 23rd Fighter Group was built.

Though Chennault was unable to build a strong Chinese Air Force, he was far more successful at putting two of the key elements of his air defense plan into place. The first was constructing airfields throughout the country. Chennault scouted hundreds of locations suitable for air operations, and Chiang's government put local laborers to work, building the fields by hand. Some of these fields rarely saw an aircraft; others became major bases later in the war. But they all played a part in Chennault's strategy.

The other vital element of Chennault's plan was intelligence. Defending fighter pilots had to know where the enemy aircraft were to intercept them successfully. Sophisticated radar systems were not yet developed, so Chennault turned to the eyes and ears of the Chinese people for his intelligence network. It came to be known as the "warning net," and it was perhaps the greatest proof of Chennault's genius as a military planner and strategist.

Chennault began to promote his ideas for a warning net as soon as he reached China, but the war progressed so swiftly that he had little chance to develop them for the first two years. Work on the net began in earnest at Kunming in 1940 under the direction of John Williams, an ex-Army radioman who had known Chennault since they served together in the early 1930s. Four stations equipped with radio transmitters and receivers in a ring about forty kilometers outside Kunming reported to the control center in Kunming. Each radio station also was connected by telephone to eight reporting points, each responsible for watching a twenty-kilometer square of sky and reporting aircraft sightings.[6]

Soon thereafter, two more nets opened in Yunnan Province, with command centers at the Yunnanyi and Chanyi airfields. All three nets were interconnected to form, in effect, one big net. The net continued to be extended until it reached virtually all over Free China and in some cases even behind Japanese lines. It was not infallible, as subsequent events would prove, but the warning net became a major weapon in Chennault's arsenal.

Though originally conceived to provide direction for defending fighters, the net soon proved to have other purposes as well. First, obviously, was its ability to warn the civilian population of air attacks. This was much appreciated in the cities of Chungking and Kunming, which were subject to regular bombings by the Japanese. Though the Chinese were unable to fight back, at least the net gave them time to take shelter from the falling bombs. Civilians, just as the pilots of the AVG and the 23rd Fighter Group, learned to watch the *jing bao* pole closely and listen for the warning gongs that were sounded at night.

Later, when air traffic increased over China, the net also served as a navigational aid. If a pilot got lost, he could circle the nearest village, and more than likely someone would spot his plane and report it to the net. Within a short time, the pilot would receive instructions from a ground radio operator on the proper direction to steer in order to reach his destination. Similarly, the net provided information about the location of downed aircraft, friend and foe alike.

When Colonel Scott returned to the United States in January 1943 and was debriefed on the situation in China for the War Department, he spoke at length about the warning net. In that interview he said, "In no other part of the world is there such a warning net. We knew when the Japs warmed their planes at Canton; we knew when the doors of the hangars were opened at Canton—and we could control our own actions accordingly. Gasoline is gold in China. . . . We used to wait until the last possible moment we could to take off in order to gain proper elevation to engage the enemy, thereby having more gasoline left than if we had taken off sooner, or tried to maintain patrol all day."

Later, he was asked how the 23rd managed to gain sufficient altitude in its P-40s to be able to intercept enemy formations. His reply: "Always by relying on the air warning net."[7]

★ ★ ★ ★

On the morning of July 3, 1942, the 23rd Fighter Group suffered its first casualty. Private Marshall F. F. Brown was working on the wing guns of a P-40 at Kunming while another enlisted man, Frank Wamsley, worked in the cockpit of the aircraft. Brown was standing directly in front of a pair of .30-caliber machine guns when Wamsley accidentally tripped the trigger on the plane's control stick. A short burst of bullets roared out of the guns, and two slugs struck Brown in the head, killing him instantly. He was buried in the local cemetery two days later. The group's chaplain, 1/Lt. James E. Tull, officiated.

Madame Chiang Kai-shek hosted a farewell party for the few AVG members in the Chungking area before they went home, but there was no other event to mark the AVG's passing. Likewise, there was no ceremony at Chennault's headquarters in Kunming on July 4, 1942, for the official activation of the 23rd Fighter Group and its three fighter squadrons—the 74th, 75th, and 76th. A formation of P-40s went up and made several passes over the field for the benefit of the press photographers on hand, but that was it. There was a war on, after all. The *jing bao* pole could come alive at any moment, as it had at Hengyang for Major Rector that morning.

2

China Air Task Force

On the morning of July 5, 1942, Maj. David L. Hill led a flight of nine P-40s east out of Kunming and headed toward Kweilin more than 400 miles away. The flight was a mixture of new P-40Es and refurbished ex-AVG aircraft. Some of the planes would be staying at Kweilin to reinforce the 76th Fighter Squadron. In a couple of days Hill would take the rest 190 miles farther up the line to his base at Hengyang.

Hill, a tall, sandy-haired man who would turn twenty-seven in two weeks, was known to one and all China hands as "Tex." He, like his buddy Ed Rector, was a former Navy dive-bomber pilot who had flown in the AVG and decided to stay in China with the Army.

It would fall on Tex Hill's shoulders to lead the bulk of the 23rd Fighter Group's missions during the next few weeks. That would pose no problem for Hill, an aggressive and skillful fighter pilot with eleven downed Japanese planes to his credit already. Born of missionary parents in Korea, Hill grew up in Texas, attended a military high school, and graduated from college before joining the Navy in 1938. A big man at six feet two inches tall, he had played football and boxed as a youth and had even fought professionally once. With his slow drawl, colorful language, and gifts as a storyteller, Tex Hill was a natural leader.

General Chennault chose Hill to command the 75th Fighter Squadron, which was to be stationed at Hengyang for the time being. Assisting Hill as vice commander would be another AVG veteran ace, Maj. John G. ("Gil") Bright.

Some of the AVG pilots who extended their contracts for two weeks were to fly with the 75th out of Hengyang. These included Pete Wright, Arnold Shamblin, Freeman Ricketts, and John Petach. The squadron also had five of the Army pilots who had come to

China in June to fly with the AVG: Capt. Albert ("Ajax") Baumler, who was a veteran of the Spanish Civil War, and Lts. Burrall Barnum, Lee Minor, Dean Carter, and Leonard Butsch.

Hill recalled those early days: "The 23rd was unique in that it was formed in the field under combat conditions. For instance, in my case I was a squadron leader in the American Volunteer Group. I came down off a flight, and they said, 'Take the oath and sign here. You're now Major Hill, 75th Fighter Squadron.'

"Chennault's directions were very, very simple. He said, 'Just try to kill every damned Jap you can find any way you can.' The American people, being very resourceful, we dreamed up all kinds of ways to do things.

"We were pretty much on our own. Our squadrons were all separated, especially in the early days. Later on they got better organized. What we would do, is move up into these advance bases. All we'd have is fuel, bombs, and ammo. Of course the Japs would know the minute we got there, and they'd be there the next morning. We'd fight out of those bases until we'd lose our combat effectiveness, then we'd move back to the rear echelon and regroup. If we could have sustained our positions, I believe we could have attritioned the Japanese Air Force from our China bases. But we had no replacements. We just could patch 'em up."[1]

Ed Rector's squadron, the 76th, would be stationed at Kweilin. While Tex Hill flew east from Kunming on July 5, Rector and his vice commander, Capt. Charlie Sawyer, returned to Kweilin to join the 76th. Actually, the 76th did not amount to much of a squadron yet. Besides Rector and Sawyer, it had only three other Army pilots: Lts. James Dumas, Romney Masters, and Jesse Carney. They had been in Kweilin for about a month, flying with the AVG on occasion. The 76th would be brought up to strength when more pilots became available, but for the next two weeks, AVG holdover pilots would fill out the flight roster. Rector did have a good nucleus of AVG ground personnel in the 76th, however. One of them was a German expatriate, Staff Sgt. Gerhard Neumann, whose amazing mechanical skills would prove invaluable in the months to come. Not only was he a whiz at patching up damaged P-40s, but once he also completely rebuilt a captured Japanese fighter so that it could be sent to the United States for a combat evaluation.

The third squadron of the group was the 74th, which Chennault elected to keep in reserve at Kunming. The 74th, like the others, was commanded by a former AVG pilot, Maj. Frank Schiel Jr. Of Chennault's three squadron commanders, Schiel was the only one who had served in the Army Air Corps prior to joining the AVG.

The Army pilots who had arrived in Kunming over the previous few weeks varied considerably in experience. Some had virtually no

P-40 time at all and little fighter training of any kind. The least experienced men were assigned to Schiel's 74th Squadron so they could familiarize themselves with the P-40 and Chennault's tactics in an area that was less likely to be subject to Japanese attack. The 74th was dubbed the "School Squadron."

Besides the three permanent squadrons of the 23rd Fighter Group, Chennault had another ace in his hand. Realizing he would need more fighter strength, he had convinced Tenth Air Force headquarters in India to let him "borrow" one of its P-40 units for temporary duty in China. That outfit was the 16th Fighter Squadron, and it was a good one. The 16th would be taking up residence in Lingling as soon as the small air base could be prepared to handle a full squadron. Never permanently assigned to the 23rd Fighter Group, the 16th would remain on "attached" status with the group for more than a year.

Finally, Chennault had under his command the 11th Bomb Squadron, an understrength unit of North American B-25 Mitchell medium bombers that arrived in Kunming in June. Commanded by Maj. William F. Basye and under the direction of Col. Caleb V. Haynes, the 11th had eight aircraft and flew its first mission from China on July 1. At present, the B-25s were stationed at Kweilin.[2]

Brigadier General Claire Chennault's command—four ragtag P-40 squadrons and half of a B-25 outfit—defended a line that ran one thousand miles from Changsha in Hunan Province to the Salween River gorges on the Burma border. The name of this patched-together outfit was the China Air Task Force (CATF). It was not much, but the CATF would have to do until Chennault could convince the War Department to give him more forces. That was not going to happen any time soon.

★ ★ ★ ★

The 16th Fighter Squadron was a prewar unit, having been activated as part of the 51st Pursuit Group at Hamilton Field, California, on January 15, 1941. The first four pilots were assigned on April 30: 1/Lt. Harry B. ("Hal") Young, the CO, and 2/Lts. Elmer F. Kingen, Heath H. Wayne, and John D. Lombard. The squadron moved to March Field at Riverside, California, a month later and received its first P-40 on June 23. Four more pilots were assigned in July, bringing the total to eight, and from August 18 to August 27 the 16th participated in a large field exercise at Big Bear Lake, California, recording ninety-nine hours of flying time.

One of the pilots joining the squadron that summer was 2/Lt. George R. Barnes, who graduated from flight school in class '41-E (the fifth class to start that year) on July 11, 1941. He described his experiences.

"During the period July to December 1941 we flew P-36s, P-40s, BT-13s, and PT-13s. Flying time was generally limited—some months only three or four hours with ten landings. My total was approximately 125 hours, including B-18 time preparatory to P-38 checkout.

"We did have a few days of gunnery and bombing at Muroc [now Edwards Air Force Base]. We were permitted about 200 rounds of .50-caliber ammunition on ground targets and three or four dummy smoke bombs. At that time the P-40 only had two .50-caliber machine guns synchronized to shoot through the prop. On one occasion my system went out, and I fired into the prop (hollow blade), the bullets being forced to tear the blade tip, and the out-of-balance propeller resulted in a teeth-chattering vibration.

"At March Field, we young 'hot pilots' thought we had the world by the tail. First job, uniform, wings, airplanes, independence, little work, enough bucks to do our own thing, new car, and most important we attracted a lot of super young ladies. As a matter of fact, I married one of the best.

"During November 1941, another officer and I were sent on temporary duty to Los Angeles to work with other members of the Army and Navy setting up a telephone net. The real feeling of possible war came to me at this time. When I left Los Angeles to return to March Field on December 7, 1941, I stopped by my girl's house and was told of the Pearl Harbor attack. Near the end of December we were advised of our departure for overseas on January 11, 1942."[3]

Colonel Homer V. Sanders, commander of the 51st Fighter Group, began campaigning for a combat assignment for his outfit as soon as the smoke began to clear at Pearl Harbor, proclaiming the 51st fully trained and ready to go. Whether this was true or not, orders came quickly. Later, when the fame of the American Volunteer Group had spread, the men of the 51st took to calling their unit the "HVG"—Homer's Volunteer Group.[4]

The 51st Fighter Group left San Francisco aboard the USATSS (U.S. Army Transport Ship) *President Coolidge* at 4:30 P.M. on January 12, 1942, in a convoy with another transport, a cruiser, and two destroyers. The convoy zigzagged west and south, crossed the equator on January 19, and landed at Melbourne, Australia, on February 3.

The men left the ship and rode a train to Bacchus Marsh, thirty-two miles away. From there it was a five-mile march to Camp Darley. On this march the 16th Fighter Squadron suffered its first casualty of the war when Sgt. John A. Sabat collapsed from heart failure and died. The unit stayed at Camp Darley for a week, and during that time five new pilots were assigned.

Then the 16th returned to Melbourne on February 12, boarded the TSMV (twin-screw motor vessel) *Duntroon*, and departed for an unknown destination. This trip was a bit more comfortable than the Pacific crossing. The officers were assigned to regular staterooms, and houseboys served fresh pineapple and orange juice with crumpets.[5] The ship arrived at Perth, in western Australia, on February 18. There, antiaircraft guns were mounted on the *Duntroon* while aircraft mechanics were sent ashore to help assemble P-40s at the local airport. On February 22 the ship left Perth in a convoy that included the old aircraft carrier USS *Langley*. Loaded with P-40s and pilots bound for Java, the *Langley* left the convoy the next day and was sunk by Japanese bombers before it could deliver its precious cargo.

The TSMV *Duntroon* arrived in Karachi, India, on March 12, 1942. The passengers left the ship the next morning, and the 51st Fighter Group went to a British reinforcement camp two miles outside the city. The living conditions in the camp were horrible, and the food was even worse. Many of the men got sick.[6]

Relief came on March 27, when the 51st moved to a semipermanent camp at Karachi Airport, the big field at New Malir. Three P-40Es were assigned to the 16th Fighter Squadron while its own aircraft were being uncrated and assembled. One of these aircraft, number 14, experienced engine failure on takeoff the very next day and crashed. The pilot, 2/Lt. Edward LaCour, was unhurt, but the plane was a total loss. Then on March 31, 1/Lt. George A. Chipman, who had joined the squadron in Australia, got into an inverted spin at five thousand feet in number 11 and crashed to his death.

The next two months were spent preparing the pilots and aircraft for combat. AVG pilots on a mission to ferry new P-40s to China stopped long enough to give a lecture about their combat experiences, and a Chinese major gave a briefing about Japanese culture. The pilots flew practice missions and tested new P-40s as they were delivered from the assembly area. One pilot, a wild Wyoming boy named Lt. Dallas Clinger, even accompanied AVG pilots to Africa and ferried back a new P-40. Tragically, Lieutenant LaCour was killed May 20 in his second P-40 crash. Then on May 26 the unit received the first of more than a dozen new pilots from the group that flew new P-40s off the USS *Ranger* in Africa.

A final addition to the pilot strength came on June 17, and it proved to be an important one. Captain John R. Alison was a highly experienced fighter pilot who had just come from an assignment in Russia, where he taught Red air force pilots to fly lend-lease P-40s. He was a small man with the face of an angel, but the Japanese would soon learn that in the cockpit of a P-40 Johnny Alison was an absolute terror. One pilot who served with him remembered seeing Alison do six rolls in a climb and roll out on top, quite a feat in any airplane of that period but especially remarkable in a P-40.[7]

By June, the 16th Fighter Squadron was up to full strength, and the men were anxious to get on with the war. Then the word came down from group headquarters that one of the squadrons would be sent to China. The 16th got the call, and orders were issued on June 23, transferring the squadron to Kunming.

Robert L. Liles, one of the *Ranger* pilots who had been assigned to the 16th, recalled, "When they decided they needed one extra squadron in China, they were going to take one of the three squadrons from the 51st Fighter Group. There were three squadron commanders. So they decided the fairest way to do it was to roll the dice to see whose squadron went off to China. It was a plum to go to China, because the others weren't going to get to go forward to northeast India for quite some time. My squadron commander, Major Hal Young, won, so in late June we started for China.

"The en route stop was Calcutta. Some of the people had aircraft trouble, including me. The rest of the squadron went on to Dinjan, and I think they had an AVG pilot leading them across. Major Young, George Hazlett, and Hal Pike were the flight commanders who took the other airplanes on in to China.

"When I got ready to leave, there were four of us: Ed Goss, Jack Best, Heath ("Tiger") Wayne, and me. We left Calcutta with some AVG pilots. One of them was named Cross, Lawlor was another, and I can't remember the third. They were flying P-66s, which were Vultee aircraft [being delivered to the Chinese Air Force]. There were twelve of them, and the other nine were all flown by Chinese pilots. So we flew to Dinjan, spent the night there, and then the following day took off for China.

"The weather was terrible going over. This was on the third of July. Thunderclouds, cumulus clouds real high. We wandered around all over, and the Chinese pilots could not fly [on] instruments very well. They were fairly new pilots. The AVG leader didn't want to take them through any clouds, so we wandered all over. Their airplane performed better at [higher] altitude than ours did. The four of us had a hell of a time keeping up with them in our P-40s. Finally, two of our pilots got disgusted: Jack Best and Heath Wayne. They just took off on their own, bored through the clouds, and landed at Kunming.

"Goss and I stayed with these AVG people. The only way we could keep up with them was, when they hit a line of clouds that they had to go around, we'd go through and cut them off to catch up. Then the engines started running rough; we were low on fuel. We were clear down over Burma part of the time. Finally I suggested to Ed that we drop our belly tanks because they were slowing us down. We punched our tanks off.

"When we got to Kunming, we were quite low on fuel. We would let the Chinese pilots land first. The AVG pilots landed. The first Chinese pilot that landed nosed up right in the middle of the runway. The second guy ground-looped to the left; he was still on the runway. The next guy ground-looped to the right and left his plane on the runway. Goss and I were desperate to land, so we went over and landed on the grass. Came in over the hangar line and put ours down on the grass. I asked the crew to check when they put fuel back in my airplane, and I had about thirteen gallons of fuel left when I landed. I was about ready to bail out. That's how we got there."[8]

Liles, who graduated from flight school in the summer of 1941, had been assigned to the 77th Fighter Squadron prior to being selected for the *Ranger* mission. On arrival at Karachi, he was pleased to be reunited with his best friend from flight training, Lt. Bob Mooney, who had gone straight to the 16th after receiving his wings. The two of them remained close until Mooney's death in December 1942. Liles went on to command the 16th Fighter Squadron and did not return to the States until July 1944.

Meanwhile, the ground personnel of the 16th had left for China via air transport on June 23 and followed the same route taken by the P-40s. On arrival at Dinjan, they found the monsoon season in full force. Bad weather delayed their departure for China a couple of days. Finally, the men boarded C-47s for the trip over the Hump. It was an uncomfortable four-hundred-mile flight, because C-47s did not carry oxygen for passengers. The planes had to climb to altitudes of nearly twenty thousand feet briefly to clear the highest peaks along the route, and the altitudes made the men woozy and achingly cold.

One of the last ground crewmen to reach Kunming was Corp. George F. Aldridge. He wrote, "Four of us mechanics were dropped off at New Delhi, India, to service and repair P-40s if need be as they came through en route to Kunming. They had two other stops before flying over the Hump into China. After the last P-40 came though, within a couple of days a C-47 picked us up and dropped us off in Assam. We were delayed there from going into China because the C-47 had to be used to drop rice to Chinese troops who were cut off from their supplies by the Japanese somewhere down in Burma. However, on July 6, 1942, we finally arrived in Kunming. A small group of AVG people arrived at the plane as we unloaded our supplies and baggage. They were anxious to leave China; so much so, in fact, that they sold six of us their jeep for a couple of rupees. The six of us kept the jeep until we left Kunming for Lingling."[9]

The 16th Fighter Squadron only stayed in Kunming long enough to regroup from the trip over the Hump. On July 9 an advance detachment was sent up to Lingling, which was seven hundred miles east between Kweilin and Hengyang, to prepare the remote air base for the squadron. Leading the detachment was 1/Lt. Bob Liles.

According to Liles, "They were getting ready to send the squadron over to Lingling. Major Young sent me and a noncom—I can't remember his name—to Lingling to get the base prepared. My sergeant drew plans for a multiple-holer shit stall for the Chinese to build so we'd have a latrine, but he didn't put dimensions on it. How high was the box seat? They went on ahead and built it. I got down there and it was comical when I saw it. The seat was so high that we had to build three steps to get up to it. And around each hole they had little foot pads because when the Chinese went to the toilet they put their feet on the pads and squatted over the hole. We had to take the foot pads off so we could use it. They did all this very quickly, just a couple of days. They added onto a sleeping facility and had that all fixed.

"When everything was ready—extra cots and stuff for everybody—we let the squadron know, and they came flying in. As I recall, it was that very night we had fish for dinner. Everybody got sick. They had diarrhea, vomiting. There were only two people who didn't get sick and were able to fly the next day: me—I didn't feel too good but I was OK—and Johnny Alison.

"They found out what happened. They sent one of the cooks to town to get the cooking oil. Instead of buying good cooking oil he bought some tung oil—what they use in paint. That's what upset everybody's digestive tract.

"If the Japs had come in that next day, not many of us would have been able to do much. In another 24 hours they were all feeling better.

"But I believe they [the Chinese] took the cook out and shot him. Another time they caught a room boy there stealing toothpaste and other little odds and ends—toilet articles. They took him out behind the hostel. They shaved a bamboo pole down into thin strips and practically de-skinned [sic] him. Beat him with it until he was a bloody mess."[10]

On July 12, half the men at Lingling were still feeling ill. But the war would not wait. An alert came in after lunch, and pretty soon the balls starting climbing up the *jing bao* pole. Two P-40s took off at 3:30 P.M. to attempt an intercept, but they made no contact with enemy aircraft. It was an inauspicious beginning to a long and distinguished combat record for the 16th Fighter Squadron.

★ ★ ★ ★

It did not look like much of a day for flying at Kweilin. The morning of July 6 had dawned with a low overcast hanging not far above the tops of the mountains surrounding the air base. Kweilin was legendary for its mountains, limestone karsts sticking up like ice cream cones for miles and miles in every direction. For thousands of years, the area had drawn China's finest artists, who found inspiration in the beautiful surroundings.

For pilots of the 23rd Fighter Group, however, the mountains were a mixed blessing. On one hand, their unique geological make-up left them honeycombed with caves, which served as useful shelters when enemy bombers arrived. In fact, the warning net center at Kweilin was built inside a cave on the edge of the air base. In bad weather, on the other hand, those same mountains presented a serious hazard, because just like mountains everywhere, they did not give when an airplane ran into them. If the weather was lousy, which it tended to be in south-central China for weeks at a time, the airplanes had to sit.

By mid-morning, the cloud deck had lifted enough for flying. Tex Hill would lead four P-40s escorting five B-25s on a bombing raid against enemy installations at Canton. It probably did not seem significant to Hill or his pilots at the time, but this flight would be the first offensive mission ever flown by the 23rd Fighter Group.

Canton was a little more than an hour's flight southeast from Kweilin for the raiders. Hill's P-40s spread out in a line-abreast formation, with their leader slightly in front. They stayed above and just behind the B-25s to protect them in case Japanese fighters attacked from the rear. The weather improved as the planes flew south unmolested, and when the bombers reached the target, they were able to drop their loads from five thousand feet through broken clouds. The bombs slammed into docks and warehouses along the Pearl River as the B-25s put their noses down and began their dash toward home.

This was not going to be a milk run, however. About thirty miles out of Canton, one of the P-40 pilots spotted a formation of Ki-27 Nate fighters approaching to take a crack at the B-25s and called them in. Hill quickly checked the sky to make sure other Japanese fighters were not hiding somewhere in the clouds and then turned toward the approaching Ki-27s. With his wingman sticking close to guard Hill's tail, the young major lined up on one of the Nates and let fly with his guns. His aim was true, and the Nate went down in flames.

Meanwhile, John Petach, leading the second element, put a long burst into another Nate and saw it go down as well. This Nate's wingman attempted to draw Petach away from his victim but was a second too late. Petach turned into the second Ki-27 and gave it a blast from his guns, too. This fighter went into a spin and dropped down through the clouds, but Petach did not follow. By this time, the bombers were well clear of danger, and the P-40s were getting low on gas. It was time to go home.

The weather cooperated, and all nine aircraft returned to Kweilin undamaged. Hill and Petach each got credit for one confirmed victory, and Petach also was credited with a probable victory on his second Nate.

Petach was a New Jersey boy, one of the AVG pilots who had elected to stay the extra two weeks. He and AVG nurse Emma Jean ("Red") Foster had fallen in love the previous summer aboard ship en route to Burma, and they got married in Kunming on February 17, 1942.[11] The new Mrs. Petach was working in the hospital at Chungking, waiting for her husband to finish his two-week extension so they could go home together.

Unfortunately, Johnny Petach would not be going home. Neither would Arnold Shamblin, another of the AVG pilots who stayed on the extra two weeks. On July 10, both men went down during a four-plane mission Petach had led out of Hengyang to dive-bomb the town of Linchuan. Captain Ajax Baumler, who was leading the second element, reported that Petach was just pulling out of his dive when his plane burst into flames. The P-40 went into a violent tumble, and one wing broke off before the plane slammed into the river bank just beyond the city's wall and exploded. Petach had no chance to bail out. Neither Baumler nor Petach's wingman, Lt. Leonard Butsch, saw Shamblin go down, but word was received later that he, too, had been hit by ground fire over Linchuan. Apparently, Shamblin bailed out and was captured by the Japanese, but he did not survive his imprisonment.[12]

This was the saddest event in the history of the AVG, made all the worse when the men found out Mrs. Petach was pregnant. Chennault's trusted recruiter and supply officer, C. B. Adair, prevailed on two of the AVG's most trusted men, Bob Neale and Charlie Bond, to take care of Emma Jean Petach on their long journey back to the United States. They were among the last AVG personnel to leave China, heading out of Kweilin on July 18, the day after Colonel Scott arrived to assume command of combat operations.

Tex Hill offered this assessment of Scott nearly fifty years later: "After we were formed, Scotty called us together. I'll be forever grateful. This guy was controversial to say the least. But I'll say this: He was a very, very good group commander. He also was a hell of a good pilot. He knew what he didn't know. He called us together and said, 'Look, you guys have been out here doing all this. The Old Man wants us to run this mission. So how do we do it?' We told him how we thought we should do it and he said, 'Fine, let's do it that way, and put me on a wing slot.'

"I thought that was pretty damned good. There were a lot of guys who came over with a lot of rank and had preconceived ideas of how to fight a war, and got a lot of people killed. Scotty was very loyal to the people who worked for him, and he was a good pilot. He meant no harm. He had a lot of pluses."[13]

Colonel Scott would need all the pluses he could find, because now the 23rd Fighter Group was on its own.

3

Hengyang in the Crosshairs

The Curtiss P-40 was a hybrid from the start. First ordered by the Army Air Corps in 1937, the P-40 mixed the airframe of its predecessor—the classic mid-1930s P-36 Hawk—with a new engine, the liquid-cooled Allison V-1710.

The new power plant, a V-12 design, put out 1,160 horsepower, which was a substantial improvement over the P-36's radial engine. The V-1710 also allowed designers to graft a streamlined nose onto the P-36 fuselage to replace the blunt open cowling that its air-cooled engine had required. The idea worked, and the new P-40 boasted a top speed more than forty miles per hour faster than the P-36. Other aspects of the P-40's design were not so successful. The lighter P-36 was more maneuverable than the new fighter, and it had a better rate of climb.

Speed counted most in the late 1930s, however, as the latest fighter designs from Europe were producing top speeds in excess of 350 miles per hour. The Air Corps ordered the P-40 into mass production. Soon Army pilots were checking out on the new plane, and export models of the P-40 were being shipped lend-lease to several Allied air forces.

If the P-40 was not a top performer of its day, it was at least a handsome aircraft. The main wing featured the classic Curtiss tapered trailing edge capped by a rounded wingtip. The tail surfaces also featured pleasantly rounded contours, and the landing gear was fully retractable.

But the nose of the P-40 was its most distinctive feature. Mounted under the engine were the radiators for the engine coolant, as well as the oil cooler. All three were fed by a large scoop that gaped open under the pointed propeller spinner.

When the pilots of No. 112 Royal Air Force Squadron in North Africa saw their new P-40s in 1941, the nose reminded one of them of a shark. He painted a fearsome shark's mouth on the cowling with an eye just forward of the engine's exhaust stacks. Soon the rest of the squadron copied his design. A magazine photographer shot a picture of one of the planes that was widely circulated, and when the AVG pilots in Rangoon saw the picture, they adopted the shark's mouth marking for their own P-40s.[1] The practice was carried forward by the 23rd Fighter Group, and in fact, it became a standard marking for P-40s in China throughout the war. Before long, the combat reports began to refer to the planes not as P-40s but as "Sharks."

The P-40 was a competent fighter for its day. The top speed in level flight varied a little from one model to the next, but it was around 350 miles per hour. This was considerably faster than the Japanese fighters and bombers it encountered during 1942. The P-40 also was highly superior to Japanese planes in diving speed due to its weight, power, and streamlined nose. The P-40 was limited in altitude performance, however, because the Allison engine had only a single-stage supercharger. Its best speed came at fifteen thousand feet,[2] and once a P-40 got above twenty thousand feet, the supercharger was increasingly unable to compress the thin air going into the engine enough to allow the V-1710 to deliver full power. The service ceiling was listed at just under thirty thousand feet, but few P-40s ever flew that high in China.

Two features that endeared the P-40 to its pilots were its heavy armament and its durability. The early P-40s mounted two .50-caliber machine guns in the nose, firing through the propeller, plus four lighter machine guns in the wings. From the P-40E version on, most of the fighters carried six .50-caliber machine guns, three in each wing. Standard practice was to aim the guns so their fire would converge at a range of two hundred to three hundred yards. An accurate two-second burst from this arsenal would pour more than twenty pounds of slugs into the target—enough to shatter the lightly built Nakajima Ki-27 Nate and Ki-43 Oscar fighters and in strafing attacks to devastate ground targets such as trucks, boats, trains, airfields, and troop concentrations. The P-40 also had provisions for carrying a droppable auxiliary gas tank or a bomb under the fuselage, and later models were fitted with bomb racks and even bazooka tubes for rockets under the wings.

The toughness of the P-40 was legendary. Time after time, pilots would return from missions with their planes riddled with bullet holes or damaged from antiaircraft shells. Some even brought their planes home safely from midair collisions with enemy aircraft. The 23rd's ground crews would patch up their P-40s and send them back out to fight again. If the plane crash-landed or was too badly damaged to be flown in combat again, the mechanics would strip it of parts that could be used to keep other P-40s in flying condition. It was not unusual to see a P-40 with the fuselage from one aircraft, the wing of another, and the rudder or elevator of a third. That is the way it was in China, where every nut, bolt, screw, and washer had to be flown in over the Hump.

Also contributing to the P-40's survivability was the designers' decision to mount the radiators and oil cooler in the nose under the engine. A liquid-cooled engine is most vulnerable to failure in its cooling and lubrication systems. The radiators are heavy, however, and many fighter designs of World War II mounted them in the wings or farther back in the fuselage to place them closer to the airplane's center of gravity. Thus, lines ran from the engine back through much of the aircraft structure, and any stray bullet or flak burst nicking one of these lines (much less the radiators or engine themselves) was likely to result in engine failure in a matter of minutes. The P-40, with its engine and cooling system all mounted in the nose, presented a much smaller target of its vital systems. Pilots of the 23rd Fighter Group would learn this fact the hard way later in the war when their Sharks were replaced by more modern P-51 Mustang fighters.

One other drawback: the P-40 was not designed to fight at night. In fact, flying the P-40 on instruments in the daytime was not even considered a good idea unless the pilot really knew what he was doing. But in China in the summer of 1942, the P-40 was the only aircraft the 23rd Fighter Group had. If there was fighting to be done at night, the pilots would have to do it in their Sharks.

★ ★ ★ ★

As July 1942 wore on, men and aircraft continued to arrive for assignment to the 23rd Fighter Group. Eight new pilots joined the 76th Fighter Squadron at Kweilin on the 16th, and enlisted men came most every time a transport landed. One mechanic recalled Major Rector hugging each new man as he greeted him in front of the operations cave.[3] Likewise, the new men were warmly greeted at Hengyang, Lingling, and Kunming.

The Japanese were building up as well in preparation for the transfer of the 3rd Air Division headquarters from Singapore up to Canton. Once sufficient forces were in place, the Japanese Army Air Force (JAAF) planned to engage Chennault's air units in a decisive battle for air superiority over China. In the meantime, they were cooperating with Japanese ground forces in a minor campaign to capture and destroy Chinese air bases in the unoccupied area of

Chekiang Province, near the coast south of Hangchow.[4] These three bases—Lishui, Chuhsien, and Yushan—were to have been used by the Doolittle Raiders to refuel their B-25s after their historic raid on Tokyo back in April, but none of the planes reached the bases. Since then, the bases had not been used. With the closest of the three nearly four hundred miles east of Hengyang, they were much too remote and vulnerable to be used for operations. So their destruction was no great loss to the CATF.

Japanese offensive operations only consisted of occasional night raids against the 23rd's advance bases following the July 4 fight over Hengyang, but that was about to change. Soon the night attacks occurred like clockwork when the moon was bright and the sky clear enough to illuminate the target areas. They usually followed daytime incursions by high-flying Mitsubishi Ki-46 Dinah reconnaissance aircraft of the 18th Independent Air Squadron that operated out of Canton and Hankow.[5] The Dinah was a two-seat, twin-engine aircraft with a good turn of speed and excellent high-altitude capability. They were not completely immune to interception, but it was a rare day when a P-40 pilot could catch up with one of them long enough to get a shot off.

The information that the Ki-46 crews brought back to their commanders was used to plan the night missions for the bombers. Chennault's tactics and the effective use of the warning net, however, made that information of little value for planning specific missions. For one thing, the 11th Bomb Squadron regularly scrambled all its B-25s on two-ball daylight alerts. The planes would withdraw in the opposite direction from the incoming enemy aircraft and not return to land until the coast was clear. That burned up precious gasoline, but the Japanese rarely spotted more than one or two unserviceable B-25s on any base. The P-40s were a different matter. Only a few of them would take off to challenge a reconnaissance flight, and the rest might be spotted on the ground. Chennault constantly shifted most of his forces from one base to another, however, so that some or all of the planes photographed on the ground at Kweilin during the day, for example, might be at Hengyang, Lingling, or even Kunming by nightfall.

In a general sense, though, the Japanese could see that the CATF was building up its strength. But even this information was inaccurate, because Chennault's rapid deployments gave the impression that he had more aircraft than was actually the case. That was part of Chennault's genius: the ability to tackle a difficult problem with limited resources and come up with a simple solution that worked.

The pilots of the 23rd Fighter Group did not take long to start thinking like the Old Man did. During the long hours spent in the alert shacks at their bases, waiting for the *jing bao* balls to go up or for the weather to clear so they could run a mission somewhere, they talked about flying and tactics. They schemed about new ways to make their P-40s fly higher or carry more weapons. They discussed air-to-air shooting techniques, dive-bombing angles, and engine settings that would increase their range. The newer pilots pumped old pros like Tex Hill and Ed Rector for tips that would help them shoot down Japanese aircraft and avoid getting shot down themselves. And with the full moon approaching late in July, the subject of these bull sessions turned to night interceptions of enemy bombers.

At Lingling, the pilots of the 16th Fighter Squadron were especially anxious for action. The unit had been in China for a month, and so far not one of the pilots had even seen an enemy aircraft, much less fired on one. Meanwhile, the 75th up at Hengyang had flown a couple of good offensive missions and was eager for more. One of its pilots, Lt. Henry Elias, shot down Ki-27s on July 10 and July 26 and recorded the first confirmed kills by any of the new Army fliers in China.

Now at every base the pilots knew they could expect night visitors from Hankow or Canton, and they wanted to greet the Japanese bombers warmly. This would not be easy, even for the more experienced P-40 pilots. Takeoff would have to be accomplished without lights, which was difficult enough under any circumstances. The P-40 presented an additional challenge because the twelve exhaust stacks of its Allison engine were right in the pilot's line of sight on the takeoff roll and shot back bright blue flames that dazzled his eyes. It took all of his concentration to avoid getting blinded while trying to get off the ground.

Once in the air, the pilots would have to rely on radio instructions from the ground and a big dose of luck just to spot any enemy aircraft, much less to get off an accurate shot. In bright moonlight it was fairly easy to find an airfield below, because most of them were located near the river, which put off a silvery reflection. But the sky itself was inky black. The pilot's best hope for spotting another aircraft was to see its black shadow blot out the stars above or the river surface below as it crossed either of them. Then he might be able to follow the light put off by the target aircraft's engine exhausts long enough to close in to firing range and take a shot. But once the P-40's guns fired, the flashes from their muzzles would blind the pilot momentarily. Unless he hit the target and set it afire, he would find it difficult to relocate the target for a second attack. Then when the action was over, the P-40 pilot might be many miles away from his base and have trouble finding it again in the darkness.

These were big problems, and the odds against bringing down an enemy aircraft at night were long. But these pilots felt anything was better than shivering helplessly in the bottom of a slit trench while a Japanese bomber cruised overhead undisturbed, its bombardier trying to drop a couple hundred pounds of dynamite into their back pockets.

Two of the 16th Squadron's top pilots, Capt. Ed Goss and 1/Lt. John Lombard, got the first crack at a night interception. The alert came in at 12:45 A.M. on July 27: three bombers headed toward Lingling. The two pilots were at the hostel and rushed down to the field where their two P-40Es were at readiness just outside the operations shack. Goss got off first, with Lombard about fifteen minutes behind. As Lombard was making his takeoff run, the three enemy bombers arrived over the field. Surprisingly, they all had their navigation lights on, obviously not expecting to be intercepted.

Goss spotted the bombers and made three passes at them in his P-40. He felt certain that he had hit one of them and knocked out its tail gunner, but then the raiders turned off their lights and disappeared into the darkness. They dropped several bombs a mile away from the field but did no damage. Both P-40s landed safely. Although this first interception did not result in any confirmed kills, it did let the Japanese know that they would not be free to roam the night skies in safety any more.

Captain Goss and 2/Lt. Dallas Clinger tried another night interception later that evening. Most of the men in the 16th climbed a hill near the base to watch the expected fireworks, but the enemy bombers did not approach the base and the two P-40s landed without contacting them.

In the early morning of July 30, Goss went up for a three-hour patrol but again came back with nothing to report. Major Ed Rector went up at Kweilin and had the same experience. However, on this night the story was different at Hengyang.

Tex Hill had a new weapon in his 75th Fighter Squadron: John Alison, who had transferred from the 16th Fighter Squadron to the 23rd Fighter Group earlier in the month when his promotion to major came through. Alison had been assigned to fly with Hill in the 75th at Hengyang and led a successful dive-bombing mission against Nanchang Airport on July 26. When word reached Hengyang of Goss's night action at Lingling, Johnny Alison could not wait to take a crack at night interception himself. He had some definite ideas on how the feat might be accomplished, and he was anxious to try them out.

Alison got his chance on the night of July 29–30. He and Capt. Ajax Baumler had decided that they would oppose the next raid by climbing to twelve thousand feet, circling the field, and waiting for the enemy bombers to come in below them. The height advantage would give the P-40s sufficient speed to overtake the bombers once spotted. The alert came in as expected at about 2:00 A.M., and the pilots took off with sufficient separation to avoid a collision.

Alison got off first. He climbed as rapidly as his P-40E would go, his eyes straining in the darkness to pick up any sign of another aircraft. He fought off the temptation to check his instruments, because even the pale lights illuminating them would cut down on his night vision momentarily. At nine thousand feet he passed through a thin layer of haze. He knew it could pose a visibility problem if the enemy came in below it while he was on top. After about five minutes of climbing, Alison reached twelve thousand feet and leveled off. He throttled back slightly and listened through the crackling static in his radio headset for a report on the intruders.

Before long he got the word: enemy aircraft over the field, passing north to south without attacking. These were probably Ki-21 Sally heavy bombers of the 62nd Air Regiment, which had a detachment stationed at Wuchang. A moment later the radio operator came on again with the report that the twin-engine bombers had made a turn and were now heading back north toward the base. Alison scanned the sky below him as he crossed the field from east to west, but he saw nothing. Then it occurred to him that perhaps they had thrown him a curve and were actually higher than he was. He looked up to his left, and there they were, shadows crossing against the stars, with the glow of their engine exhausts faintly visible. Alison firewalled his engine and called in the sighting to Baumler as he climbed into position behind the enemy aircraft. Just as Alison reached fifteen thousand feet and pulled in behind his targets, they banked to the right and made a 180-degree turn that would put them in position for a third run over the field. That turn placed Alison's P-40 between the bombers and the moon, and one of the Japanese tail gunners spotted him as he lined up behind the aircraft on the left of the vee formation.

The gunner, who was in a plane to Alison's right, opened up with an accurate stream of fire. Tracers reached out toward the P-40, and Alison could feel slugs slamming into the nose of his fighter, then working their way down the fuselage. With no time to lose, he opened fire on the bomber in front of him. The six .50-caliber guns roared, and within two seconds the badly crippled bomber pulled up, then fell away from the formation.[6]

One of the ground crewmen watching from below was Sgt. Bill Harris, a mechanic and painter in the 75th. He described what he saw.

"It seemed as if the Jap bombers were a long time coming in. Then we could hear the faint typical drone of their unsynchronized engines. As it got louder we could see the bomber formation coming in with their running lights on, of all things! They were so cocky because of no previous night fighter opposition. To the dismay of all of us on the edge of the field, it seemed the P-40s were in the opposite direction, and we were foolishly but enthusiastically yelling, 'Over here! Here they are! Get them!' The P-40s put on full power and we knew they had seen the bombers.

"All of a sudden there was a stream of yellow/green tracers arching back at the P-40 of Alison. Then a terrific roar of his .50 calibers, and the bright orange flash from six guns lit up the sky. Almost immediately the sky was lit again with a fireball as the first bomber went down. The Japs immediately high-tailed it for home and the second and third blasts of .50s grew fainter as the action was carried on out of our sight."[7]

It is likely that the bomber Harris saw coming down on fire was actually the second one Alison shot. Soon after sustaining the hits in his P-40, Alison felt his damaged engine beginning to lose power. But the bomber closest to his right was still within easy striking distance. He turned toward the source of the tracers that were still coming his way. Again Alison pressed the trigger, and again his aim was on the mark. The second bomber caught fire and then exploded before falling in pieces from the sky. Now Alison's engine began to smoke and spew oil back over the P-40's windshield.

Several thousand feet below, Captain Baumler saw Alison's first target turn away from the formation and start down. He was determined that the bomber would not get home. After a short chase, Baumler pulled into firing range and let fly. The bomber staggered as it erupted in flames, then began its death dive. Now a gunner in another bomber took a shot at Baumler, alerting him to its heretofore unknown presence. Baumler turned to give chase. He caught up with his quarry about thirty miles north of Hengyang and shot it down.

Alison might have been wiser to head for home after attacking his second bomber, but his engine was still running a little and a third Japanese bomber remained in sight. He reached firing range just after the plane in front of him dropped its bombs. In the last seconds before his P-40 quit running, Alison opened fire for the third time. This time his gunfire must have ripped directly into the bomber's unprotected gas tanks, because the plane literally exploded in flames. Then Alison's engine quit altogether, and he had no choice but to land.

In the sudden silence, Alison spiraled as slowly as possible to stretch out the P-40's glide while he looked for the airfield at Hengyang. Spotting the base, Alison opened the canopy to give him better vision, as the windshield was dotted with oil. Then, just as he was trying to set up for a dead-stick landing approach, flames belched out from under the engine cowling. Distracted briefly and with his vision obscured, Alison overshot the field. He pulled back on the stick gently to gain as much altitude as possible, then practically willed the airplane to stretch its glide over some buildings and trees until he reached the river.

He skimmed the plane down "like a PBY" onto the surface of the river.[8] The plane bounced a couple of times, once hard enough to slam Alison's forehead into the gun sight mounted on the cockpit rim and cut a gash in it (a common injury for P-40 pilots making wheels-up landings). Then the plane slowed to a stop and began to sink. Alison pulled himself out of the cockpit and swam to shore on the city side, which was on the far side of the river from the airfield but a shorter swim for the exhausted pilot. There he was detained by Chinese soldiers until his identity as an American pilot could be established. About daylight they commandeered a boat and took him back across the river to a landing near the U.S. hostel. Later, when Alison was awarded a Distinguished Service Cross for his exploits that night, he would complain to General Chennault that he would have preferred to have movie star Lana Turner pin the ribbon on his uniform.[9]

One more bit of heroism took place that night, not in the sky but on the field at Hengyang. While the pilots had little trouble taking off from the field in darkness, landing was something different. It was nearly impossible to make a good approach to the runway with the field blacked out, so it was arranged for Chinese coolies to place lanterns down each side when it was time for the P-40s to return to their base. However, that night the Chinese had all fled during the bombing. Second Lieutenant Martin S. Cluck and 1/Sgt. Thomas L. Irwin of the 75th Fighter Squadron took it upon themselves to set out the boundary lights, even though the *jing bao* warning was still in effect. Thanks to them, Baumler was able to land safely after the engagement. And Alison was able to find the field, too, even if his landing went a bit long.[10]

Alison got himself cleaned up at the hostel, then headed back to the airfield. He arrived around 9:00 A.M., just in time to see a two-ball alert go up on the *jing bao* pole. The pilots at the alert shack were surprised and relieved to see Alison, because most of them figured he had been killed after seeing his flaming P-40 skim across the field and crash into the river. There was not much time to talk, however, because the net was reporting a force of enemy fighters coming in from the direction of Hankow. The night raids of the past few evenings had been the opening rounds in a major effort to run the China Air Task Force out of its eastern bases. The American pilots would have their hands full for the next few days.

Soon ten P-40s, a mixed formation that included pilots of the 75th and 16th squadrons, were climbing away from Hengyang with Maj. Tex Hill in the lead and Maj. Gil Bright leading the second flight. Hill was anxious for action, because he had spent a frustrating and unsuccessful hour and a half probing the dark for a second Japanese night raid after Alison and Baumler came down from their spectacular fight.

This time Hill would find plenty of targets. The P-40s had reached nineteen thousand feet when a formation of about forty Japanese fighters was spotted not far from the field. Hill led his P-40s straight into the mixed formation of Ki-27 Nates and Ki-43 Oscars, and a tremendous fifteen-minute air battle ensued. Down on the field, Bill Harris and the rest of the ground personnel had a clear view of the whole thing.

As Hill approached the enemy fighters, he and one Ki-27 pilot appeared to pick each other out. They approached head-on directly over the airfield with a closing speed in excess of five hundred miles per hour. The Ki-27 pilot opened fire first, but his two light machine guns were no match for the .50-caliber guns in Hill's P-40E. When he judged the enemy fighter was in range, Hill cut loose with a burst of fire that hit the Nate squarely in the nose. The plane went into a death dive and smacked into the ground about fifty feet away from a dummy aircraft that had been set up at the edge of the airfield. In reviewing the event, some have suggested that the Japanese pilot may have aimed his stricken plane at the dummy in an early version of a kamikaze attack. Hill did not speculate about that when he discussed the mission more than fifty years later.

"It just happened," he said." We damned near ran head-on into each other. When I hit him, he went down and I turned the other way. He crashed right on the end of the runway.

"When I did get down, I went over to look at him [the dead Japanese pilot]. The dramatics weren't all that much. I might have made some kind of remark; I don't remember. I probably rooted him around with my foot or something."[11]

While Hill was dueling with the Ki-27, the rest of the P-40 pilots began mixing it up as well. Major Bright made a pass from the rear on a Ki-43 that was flying in a flight of three. He put a two-second burst into the plane, and it nosed over. But before Bright could follow, he spotted another Ki-43 from the flight coming around to get on his tail. Using his superior speed, Bright started a shallow climb and pulled away from his attacker until he was out of range. Meanwhile, Bright's wingman, Lt. Bill Druwing of the 16th Squadron, followed the first Ki-43 down and put some shots into it before the plane crashed.

Now Bright turned back toward the fight. Soon he spotted a Ki-27 ahead of him and began to close in. The enemy pilot spotted him, however, and whipped into a tight turn that put him in position to make a head-on pass at Bright's P-40. That was a bad idea. Bright did just as Tex Hill had done a few moments earlier and put a deadly burst into the nose of the Ki-27. The damaged plane pulled up sharply, then dropped over into a spin with white smoke trailing behind it. Bright started to follow it down but had to break off when he saw yet another enemy fighter lining up on him from behind. He returned safely to base.

Other pilots getting into the action included Captain Baumler and 2/Lts. Martin Cluck and Thomas Dyer, plus 1/Lt. Bob Liles of the 16th. A flight of three P-40s from the 16th, led by Capt. Ed Goss, flew up to Hengyang from Lingling to give support, but they did not arrive in time to get into the fight.

While the pilots at Kweilin were giving their reports to the intelligence officer, word came from the warning net that one of the Japanese fighters they shot down had landed intact not far from the field. Not only that but the pilot was reportedly alive. Major Hill sent Second Lieutenant Cluck out in a jeep to take the pilot prisoner and keep the Chinese from damaging the plane, which turned out to be one of the new Ki-43 Oscars.[12] Eventually the plane was salvaged and restored to flying condition by Sgt. Gerhard Neumann of the 76th.

The Japanese came back for another round early the next morning. Again, pilots of the 16th and 75th squadrons were waiting for them. Major Hal Young, commander of the 16th, led a flight of six P-40Es up to Hengyang in the predawn light from Lingling when the warning net became active. Meanwhile, Major Bright of the 75th was leading a formation out of Hengyang to intercept the same raid.

The fight started about 6:30 A.M. Bright's formation became separated during the climb out. He spotted a large formation of enemy fighters and bored straight in with his diminished force. His first attack set a Ki-43 on fire, and then the stricken plane simply exploded. Bright swerved to avoid the blast and swung in behind another Ki-43. Again, his bullets found the target, which began to smoke. But this time the Japanese pilot was able to whip his plane around in a tight turn and avoid further damage from Bright. It headed back north in the direction of Hankow, trailing smoke. Another member of Bright's flight, Lieutenant Elias, also nailed one Ki-43.

About this time Major Young's P-40s arrived from Lingling. First Lieutenant Lombard and his wingman, Second Lieutenant Clinger, spotted three planes on the edge of a large enemy formation and attacked them with the idea of cutting them off from the main group. Within seconds, however, the two P-40 pilots found themselves in a swirling mass of more than twenty enemy fighters. One of the men reported later that the Japanese looked "like a swarm of angry hornets."[13]

Lombard continued to attack in a diving fight and claimed one Ki-43 shot down. Clinger guarded Lombard's tail aggressively, shooting down one Ki-43 and firing at several others. At one point he even feinted his P-40 at one of the Ki-43s. The Japanese pilot wisely decided to break off his attack on Lombard.

Captain Goss of the 16th also claimed one Oscar destroyed, and all of the 16th's P-40s landed safely back at Lingling. Lombard and Clinger had recorded the 16th's first confirmed victories, and both were decorated for the mission.

The most spectacular performance of the morning was turned in by 2/Lt. Mack A. Mitchell of the 75th. While the Americans were occupied at high altitude, part of the Japanese force split away and dived out of the sun for a strafing attack on Hengyang airfield. Men on the ground squeezed themselves into the bottoms of slit trenches while the Japanese pilots concentrated on shooting up P-40s that had been undergoing repairs on the field.

Mitchell was at ten thousand feet when he spotted about nine Ki-43s at seven thousand feet heading toward the field. He dived after them alone, picking up tremendous speed in the process. Using Chennault's dive-and-zoom tactics, Mitchell approached the rear of the formation, put a burst into the rearmost aircraft, then pulled back up to make another pass. He attacked again, but this time he let his speed carry him in front of two Japanese fighters and then pulled around in a sharp turn to make a head-on pass at them. This he accomplished, but then the quick-turning Ki-43s zipped around behind Mitchell and started shooting at him. Soon there was one Oscar planted squarely on his tail and four more hovering above.

Mitchell did the only thing he could do and pushed the P-40 over into a screaming dive. The Ki-43 was still firmly attached to his tail, though beginning to lose ground, when Mitchell passed near the field at very low altitude and went out of sight behind the nearby hills. But he was not finished fighting yet. He gave the following statement later:

"When I came out of the dive that Jap was so close that I saw his bifocals. The forward travel of that throttle was not half enough, but the '40 gave its all and me a little distance on that Jap. I gained enough distance to turn for a head-on pass. As I turned he pulled up, exposing his belly at which I had a good shot and observed some hits. Only the guns on one wing were firing, which caused my plane to stall, so I had to run for it again. But the Zero [it was common for pilots in China to refer to any Japanese plane they encountered as a Zero] did not follow. I pulled up but did not see him again; so I returned to the field, but the fight was over."[14] Later, Chinese civilians found the wreckage of a Ki-43 near the scene of the action, and Mitchell was given credit for destroying it.

Also that day, Colonel Scott took off from Kunming in a P-40 bound for Kweilin after a conference at CATF headquarters. The cloud cover was thick, and he had trouble finding Kweilin. When he finally landed at Lingling he was almost out of gas. Scott reported having engaged a Japanese bomber being escorted by two fighters near Leiyang and claimed credit for the bomber and one fighter destroyed.[15]

★ ★ ★ ★

As August arrived, the Chinese people of Lingling and Hengyang decided to show their appreciation for the stiff defense that the 23rd Fighter Group was providing against Japanese air attacks.

At Lingling, civilian and military leaders held a ceremony on August 1 and presented the men of the 16th Fighter Squadron with a large blue and white banner proclaiming them "The Great Wall of the Air." This banner, on which the Great Wall of China was portrayed with a shark's mouth and small yellow wings, became the inspiration for the 16th's squadron insignia. Major Young made the acceptance speech for the squadron. A similar celebration took place August 3 for the men of the 75th and 16th squadrons at Hengyang. General Shio, commander in chief of the 9th War Area, hosted the appreciation dinner.

Indeed, it had been a good first month for the 23rd Fighter Group. Even considering the inevitable vagaries of the confirmation system, the score of aerial victories far exceeded the number of P-40s lost to enemy action. In all, the American pilots had received credit for twenty-three enemy aircraft destroyed, ten probably destroyed, and two damaged in aerial combat. More important, the presence of a creditable fighter defense had forced the Japanese to concentrate their air attacks on the air bases at Hengyang and Lingling, leaving civilian targets alone.

And best of all, the 23rd Fighter Group had suffered no casualties at the hands of the Japanese after the deaths of AVG civilians Petach and Shamblin. Death is an inevitable part of war, however. The 76th Fighter Squadron lost a new pilot, 2/Lt. Leon C. Allen, on July 21 during a test flight at Kweilin. Observers saw Allen's P-40 dive low and pull up before it flipped over on its back and fell into a rice paddy near the airfield. And soon the first U.S. Army pilot would fall in combat over China.

A mixed formation from the 75th and 16th squadrons flew a successful dive-bombing mission against Linchuan on August 3. Many hits were observed inside the target area of the town, and no Japanese fighters attempted to intercept the twelve Sharks.

The Japanese retaliated two days later with yet another attack on Hengyang. Nearly fifty Japanese fighters, a mix of Ki-27s and Ki-43s, swept over the field in a loose formation at 6:00 A.M. Only eight Sharks, led by Major Alison, were able to get airborne in time to challenge them. The fight spread broadly across the sky, with Major Alison and 1/Lt. Lauren R. Barnebey of the 16th claiming victories.

A further victory was claimed from a trench on the field, where Technical Sgt. John W. Brewer was behind the gun sight of a machine gun. Brewer, flight chief of the 16th Squadron, had supervised the takeoff of the squadron's P-40s before adjourning to his volunteer gun position. When two enemy fighters buzzed low over the field on a strafing run, Brewer was the first to open fire on them. His efforts attracted the Japanese pilots' attention, and they turned to attack him.

Pilot Bob Liles of the 16th recalled, "My airplane was broken. We knew the Japs were coming in, so they put the plane in a revetment. Brewer and another guy were working on it, and I went off to the edge of the field.

"The Jap fighters came in right over my head, strafing. I had a .45 with tracer [bullets] in it. I was standing out there shooting with this .45, and I hit one of them. I hit him right behind the ring cowl on his engine. I knew what it did because of the tracer. I didn't know it, but that son of a bitch was strafing at my airplane.

"Brewer and this other guy were in a slit trench right by my airplane. Brewer had a Browning Automatic Rifle and he was shooting at these Japs. They saw him shooting at them, and they started coming over and rolling straight down, trying to hit him in that slit trench. There were 20-millimeter pock marks all around him, but they didn't hit him.

"One of the Japs came down to make a pass, and Brewer shot him right in the fuselage. I mean he hit him hard. The guy wobbled around the damned airfield, rolled over, and dived into a building; I believe it was the armament shack. Set it on fire. The Chinese went in there and pulled him out—stole his clothes and threw them on the fire. My doctor, Major Voss, went over and hauled the guy's body out."[16]

Brewer was awarded a Silver Star for his show of courage in the face of enemy fire.

The day was touched by deep sadness, however, when word was received at Hengyang that 2/Lt. Lee Minor of the 75th Squadron had been killed in the air battle. Minor's P-40 was hit from the rear, and he bailed out. At some point Minor suffered a head wound, and he was dead when the Chinese found him, still strapped in his parachute. In all, nearly 150 men of the 23rd Fighter Group would die during the course of the war, but Lieutenant Minor was the first of them to be killed in action.

★ ★ ★ ★

The 76th Fighter Squadron did not see as much action as the 75th and the 16th during this period, but Major Rector's unit was not altogether idle, either. Besides training new pilots and ground personnel as they arrived at Kweilin, the 76th ran offensive missions on July 16 and August 6. Both missions were escorts for B-25s of the 11th Bomb Squadron attacking Tien Ho Airdrome at Canton, and neither run resulted in contact with enemy aircraft. Bad weather limited operations at Kweilin, as did the lack of Japanese raids on the 76th's base.

The squadron finally saw some action on August 8, however, when Capt. Charlie Sawyer led Lts. Patrick Daniels, Charles Dubois, and Harold Stuart on yet another escort mission to Canton. This time the target was White Cloud, another airdrome at the port city, and the 16th Fighter Squadron also contributed four Sharks to the escort chores.

The B-25s hit dropped their bombs on the target at 11:36 A.M. Just then, Lieutenant Daniels spotted three Japanese fighters from the 24th Air Regiment below him and peeled off to attack them. His inexperience showed, as he spun out during his attack and wound up with the three Ki-43 Oscars on his tail. Daniels gave his Shark full throttle and began racing for safety. Two of his pursuers gave up and turned away as he outdistanced them, but the last one continued to follow. When Daniels judged that he had put sufficient distance between the two fighters, he whipped his P-40 into a tight turn and came back for a head-on pass at the Ki-43.

When Daniels started shooting, the Oscar pilot pulled up in a steep climb to avoid his fire and to maneuver for a shot at the P-40. Instead, Daniels followed him into the climb, continuing to shoot. The Oscar doubled back from the top of his climb, but a burst from Daniels's guns hit it at a crucial moment and the plane caught fire as it dived past him. Daniels reported that he saw the Japanese pilot climbing out of his cockpit, attempting to bail out, just before the stricken plane crashed into a mountaintop.

On the return flight to Kweilin, Captain Sawyer saw nine enemy fighters climbing up toward the bombers. He rolled over to drop down on the attackers, with Lieutenant Dubois right behind. In the fight that followed, Sawyer destroyed one Ki-27 and shot at three others. When the enemy fighters dispersed, Sawyer and Dubois rejoined the formation, and Sawyer led his flight back to Kweilin.

The 23rd Fighter Group ran two more missions on August 10 and 11, but the pace of action soon slowed. Bad weather increasingly hampered operations in East China, personnel were tired, and the supply situation on the bases was becoming critical. Fighters cannot fight without sufficient pilots, gasoline, and ammunition. All three were in short supply, especially at Hengyang and Lingling.

In mid-August, the squadrons got their marching orders. The 16th would pull back to Peishiyi, a base not far from Chungking. The 76th joined the 74th at Kunming, and the 75th moved to Chanyi, a remote base in a small valley eighty miles northeast of Kunming. It was time for a short rest before General Chennault turned the 23rd Fighter Group loose on a new set of targets. For the time being, low clouds and rain would have to provide protection for the cities along the Hsiang River valley.

4

The School Squadron

At just past noon on July 16, 1942, two pilots of the 74th Fighter Squadron hurriedly took off from Kunming. They were attempting to intercept a Japanese reconnaissance plane that was reportedly heading their way. Within minutes, the inexperienced Americans became separated in the clouds.

One of the pilots, 1/Lt. James C. Reed, circled for a while without seeing anything, then landed uneventfully. His wingman, 2/Lt. Joseph L. Mikeworth, climbed to twenty thousand feet above the field. There he spotted a twin-engine airplane fleeing southward in the distance. Mikeworth began to give chase, but soon the engine in his P-40 started cutting out. Unable to close on the Japanese aircraft and fearful that his engine might quit at any moment, Mikeworth turned back toward Kunming.

Mikeworth could not make it. His engine gave up before he reached the air base, so he attempted a dead-stick landing in a field. The P-40 hit the ground with a thud, driving both main landing-gear struts up through the top of the wings. The pilot walked away, but the airplane was junk.

So ended the 74th's first encounter with the enemy. It was about what might have been expected from a unit referred to as the "School Squadron."

Five weeks later, Lieutenant Mikeworth was killed when his P-40 entered a spin during a test flight and crashed into Kunming Lake. The week after that, Lieutenant Reed was among four pilots sent back to India for additional training.

All fighter pilots are not created equal. Some have better eyesight than others. Some are born navigators, and others excel at marksmanship. Very few can do all things well. But the most important asset any pilot can have is seat time. The more hours he gets in the air, the better the pilot he becomes.

The pilots who joined the 23rd Fighter Group in the summer of 1942 all had graduated from Army flight training, but the amount of flight time and operational training in their logbooks varied greatly. Those who were judged least ready to begin flying combat missions were lumped into the 74th Fighter Squadron, which was stationed at Kunming. There they would be able to build up experience gradually while providing air defense for this key base at the eastern end of the Hump's transport route.

The man in charge of turning the School Squadron into a combat-ready unit was Maj. Frank Schiel Jr., twenty-five, commanding officer of the 74th. A dark-haired Arizona native with a pencil-thin mustache, Schiel bore a resemblance to a popular movie star of the time, Robert Taylor. Schiel had been credited with four Japanese planes destroyed in the air and three more on the ground while flying with the AVG, but he was most noted for the reconnaissance missions he flew in a special stripped-down P-40 fitted with an aerial camera.

Schiel had much ground to cover with his pilots. Even the men who were flying combat in the other squadrons were hardly what you would call "old hands." Bob Liles of the 16th recalled the problem vividly.

"A lot of us had never had any gunnery training. I had never had air-to-air gunnery training at all. The first round I ever fired air-to-air was at a Jap Zero, at Hengyang in July of '42. My ground gunnery consisted of somebody throwing aluminum powder on the ocean surface. It spread out about the area of two houses, and if you hit it, that was pretty good. That was our ground gunnery training.

"Some of the other people had had gunnery training. Where they got it, I don't know. Quite a few of the younger pilots were graduates of class '41-I, which meant that they graduated from flight training in December '41 or January '42. They had about six months' experience.

"I would say it took a couple or three months in China before we became what I would consider proficient. Probably six months before people got really, really good at being fighter pilots. That's my opinion.

"Two of the toughest things about flying and running missions in China: the weather was a hell of a factor, and the maps were bad. It was very bad a lot of the time. The mountains were there in many areas, and we had very few navigation aids the fighters could use. You couldn't do let-downs. If you got caught above the overcast, you couldn't get down to the ground. You'd either find a place to let down, or just bail out.

"Haze depended on the time of the year. Other times, over West China it would be clear as a bell. It was just like our western states. You could see Mount Everest for two hundred miles. You could use Everest as a little bit of a checkpoint to keep your orientation because you could see so damned far.

"Being able to navigate and cope with the weather and the lack of navigational aids was one of the prerequisites of being a good flight commander. Being able to keep track of where you were. Being able to get from Point A to Point B without losing airplanes.

"And the maps were not very good. Sometimes the railroad tracks would be on the wrong side of the river. They were not accurate, and you had to be there awhile to find out some of this. Over in East China, somewhere down around Liuchow was a railroad track on the wrong side of a river. There were a lot of places where you had to learn those things, and then pass them along to the guys who were coming along behind you.

"Basically we'd give a new pilot a briefing, but you couldn't take him out and fly him around to see if he was any good. We'd tell him how to do what was expected of him—tactics. That was turned over to the flight commanders."[1]

Tex Hill of the 75th expanded on that final point. "Most of the flying was done by AVG pilots during the first couple of weeks. However, some of the other guys they got in there came out of [previous assignments in] Panama, and, boy, they were very well trained. These guys—Elmer ["Rich"] Richardson, Joe Griffin, [Hollis] Blackstone, [Jesse] Carney—for some reason the people who came out of these foreign areas were better trained. I don't know if it was because they were out there in the boonies or what. Then we got some replacements out of Puerto Rico that were good.

"The new pilots picked it up very fast, though. They were seasoned pilots. All we had to do was give them our tactics. Our tactics were really very simple: *You just don't turn with the guy.* They picked up on it real good, and we did very well there in those first six months.

"Unfortunately, Frank Schiel got stuck up there in Kunming when they were activating the group. He got the 74th. Anything close to headquarters, Jesus, you were in deep trouble. So they didn't get to see much action. Later on, they became one of the best squadrons in China."[2]

★ ★ ★ ★

During the first three weeks of July 1942, the 74th was kept busy doing maintenance on its AVG hand-me-down P-40s. These planes were all early model P-40s, as the more modern P-40Es were needed by the squadrons in East China. Mechanics, radio technicians, and armorers worked over the weary warriors, and when one was ready for a test flight, there were always plenty of pilots in the operations shack eager to take it up.

It was not uncommon for problems to occur on these engineering flights. The landing gear collapsed on a Shark flown by 1/Lt. Thomas R. Smith on July 18, and 2/Lt. Eugene F. Wanner ground-looped another one while landing on July 22. Six more accidents were recorded during the following month, some mechanical and some caused by pilot error. Then came August 21, the day Lieutenant Mikeworth spun Shark number 40 into Tien Chih Lake, which the pilots called Kunming Lake, and was killed.

Five days later, on August 26, a *jing bao* alert sent a flight of Sharks from the 74th off at 6:15 P.M. to intercept a reported incoming raid. Instead of enemy bombers, the 74th pilots found a flight of P-40s from the 75th and 16th squadrons coming into Kunming after an uneventful mission. The 74th Sharks had more gas, so they let the other planes land first. A new pilot in the 16th Squadron, 2/Lt. Richard C. Gee, had just landed and was taxiing on the runway when 1/Lt. T. V. Skelly of the 74th landed his P-40 from the other direction and immediately collided head-on with Gee. The planes erupted in a ball of flames, and both pilots perished. The realities of war were beginning to sink in on the men of the 74th.

One of the problems that made it so difficult for pilots to get flying time was the shortage of supplies and equipment. The pilots rarely got a chance to fly training missions because gasoline could not be spared and the planes had to be preserved for operational uses. Again, Bob Liles remembered, "one factor that worked against us was that we didn't get to fly very much in China. Practically every time you flew it was on a combat mission of some kind. We never had the fuel to go out and practice. We couldn't even go get gunnery practice. It cost too much to haul the fuel and ammunition over to China. If we were going to shoot the guns, we had to shoot them at something. That didn't change while I was there."[3]

As a result, the decision was made henceforth to have operational training done by the Tenth Air Force in Karachi before new pilots ever got to China. And four pilots with the least experience in the 74th, including Lieutenant Reed, were sent back to Karachi on September 1 for additional training.

Then on September 8, 1942, came the day that everyone in the 74th had been waiting for: the squadron's first confirmed kill. First Lieutenant Thomas R. Smith was on alert duty when the warning net reported an enemy aircraft approaching Kunming from the southeast. Smith ran out to P-40 number 46 and took off. The Shark quickly climbed out of sight, and the men on the ground waited a frustrating fifteen minutes for the young pilot to report in on his radio.

"There's the bastard now!" was Smith's first call.[4] He had spotted a twin-engine Ki-46 Dinah reconnaissance plane at twenty-four thousand feet. The young pilot pulled his laboring Shark in close behind it before opening fire. The first burst from Smith's guns hit the Dinah's left engine. Then he pumped five short bursts into the right engine and saw the enemy plane begin to trail flames.

By this time, Smith was so close behind his target that oil from the damaged Japanese aircraft sprayed back onto the leading edges of his Shark's wings and tail. Then he watched as the Dinah nosed over and dived straight into the ground.

When Smith returned to Kunming, he flew right across the field and did a victory roll fifty feet off the runway. General Chennault and Colonel Scott were waiting to congratulate Smith when old number 46 rolled to a stop and he shut it down. Smith later was awarded a Silver Star for the mission.

Four days later, Major Schiel flew the 74th's second Silver Star mission. Schiel, the reconnaissance specialist, was assigned to fly to Hanoi, 340 miles south of Kunming, and photograph the Japanese airfield there. He flew the mission not in a P-40, but in a Republic P-43A Lancer fighter equipped with an aerial camera.

The P-43 was a stubby, radial-engine aircraft that looked like a shrunken P-47 Thunderbolt. The plane was built in limited numbers by Republic in 1941 while the Thunderbolt was under development, and 108 of them were sent to China under the lend-lease program for the Chinese Air Force. General Chennault had arranged to "borrow" a handful of them for the 23rd Fighter Group to fly.

On paper, the P-43A appeared to have a slight edge on the P-40E. On the one hand, the planes were very close in operational range and maximum speed. The P-40E had a slight advantage in armament with six machine guns to the P-43A's four. On the other hand, the P-43A was equipped with a turbo-supercharged engine, which gave it a faster climb and a service ceiling of thirty-six thousand feet, far above any model of the P-40.

But for combat operations, the P-43A clearly was not up to the durability standards set by the P-40. For one thing, the P-43A had insufficient armor plate behind the cockpit to protect the pilot. More important, its gas tanks were not self-sealing, and in many of the planes they tended to leak. This made the Lancer a virtual flying bomb, ready to explode at the first strike of enemy gunfire. So the 23rd Fighter Group used P-43s sparingly, often in a reconnaissance role.

Schiel flew south out of Kunming and crossed the border into French Indo-China near Lao Kay. Following the Red River, he continued deeper into the French colony, which had been controlled by the pro-Japanese Vichy government since France surrendered to Germany in 1940. Schiel was 175 miles deep in enemy territory when he began his sighting runs over Gia Lam Airdrome at Hanoi. He could see Japanese fighters taking off below him and knew they would be climbing up to his altitude within minutes. Still, he turned and made a photo pass over the airdrome.

Major Schiel continued to take photos until three Ki-43 Oscars reached his level and drew near firing range. Schiel resisted the temptation to engage, knowing how valuable his photos would be to General Chennault's mission planners. So he turned the Lancer north and gave it full throttle. Before long, the speedy fighter outdistanced its Japanese pursuers, and Schiel was able to return safely to Kunming with his photos. A few days later, four B-25s of the 11th Bomb Squadron made a highly successful attack on the airfield at Hanoi, using the information Schiel had gathered.

Major Schiel followed the September 12 mission with another long one on October 7. This time, he flew a stripped-down Shark down to China's coast to observe installations and shipping. He was gone from Kunming no less than eight hours, and he was awarded a Distinguished Flying Cross for the flight.

As the fall of 1942 progressed, the School Squadron's primary mission continued as air defense for Kunming. Strafing and escort missions came up occasionally, but bad weather and the pilots' inexperience were limiting factors.

Also during this time, more new pilots were arriving in all of the 23rd's squadrons. Quite a few of these men had served in Central America for a number of months and had logged substantial flying hours before coming to China. One of these men was 2/Lt. William B. Hawkins Jr. Not long after graduating from flight school in December 1941, Hawkins was sent to Panama to fly P-39 Airacrobras with the 53rd Pursuit Group. From there he was transferred to Karachi, where he completed about twelve hours of transition training in the P-40 before ferrying a new Shark to Kunming in early October 1942. Perhaps because of his limited experience flying P-40s, he was assigned to the School Squadron. Now a retired Air Force colonel, Hawkins recounted his China experiences in 1987.

"I spent the first winter with the 74th at Kunming. It was in a big valley with six-thousand-foot mountains all around, especially west over the Himalayas. I have vivid recollections of it being very cold. We were short on fuel and didn't fly very much. We sat alert all the time in our P-40s.

"The aircraft were dispersed around the field every evening so they wouldn't be parked in a row and make an easy target for night bombers. We'd get up a couple of hours before daylight and have a breakfast of hotcakes and eggs. I think I had that for breakfast every day I was in China. Then we'd go out and find our P-40s, clear the frost off their windows, start the engine, and let it warm up. We'd taxi over to operations so we'd be ready in case there was a *jing bao*.

"As soon as an aircraft was seen in the warning net, the Chinese would call in, and we'd have a one-ball alert. . . . We'd get ourselves all emotionally ready to go. A little while later two balls would go up. That was the time for action. We'd run to the aircraft, get in, and take off. The leader would go first, and we'd form up on his wing. When the third ball went up, that meant the Japs were directly overhead. Everyone on the field was supposed to take cover in the slit trenches.

"We had lots of alerts, and Kunming was bombed frequently, but never while I was there.

"The biggest thing that happened that first winter was the Red Dog game. We'd clean up in the morning and taxi the ships to the line. But weeks would go by when we didn't fly. As soon as we got the planes set up, we'd start playing Red Dog.

"I don't remember how it was played, but as many could play as wanted to. The money that was riding on that: God, there'd be thousands of dollars on the Red Dog game. Everybody—especially the old heads—had a lot of money.

"There were so many guys killed. I've read where we had a 12-to-1 victory-to-loss ratio and that may be so, but that doesn't take into account all the guys who were killed in other ways.

"The pilots weren't trained in instruments and there weren't any navigational aids. Plus, the P-40 was a lousy airplane to fly weather in. For one thing, the gun sight was in the way, so you had to tilt your head to see the instruments. Then, any time you turned, the engine torque threw the aircraft out of trim.

"You were just fighting that aircraft all the time. Otherwise it would do something squirrelly. It took experience to do it, and the most difficult thing about being in China was there wasn't anyone to teach us. Nobody had any experience in weather flying.

"In the 74th we had [James D.] Procter, [William R.] Crooks, [Truman O. ("Clyde")] Jeffreys, and some others. These were captains and experienced guys. But the group I came with had very little gunnery training and very little tactics. When I first got there in '42 there were still a couple of AVG guys. We had Frank Schiel, who was an excellent pilot and a wonderful guy on reconnaissance work. But he didn't teach us tactics. The most I learned was from an article in *Reader's Digest*. It explained a little about the two-element thing.

"If you could learn something around there, well fine. If you didn't, well that was your tough luck. That was the way it went. When I became a flight leader I probably wasn't any better than the rest of them about passing on information. By the time I got in that exalted position the pilots coming in from the States had better training. They knew formations and gunnery, and they were generally more experienced than we had been."[5]

★ ★ ★ ★

On November 26, 1942, three odd-looking airplanes appeared over Kunming Airfield and joined the landing pattern. From below, these planes looked like flying rectangles, with two long engine booms trailing back from the wing and joined crossed at the rear by the horizontal stabilizer. The planes had no fuselage, per se, just a pod between the engines for the cockpit.

As the three planes peeled off in a standard fighter break and came in to land, most men on the field assumed they were watching the arrival of the first Lockheed P-38 Lightnings to reach China. They were almost right, but not quite. The three gray airplanes were F-4As, unarmed versions of the P-38 that carried cameras in the nose in place of guns.

The F-4As belonged to A Flight of the 9th Photographic Reconnaissance Squadron, and they were flown by Maj. Dale L. Swartz, 1/Lt. John W. Robinson, and 2/Lt. Lester C. Pagliuso. On arrival at Kunming, they were attached to the 74th Fighter Squadron for rations and housing.[6] As it turned out, the three photo pilots had arrived just in time to share a fancy Thanksgiving dinner of duck with their host unit.

The F-4A had by far the highest performance of any aircraft in China at the time. It shared all the flight characteristics of the P-38F—a top speed of nearly four hundred miles per hour, a service ceiling of thirty-nine thousand feet, and exceptionally long range. In the place of guns, the F-4A mounted four K17 aerial cameras, and it also was equipped with an autopilot.[7] Before long Major Schiel got himself checked out in the new planes, and on December 1 Major Swartz and he flew their first mission in them, a four-hour run down to Thailand. They photographed Chiangmai and other places including Kengtung, Burma, where they noted a half-completed airfield.

Schiel and Swartz flew again on December 3 and 4. Then on December 5 they took off in bad weather with plans to photograph Formosa after a stop at Kweilin.

They completed the mission, returned to Kweilin, and then took off again, bound for Kunming. The two planes became separated in the clouds, and Major Swartz eventually landed at Tsingchen, about two hundred miles northeast of Kunming.[8] All evening they waited at Kunming for word on Frank Schiel, but none came.

Swartz returned to Kunming on December 8, but still no one had heard from Schiel. By this time it was certain that the 74th's commanding officer would not be coming back.

On December 18, some Chinese civilians found the wreckage of an airplane on a mountainside near Suming, not too far southeast of Kunming. It was Schiel's F-4A, which apparently had crashed at full speed and burst into flames. The major's body was brought out from the crash site and buried in the old AVG cemetery at Kunming on December 20. Major Frank Schiel was the first of six squadron commanders in the 23rd Fighter Group to be killed in the line of duty during World War II.

With Frank Schiel gone, the 74th needed a new CO. The man chosen for the job was none other than Capt. "Ajax" Baumler, who had been serving as operations officer in the 75th. Baumler, a twenty-eight-year-old native of New Jersey, was a seasoned combat veteran. He graduated from flight school at Kelly Field, Texas, in 1935, then left the Army to fly on the Loyalist side in the Spanish Civil War and was credited with eight victories there. Returning to the Army in 1939, he served as an instructor and then was caught in Hawaii during the Pearl Harbor attack while on his way to China to join the AVG. He eventually reached China and began flying with the AVG in April 1942.[9]

Captain Baumler assumed command of the 74th on December 11 and immediately called a squadron meeting. At the meeting, he briefed the men of the 74th on his tactics and philosophy. Then he told them the news they had been waiting for months to hear: As far as Baumler was concerned, school days were over. His 74th was a fighter squadron, and he promised the men they would be seeing more action soon.

Baumler was as good as his word. The next day he sent five Sharks led by 1/Lt. Joe Hinton out on an escort mission to Tengchung, Burma. Then on December 14, Captain Baumler himself led six Sharks, new P-40Ks, on another escort mission. This time the 74th would team up with the 76th to cover a flight of six B-25s hitting Gia Lam Airdrome at Hanoi.

Bill Hawkins, one of the 74th pilots who flew the mission, remembered, "The way the B-25s would do it is they'd go past the target, then turn back, and drop their bombs on the target while they were on a heading for home. The B-25 was a fast airplane. Jap fighters could choose to chase them or engage the P-40 escorts, but they couldn't do both. If they tried to turn with the P-40s, they couldn't catch the B-25s; if they chased the B-25s from behind, the P-40s would jump them.

"When I was assigned to China, I knew nothing about combat tactics, flying P-40s, or anything. We were so inexperienced that we even had big problems just landing the planes. This day I was flying number four in the second flight—tail-end Charlie. We were above and behind the B-25s. I saw them drop their loads, and I could see the Japs taking off down below. Boy, they could really come up. By the time we got over the target they were right underneath me.

"I called my flight leader. Our radios were little RCAs, not as good as the radio in a cheap car, and we couldn't check them en route to the target because we kept radio silence. I called the leader, but there was no response. I could see two Japs underneath me, and they were just coming on up. I peeled off and went down. They were all mine.

"I really didn't know how to make a gunnery approach, so I was just hanging by my seat. All this dust and junk were flying up from the bottom of my aircraft [because of the negative G forces in the dive]. I was above and behind the B-25s. As I was going down, I saw tracers flying all around me. It was the B-25 gunners shooting at me. They shot at anything that came close. Boy, it really discomboober-ated [sic] me.

"I pulled the release for my belly tank, and the plane gave a big lurch. I thought I'd been hit for a second. Then I got worried about where the Japs were. They were right behind me, and their tracers were going right over my canopy—I could have reached out and grabbed them. But I'd been going down, and they were shooting over me. The P-40 could dive faster than they could, so I dove out to get away. But instead of heading toward Kunming, now I was going east toward the China Sea. That was the wrong way to go, and I didn't have much fuel.

"A stratus bank had built up over the ocean, so I punched into that thing. The Japs were still right on my tail. But I had another problem because I didn't know how to fly on instruments. Finally I got control of the aircraft and climbed up out of the clouds to take a look. God, there were two Japs, thirty to forty yards off my wing. I popped back into the clouds.

"I was really in a fit now because I couldn't go any farther out across the ocean. I thought, well, I'll pull up out of the cloud and ram into them. I came steaming out of the clouds in a big turn, ready for whatever. But fortunately for me—or them—they'd given up and were heading back for Hanoi.

"I headed back toward Kunming, but there were no navigational aids, homers, or any of that stuff. I looked at the map and looked at the ground. I really didn't know where I was. I figured Kunming must be that way, so I headed for it. Somehow I found the field and landed. Just as I got to the end of the landing roll and was ready to turn off the runway onto the taxi strip, the propeller stopped. I was out of gas."[10]

Missions continued steadily the rest of December, during the course of which three confirmed victories were credited to pilots of the 74th. The School Squadron no more, it was now a full-fledged combat outfit.

5

Branching Out

During its first two months of operations, the 23rd Fighter Group proved itself as a combat unit, fully capable of carrying on in the tradition of the American Volunteer Group. But life in a fighter outfit during wartime is more than a series of heroic air battles fought on a field of blue. Mostly, it is grueling work, whether one's job is in the cockpit or on the ground.

Of the personnel in the 23rd Fighter Group a small percentage were pilots who had to accept the dangers of combat in exchange for what little status or glory went along with the job. The rest of the men—during World War II, U.S. combat squadrons were strictly males only—carried out their duties for the most part in safety, far from the scene of battle. Maintaining and repairing aircraft; acquiring, storing, and dispersing supplies; gathering and disseminating intelligence information; caring for and feeding personnel; and administrative functions—these were all part of squadron life.

For most personnel with ground duties in the 23rd, life was primarily hard work and boring routine. Major events were mail call and the arrival of new men in the unit. Still, they experienced breaks in the routine that set their hearts pounding in excitement and fear. Nearly every man who served in China, especially those who were there during the early days in 1942, remembers an event like that. Dick Lee, who as a young sergeant served as a crew chief on Sharks in the 16th and 74th squadrons, told the story of watching an amazing display of courage by a young fighter pilot at Hengyang on September 6, 1942.

"If you're familiar with aircraft, you know that you don't change major components—engines, propellers—or do any major maintenance without accomplishing a test hop afterward to make sure the aircraft is OK for service.

"I had myself and Kruces, a weapons man I think in the 76th. I was out of the 16th. Hengyang was about out of fuel and everything else. We'd been operating out of there for a while [since September 1]. Logistically, we were just about exhausted.

"All our P-40s had come back off a mission except one. I thought that perhaps we'd lost him, but the pilots said no, they knew he was with them, but he'd had some engine problems. Just about that time we heard this P-40 coming, and man, he came right in, hopped right over the hill, and sat down.

"I climbed up on the wing, and the pilot said, 'Damn, I can't get over thirty inches [of manifold pressure in the engine] out of this thing. I don't know what's wrong with it. I just did make it in here.' So he got out and I got in; cranked the thing up to full power. Sure enough. We used to be able to draw sixty-six inches of mercury on those engines in a P-40. I couldn't even get thirty inches. Something was haywire, so I pulled the carburetor off. I reached down, and I saw some oil down by the drain. I reached down there with a rag, and the whole impeller spun just as free as could be. So I put the carburetor back on and taxied the plane off the field.

"I taxied it down a road, a very narrow road, too, and put it in a hangar. The hangar was really a dugout in the side of hill, roofed over with sod on it. I pushed the P-40 in there and pulled the carb off. By then the whole squadron had left, everyone except myself, Kruces, and this pilot Barnum [of the 75th]. He was going to fly the airplane out when we got the thing fixed. Captain Barnum was a hell of a nice guy, an eager joe. He came from a well-to-do family. We'd overheard him talking about when he was in flight school, flying home to New York and landing on his dad's estate.

"I went ahead and pulled the whole ass end of that Allison engine off, and what I found was that a nut had come off that had not been safetied. It had dropped down into the impeller drive gears, and there wasn't a tooth on any of them. Nothing chewed up, just broken. All the pieces were lying there, so I scrounged all them. This was what they call a dry-sump system with an oil strainer on it. So I cleaned the strainer. Then I went down to this shed where this engine was sitting that had been sunk in the river. It had come off of Major Alison's aircraft [which was salvaged soon after he crash-landed on the night mission July 30]. I pulled the ass end off of this engine, and everything looked real great in there. I got the drive gear, the intervening gear, and the impeller gear. I took them out and put them in this other engine and put the thing back together. I didn't have to take the engine out of the airplane to do this. I did it all with the engine right in the mounts.

"Everybody was gone. I rolled this thing out of the hangar and cranked it up. Ran it for about fifteen or twenty minutes. It ran like a champ, so I shut the thing down; checked the oil strainer. The oil strainer was all clean—no metal contamination—so the airplane was fit to go on a test flight.

"Early the next morning, Kruces and I got up. We got in this Ford station wagon that we had. I think it was a 1939 model, and it used to run on alcohol, so you know it was a real bomb. I taxied the airplane up on the line out in front of ops [operations] and ran it up for preflight. It checked out perfect. Kruces and I were sitting around there, and pretty soon here came a cloud of dust up over the hills. It was Barnum riding in the sidecar of this German motorcycle with a Chinese driver.

"'Goddamn,' he says, 'the Japs are coming!'

"I said, 'You want me to taxi this plane back off the field?'

"'No, no. Hell no,' he says, 'I'll take it.' He hopped in the airplane and away he went.

"The Japs came, all right. There were sixty-six of them, and he tangled with them twice. They never got him. I don't know if he shot any of them down [he didn't], but I know for guts, there was no doubt about it. The guy had plenty of moxie.

"While he tangled with them, we were in a net radio station that was in a bunker underneath the railroad tracks. We heard from Barnum that he was coming back in. The Japs were reported leaving the net. They were going back out. Barnum needed fuel and oxygen.

"Kruces and I got in the station wagon and went looking for this charging line that we had for the oxygen bottle. We got up there in front of operations and started looking for this copper line. In those days we didn't have any radios in the damned vehicles or anything like that, so all of a sudden I heard this rumble. If ever you heard Jap airplanes, you knew what it was. They were coming back.

"I looked at routes of escape from the airfield. If we'd gotten in the car and gone down the road, we'd have left a big trail of dust. So that was that. There was no place to go. Safety was too far away. But directly across the field was a row of poplar trees, and off to one end of them was a little shack that held a little plane like a Fleet biplane, a little trainer the Chinese used. In front of that, facing the field, was our mechanics' line shack. Kruces and I hopped in the station wagon and headed out across that field. Foot in the carburetor, and away we went. I didn't think we'd ever get over there. I drove up behind those poplar trees, and we jumped out. I saw the morning sun was glancing off the car's windshield. I reached down and grabbed two handfuls of grass and threw them over the windshield to break up the glare from the sunshine.

"The Japs came right down over this hill to the east of the field and started shooting. What they thought was that we had run in the line shack, so they filled the place full of holes. Anyway, they didn't get us. They didn't see us, I guess. They made the one pass and left; headed on out.

"We went back down to the radio station and found out that Barnum was headed back in. So I found the oxygen charging line. He came in, parked the plane, sat in it with the battery switch on, listening to the radio. We used a hand pump out of a fifty-gallon drum pumping gas into the fuselage tank, and we also serviced him with oxygen.

"Then he says, 'Japs are coming back! Gotta go.' We unplugged everything, and he cranked the plane up. I thought he was going to taxi the plane down to the end of the field and take off, the way he did before. He didn't. He just turned the airplane and took off downwind. He was already almost halfway down the damned field, downwind and kind of catawampous. He wasn't actually on the runway.

"There was a lot of dust blowing behind him, but gradually the dust worked off to one side, and I could see the airplane coming to the end of the field. Then I saw him hike it into the air, and then it looked like it kept mushing right straight ahead. There were some old bombed-out buildings and railroad companies down there. At the last second, he just eased up slowly and away he went.

"That was quite a test hop for an airplane.

"But old Barnum later was shot down and killed. He was a nice guy."[1]

Captain Burrall Barnum, a graduate of Yale University, was a well-known yachtsman before the war and very popular in the 75th. Awarded a Distinguished Flying Cross for his heroics on September 6, he went down during a dogfight over Lingling on April 1, 1943. According to one account, pieces of a Japanese fighter were found intermingled with the wreckage of his Shark, indicating the two planes had collided.

★ ★ ★ ★

General Chennault kept the units of the 23rd Fighter Group deployed close to Kunming through most of the fall of 1942, though occasional deployments in squadron strength (or individual flights from several squadrons) went to Hengyang to the east and Yunnanyi to the west. That did not mean the group was restricted to defensive duties, however. In fact, the first of the group's truly spectacular long-range strikes were made during this period.

Also during this period the 23rd's pilots began to appreciate one of the benefits of serving a combat tour in China: a pilot had a good chance of getting back to his unit if he went down on a mission, because so much of the territory over which the pilots flew was either held by their Chinese allies or very loosely controlled by the Japanese. In either circumstance, the Chinese people were extraordinarily helpful and friendly to downed American pilots, even to the point of risking their own safety and sharing their meager belongings if it would assist their American friends. For the most part, the Chinese people understood and appreciated the efforts of the Americans to protect China from Japanese air attack.

Major Bruce K. Holloway was one of the first airmen of the 23rd Fighter Group to make a long walk home from a mission. Holloway, a soft-spoken twenty-nine-year-old from Tennessee, had been sent to China in May 1942 to observe AVG operations.[2] The tall, lanky West Point graduate stayed on after the AVG disbanded and worked under Col. Bob Scott as the group's executive officer. Holloway maintained contact with the squadrons and flew with them as often as possible, especially with the 76th. He made his first combat claim, for a Ki-27 probably destroyed, while flying with the 76th at Hengyang on September 3. After returning to group headquarters at Kunming, he flew a number of solo recon missions into Indo-China and Burma, gathering helpful information for planning offensive missions into those areas.

Bad weather kept flying to a minimum at Kunming for the first three weeks of September. On the morning of September 22, 1942, Holloway went to his office and attended to some odd jobs while waiting for the weather to improve so he could fly a mission. Just after lunch, the skies lifted enough that he decided he could take a flight of Sharks down to the Salween River gorge on the chance it might catch some Japanese trucks to strafe on the Burma Road.[3]

The flight of four Sharks lifted off the main runway at Kunming about 1:00 P.M. Holloway led the first element, he and his wingman flying early model P-40s, while Maj. Ed Rector and his wingman followed in two P-40Es. They made the 150-mile run west to the field at Yunnanyi, where they stopped to refuel. Holloway's Shark burned thirty gallons of fuel on the hop, but when the station operations people asked him to sign the chit for his refueling, they had recorded the amount as sixty gallons. Bad idea. Holloway was not the kind of guy who would overlook such a detail. The major straightened the matter out in no uncertain terms before leading his flight off again at 2:30 P.M.

The flight was headed for Mangshih, a Chinese town on the Burma Road just inside the border with Burma but west of the Salween River gorge. The Japanese had held the town—an important supply center for them—since the previous spring. Holloway encountered an imposing cloud formation in his path, so he led the Sharks south to go around it.

"We crossed the Salween just below Mangshih and headed up the [Burma] Road, looking for trucks. Didn't have to look very far," he noted in his journal.[4]

The trucks looked like toys from Holloway's tight perch in his Shark several thousand feet above. The Japanese driver of the first one probably did not hear the P-40s coming over the roar of his truck engine, because the vehicle was still moving as Holloway dived toward it, with his wingman lagging behind in line-astern formation to make his own attack after his leader's run. The truck loomed larger and larger as Holloway lined it up in the ring-and-bead gun sight mounted on the cowling of his Shark. He had to be careful not to overconcentrate on the target, because at his speed if he waited a split second too long before pulling out of the dive, he would have splattered himself all over the countryside.

Holloway's Shark was about a quarter of a mile behind the truck and not much above it when he pressed the trigger button on his control stick. Tracer rounds arrowed out from his two .50-caliber cowl guns, and he watched as the bullets kicked up sprays of dirt in a deadly line down the road and into the truck. Holloway flashed over the target, and behind him his wingman could see the truck swerve crazily off the road and burst into flames.

This scene repeated itself perhaps twenty times along the thirty-mile stretch, and Holloway reported seeing seven trucks either burst into flame or explode outright. He got so close to his target on one attack that debris from the explosion rattled against his plane as he flew through it. On another, he witnessed the grisly sight of a soldier's body being thrown like a rag doll fifty feet up the embankment next to the road. He allowed no quarter during the attacks; five people jumped out of one truck as it caught fire, and he blasted them, too.

At one point, Holloway spotted a small encampment off the road, where empty drums were stored under some trees. He made an especially low strafing pass over this target, brushing the trees with the belly of his Shark as he pulled off the target.

Holloway felt his Shark take a couple of hits from ground fire during these attacks, but the plane was showing no ill effects when he reached the Salween River bridge. The bridge marked the line between territory held between the Japanese and the Chinese, and it was Holloway's prearranged rendezvous point with Rector. But when Holloway and his wingman arrived, Rector was not there. They circled a few times, then Holloway decided to head back down the road because he still had a little ammunition left.

Within a few minutes, Holloway spotted a staff car and a couple of trucks driving down the road. That surprised him, because he thought he had seen everything on his flight up the road. The two Sharks must have surprised the Japanese as well, because Holloway was able to drop down and make a strafing run on the staff car before its occupants could stop and get out. His gunfire "annihilated" the car and its occupants, then carried farther down the line, and tore up a truck as well. Meanwhile, his wingman was making a run from another direction. Holloway could see that P-40's tracers ricocheting off the road surface, though the plane itself was on the far side of a hill from him.

Holloway pulled up from his first run at the convoy and swung around in a wide turn about a mile and a half west of the road, getting lined up for another attack. He recorded:

"I felt them hit me with some ground fire. It was a pretty solid sounding slug, probably 13 mm [millimeters], but they had already hit me a couple times and I thought nothing of it. Completed the pass on the truck and was pulling up toward the river when I noticed that I had no oil pressure.

"Well, I figured this was the end. The Japs would certainly give me a warm welcome after I had just finished shooting them up. My greatest hope was to reach the river and land in it, so I eased her back to a slow cruising speed and waited for the rods to start coming through the sides of the engine. I made the river and she was still running, so I headed over the mountains toward Paoshan. The oil temperature was steadily dropping, which indicated without any doubt that there was no flow on the gauge or intake side of the pump. The coolant temperature remained normal. Just as I reached the top of the ridge on the east side of the river, the engine froze. First it sounded as though a couple of rod and main bearings let go and the engine started vibrating convulsively, and in a couple of minutes it froze solid—probably the thrust bearing. I don't ever want to hear anyone say anything against the Allison engine to me. It would be fighting words. This one ran for three whole minutes with no oil pressure—enough to get me back over Chinese lines on the east side of the Salween. And it never did catch fire."

When the engine finally quit, Holloway was at the top of the ridge facing the Paoshan Valley from the west. The town of Paoshan was about twenty-five miles north, and Holloway knew there was no way he would be able to glide that far. So he started looking for a place to put his Shark down and chose an area of rice paddies not far away.

As Holloway glided down at 130 miles per hour he decided to come in with his wheels up, because he was afraid that the P-40's sturdy landing gear would catch on some obstruction and cartwheel the plane over onto its back. It was a good decision. He set the plane down without flaps at one end of a rice paddy, and it slid smoothly across it, throwing water and mud out behind. At the far end, the plane punched through a dike, spun sideways, and kept on sliding through the paddy on the other side. He was still moving pretty fast when he took out another dike on the far end. This impact spun the plane 180 degrees and slowed it down. The plane splashed to a stop

in the middle of the third rice paddy. Both wings were badly mangled, and the fuselage had buckled behind the cockpit. Holloway,
however, was unhurt. He unbuckled, climbed out of the cockpit, and
slogged over to a dry area at the edge of the rice paddy, where
immediately he was surrounded by dozens of Chinese farmers who
had witnessed his dramatic landing.

The Chinese were by no means friendly for the first few moments,
because they did not know if Holloway was friend or foe. He certainly was not Chinese, but was he an American or a Japanese?
Fortunately, Holloway was wearing his flight jacket, for on the back
of it was a large standard-issue patch for American pilots flying in
China. It displayed a Nationalist Chinese flag, and a message written
in Chinese that the wearer was an American pilot flying for China
and to give him whatever help he needed. It was signed by
Generalissimo Chiang Kai-shek. Once the Chinese surrounding
Holloway got a look at the patch and understood who he was, they
became very friendly and led him to a village nearby.

According to Holloway, "Eventually the head man took me in tow
and led me to his house. It was a very nice house, and they summoned a council of all the bigwigs in the neighborhood to look me
over. They broke out choice things to eat—such good things as tins
of pineapple and candy and cakes—things that are like gold to them
and that they treasure even more than we do 30-year-old whiskey.
We had a feast, and from then on there was nothing too good for me.
They continually gave me too much to eat and fixed up the best bed
in the house, of good pine boards, for me to sleep in all by myself.
They gave me a basin of water for my face and a basin for my feet—
and a toothbrush and paste. The paste was labeled 'Kiss Me
Toothpaste' and was a Shanghai product.

"After about three hours a captain of the Chinese Seventy-first
Army arrived. He spoke English after a fashion and was a secret service man, so I immediately tackled him for all the intelligence he
had relative to Japanese installations. It wasn't much, so I went to
bed and they all sat around discussing me and my plight and my airplane while eating some sort of nuts and spitting hulls on the floor.
Until now they had never seen an airplane on the ground."[5]

Early the next morning, Holloway returned to the rice paddy
where his crumpled P-40 was sitting. He cut the battery ground,
detached a few small items from the plane, including his parachute,
and arranged for a Chinese Army guard in hopes that the plane
could be salvaged for parts. Then about 9:00 A.M. Holloway left the
village and headed for Paoshan in the company of Captain Mah (the
secret service captain), his host's grandson, several soldiers, and

three small horses. One of the soldiers had the unpleasant task of carrying Holloway's heavy parachute. Progress was slow, perhaps one mile an hour, and in each village they passed all the people turned out to give Holloway a hero's welcome, complete with banquets and lots of rice wine. Before long, Holloway was so full of wine that he could hardly stay on his horse.

Niuwang was the first town of any size that they reached. There, Captain Mah placed a phone call to his headquarters in Paoshan and arranged for a car to meet them down the road to pick up Holloway. Meanwhile, the mayor of Niuwang gave Holloway his personal horse, which was an improvement because it was bigger than the others and could walk a little faster. The group headed out over a narrow cart path that led to an intersection with the Burma Road. The men reached the Burma Road at the 707 kilometers marker, which meant they were 707 kilometers, or 440 miles, from Kunming. They turned right and headed up the road toward Paoshan.

Technically, this was Chinese-held territory, but there were very few Chinese troops in the area, as they had pulled back to defensive positions closer to Paoshan after halting the Japanese advance in the spring. The Chinese had blown out large sections of the Burma Road during their retreat, so Holloway and his troop had to continue on horseback for several miles before reaching passable roadway. The sun had set by then, but they were able to continue traveling under a full moon through the beautiful hills. Finally, the car from Paoshan pulled up. Holloway bid farewell to his traveling companions, with a special note of pity for the exhausted soldier who had carried his parachute all day. Holloway rode the rest of the way to Paoshan in the car with three Chinese staff officers and a postmaster. He spent the night in the quarters of General Tsung, commanding general of the Seventy-first Army.

September 24 is the day of the Chinese mid-autumn festival, the equivalent of Thanksgiving in the United States, so the only thing happening in Paoshan was an all-day feast. Major Holloway was anxious to be on his way back to Kunming, but the Paoshan airfield was inoperable due to the recent rains, and no ground transportation was available on the holiday. He had no choice but to join the feast, and feast he did to the point that he began to feel ill. He spent the night at the local field hospital, where he checked in on Captain Kit and Lieutenant Sykes of the radio warning net, who had been injured recently in a jeep accident. A truck belonging to the Friends Ambulance Unit was leaving for Yunnanyi the following day, and he would catch a ride on it. Holloway recounted the rest of the story.

"The truck didn't leave until 1:30 P.M. It was a six-wheel Chevrolet charcoal burner and was loaded to the gills with a bunch of truck engines, drums, four Britishers, Capt. Kit, me and a bunch of other junk. It was quite a ritual to get the fire going—we ran shifts cranking a hand blower for about twenty minutes and finally got her rolling. Everybody gathered around and said good-byes. It was almost like a boat sailing. We bumped along for awhile, packed in like sardines, and right in the middle of one downhill stretch we ran out of brakes. Of all predicaments I can think of, running out of brakes on the Burma Road is one of the highest ranking. Anyhow, the driver got her stopped and we found a leak in the right rear cylinder. Taking it apart, we found that somebody had put the rubber expander piston in backwards, so of course all the fluid eventually leaked out during brake applications. We put it back together, filled the master cylinder reservoir up with water, and proceeded on winding around the cliffs. Stopped for supper just before reaching the Mekong River stretch. The food was pretty good—filthy but sanitary. Went on to Yungping from there. At the Mekong River bridge, the stationmaster tried to load on some soldiers, but we booted them off and proceeded on up the hill. For all grades in excess of a slight rise we had to use gasoline [to give the engine more power]—this was essentially half the time as the road went either uphill or downhill and there were very few hills that could be called slight rises. Slept on the floor of the truck at Yungping; arrived there about 11 P.M.

"September 26: Kit complained of his wounded finger hurting badly, so I had a look at it. It was swollen badly and there was a red streak up his forearm. The nearest doctor was at Siakwan, which we wouldn't reach until that night. Blood poison is bad when it gets a start, so I had the female manager of the so-called hostel get me the sharpest knife available and some hot salt water—lanced his finger and soaked it for awhile. This relieved the pain and probably kept the condition under control.

"We proceeded on our merry way again and reached Tali about 5 P.M. That is a beautiful place. We stayed with a missionary and his family and mission members that night. His name was Snow, and he was head of the China-India mission at Tali—sponsored by Great Britain, bless her. The doctor lanced Kit's hand again and pronounced it well under control. I slept on a good rope bed and was even given a blanket. Mrs. Snow served us a wonderful supper.

"September 27: Went to Siakwan and fiddled around there all morning working on the truck. . . . We left Siakwan about noon and breezed on up the road to Yunnanyi, reaching there about 4:30 P.M. Three days to cover a stretch that takes about 25 minutes in a P-40. I had not realized before what a problem travel is in China to people without airplanes. Just after we arrived I saw a BT [two-seat training plane similar to an AT-6] taking off for Kunming. I had the radio station call him to come back. He couldn't contact the plane, but McDonald of CNAC [Chinese National Aviation Corporation, which flew transport planes over the Hump route] was coming along and heard the call so he stopped and picked me up. He sent a wire ahead and everybody was out to meet me. It was good to see everybody so glad to see me."[6]

★ ★ ★ ★

Majors Holloway and Rector both were awarded the Silver Star for their exploits during the September 22 mission. Rector, after splitting away from Holloway, carried out similar strafing attacks on truck traffic. Then he turned south and flew through heavy rain to the Japanese encampment at Chefang, where he strafed barracks in the face of heavy ground fire before returning to Yunnanyi. Then on September 25, while Holloway was making his way up the Burma Road, Rector led an escort mission to Hanoi that encountered stiff resistance from Japanese single- and twin-engine interceptors. A swirling air battle ensued in which the American pilots claimed six enemy planes destroyed for no losses of their own. Rector fought a solo rearguard battle while the rest of the fighters escorted the bombers to safety, and he was awarded the Distinguished Flying Cross for this feat.

Strafing and reconnaissance missions continued against Japanese traffic and installations along the Burma Road through the middle of October. By that time, the Japanese had virtually ceased trying to use the road during daylight hours because of their heavy losses to the 23rd Fighter Group's marauding Sharks.

6

Duel in the East

It was a pitifully small force, really, considering the strategic importance of the target about to be attacked, but that was beside the point. The harbor at Hong Kong, the great port city on the southern China coast, was reportedly chock-full of Japanese shipping. Chennault would hit it on October 25, 1942, with all the strength he could muster—even if that only amounted to twelve B-25 medium bombers with nine P-40s of the 23rd Fighter Group to provide escort protection.

Hong Kong: Just hearing the name conjured images of the "mysterious East"—narrow streets teeming with color and commerce, smoky opium dens and gambling rooms, noisy restaurants and outdoor markets, and exotic women with long dresses slit way up the side. And one always thought of Hong Kong's harbor, where tiny sampans and antiquated junks shuttled around great oceangoing ships carrying mountains of cargo into and out of China.

Hong Kong had been a British colony for a full century prior to World War II. During those years, English government officials and merchants built the city from a small island settlement on the eastern edge of the Pearl River estuaries to one of the busiest ports in the world. By 1941, the cities of Singapore, Manila, and Hong Kong constituted a triangle of Western power and economic influence in the Far East. It came as no surprise that Japan targeted all three cities for quick capture when it set out to conquer Asia. What surprised the Western world was how quickly Japan succeeded. Hong Kong was the first to fall, surrendering on Christmas Day 1941. By February 15, 1942, all three were in Japanese hands.[1]

In Hong Kong the Japanese went about their business undisturbed during their first ten months of occupation. They used the port to ship military troops, supplies, and equipment into China for their occupation forces and to extract food and raw materials from southern China that were needed in Japan. The port also served as a refueling point and safe haven for shipping throughout the South China Sea. Nearly all of this activity supported Japanese war efforts in one way or another.

By October 1942 Chennault felt he had sufficient forces in China to mount an effective attack on Hong Kong. He put his chief of staff, Col. Merian C. Cooper, to work planning a major strike against vessels and shipping facilities at the port. It would set off a month-long aerial duel between Chennault's forces at Kweilin and the Japanese at Hong Kong and Canton.

Planning the Hong Kong mission was a more difficult task than might first appear. Flying in a straight line from Kweilin to Canton and then an additional 75 miles to Hong Kong makes a 325-mile trip, one way. Every combat aircraft in the China Air Task Force had sufficient range to make the hop from Kweilin to Hong Kong, but on combat missions a pilot also has to turn around and come back. That alone turned the run to Hong Kong into a 650-mile mission, but there was the additional matter of Canton to figure. The two airfields there, Tien Ho and White Cloud, were full of Japanese fighters, so the CATF would have to give them a wide berth. The long trip just got longer. And what of the Japanese fighters in Hong Kong's own Kai Tak Airdrome? If they engaged the formation, as they were sure to attempt, that would cost the U.S. planes precious fuel needed for the return trip to Kweilin.

Colonel Cooper had to enter all this into his calculations. Even the winds would have to be right to avoid even greater fuel losses. The first obvious challenge was to stock up sufficient supplies of gasoline at Kweilin so that all the planes could leave with full tanks. Ground crews also would be needed at Kweilin to service and load the planes. And the payloads of the B-25s would have to be calculated carefully to determine the optimum ratio of gasoline to bomb tonnage.

Another factor was the fighter escorts. The Sharks used for this raid all would have to be P-40Es, because the earlier models could not carry auxiliary belly tanks. These teardrop-shaped tanks provided an additional seventy-five gallons of fuel capacity and could be dropped from the plane to improve its performance when engaging enemy aircraft. The Shark pilots would need every drop of gas they could carry if they expected to reach Hong Kong, get in a scrap, and still get home to Kweilin. So the mission could not go until a sufficient number of P-40Es were operational and based at Kweilin. In the 1990s nine planes might not sound like many, but in October 1942 the 23rd Fighter Group considered a formation that big an armada.

Colonel Merian Cooper was an extraordinary man. He flew with the American Expeditionary Forces in France during World War I and then joined the Polish Air Force to fly in the Kościuszko Squadron against Russia in 1919. Later he became an explorer and helped form Pan American Airways. In the 1930s he went to Hollywood to produce motion pictures, his most famous being the epic *King Kong*.[2] Tex Hill described him as an innovative thinker who once suggested a plan for the Chinese to capture Canton and reopen its seaport, which would have relieved pressure on those bringing in China's supplies by air over the Hump route.[3]

It took Colonel Cooper most of a week to put all the pieces together for his strike against Hong Kong.[4] Then he had to wait for the weather to cooperate and for his intelligence sources to let him know when traffic in the harbor presented a juicy target. On October 24 the word went out to Chennault's key bomber and fighter leaders: Attack Hong Kong tomorrow.

The clouds cleared early at Kunming on Sunday morning, October 25. Soon twelve B-25s took off for the five-hundred-mile trip to Kweilin. Colonel Bob Scott and Major Holloway of the 23rd Fighter Group led a flight of P-40s behind them at 6:30 A.M. The Sharks flew up to Chanyi, where they rendezvoused with Majs. Tex Hill and John Alison plus a few other pilots in the 75th Fighter Squadron. The formation of eleven Sharks and one P-43 proceeded to Kweilin, arriving at 9:30 A.M. The slower B-25s took longer to reach Kweilin, but by 11:30 A.M. everyone was refueled and ready to go.

All twelve B-25s were led by Brig. Gen. Caleb V. Haynes, who had been promoted in October. His flight took off cleanly and proceeded southeast toward the target. Problems started for the Sharks immediately, however. One P-40 refused to start, and the pilot of a second one taxied into a hole and damaged his plane before it ever left the ground. Major Holloway led the nine remaining P-40s off, with Colonel Scott on his wing.

Major Holloway flew for only about half an hour before his engine began acting up. Disgusted, the eager fighter pilot handed off the leader's spot to Colonel Scott and banked away to return to Kweilin. Not long after Holloway landed, he saw Major Alison come in as well. Alison's belly tank had refused to feed, forcing him to abort the mission, too. Now there were just seven Sharks to protect the twelve bombers.

The bombers went into tight battle formation half an hour north of Canton and turned slightly to the right, steering them thirty miles west of Canton. Fortunately, Cooper's plan worked. No Japanese interceptors rose from Canton to challenge the Americans. The bombers climbed to seventeen thousand feet, while Colonel Scott's

P-40s flew slightly behind and three thousand feet above them. Visibility was unlimited in the cloudless sky.

Once the bombers had cleared Canton, they made a shallow turn to the left and bored straight in on Hong Kong. Before long the harbor stretched out below them. From his Plexiglas office in the nose of General Haynes's B-25, lead bombardier Lt. Col. Herbert ("Butch") Morgan could see Kowloon Peninsula on the mainland dead ahead and the mountainous outline of Hong Kong Island in the distance. Morgan looked closely for a convoy of Japanese transport ships that had been reported in the mile-wide harbor separating Hong Kong and Kowloon. He did not find a convoy, however, so he turned his attention to the dock areas on Kowloon. If the ships had fled, Morgan at least could bomb the cargo they left behind.

Meanwhile, the fighters spread out. Colonel Scott took his flight of four—Major Hill and Capt. John Hampshire of the 75th plus 2/Lt. Morton Sher of the 76th—to one side of the B-25s, while 1/Lt. Mortimer Marks led fellow 76th pilots Charles DuBois and William E. ("Bill") Miller to the other. Every pilot kept a sharp lookout in the clear blue sky. Below them, Japanese fighters were taking off and climbing rapidly from Kai Tak. These may have been Mitsubishi A6M Zeros of the Japanese Navy, but more likely they were Ki-43 Oscars of the Army's 24th Air Regiment.

Lieutenant Colonel Morgan lined up the B-25s for a bomb run over the docks opposite from Stonecutters Island, a key landmark in the harbor. As he sighted through the bombsight, Morgan identified docks, warehouses, and oil storage tanks. Nasty puffs of smoke from exploding antiaircraft shells appeared around the bombers as they unloaded their cargoes of five-hundred-pound bombs on the target. Within seconds, seventy-two of the high-explosive bombs were whistling down toward the dock area. Records of the 11th Bomb Squadron indicate the bombs exploded in three evenly spaced strings across the warehouses and onto the docks, throwing up clouds of dust, smoke, and debris.

The B-25s made their standard combat break off the bomb run, a diving right-hand turn toward home, and ran smack into about two dozen Japanese interceptors that had climbed up to meet them. Colonel Scott's P-40s swooped down from above, dropping their belly tanks as they came, and the fight was on.

Major Hill was the first Shark pilot to reach the fight. He quickly latched onto the tail of an enemy fighter and opened fire. Hill's quarry may have been lining up for his own shot on the bombers, as he turned in their direction. Tracers zipped toward the enemy plane from the turrets of several B-25s, but Hill's guns found the mark first. The Japanese fighter burst into flames and fell from the sky, trailing a long plume of smoke. For the next few minutes Hill twisted and turned for all he was worth, trying to disrupt the Japanese fighters rising to intercept. Firing snap bursts whenever he got the chance, Hill was able to damage three more Japanese fighters.

Seconds after Major Hill made his first attack, Colonel Scott pulled in close behind an enemy fighter and fired a burst right into its engine and cockpit. He saw smoke pouring back over the plane's canopy as he passed. By the time he had made a sharp turn to clear his tail and had chosen a second target, he could see four aircraft falling in flames toward the harbor. He also recalled shooting a Japanese fighter off the tail of a P-40, firing at others, and even encountering several twin-engine fighters, which he referred to as "Japanese Messerschmitts" but more likely were Kawasaki Ki-45 Nicks.[5]

Lieutenant Marks's flight of three Sharks also got into the action quickly. Marks, a former enlisted man from New Jersey, pulled in at the end of a string of Japanese fighters and attacked the plane in front of him. His tracers ripped into the nose of the plane. It immediately caught on fire, flipped over on its back, and dived straight down, out of control. A few moments later, he and Lieutenant Miller caught up with some enemy fighters that were attacking a lagging B-25. Marks and Miller each shot up one, then Miller attacked another and hit it dead center, sending the stricken plane down in a spin.

Lieutenant DuBois also was successful. He attacked a mixed gaggle of single- and twin-engine planes out of the sun and got good hits on an engine of one of the twins. As that plane dropped away in a spin, the others turned on DuBois, but he was able to use his superior speed to zoom up above them and make another pass.

On his second pass, DuBois sent a single-engine fighter down smoking but then came under attack from behind himself. By this time he had become separated from the rest of his flight, and his fuel supply was beginning to worry him. He dived away from the fight and headed for home at top speed. The Japanese fighter clung to his tail for several miles, but the P-40 eventually pulled away and the Japanese pilot gave up the chase.

The last plane in the B-25 formation was piloted by Capt. Howard O. Allers of the 22nd Bombardment Squadron, a new unit that had just arrived in China on temporary duty. His plane was hit hard by the Japanese fighters on their first pass; its right engine caught on fire after an oil line was severed. Unable to maintain airspeed, Allers fell behind the rest of the formation and soon was singled out by at least seven enemy fighters that began making passes. Allers called for help on his radio, and Captain Hampshire responded with Lieutenant Sher on his wing. The two P-40 pilots piled into the fray just as a Japanese fighter was pulling in behind the B-25 to finish it off. Hampshire got there first and blasted the plane while Sergeant

Webb in the top turret of the B-25 fired back from the other direction. The Japanese fighter came apart under the barrage and went down in a spin.[6]

Hampshire and Sher each had knocked down one fighter in the preceding moments, and now Sher fired on another one before he, too, was hit. Sher dived out of the fight and nursed his dying Shark as far north as it would carry him before he had to belly-land the plane. Fortunately, he made it far enough to reach Chinese-held territory and was unhurt in the landing. Sher rejoined the squadron several weeks later.

Meanwhile, Captain Allers had taken hits in his good engine and was unable to keep his B-25 flying any longer. Two crewmen bailed out, and the others rode the plane down to a belly landing in a rice paddy. Eventually, the copilot and navigator were able to escape to Chinese-held territory. Captain Allers and the rest of the crew were captured by the Japanese.[7]

The surviving aircraft returned to Kweilin in ones and twos late in the afternoon. Combat crews sat down with the intelligence staff and gave their reports. When the tallies were finished, the totals were remarkable. The Shark pilots confirmed eleven enemy aircraft destroyed, and the gunners in the B-25s claimed an additional seven. And this was a bonus on top of the damage done by the bombing.[8]

Tex Hill, who won a Distinguished Flying Cross for his exploits that day, remarked about the mission years later, "That damned sky—you could see airplanes burning everywhere. It was a good one."[9]

The action was not over for the day, however. About the time that the Hong Kong mission aircraft were landing at Kweilin, a flight of Sharks from the 76th Fighter Squadron based at Kunming intercepted a raid by Japanese fighters coming out of Indo-China. They met in the sky over Mengtze, in southern Yunnan Province, about 3:15 P.M. The Shark pilots destroyed several raiders and forced the rest to withdraw, without any losses themselves.

Then, at 9:00 P.M., six of the 11th Bomb Squadron's B-25s took off for another trip to Hong Kong. They dropped their loads on the Hong Kong powerhouse in the face of a fierce antiaircraft barrage and returned to Kweilin. Finally, three B-25s raided Canton after midnight to round out the one-day blitz from Kweilin. The B-25s returned to the relative safety of Kunming early the next morning.

General Chennault's aircraft would hit Hong Kong many more times during the war—in fact, four P-40s from the 75th hauled five-hundred-pound bombs to attack shipping there just three days later—but the October 25 mission was the first. As such, it stands as one of the high points in the 23rd Fighter Group's history. It also touched off a month of air combat over eastern China, a month in which the P-40 pilots would completely dominate the Japanese in the skies over Hong Kong, Canton, and Kweilin.

The return mission to Hong Kong on October 28 was another brainchild of Colonel Cooper. Lieutenant Jack Best of the 16th Fighter Squadron, which had moved to Kweilin October 26 on orders from Chennault, was one of the P-40 pilots who flew the mission. He remembered the mission vividly. "Cooper decided that since Hong Kong was out of our range with the P-40 [without a drop tank], we could go down there and run a dive-bombing mission and land at a field called Namyung, which was up north of Hong Kong. Apparently it was under Japanese control for the most part, but it would be taken over for our mission by the Chinese ground forces long enough so we could refuel and then get home. My old logbook reads, 'Four hours from Kweilin to Namyung, dive bomb Hong Kong, and then an hour and fifteen [minutes] from Namyung to Kweilin.' That was quite a mission.

"The object of the thing was that there was a probable aircraft carrier in Hong Kong harbor that we might be able to do some damage to. It turned out it wasn't a carrier, it was a freighter with a canvas deck on it, apparently. We came in above a broken cloud ceiling. When we came underneath it, there was a whole bunch of Zeros waiting for us. That was the first time I actually saw one of my mates get hit and go in. That was P. B. O'Connell [a captain in the 75th Squadron], who was hit as soon as we came under the clouds and went straight into the harbor without pulling out. That was quite a shock to me.

"At any rate, we did our mission. I can remember trying to get onto some guy taking off from Kai Tak Airdrome and almost went into the runway myself trying to pull my plane around in order to get my sights on him, but I never did. We got out of there eventually, and we landed at this little field of Namyung. The only identification we knew was that the field itself was shaped kind of like a Chevrolet sign. We found it—at least some of us did. Some of the guys didn't find it and had to belly-land on the way back to Kweilin because they just ran out of fuel. But we were able to refuel there and get on back to Kweilin."[10]

★ ★ ★ ★

Late in August 1942, the 3rd Air Division of the Japanese Army Air Force had received direct orders from the high command in Tokyo: Engage the American air forces in China in a decisive air battle, and destroy them. That simple order was proving extremely difficult to carry out. In fact, the October raids on Hong Kong were clear evidence that Chennault was stronger than ever. The Japanese would have to respond, and their target would be Kweilin.

Waiting at Kweilin was the 16th Fighter Squadron, now under the command of Maj. George W. Hazlett. The 16th was particularly hard hit by illness during its first few months in China, and one of the victims had been its previous CO, Maj. Hal Young. Many of the 16th's early pilots suffered from amoebic dysentery in China (Bob Liles lost forty pounds in two and a half months during his bout with it), perhaps because they had spent more time in Karachi than the pilots of the other squadrons. Young was unable to shake his case, however, and became so weak by early September 1942 that he had to be sent back to India for hospitalization. He never returned to combat in the squadron. Several other pilots also had to be removed from active duty and sent to India. It was not until October 22 that the 16th could boast "all pilots on flying status today for the first time since the squadron arrived in China."[11]

Major Hazlett was a twenty-nine-year-old former Braniff Airlines pilot with a degree in aeronautical engineering from the University of Pittsburgh. The father of two was very popular with the pilots, several of whom had flown with him in the 33rd Pursuit Group before the war. He was an excellent administrator and a good pilot, but his airline experience showed in his flying style, which was perhaps too smooth and safety-conscious for fighter operations. That was of little concern, however, because his flight leaders—John Lombard, Hal Pike, Clyde B. Slocumb Jr., and Ed Goss—were plenty aggressive. All four officers would command squadrons of their own in the months to come.

The 16th did not have long to recover from its October 28 attack on Hong Kong. On that mission, three of its P-40Es had gone down near Hengyang because of fuel exhaustion, but the squadron still had sixteen Sharks and one P-43 to scramble early on the morning of October 29 when a Japanese formation was reported coming in from Canton. Unfortunately, the enemy formation was able to elude the 16th's fighters and strafe the airfield, but little if any damage was done. A Japanese bomber attacked the field again at 3:30 A.M. on October 31, dropping two sticks of bombs east and southeast of the runway, but again doing no damage.

The Japanese came back yet again on November 2, and this time the 16th was ready. Twelve Sharks got off at 7:50 A.M. and had an hour to gain plenty of altitude before the enemy raiders arrived. When they finally did come into view, the Japanese made for an impressive if frightening sight: twelve bombers were being escorted by an estimated forty-eight fighters. The P-40 pilots did not hesitate. They dived into the fighter escorts and hit them at about ten thousand feet, knocking down three in the wild air battle that ensued. Meanwhile, the bombers were able to unload forty-nine bombs—

mostly incendiaries and antipersonnel—on the field, though again the damage was inconsequential. Two P-40 pilots boldly chased down the bombers as they withdrew, and each shot one down. The 16th did suffer one loss: 2/Lt. Walter Lacey was shot down by the bombers' defensive fire and killed.

Bad weather shut down flying for the next week at Kweilin. As soon as it broke on November 9, the Japanese came back, but the attack was smaller, with just eight fighters. And for the first time, the 16th—with nine Sharks—was able to put up a defensive force that was superior in numbers to that of its attackers. Battle was joined at 12:45 P.M. The Japanese employed a looping "squirrel cage" formation and maintained good discipline, but still lost three of their fighters to Lts. Melvin B. Kimball, Robert E. Smith, and John D. Lombard. All Sharks returned to Kweilin safely.

These two missions were only warm-ups, however. The Japanese tried a new tactic against Kweilin on November 12. They sent successive waves of aircraft all day in a maximum effort to catch the 23rd Fighter Group in a vulnerable position and destroy it. Again, the Shark pilots were ready for them, thanks to the warning net and some good calls by the ground controllers in the cave at Kweilin.

The first wave of enemy aircraft was reported coming from the direction of Wuchow to the southeast at 5:45 A.M., and eleven Sharks from the 16th Fighter Squadron took off at 6:25 A.M. to meet it. Captain Pike soon was forced to land with a bad engine, but the remaining ten Sharks engaged the Japanese fighter formation over the airfield at 7:15 A.M. During the dogfight that followed, another flight of eleven Japanese fighters was able to sneak in and make a strafing attack on the field. Lieutenant Don Bryant caught one of the strafers over the field and shot it down in a smoking spin from low altitude. Lieutenant Dallas Clinger also knocked down one, and other pilots were able to claim probables and damage.

After the fight ended, ground control ordered the pilots to land at the nearby fields of Lingling or Chihkiang, which was about 140 miles north of Kweilin. Lieutenant Clinger, however, had to make a forced landing at Kweilin, here he was strafed by the third wave at 8:03 A.M. Clinger was not hurt, and his P-40 was only hit a few times. The strafers finally departed about 8:30 A.M.

Six of the 16th's Sharks took off from Lingling at 8:45 A.M. and met another Japanese fighter formation over that airfield at 9:00 A.M. During this fight, Lt. George Barnes dived through a beehive of eight enemy fighters and then met one head-on as he pulled up. He gave it a long burst, which ripped through the fuselage. The plane did a slow wingover, obviously out of control, and plunged into the ground. Lieutenant Heath H. Wayne also was credited with a victory during this scrap. Again, the P-40 pilots were directed to land at Chihkiang.

Yet another flight of strafers attacked Kweilin at 9:45 A.M. Nine Japanese fighters set up a gunnery pattern over the field, with the top-cover planes doing slow rolls and other aerobatics while the rest made strafing runs. But the combination of the small-caliber machine guns on the Japanese fighters and the fact that the few Sharks on the field were well protected in revetments neutralized the attack. Everyone also kept his head down, so no one got hurt.

The Shark pilots returned to Kweilin late in the afternoon, and at 5:50 P.M. the field was declared secure. In all, the Japanese had sent six formations, totaling fifty-seven aircraft, to Kweilin during the day. The eleven Shark pilots of the 16th Fighter Squadron who opposed them were credited with four confirmed kills, six probables, and five damaged. Not a single P-40 was lost during the long day's fighting.

The Japanese would not risk another encounter with the 23rd Fighter Group's P-40s over Kweilin or the other eastern air bases in daylight until after New Year's 1943. Chennault, on the other hand, was emboldened by the 16th Fighter Squadron's success and planned some final blows against the coastal ports before winter weather arrived to shut down flying. He flew up to Kweilin with Colonel Cooper to organize the assault personally.

One more action would take place over Kweilin this month, though. On November 22, ten B-25s of the 11th Bomb Squadron and eleven P-40s of the 75th and 76th fighter squadrons flew to Kweilin from Kunming to prepare for operations against Canton and Hong Kong. The field was bone dry and windless when they landed, creating a cloud of dust that seemed to hang over the field for days on end. Three B-25 missions went off to Hon Gay in French Indo-China that afternoon.

Japanese intelligence must have been on top of the situation, because a two-ball alarm gonged at the ungodly hour of 1:20 A.M. on November 23. Major Pike and First Lieutenant Lombard of the 16th, plus 1/Lt. Joseph H. Griffin of the 75th took off in the dark at 1:35 A.M. and caught three enemy bombers over Kweilin about 2:00 A.M. The bombers were able to drop their loads before the fighters attacked, and they blew a couple of holes in the runway.

Lombard made the first attack, from the rear, and one bomber went down in flames. He pulled into position for a shot at a second bomber, but the Japanese rear gunner got him first. Slugs ripped into the gas tank behind Lombard in the fuselage, and soon it burst into flames. Just as Lombard was reaching up to pull back his canopy and bail out, he saw a bullet hole in the Plexiglas just above his head. He had no time to ponder his near-miss, though. He leaped from the burning plane and parachuted safely to the ground not far from the airfield.

Pike shot a second bomber down in flames, and then Griffin caught up with the third just east of the field. He filed the following report:

"At first I thought the plane was another P-40 and I pulled up on his wing, but fire from the rear gunner identified the plane immediately. I passed it too quickly to get a shot and pulled up for another run. I made about 10 runs at the plane, which was flying about 50 feet above the ground, seeking cover in the numerous hills. On my third pass I felt bullets hit my plane but noticed no damaging effects. After a few more passes there was no return fire from the bomber and I closed to within 75 yards, noticing that the plane was being hit. The plane seemed to lose altitude and I lost it as it went low behind a hill. I circled the area for about five minutes and could no longer make contact. I returned to the field in ten minutes."[12] The wreckage of the plane Griffin attacked was found the following morning about thirty miles from Kweilin.

When daylight arrived, the Kweilin task force sent off a mission against the airfield on San Chau Island near Hong Kong. The planes had to dodge the holes in the runway to get off, but all of them did so successfully. Chinese workers filled the holes while the mission was away, and the planes later landed without trouble.

The next day, November 24, eight B-25s and four P-40s fitted with bombs were escorted by twelve more P-40s to their target—an aircraft assembly plant at White Cloud Airdrome in Canton. Major Holloway, leading the escorts, and 1/Lt. Marvin Lubner of the 76th, one of the dive-bombers, each shot down a Japanese fighter. The mission exacted a heavy price, however. First Lieutenant Patrick H. Daniels of the 76th, leader of the dive-bombing flight, was killed when the bombs under one of his wings exploded during his bomb run. The wing of his P-40 was blown off, and he spun straight into the ground near Tien Ho, the other airdrome at Canton. Lubner suggested that Daniels probably was in a skid during his dive, causing the bombs to hit each other and go off when he released them. Japanese radio later claimed Daniels had been shot down. Whatever the cause, the 76th had lost one of its most effective and aggressive flight leaders.[13]

That was not all the action for November 24. Later that night, under the cover of darkness, Maj. John Alison led six P-40Es, each loaded with two fifty-kilogram demolition bombs, up to Hankow for bombing and strafing attacks on river traffic. This was dangerous work, but all the planes returned safely.

Then the next morning, eight P-40s went up to Hengyang to refuel before escorting B-25s to Sienning, just south of Hankow. Heavy overcast caused problems during the approach to the target, but the mission got straightened out and went off without opposition. A similar mission went to Yoyang, a river town 180 miles northeast of Hengyang.

November 26 was Thanksgiving—a day for eating, not fighting. To that end, 150 pounds of turkey and a couple of hams had been flown in to Kweilin for the feast. In all, about 225 men shared dinner, including General Chennault, the combat pilots, ground personnel, and even a couple of news correspondents. Everyone ate heartily. They knew that the mission planned for the following day was going to be a doozy.

★ ★ ★ ★

General Chennault's original plan for the Thanksgiving Day-plus-one raid was to hit Hong Kong one last time before withdrawing his forces to the Kunming area. The forces of nature and supply conspired against him, however, and he was forced to make a change at the last minute. A strong wind came up Thanksgiving night and persisted the next day. This, along with a dwindling supply of seventy-five-gallon belly tanks, would have made the long flight to Hong Kong difficult for the Sharks. On the morning of November 27, the general decided to play it safe and hit Canton instead.

The CATF force that set out from Kweilin was the biggest yet. Led by Lt. Col. Butch Morgan, all ten B-25s of the 11th Bomb Squadron at Kweilin participated. Their escort was made up of twenty-three P-40s from the 16th, 75th, and 76th squadrons. They took off starting at 8:45 A.M., and only one plane, a P-40, had to abort the mission.

Ever eager Colonel Scott led the P-40s. Flying with him was Lt. Col. Clinton D. ("Casey") Vincent of CATF headquarters. Vincent, a West Point graduate two days shy of his twenty-eighth birthday, had arrived in China just two weeks earlier and already was on his seventh mission. The commander of the Tenth Air Force, Brig. Gen. Clayton Bissell, had sent Vincent to China as the CATF's executive officer with orders to organize Chennault's administrative structure. Chennault, contemptuous of his boss's meddling in his affairs, named Vincent operations officer instead. This put Vincent on combat status, which suited him just fine. The paperwork could come later.[14]

The Shark escorts were divided into three echelons of seven or eight each, one on each side of the bombers and a third for top cover. Scott led one echelon, while Major Alison of the 75th and Major Holloway, now assigned to the 76th, led the others. Holloway was instructed to hold his top-cover flight in position during the bomb run and clean up the remaining Japanese opposition afterward.

The big formation approached Canton from the north in mostly clear skies at nineteen thousand feet. If the Japanese high command still was anxious to engage the Americans in an air battle, this would be the perfect opportunity. The bombers split into three groups about fifteen miles from the city. One would hit the aircraft factory, another would go after Tien Ho Airdrome, and the third would attack shipping on the Pearl River.

The Japanese responded in force, much to the Shark pilots' satisfaction. The air battle began a few moments after the bombers split up and lasted long after they completed their runs. During the engagement, the Americans noted two distinct types of Japanese fighters: fixed landing gear Ki-27 Nates (which the Americans called "I-97s") and sleeker Ki-43 Oscars ("Zeros").

The first Japanese run against the B-25s was made from the left by ten Oscars and Nates. A flight of P-40s led by Capt. Ed Goss of the 16th met them, and the fight began. Goss claimed two kills in this opening engagement, and the B-25s continued unmolested toward their targets. The bombers, looking for targets in the river, blew an eight-thousand-ton ship to pieces. The other B-25s found their targets, including the wharves on Whampoa Island, as more Japanese interceptors began to reach their altitude. A huge dogfight ensued, in which all but two of the P-40 pilots would inflict damage on the Japanese interceptors. Bruce Holloway made the following report of the battle:

"I stayed with the [B-25s] who bombed a ship of about 8,000 tons. They made several direct hits and practically tore it to pieces. Right after this another fight started right under us—Alison got his flight into this one, and by this time the radio conversation was getting good and everybody was shouting for everybody else to shoot a Jap off his tail. I heard [Lt. Dallas] Clinger say to [Lt. Jack] Best, 'I just knocked one off your tail but you ought to move over. I almost hit you, too.'

"About this time I saw a parachute descending directly ahead, and since the bombers seemed to be getting away all right, I went on to investigate the parachute, thinking it was a silver-colored aircraft in the distance. By this time I was right over Tien Ho Airdrome, so I dived down into the fight. It was really going strong and my flight pitched right into the middle of it. I made a pass on a Zero and it burst into flames. Didn't see it hit the ground but started to look for others. They were all over the place, and you could see burning tracer bullets going in every direction. I saw burning Japanese airplanes falling all over the sky.

"I made several more runs on Zeros and I-97s and finally got into a good position on an I-97 and gave him a long burst. I don't know whether he went down or not—claimed him as a probable. After this I climbed back up for a little altitude on the outside of the fight, expecting to be jumped on from above at any instant. I got back to about 8,000 feet and barged in again.

"By this time I could see only about three Japs left milling around over the field like mosquitoes. All the P-40s had either left or were chasing some Jap out over the countryside. The three that were left were very elusive and I didn't get a good pass at any of them. Finally, two of them got on my tail so I left the vicinity in somewhat of a hurry and started for home. I could hear everybody talking about how many they shot down, and it certainly sounded good.

"I proceeded on toward home all by myself, looking around behind me all the time, when I saw an aircraft off to my left going back toward Canton. It was a twin-engine light bomber and was very low over the hills. I turned in behind him and gave chase. Apparently he never did see me. I pulled on up to within about 100 yards behind him, expecting the rear gunner to open up on me at any instant. Either there was no rear gunner or he was asleep. I opened up from directly astern and poured the lead into him. The whole right side of the plane burst into flames and immediately thereafter there was an explosion which tore off the entire right wing. The flaming wreckage fell off to the left and crashed into the ground. It made a beautiful fire, and the whole thing took less time than it takes to tell about it.

"Again I expected to be jumped on from above. There is no more lonely feeling than to be at low altitude all by yourself over enemy territory with enemy planes in the vicinity. Nobody bothered me, though, so I turned around and went on home. Didn't have a single bullet hole in my plane.

"I was one of the last to get home and was overjoyed to find that my entire flight found their way back without getting lost. What's more, every one of them got at least one Japanese airplane."[15]

Holloway's experience was typical of the P-40 pilots. Once all the combat claims were tabulated and cross-checked, the total score for the day was twenty-three enemy planes confirmed destroyed, four probably destroyed, and one damaged in the air, plus one plane destroyed on the ground at Tien Ho by Colonel Scott. Only one Japanese fighter was able to break through the escorts and attack the bombers, and it put just a single bullet hole in one of the B-25s. Moreover, none of the P-40s were lost. Though two pilots made forced landings on the way home due to low fuel, Lts. Chuck Tucker and Ed Calvert of the 75th, but both flew home to Kweilin later.

An interesting sidelight to the mission was that one pilot in each of the three participating squadrons scored his fifth confirmed victory on November 27, making them their units' first "homegrown" aces. The pilots were 1/Lt. John Lombard of the 16th, Capt. John Hampshire of the 75th, and 1/Lt. Charles DuBois of the 76th. The other aces in the squadrons—Hill and Bright in the 75th and Rector in the 76th—had scored most of their kills in the AVG.

The November 27 mission capped an outstanding CATF campaign for control of the skies over southeastern China. It is difficult to assess the accuracy of the combat claims from such a large, free-wheeling air battle, but undoubtedly the pilots of the 23rd Fighter Group scored a lopsided victory. Now, however, it was time to fold the tents at Kweilin and pull back to western China. Supplies of gasoline, ammunition, and drop tanks were running low, and the P-40s needed major servicing.

Holloway recalled having a quick lunch after returning from Canton on the twenty-seventh, climbing into his P-40 again, and leading the 76th Fighter Squadron all the way back to Kunming. The 75th did likewise. The 16th moved to Chanyi the next day, leaving just five P-40s and pilots at Kweilin to escort four B-25s on a final strike against Hon Gay before moving out. By December 1, the base at Kweilin was virtually deserted.

The Hon Gay mission closed the Kweilin campaign for 1942. At the same time, the former AVG personnel still serving in the 23rd prepared to go home to the United States. The 76th threw a party for Maj. Ed Rector at Kunming on November 29, during which General Chennault presented him with a Distinguished Flying Cross. Major Tex Hill gave a farewell speech to the 75th the following day, telling his men he hoped to return to the squadron after his leave. Hill recalled, "Ed [Rector] and I came home in December 1942. My health was terrible. My first physical, I was down to 147 pounds. I had malaria real bad, and it took me quite a while to get over it. I dropped Ed off in Bombay. He went into the hospital there with pneumonia. He damned near died.

"I did a little bit of bond sales when I got back to the States. But not much. They sent me down to . . . Orlando. We checked out in Jugs [P-47s] down there. Then I came on up to Eglin. I took over the proving ground group from [Col. Winslow] Winnie Morse. Later on, I got Ed Rector down there. I tried getting all the China hands I could get."[16]

Neither Rector nor Hill was finished fighting in China. Both would return to command the 23rd Fighter Group later in the war.

7

The First Winter

At about two o'clock in the gloomy afternoon of December 5, 1942, a C-47 transport took off from Kunming Airfield bound for India. Aboard the plane were Majs. Ed Rector and Tex Hill, both shipping out for a well-deserved rest in the United States after almost a year of combat in Burma and China. Three P-40s took off right behind the C-47, with Maj. Bruce Holloway leading. The fighters escorted the slow transport for a short distance, hoping to do some stunts for the enjoyment of its honored passengers, but before long, the bigger plane rose into the low overcast. Holloway flew for a short distance on the wing of the transport, trading waves with Rector and Hill before turning back and landing at the field.

After Rector and Hill left, Maj. Frank Schiel of the 74th Fighter Squadron was the last remaining veteran of the American Volunteer Group still flying in China. However, only a couple of hours later, Schiel piled his F-4 reconnaissance plane into a mountainside not far from Kunming and died that same day. Now the 23rd Fighter Group was really on its own.

With Schiel, Hill, and Rector gone, General Chennault needed three new squadron commanders. He did not have to look hard to find ready-made replacements already flying in the 23rd Fighter Group. In addition to Capt. Ajax Baumler, who took over the 74th a few days after Schiel went down, he chose Maj. Johnny Alison for the 75th and Major Holloway for the 76th. With these experienced pilots in charge, all three of the squadrons would be able to continue operations without missing a beat.

Following the intense period of operations at Kweilin, Chennault had pulled all of his forces back to the Kunming area. This was partly due to the continuing problem with keeping the forward bases adequately supplied. Intense lobbying of Washington by Chennault and Generalissimo Chiang was beginning to pay off with increased flights over the Hump, but the tonnage arriving in China remained pitifully small at about one thousand tons a month. And the Old Man's China Air Task Force still only amounted to four fighter squadrons and a handful of B-25s.

Weather also played a part in Chennault's decision to move his forces. The eastern front was expected to stay mostly socked in through the winter, while the flying weather would be better down toward Burma and Indo-China. It made more sense to shift the CATF's operations to the south for awhile. As he had done previously and would do again repeatedly, Chennault used mobility to spread his forces and obscure his numerical weakness from the Japanese. The Old Man knew how to keep them guessing.

As it turned out, bad weather the first two weeks of December prevented much flying anywhere in China. Major Hazlett kept his 16th Fighter Squadron busy at Chanyi painting the P-40s, repairing engines, and performing other heavy maintenance on the ships. The pilots had little to do except routine check rides, but after the hectic month they had just completed at Kweilin, no one complained too much.

The other squadrons went through much the same routine at Kunming. Major Alison's crew chief in the 75th, Sgt. Bill Harris, wrote about that period: "John Alison assigned me as his crew chief when he became the 75th's squadron commander. I painted his new P-40 with the two white commander's stripes [vertically around the fuselage, just forward of the tail], the shark's mouth and eyes, and his three 'kill' flags and name on the left side just forward of the cockpit. . . .

"I also was assigned squadron painter but didn't have much time for painting insignia. I did paint a Petty girl nude on Lt. [James W.] Little's P-40. The rendition was a 'knock out,' but someone in head-quarters didn't think it was appropriate for a fighter plane. When a lot of P-40Ks came in over the Hump, Sergeants Don Van Cleve and George De Boer helped in getting all the painting done. I painted a lot of shark's mouths and eyes to look more vicious with longer teeth in the front and an inverted eyebrow over the eye on some."

Harris also recalled an incident a few weeks later, after the 75th moved to Chanyi: "Johnny Alison gave us a real scare when he took off from Chanyi and buzzed the field. It was right before Christmas, and we were all down in the dumps—no mail or packages, no action, and we were down to only five flyable P-40s. Alison took off for headquarters, Kunming, to see what he could do. After takeoff he turned and buzzed the taxi strip directly in front of the alert shack. He was so low I thought he was belly-landing at high speed. He was so low he left prop-tip tracks in the dirt and a long scratch mark made from the bottom of the drain cock on the belly tank. A close call!"[1]

One diversion for the pilots was occasional trips down to India to ferry new P-40s up to China. A group of pilots would pile into a C-47 and ride it across the Hump. Sometimes the new planes would be waiting for them at Dinjan, the western terminus of the Hump. More often they had to go all the way across India to Karachi to get them, spending a week or two in the process.

The new planes they were bringing in in late 1942 were P-40Ks. Outwardly, these planes were similar to the P-40Es, with the exception of a small curved addition to the vertical fin and bell-shaped exhaust pipes exiting from the cowling. Both of these changes were due to the P-40K's improved Allison engine that produced 1,325 horsepower, up about 200 from the previous power plant. P-40s' noses tended to swing left during takeoff due to the torque of the engine, and the additional horsepower exacerbated the problem. So the additional fin area was fitted to give the plane slightly better directional stability.

The P-40K offered only a slight increase in speed over the E-model, but the pilots appreciated any improvement. Mostly they liked the fact that the planes were newer, without the nagging problems like bald tires, touchy electrical systems, leaky hydraulics, and tired engines they had become accustomed to with their older Sharks. One pilot, Bob O'Neill of the 16th Fighter Squadron, had to take off from Yunnanyi once "with rope wrapped around one wheel to act as a tire, to save the airplane just prior to a Japanese attack. It took full right rudder and right aileron to maintain directional control on takeoff and landing."[2] In time, the P-40Ks would become war-weary, too, but for now they boosted the confidence of the men who flew them.

Operations were extremely limited at first. On December 6, 1942, a recon mission to Gia Lam Airdrome at Hanoi revealed a number of Japanese bombers and fighters parked there; but the weather closed back in before an attack could be mounted. A week later, Sharks escorted B-25s on an uneventful mission to Tengchung, Burma. Finally, on December 14 the weather cleared enough to allow the attack on Gia Lam. Bruce Holloway recorded the following account of the mission, which occurred on the day he was promoted to lieutenant colonel.

"Went to Hanoi with six bombers, 14 P-40s and four P-43s. I led the pursuit. We went in at 17,000 feet, and the bombers plastered Gia Lam Airdrome. Apparently they had only about four or five planes up after us. I didn't see any myself, but the bombers did, and somebody in the 74th made a pass on one of them and they all scattered. I stayed around for about 10 minutes watching for anybody taking off from Gia Lam that I could go after. None took off. The anti-aircraft was very heavy and very accurate. Everybody got pretty well split up, and I started home with [2/Lt. Robert S.] Ellis on my wing.

"Came up the Red River and saw no activity on any of the air-dromes. Halfway between Dong Cuang and Lao Kay, I saw an old French biplane going toward Hanoi at low altitude. The Chinese intelligence stated the other day that the Japanese are not allowing the French to fly anymore, so I didn't hesitate about shooting this airplane down. Turned around and dived on the old crate—one short burst tore it apart and set off the gasoline. It made a good blaze. One man bailed out and I watched him land in the river.

"Proceeded on toward home and saw a long train going north—didn't strafe it because I was afraid I might miss some more easy meat going down the river. Came on home without further event."[3]

Holloway shot down another French biplane a week later, but weather continued to hamper operations. On December 19, high winds from the southwest—80 to 100 miles per hour at fifteen thousand feet—caused Holloway to spend two hours and ten minutes making the 350-mile flight from Kunming to Lashio, but it only took him an hour and five minutes to get home.

These turned out to be winds of change.

★ ★ ★ ★

On the morning of Christmas Eve Day, the China Air Task Force held an awards ceremony outside at Kunming. As Lieutenant Colonel Holloway read the citations, General Chennault handed out three Distinguished Flying Crosses, three Silver Stars, and a Purple Heart to men of the 23rd Fighter Group, plus some medals for the 11th Bomb Squadron. Holloway recorded in his diary that "everything went off fairly smoothly considering we never have any military formations around here." Later, a Chinese general hosted a dinner for the men at Hostel Number Two, where each officer was presented with a red tie from the Generalissimo and Madame Chiang. After that, the squadrons adjourned to their own areas for parties of a more raucous nature.[4]

Everything went off smoothly for A Flight of the 16th Fighter Squadron on December 24, too, but its formation was in the sky, not on the ground. Major Hazlett led the flight of six P-40s from Chanyi west to Yunnanyi, where they had been ordered to set up combat operations. With him were Lts. Llewelyn Couch, W. S. Butler, Melvin Kimball, Aaron Liepe, and Bob Liles. The rest of the squadron would follow the morning after Christmas.

Yunnanyi was a small airfield in the high country about 150 miles west of Kunming, in the Himalayan foothills. It had been operating as an emergency strip for months, but about the only planes that landed there were occasional C-47s en route across the Hump and

P-40s staging to and from missions into Burma. That was about to change. To increase tonnage crossing over the Hump, the Air Transport Command decided to start using the field as eastern terminus for the Hump route.

Yunnanyi was well suited for its new role. It had a 5,864-foot runway made of crushed gravel, and flying conditions were good nearly year-round. Precipitation was light, even during monsoon season, though heavy winds could kick up during the winter. The high altitude at Yunnanyi—6,480 feet—required some care in figuring take-off loads for the aircraft, but it also meant cool evenings in the dead of summer. Also, the field was easy to find. Picturesque Yehching Lake was just west of the town of Yunnanyi, two 10,000-foot mountain peaks were about twenty miles away to the west and south, and the Burma Road circled the airfield from the west, around the north end of the runway. All made excellent landmarks. Finally, the Burma Road's proximity to the field also meant that transport planes could be unloaded at Yunnanyi and their cargoes trucked the rest of the way to Kunming, cutting flight times over the Hump by about an hour each way.

Yunnanyi had one shortcoming: The base was extremely vulnerable to Japanese air attacks. Not only was Yunnanyi within easy flying distance of Japanese airfields in Burma, but also the Chinese air warning net was less reliable in this area than it was in other parts of Free China. From now on, Chennault deemed it necessary to station some of his fighters at Yunnanyi at all times to provide air defense.

Once more, the Old Man's instincts proved correct. Major Hazlett and his pilots of the 16th Squadron spent only one night at Yunnanyi before Japanese bombers roared across the field in a sneak attack on Christmas Day. They caught the 16th flat-footed, and not a single P-40 was able to take off in time to challenge them. Fortunately, none of the Sharks were damaged in the attack, either, because the bombs fell beyond the airfield. Major Hazlett led a flight of Sharks off to chase the enemy bombers, but they were long gone by the time the P-40s reached altitude.

Colonel Scott, the 23rd's group commander, flew in from Kunming that night with instructions from General Chennault on how to prevent getting caught on the ground again. Scott placed all the pilots at Yunnanyi on alert, and at 7:00 A.M. on December 26 he sent two Sharks up on patrol. At 9:00 A.M. the patrol was doubled, and from 11:00 A.M. on, Scott kept at least eight P-40s in the air. If any Japanese planes tried to come back, they were not going to get a free ride.[5]

The first sign of trouble came in mid-morning. Two pilots in the 74th Squadron, Lts. Thomas J. Clark and Arthur W. Cruikshank Jr., encountered an enemy twin-engine recon aircraft near the Salween River while they were returning to Kunming from an escort mission to Lashio. They gave chase, and Lieutenant Clark was able to shoot the Japanese plane down in flames.

At Yunnanyi, Colonel Scott waited and fretted. At 2:00 P.M., he ordered the rest of his fighters to take off and set up patrols. The Old Man had told him that if the Japanese were coming back, they were likely to return at the same time they attacked the previous day, 2:45 P.M.

Sure enough, the raiders came in from Burma across the Mekong River just before 3:00 P.M. Nine twin-engine bombers flew at seventeen thousand feet in three vees of three, with about ten escort fighters above and behind them. The first Sharks to make contact were a flight of four led by Maj. Hal Pike. The Sharks concentrated on the escort fighters, downing several and drawing the rest away from the bombers.

Colonel Scott and Major Hazlett led the rest of the Sharks in an attack on the bombers a few minutes later. The sky erupted in gunfire, but the bombers held their positions. Scott concentrated his fire on the lead vee of bombers, hitting all three of them on his first pass. His second target exploded as he pumped slugs into the third. He made another pass from underneath the bombers but was unable to confirm the results because he was flying directly into the sun at the time.

By the time the bombers reached Yunnanyi, only six were left. They dropped their bombs on the field but only left minor damage and no injuries. The P-40 pilots continued to attack, and more airplanes fell from the sky as the Japanese attempted to withdraw to Burma. The Sharks' final victory tally was ten confirmed destroyed, five probables, and one damaged. On the negative side of the ledger, two P-40s were shot down and one pilot killed.

One of the Shark pilots taking part in the mission was Capt. Bob Liles of the 16th. Liles and another 16th pilot, Bob Mooney, went through flight school together and were great friends. Liles went to the 77th Squadron out of flight school, and Mooney went to the 16th. They met again in India when Liles was assigned to the 16th, and they had a big reunion. Liles recalled December 26, 1942, vividly. He reminisced, "Bob Mooney was a very aggressive pilot and a damned good one. He was supposed to go with us [when the 16th left Chanyi], but his airplane had had an engine change and he had to slow time it—wear the engine in a little bit. He didn't come over that day.

"Just as I was taxiing out to take off [on December 26], I saw Bob Mooney land. I saw him pull his clothes bag out of the plane. He was trying to get refueled so he could back in on the mission. I left. We were patrolling some miles south of the field anticipating the Jap attack.

"Major Pike was leading my flight, and Hazlett, the other. Just as we were about ready to sail into them, a lone airplane came streaking up from the base, and it was Mooney. I recognized his airplane. He went past me going pretty fast. At that point we went right into these Zeros and bombers.

"I was getting ready to shoot at a Zero, moving to the right. Mooney picked on one going to the left. We never did actually form up as an element and start fighting together. That was the last time I saw him. He was shot down that day. Most of the Jap airplanes that came in that day were shot down, too.

"When I landed, someone told me Mooney was down. So I got a jeep and driver, and we went out west of Yunnanyi to look for him. We knew only approximately where he was. The Chinese had told us about the location. So when we got there, I saw him being carried on a door. An elderly Chinese man—black clothes, long beard—was leading the group. Looked like he was about sixty-five years old. Probably twenty or thirty Chinese walking along.

"I went up to the group and learned Mooney was still alive. But he had a big bruise behind his left ear. The Chinese said that he had shot a Zero down in a head-on pass, but he was shot by another one. He bailed out and landed in a Chinese cemetery. Apparently, he struck his head on a tombstone or something. Prior to this, however, he'd shot down a Jap bomber.

"They took him into the doctor's house. The doctor had gone to . . . a British medical school in Shanghai, so he informed me. Then he dragged out a medical book, talking about concussion. He told me he really had a concussion. Showed me in this medical book some drug; you were supposed to give an injection of this drug to counteract the effects of the concussion. He asked my permission to give it to Bob. I was very reluctant to do that, but I didn't know what else to do. I knew our doctor had gone out to another crash, where Llewelyn Couch bailed out. I had no idea when Doctor Voss would get there, so I told him to go ahead and give him the shot. The Chinese doctor's wife sat there and held Bob Mooney's tongue to keep him from swallowing it. For hours she sat there.

"He died as midnight approached. About ten minutes later Doctor Voss and another driver showed up. I couldn't wait to ask him about what this guy had given Bob. I asked him to talk to this Chinese doctor, which he did. He said the doctor did the only thing he could do. I asked him if I was right to authorize this guy to give him the shot and he said, 'Certainly; it was the only thing you could do.' I was much relieved.

"Not too long after that the squadron left and went to East China. We were over there for some time, and later we came back to Yunnanyi. Then, shortly after I became commander of the 16th, the Chinese asked if I would come and participate in a ceremony that they were going to have. I had no idea what it was, but they asked me to go so I was going.

"They had erected a monument, probably twelve feet tall, that was kind of a replica of the Washington Monument except that up at the top was some kind of a star. On two sides, in English, it told what (Mooney) had done that day, and on the other two sides was the same story in Chinese. They had this ceremony, and this same old outfit was there. We renewed acquaintances. The peasants in that valley had made contributions to pay for this ceremony. It was right on the Burma Road, and there was another road that came down that they referred to as the Lincoln Highway. The monument sat right in the intersection. I don't know if the communists have knocked it down."[6]

In fact, the monument was destroyed during the Cultural Revolution of the 1960s. But following a visit to the site in 1991 by Mooney's sister, Ena Lee Davis of Kansas City, a new monument honoring Lieutenant Mooney was constructed. It was dedicated in 1993.

The 16th Fighter Squadron continued to stand alerts at Yunnanyi after New Year's 1943, but the enemy stayed away. Meanwhile, P-40s of the 74th and 76th squadrons ventured down to Burma almost daily to hit targets in the Lashio area.

On the afternoon of December 30, 1/Lt. Mortimer Marks of the 76th led a flight of five Sharks to Lashio and met up with six Ki-43 Oscars that attacked the P-40s from different directions. Marks got off shots at two of his attackers and damaged one of them before two more got on his tail. He whipped his P-40 over and dived for safety. Meanwhile, 2/Lt. William E. ("Bill") Distefano got behind one of the Oscars and hit it hard in the wing. A wingtip and aileron tore off the Japanese fighter, and it nosed down out of control. Distefano's destroyed Oscar was the 23rd Fighter Group's last confirmed victory of 1942.

War does not observe the calendar, however. Operations continued at the same pace as 1943 opened. P-40s flew missions out of Kunming nearly every day, while the 75th Fighter Squadron dispatched a flight to Yunnanyi to bolster the 16th's defenses there and prepare for moving the entire 75th into the western base.

The quiet period at Yunnanyi lasted until 5:30 A.M. on January 16, 1943, when the warning net came to life with word of a big enemy attack taking shape over Burma. Captain Liles and Lt. Aaron Liepe took the early patrol and spotted the Japanese formation approximately thirty miles southwest of Yunnanyi at about 9:00 A.M. It was a big one: eighteen twin-engine bombers and twelve Oscar escort fighters in the first wave, with another dozen or so Oscars above them and several miles behind. Liles radioed the sighting to the field, where eight more P-40 pilots were sitting in their planes with engines running, waiting for the signal. They scrambled quickly and caught up with the enemy formation over Yunnanyi. Again, though the Japanese bombers were able to drop their loads on the air base, they did very little damage, and then they headed north in a long turn that took them nearly over Lake Tali before turning for home. Two ground crewmen, Technical Sgt. Theodore Johnson and Staff Sgt. Rudolph Brlansky, were wounded on the field. Brlansky had stayed out on the flight line to help his pilot prepare to take off and ran out of time to take cover. A bomb fragment hit him while he was running for the slit trenches, and he was later awarded the Purple Heart.

Once more the Shark pilots made the Japanese pay. Liles and Liepe attacked the escort fighters, with Liles downing two and Liepe a third. Captain Lombard, leading the rest of the fighters, made two passes on an Oscar and shot it down, while 1/Lt. James Little of the 75th shot down two more. Captain Bob Smith of the 16th led the attack on the bombers with 2/Lt. George V. Pyles on his wing. They attacked head-on at sixteen thousand feet, and Smith saw his fire rip into the nose of one bomber. His line of flight carried him through the bombers and into the Oscars, where he made another head-on attack and saw his target go down in flames. Unfortunately, Lieutenant Pyles was shot down and killed during the encounter.

After the P-40s landed and the pilots filed their reports, twelve more victories were tacked on the 23rd Fighter Group's growing score. Lieutenant Pyles's death was even more troubling as the 16th had lost another pilot less than a week before. First Lieutenant L. F. ("Chip") Myers was killed when his P-40 crashed on January 12 while he was bringing mail from Kunming.

Another pilot in the 16th, Jack Best, shared his memories of Pyles's death. He said, "George Pyles was shot down somewhere near the headwaters of the Mekong River, up toward the Tibet border almost. We knew approximately where he was, so our squadron flight surgeon, Doc Voss, and myself volunteered to go out and try to recover the body. We had an escort of a few Chinese soldiers. We left from Lake Tali with two donkeys and these Chinese GIs and started across the mountains. I can remember that we were up over seventeen thousand feet going across the passes. It took us two days.

"As Doc and I would get saddle sore from riding those donkeys, we would get off and walk for awhile. We still had trouble even with the aid of donkey transportation keeping up with those soldiers.

"We finally got out to this area that we were looking for on the Mekong, a little place called Meiling, as I recall. When we got there, the soldiers disappeared because they didn't know what kind of people they were running into—and neither did we, of course. We got into this village with our two donkeys. As we went down the street it was late in the evening, and there was not a sign of life anywhere. It began to get more spooky as we went further in the village. Sooner or later the people showed up, and it turned out that the mayor was there to greet us. One of the first things he did was show me a casing from what was obviously a .50-caliber machine-gun bullet, probably one of ours. I assumed what he wanted to know was whether it was Japanese or American. With our pointee-talkee [translation] book, we said, 'Japanese, Japanese.' Anyway, we got away with it.

"It turns out, they had found the body of George. They had among the remains his ID card with a photo on it. They had made a tremendous poster picture of him, and we were there for a three-day funeral. No way could we get away. They had built a teak coffin, which must have weighed five hundred pounds. Of course, George was not light, either. They gave us an escort to take us back, and those guys (six of them) carried that coffin all the way across those mountains and back to Lake Tali. That was an experience I'll never forget."[7]

Another pilot in the 16th who had an unforgettable experience on January 16 was Lt. Bob O'Neill. During the air battle, he met three Japanese planes on their way home and turned his guns on the last one. He hit the enemy fighter hard, and it crashed into a field southwest of the air base. O'Neill went out again later that day in his P-40, named "Deanie" for his girlfriend, to patrol along the Mekong River in case the Japanese came back. During that mission, his plane's propeller malfunctioned, and O'Neill had to bail out. He parachuted safely and was met by a band of Chinese tribesmen. As he recalled, "It was only 40 miles from the base, but because of the rough terrain it took my rescuers and me seven days to get back. Their treatment and care was true 'southern hospitality.'"[8]

On January 20, the pilots of the 16th Fighter Squadron packed up and flew back to Chanyi to rest and regroup. Trading places with them were the eager men of the 75th. The 16th had defended Yunnanyi so effectively during its month there, however, that the Japanese did not attempt another raid on the base for the rest of the winter.

★ ★ ★ ★

The new year 1943 brought more leadership changes for the 23rd Fighter Group. The first one came right at the top, as Col. Robert L. Scott received orders sending him back to the United States just after New Year's Day. He departed Kunming on January 9. Replacing Scott as group commander was Lt. Col. Bruce Holloway, who had been commanding the 76th Fighter Squadron for the previous month. Holloway described Scott's departure in his diary:

"Colonel Scott left today and I was appointed c.o. of the group. Very honored. Scotty left in a C-87 [a cargo version of the B-24 Liberator heavy bomber] and we gave him a razzmatazz farewell flight. First, we took off with five planes and went low in a five-plane 'Vee' over the C-87 as it taxied out on the field. Then, after it got in the air, we came up alongside the transport with the apex of our 'Vee' directly under the big plane. They said that looked very good from the ground. After this we got in string and dived past the transport, doing a slow roll around it as we went by. He got a lot of pictures of us, and it was a good farewell."[9]

Bob Scott probably is the most controversial character who ever served in the 23rd Fighter Group. When he left China, he was a double ace with at least ten confirmed victories, the highest total of any active pilot in China. After his return to the United States, Scott was debriefed extensively in Washington and then sent off in a new P-40K on a national speaking tour to promote sales of government bonds and boost the morale of factory workers. But Scott's biggest contribution to the morale of the nation was yet to come.

Following a speaking engagement at a church in Buffalo, New York, he was approached to write a book about his experiences for Scribner's. Having only a few days off from his tour to devote to the project, Scott dictated his story into a recording machine and left the recordings with Scribner's to turn into a book. The end product, *God Is My Co-Pilot*, became an immediate best-seller and made Scott a household name throughout the country.[10]

While basically factual, the book was a product of its time, meaning it was skillfully edited to produce the maximum propaganda value. Though he had been very careful to give credit for the 23rd's success in China to General Chennault and others, Scott came through in the book as an all-American, one-man-air-force kind of hero—just the kind of person the American public wanted to read about after a difficult first year of war.

As popular as the book was, many of the people who served in China before and during the time Scott was there did not like it. One former AVG pilot who read the book noted in his dairy: "*God Is My Co-Pilot* . . . is as great a compilation of lies and overstatement as it has ever been my displeasure to read."[11]

A movie quickly followed with the same title, only adding to Scott's reputation. In fact, one rumor that made the rounds in China was that Scott once returned from a solo mission and claimed to have destroyed a Japanese aircraft, but the masking tape that was applied over the gun barrels on his P-40 to keep them clean before firing was still in place when he landed. Tex Hill, one of Scott's

strongest supporters, disputes that story. He claims "that bull—
about him coming back with the guns still having tapes on them—
was totally untrue. They had an investigation later on. Here's what
happened: You come back off of one of those missions and you're
short of fuel or something, so you've got an alternate. You go into
one of those little ol' fields. The first thing they do is gas you up,
clean your guns, rearm them, and tape them. Scotty stopped off at a
little field and that happened. When he came back that story got
started, and he's never been able to shake it. I happen to know that
was wrong. He got a bum deal on that."[12]

Whatever his colleagues may think about him and his book, there
is no doubt that Bob Scott made a tremendous contribution to the
war effort with *God Is My Co-Pilot*, perhaps even greater than the
one he made in the skies over China. The book inspired millions of
Americans in every walk of life, from young men determined to follow his example in combat to factory workers and potential bond
buyers. The book is still popular in the 1990s.

When Lieutenant Colonel Holloway moved up to group commander, more personnel changes were in order. Casey Vincent was promoted to full colonel and named executive officer of the CATF, a job
formerly held by Scott along with his group command. Vincent,
despite his increased administrative load, would continue to fly on
combat missions with the 23rd whenever possible and eventually
downed six Japanese aircraft.

Taking over for Holloway as commander of the 76th Fighter
Squadron was a relative newcomer to China, Capt. Grant M.
Mahony. The new commander was not, however, a green combat
pilot. The handsome, twenty-four-year-old Californian was a flight
leader of the 3rd Pursuit Squadron in the Philippines in 1941 and
flew two combat missions on the first day of the war. A very aggressive pilot, Mahony flew a solo strafing mission and destroyed several
Japanese fighters on the ground December 14, 1941, the day after
his best friend was killed in action. Mahony also participated in the
ill-fated defense effort in Java during February 1942, scoring three
aerial victories and briefly commanding the 17th Pursuit Squadron.
Major General Lewis H. Brereton took Mahony with him to India in
late February 1942, and from there Mahony finally came to China in
early December.

Mahony took the war very seriously and did not have much
patience for anyone who did not share his fighting spirit. Consider
this opinion he noted on a monthly operations report two months
after assuming command of the 76th: "Squadron morale rises rapidly when a mission is scheduled. A few pilots have no desire to participate in missions over enemy territory. These pilots should not

remain in pursuit, but they should not be rewarded by sending them home, either. . . ."[13]

One other squadron change of command took place late in the month when Major Hazlett turned over the 16th Fighter Squadron to Maj. Hal Pike. Hazlett's combat experience, administrative skills, and maturity made him a natural for his next assignment, which was to set up and command the Karachi Operational Training Unit in India. This organization was to provide new fighter pilots arriving in the China-Burma-India (CBI) theater with real-life training in the tactics and techniques used by frontline combat squadrons. Instructors would be experienced pilots who had completed their combat tours. Unfortunately, Major Hazlett did not survive the war. He was killed in the crash of a training plane at Landhi Field, India (now Pakistan), on August 6, 1943.

The new commander of the 16th had been with the squadron since its days in India. Hal Pike was well liked and highly experienced. A prewar pilot like Hazlett, Pike had served in the 33rd Pursuit Group at Mitchell Field, New York, before coming overseas. Most pilots felt he was more combat oriented than Hazlett, an opinion that would prove accurate in the months to come.

The last command change of the winter occurred February 18, when Maj. Ajax Baumler completed his combat tour. He was replaced as commander of the 74th Fighter Squadron by Capt. John D. ("Mo") Lombard, who was the 16th Fighter Squadron's first ace and top-scoring pilot with five confirmed victories. Joining Lombard in the 74th was another top combat pilot from the 16th, Wyoming daredevil Capt. Dallas A. Clinger.

★ ★ ★ ★

February 1943 passed relatively quietly. It was the first month since the 23rd Fighter Group commenced operations that not a single Japanese aircraft was encountered. In just twenty-one missions, the group destroyed two dozen trucks, two river steamers, and four barges as the Sharks beat up targets along the Salween River and the Burma Road. One pilot, Lt. William T. Gross of the 75th, was killed when his P-40K was shot down February 11 while strafing troops at Nan Sang.

Perhaps the biggest excitement at Kunming during the winter was the arrival and subsequent testing of a captured Japanese fighter. The plane was a "real" Zero, a Navy A6M, as opposed to the Army Ki-43s that were more commonly encountered in China. The Chinese had recovered it after a forced landing and brought it to Kunming, where mechanics of the 76th Fighter Squadron under the direction of Staff Sgt. Gerhard Neumann restored it to flying condition. On February 2, Lieutenant Colonel Holloway got a chance to fly the plane before it was shipped back to the States. He wrote in his diary, "This afternoon I tested the Zero. I gave it a rather thorough workout, and practically all of Kunming was out to watch the show. There must have been a thousand cameras.

"First, I flew alongside a B-25 so official and news cameras could get some shots. Then I tested it for climb and high speed at 10, 15, 20, and 25,000 feet. This airplane is greatly overrated. It is highly maneuverable; the P-40 and P-43 are both much faster, sturdier. After these tests, I had a series of dogfights and acceleration tests with both a P-40 and a P-43. I went along in line formation at 200 mph indicated with the P-40. On signal, we both poured on the coal. For a few seconds we stayed together, and then the P-40 pulled away so fast it was thrilling—nothing before has ever assured me so much as to who is going to win the war as comparing the Zero and P-40. The best short definition I can think of for the Zero is a 'cheesebox with an engine.'

"In the middle of an exhibition low flying series of maneuvers, five new P-40s arrived from India, so I decided to bust through the middle of them. They scattered in all directions and one of them confided that he almost shot me down—until he saw the white star."[14]

The big news for March passed almost unnoticed by the men of the 23rd. On the tenth of the month, the China Air Task Force was disbanded and the Fourteenth Air Force created to take its place. A significant organizational change, it put a second star on General Chennault's shoulder and gave his command equal status with the Tenth Air Force in India. In time, that would help Chennault lobby successfully for more combat strength and more supplies over the Hump. But for now, it was nothing more than a paper shuffle to the guys on the line.

Operations continued to focus on the Burma front in March, and the level of activity picked up with thirty-eight missions flown. Just as in the previous month, no Japanese aircraft were encountered.

The worst damage suffered by the 16th Fighter Squadron occurred on the afternoon of March 5, when a fire burned down the armament shack at Chanyi. The blaze started when a staff sergeant tossed a match away and it landed on the thatched roof of the shack. In the ensuing fire, the squadron lost all its spare gun parts, armorers' tools, and machine guns, as well as ten thousand rounds of .50-caliber ammunition, many rolls of gun camera film, and a few sidearms. The sergeant was busted down to buck private following an investigation.

First Lieutenant William Grosvenor of the 75th had a close call on March 24, when a flight of four Sharks went up to test a new skip-bombing technique at the practice range about fifteen miles from Kunming. A very accurate method of delivering ordnance against shipping, it would be used extensively by the 23rd Fighter Group throughout the rest of the war.

In skip bombing, the idea was to come in very low and skip the bombs off the surface of the water and into the target vessel. The bombs were set with delay fuses to give the low-flying fighters a chance to clear the target before the explosion. The delay fuse did not work on Grosvenor's bomb, however, and it went off just as his plane passed about forty feet above it. The Shark was riddled and an aileron was torn off, but its momentum allowed Grosvenor to nurse it up to about five hundred feet before it dropped off in a spin. Grosvenor, unhurt, was out of the cockpit in a flash and parachuted safely to the ground. It was a lucky break for the future ace.

Though air combat had petered out for the time being, the Japanese 3rd Air Division was not quiet during this winter period. Flying from the Hankow and Canton areas, Japanese raiders carried out ten attacks on the East China airfields of Kweilin, Liuchow, Hengyang, and Lingling. They accomplished little with these missions, because Chennault did not have aircraft stationed on those fields at the time. But the stage was set for heavy action in the spring and summer ahead.

8

Fighting on Two Fronts

First Lieutenant Melvin B. Kimball must have felt like the unluckiest man in the China-Burma-India theater. Here he was, flying a worn-out, old P-40 with a dwindling fuel supply over northern Burma and without any idea in what direction Dinjan was. For a seasoned fighter pilot such as Kimball, who had shot down three enemy planes and won a Silver Star for bravery since coming to China with the original contingent of the 16th Fighter Squadron, it was a heck of a predicament. But there was no denying it; he was lost.

Kimball had left Kunming mid-morning of March 29, 1943, with the seemingly simple task of delivering the old AVG warhorse to India and bringing back a new P-40K. No sweat; guys did it all the time. A combination of bad weather and bad luck, however, had gotten Kimball turned around somewhere east of the Naga Hills, and now he needed a place to land. Below him was uninviting jungle, but finally Kimball saw what appeared to be a small airstrip hacked out of the landscape. There was a 50 percent chance that the strip was held by friendly forces, so down he went to find out. He sure was not going to bail out over the jungle unless absolutely necessary.

Kimball dropped the P-40 in over the fence in a near stall. The wheels touched down, and the old Shark slowed dramatically as the muddy runway gave way under the weight of the plane. Somehow, the Shark stopped at the far end without nosing up. Kimball quickly jumped down from the cockpit and looked around but did not see anyone. He trudged over to some huts off the edge of the field, looked around, and still did not find anyone. Then he came back to the plane and got on the radio, calling for help to anyone who might be flying in the area and hear him. He had landed safely, but he was not going to be able to take off again in his P-40 from the short, muddy field.

At that moment, Capt. Charles H. ("Hank") Colwell and his wing-man, Lt. John J. Ferguson, both pilots in the 26th Fighter Squadron of the 51st Fighter Group, were returning to their base at Dinjan following a recon mission into central Burma. Colwell's P-40K had been hit by ground fire on the flight, but it was not giving him trouble. Colwell heard Kimball's distress call and headed for nearby Maingkwan, which he knew was a Japanese-held landing strip about 120 miles southwest of Dinjan. Sure enough, when Colwell and Ferguson arrived, they saw a P-40 sitting there with its pilot in the cockpit.

Captain Colwell relayed Kimball's distress call to Dinjan and then set up a patrol pattern over Maingkwan. He knew the Japanese army had an outpost not more than a mile away. Meanwhile, the 51st Fighter Group dispatched to the scene a flight of P-40s and a Stearman PT-17 biplane trainer flown by Lt. Ira M. Sussky of the 25th Fighter Squadron.

The P-40s came and relieved Colwell, and a little while later, Sussky arrived in the PT-17 to pick up Kimball. He put the plane down gently, knowing of the muddy conditions on the field. Kimball, much relieved, raced to the biplane and jumped into the open front cockpit. Sussky taxied slowly to the upwind end of the strip, turned around, and gave the little trainer full throttle. The plane began to move but then slogged to a stop, stuck in the mud. Sussky and Kimball jumped out, shoved the plane out of its rut, and tried again, but they got the same results.

By now, the situation was getting tense. The Japanese had dispatched troops to the area, and the P-40s above were making strafing passes to keep the Japanese from reaching the PT-17. Bullets began to whiz past as Sussky and Kimball tried repeatedly to take off. Finally, on their eighth try, the little trainer was able to break free from the mud and lift them into the sky. As soon as they cleared the field, the P-40s swooped down and shot up Kimball's P-40 until it caught on fire and burned.

Captain Herbert W. Davis of the 26th Squadron escorted Sussky's PT-17 back to Dinjan, where they landed after dark, almost out of gas. Kimball posed graciously with his rescuers for photographs the following morning and then continued on his ferry mission. Before long, he would be back in combat in China, where he would have quite a story to tell his buddies in the 16th Fighter Squadron. There was one sad postscript to his story, however; Captain Colwell was killed in a flying accident on June 2, 1943.[1]

Kimball's close call in the jungle showed that even experienced pilots could get in trouble in the vast, empty skies over the Hump. But by the spring of 1943, the 23rd Fighter Group was beginning to receive a steady trickle of replacement pilots. The group welcomed these men because they were needed to keep the squadrons up to full strength. And the older hands continued to be impressed by how much better trained the new pilots seemed to be.

The new pilots were not, however, cagey combat veterans like the crew cut–sporting Mel Kimball. One of the pilots arriving in China during the spring of 1943 was 2/Lt. Vernon J. Henderson, who soon would begin flying with Kimball in the 16th. Henderson, like many ahead of him, had served in Central America before coming to China. He wrote the following account of his experiences, starting in August 1942 during P-40 training in Florida.

"It was soon time to move on, and the destination was Pinellas, Florida, on the north shore of Tampa Bay. Very soon after arrival there was a call for 'volunteers' but no indication of what you were volunteering for . . . must be something exciting . . . so old dummy says, 'I'll go,' and got orders to the 53rd Fighter Group, Old France Field, Panama Canal Zone. Hardly the European or African assignment expected, but probably the best thing that could have happened from a survive-the-war point of view.

"Four months of concentrated flying and gunnery practice in early P-40Bs. Lots of air patrols, flying in and out of ill-prepared airstrips of Central America and dealing with the extreme weather conditions of the tropics; day and night. By and large, the days of errors due to inexperience were over, and losses were those to be expected in this unfriendly operating environment.

"Actually, Panama was a good tour. There were the massive pre-war quarters on base, and we all had private rooms. However, we were always on alert and usually slept in the dormitory located in the hangar. In the jungle there had to be 'pets,' so we shared quarters with a jaguar cub—mean as hell—a six-foot python, and a honey bear that usually roamed free. He was nocturnal and prone to jumping on top of you in the middle of the night. . . .

"Six of us were moved down to Talara, Peru, and into the airshow business with lightweight, highly polished P-40Bs. Show the flag in the northern countries of South America, and as I remember we did this with gusto. Flying out of Talara one day, I had a 250-pound bomb on the belly rack and was off to get us some dinner. Spot a school of tuna just offshore and dive-bomb them. The crash boat comes over to the area where the bomb exploded and collects the booty. We and the locals feast on fresh tuna for a few days. Well, this time the plan failed. I set up my bomb run and reached for the release handle: This is low enough; pull; now recover from the dive before you splat into the ocean. Pull up, roll over, and check where the bomb landed. Sorry, fella, no bomb. It's just right down there under your feet. But surprise: It's now only secured by the front shackle, as the rear one released as advertised.

"There followed many attempts to get rid of this unwanted cargo, all to no avail. Advice from our little operations shack was to bail out with the airplane headed out to sea. While the rationality of this course of action was clear, the idea of deliberately trashing a good plane—with my name on it—was an unsatisfactory solution. Since I was unable to force the bomb off, perhaps if I was real gentle, it would oblige and stay on while I landed on the smooth cement strip that was Talara. I did and it did.

"The fire trucks intercepted my rollout until they saw the bomb bouncing its tail fins along the runway. Then they almost rolled over in their haste to put as much distance between me and them as possible in the shortest amount of time. The bomb was nose-fused with the arming wire still retained. The rear fins would never be the same after being pounded on the concrete. Major Buffum, my commander at the time, questioned my sanity but commented that it was the most beautiful landing he'd ever seen anyone make in a '40.

"We were recalled to Panama and then it's time to launch for China. It is now February 1943 and I have logged some 700 hours of flying time; about 250 of it in P-40s from the early B to the C, E, and F. We fly the P-40s back to Panama and pick up new airplanes to be dropped off in Puerto Rico. It's an island-hopping series of flights to Borrenquin Field, where we bid so long to the birds and catch a transport on down to Belém, Brazil, our jumping-off place for Africa and on to India and China. . . .

"At Landhi Field, I spent thirteen and a half hours at the controls of a P-40E, most of which was devoted to aerial gunnery practice against both air and ground targets. Then picking up a new P-40E, it was time to head east again toward the final destination: China. The trip from Karachi to Kunming, China, consumed ten hours and twenty minutes by P-40. From Karachi to Jodhpur transits the Sind Desert, which I would compare to our own southwest except that towns, roads and irrigated areas were totally lacking. Refuel at Jodhpur and head on to Agra for the night. Actually, the weather turned sour and we were in Agra for two nights and had a day and a half to explore this fascinating city. The Taj Mahal—fantastic—and in beautiful condition for this was still British India. Stayed at a wonderful hotel, and we all thought we were in heaven with the great food, swimming pools and a huge manicured lawn for an impromptu football game. One of our group, Bob Maxent, turned out to be a champion gymnast, and the football game became a spectator sport as he put on a demonstration of his tumbling skills for us. Fortunately, when we went in the pool later, he did not require a game of follow the leader off the diving board. Our contribution to the war effort would have ended abruptly had that been the case. [Lieutenant Maxent, assigned to the 75th Fighter Squadron in China, was killed in a crash at Chanyi on September 5, 1943.]

"As the weather cleared we cranked the Allisons and headed farther east with a refueling stop at Gaya and an overnight at Koch Bihar. The Maharaja of 'Cooch Behar' treated us as royalty. Our ground crew caught up with us at this point, and all the airplanes received a thorough inspection and were primed for the high country ahead. We made one more refueling stop at Dinjan in Assam at the foot of the Himalayas.

"At this point, the powers that be had determined an escort to be necessary, and a B-25 with navigator was to escort us over the Hump into China. Each of four fighters was to be escorted by a single B-25, and we dutifully fell in formation as we began the long climb over the great rock pile. In and out of cloud, we were out of sight of the ground, finally breaking out on top at about 23,000 feet. In clear view to the north were the great peaks of Everest and its even higher neighbors, and our engines labored in the thin air. Flying in cirrus cloud, a ball of St. Elmo's fire would form on the propeller tip, glowing with ethereal colors. Lazily, this glowing ball would drift around the propeller arc; gently right, left, then right again. This was my first experience with this phenomenon, and I was fascinated.

"Things didn't seem right, as we were headed farther north than we believed we should. The friendly navigator insisted that he—the B-25—was on course, and as our fuel went down and down we became more insistent that he was wrong. Finally, he said, 'We're off course and correcting to the south. Good luck, we'll see you in Kunming,' and broke away from our fearless leader. Clearing the high ranges, we began a gentle descent and throttled back to conserve fuel. Ahead in the distance was Lake Tali, a most welcome sight because our proper course lay along the southern boundary of this huge, high-altitude lake.

"We arrived in Kunming soon thereafter. About 45 minutes later our noble B-25 arrived also. Had we stayed with him we would never have made it; there would have been four silk letdowns and if one were fortunate, a long walk to Kunming. We all learned a valuable lesson, and I'm sure we all did our own navigation regardless of the circumstances or composition of the formation after that.

"The day after our arrival in China, we met briefly with General Chennault. He was comfortable to talk with, but you immediately recognized that this was a man fully in command in every respect. He spent some time outlining the situation in China and the part we were to play. His tactical doctrine had been nurtured over many years, and he made clear the response expected in a wide variety of anticipated combat situations. As I recall, he not only explained how the P-40s could best be employed against the Japanese fighters, but expressed a broader point of view. Pilots, airplanes, fuel and ammunition were exceptionally precious here at the end of a very long supply line. Conceptually, do all the damage to the enemy you can, but remember there is always another day if you stay alive and your airplane remains flyable. Dead heroes have very little capacity to do further damage to the enemy. Much different from most of the European scenarios, where the 'homeland' was involved. Then it was, 'Good luck, gentlemen, you are dismissed.'"[2]

★ ★ ★ ★

By the time Lieutenant Henderson joined the 16th, the squadron had moved from Chanyi back east to Kweilin. On March 31, most of the 16th's pilots plus a flight from the 76th Squadron flew to Kweilin, and the 75th went to nearby Lingling. These moves were made in preparation for resuming operations against the Japanese in the Hankow and Canton–Hong Kong areas. This time, the 76th Fighter Squadron stayed at Kunming to provide air defense and run raids into Burma and Indo-China, while the 74th was stationed at the western end of Chennault's line, Yunnanyi, to defend the Hump route and strike at the Japanese in Burma.

This spring, General Chennault planned to hit the Japanese all along the line—from Lashio to Hanoi to Hong Kong to Hankow, with some surprises in between. With promises of more units and more tonnage coming over the Hump, he felt confident that he could widen the air war in China at least until the monsoon season hit on the Burma front. This assault would make the Japanese commit more forces against him, forces that would be badly missed in the South Pacific as the Allies began their long island-hopping campaign that year.

For their part, the Japanese were not surprised by Chennault's aggressive moves. The previous December, the Imperial General Headquarters had laid out plans for future operations in China. Stretched for resources, it planned to lie low in China through the winter while concentrating on operations in the Pacific. A major offensive to crush the U.S. air forces in China would start after the spring of 1943. In the meantime, as soon as it was available, the Japanese would introduce their new fighter design in China, the army's high-performance Nakajima Ki-44, which the Allies code-named the Tojo. A second directive from Tokyo on February 17, 1943, echoed the earlier one, but it also announced that two fighter regiments and two heavy bomber regiments were being added in China and that air bases and navigational aids were to be improved.

It did not take the Japanese long to respond to their March 31 intelligence net reports of the U.S. buildup at Kweilin and Lingling.

The 33rd Air Regiment at Canton immediately sent six Ki-43 Oscars to Kweilin on a fighter sweep, hoping to draw the Americans into a fight. In poor weather conditions, the 16th Fighter Squadron scrambled three P-40s and two P-43s to intercept, but they were unable to make contact with the Oscars.

The Japanese sent out a stronger force from Canton on April 1. The flight consisted of four Ki-43 Oscars of the 25th Air Regiment plus six Ki-43s and two of the new Ki-44 Tojos from the 33rd. The pilots flew up to Hengyang and strafed the empty airfield there, then headed southwest toward Lingling. Chennault's warning net had done its job, however, and when the Japanese got to Lingling about 9:00 A.M., the 75th Fighter Squadron had fourteen P-40s already at altitude waiting for them. It was the first time anyone in the 75th could remember having the numerical advantage going into a scrap.

The first pilot to spot the incoming Japanese fighter formation was a remarkable young man from the Rogue River area of southern Oregon, Capt. John Hampshire. "Hamp," as his squadron-mates called him, had scored his first victories the previous October, and he was now the 75th's leading ace with five kills. Hampshire dived to the attack and picked off an enemy fighter at seven thousand feet with his first shot. The plane burst into flames and fell to earth.

The aggressive attack caught the Japanese by surprise, and they attempted to turn for home, but it was too late. The 75th was all over them by this time. A wild dogfight ensued. One pilot, Lt. Chuck Tucker, set an enemy plane on fire with his first burst and then fired an additional eight hundred rounds into it for target practice. Tucker did a rare victory roll over the field when he returned to Lingling.

The 75th's final score for the day was five confirmed destroyed. Other enemy fighters were thought to have been damaged, but due to the confusion during the air battle, the pilots chose only to claim the targets they felt were surely destroyed. The score was not one-sided, however. Captain Barnum, who had performed the miraculous one-man defense of Hengyang the previous September, collided with a Japanese fighter and crashed to his death. In all, the Japanese pilots claimed four victories for the mission but counted their losses at four as well. (The confirmation process was far from perfect on both sides, and overclaims were common in every theater throughout the war.)

Bad weather hindered flight operations throughout China for the next three weeks. On April 19, the 16th was able to fly one successful strike against Fort Bayard on China's coast nearly three hundred miles due south of Kweilin. Major Hal Pike led ten P-40s though stormy skies and caught the Japanese by surprise. The Sharks strafed an administration building, a radio station, and the residence of the local Japanese commander while encountering only light and ineffective ground fire.

The Japanese finally returned to Lingling on April 24, and this time they came in force with forty-four Oscars and Tojos. Again, the warning net tracked the enemy formation in; again, the 75th had fourteen Sharks airborne at Lingling; and again, the 75th claimed five destroyed, after a fight that lasted nearly an hour. Captain Hampshire's share was two destroyed, bringing his total to eight. The 75th did not have any losses.

One of Hamphire's victims was a twin-engine aircraft that had dropped leaflets over the field at Lingling. When the pilots landed they got quite a kick out of the reading leaflets, which stated:

> To Officers and men of the United States airforce [sic]:
>
> We express our respects to you men who have taken great pains to come to the interior of China.
>
> We of the Fighter Command of the Imperial Japanese Air Force take pride in the fact that we are the strongest and the best in the world.
>
> Consequently, we express our desire as sportsman [sic] to hold a decisive air battle with you in a fair and honorable manner.
>
> We then can best prove to you the spirit and ability of our air force.
>
> With hearty wishes for a decisive battle,
> The Fighter Command of the
> IMPERIAL JAPANESE AIRFORCES

At least one historian believes the leaflet was a hoax, but the fact remains that many of the men who were at Lingling on April 24 remembered the incident. The text of the leaflet is quoted verbatim in two diaries of the time as well.[3] Further, the express "desire" for a "decisive air battle" is consistent with the orders under which the Japanese 3rd Air Division was operating at the time. Claire Chennault, however, had different ideas about how to fight an air war, and his subordinates were perfectly happy to do it his way. No one in the Fourteenth Air Force took the leaflet seriously.

Also during the month of April, one of General Chennault's efforts to bolster the strength of his force paid off when sixteen Chinese Air Force pilots were assigned to the 23rd Fighter Group (four per squadron). Most of them spoke reasonably good English and had attended flight training at Luke Field, Arizona. One of these pilots, Lt. Fu Chung Ching of the 75th, crashed while testing a P-40 at Lingling on April 9 and was killed. The first CAF pilot to fly a combat mission with the 23rd was Lt. Chiu Hao of the 76th, who went with Lt. Harold Stuart on an uneventful recon flight from Kunming to Lashio on April 22. As these pilots gained experience, they also gained the confidence of the American pilots in their squadrons. Several of them, notably 2/Lts. Cheng Tun-Yung of the 74th and Chung Hung-Chiu of the 76th, would apply the combat lessons learned while flying with the 23rd to their later assignments in the Chinese-American Composite Wing (CACW).

★ ★ ★ ★

The 74th Fighter Squadron, under the command of Captain Lombard, was well settled in at Yunnanyi by late April 1943. The outfit had taken over base defense duties on March 12 and stationed one flight on the small field at Tsuyung, which was about half the distance east toward Kunming.

Lombard was well aware of the warning net's unreliability on this end of China. For the first few weeks, he used standing patrols over the bases to ensure that his Sharks would not be caught defenseless on the ground by a surprise Japanese attack. Lombard's squadron also was able to send out offensive recon missions over the Salween River valley in northern Burma nearly every day. These flights usually consisted of two to four Sharks that would patrol the Burma Road and shoot up any worthwhile targets. The 74th lost several P-40s and pilots during these missions. Captain Raymond W. Lucia was hit by ground fire and killed while strafing a motor pool near Mangshih on March 19. Then on March 29, a similar mission to Chefang cost the life of 1/Lt. Robert E. Atkinson.

April brought more bad weather, a few more offensive recon missions, and a string of false alarms on the warning net at Yunnanyi. On twelve occasions in the first twenty-five days of the month, Captain Lombard ordered Sharks into the air in response to enemy activity reported by the net. Each time, however, they returned to base without even seeing an enemy airplane, much less taking a shot at one of them. This was frustrating for the pilots and extremely taxing on Lombard's limited supply of gasoline. All that would change on April 26.

The day began as usual at Yunnanyi. Just before sunrise, the crew chiefs taxied their Sharks out of the dispersal areas and lined them up on the flight line, where they would be ready for a quick takeoff. After a coffee break, they went to work checking their planes to make sure everything was ready: gas tanks and ammunition trays full, radios functional, windshields clean. The morning sun warmed the air and dried the dew on the grass.

In the operations shack, Captain Lombard and his pilots waited. In mid-morning, one ball went up on the *jing bao* pole. What Lombard did not know was that the radio in one of the net stations had failed. When a large formation of Japanese bombers with heavy escort left their bases in Burma and flew over the net sector heading toward Yunnanyi, the observer had no way of relaying the warning. The Sharks of the 74th sat quietly along the flight line.

By 11:30 A.M., the pilots were getting hungry and bored. Lombard had decided not to send any Sharks up until the second ball went up, and the pilots saw no point in getting excited until he gave the order. From outside the shack came the hum of an engine. Someone suggested it must be the chow wagon bringing lunch, and Capt. Bill Crooks went to the door to take a look. "Chow truck, hell," Crooks yelled, "Those are Japs!" He raced from the shack toward nearby slit trenches, and the rest of the pilots followed in a tumble of arms and legs, running as fast as they could.[4]

First Lieutenant Bill Hawkins also ran for trenches. He recalled, "By that time we could see they were closing their bomb bay doors and were already heading out. That meant the bombs were coming our way. They started hitting pretty soon. Boy, if they didn't knock the tar out of our planes. Three hundred or so Chinese [who were working on the runways] were killed and many more injured.

"As soon as I saw the bombers overhead, I started running for my airplane. It was about the length of a football field away. Normally, we'd pile in a truck to go to the planes, but since the bombers were already there we just ran to try to get away. I got to the plane and jumped up into the cockpit, but then I saw it had been hit by bomb fragments and had holes in the cowling. I was reluctant to take off, because I probably would have lost my oil and been out of luck anyway.

"At that time the Japanese fighters came down and started strafing. I got under my airplane and could hear these bullets PAT-PAT-PAT through the wing. Then I got up and ran about twenty-five or thirty yards away from the plane to a slit trench. Some other men already were in it.

"At that time I was very good with a .45 pistol. Mine was an old Colt revolver—a six-shooter. When I left for overseas that was the only gun I could get, so I took it. The Japs were coming very low to the ground, not over one hundred feet above our airplanes, and I was off to one side. I'd get two shots at them as they were coming in and two more going away. I'm as certain as I can be that I shot one of those airplanes down. One was shot down, and as far as I know I was the only one who was shooting."[5]

The pilots were lucky. None of them was hurt during the attack. The same could not be said for the ground crews, who were on the far side of the field from the alert shack. Many of them were in two tents located next to the flight line when the bombers appeared overhead.

Earlier in the year, Sgt. Dick Lee had transferred from the 16th Fighter Squadron to the 74th with Capt. Dallas Clinger to be his crew chief. Lee gave the following account of the attack:

"I think there were three armament men and three mechanics. Our P-40s were all lined up there in two rows—twenty-four airplanes. We had these old GI tents. Somebody had put up a little wind vane with a propeller on it; made a lot of racket. Two guys were in there, playing chess or cribbage. One was a guy named Lynch. One tent over—you could drive a six-by [truck] between them—was the weapons tent. One of the guys in there was named Eskridge. Everybody else was up to early chow.

"I had stepped out of the tent. All of a sudden I heard this rumbling. My God, I looked up and there at about twenty thousand feet, sitting right off the end of our runway, were twenty-two Jap bombers. When I saw the bombers, they were already at bomb release point. All I did was yell. Then I looked around for a place to go. We didn't have any slit trenches there. The ground was as hard as concrete. The only thing I did was run up in front of our tent.

"I heard the bombs coming. I heard one bomb hit way down at the end of the field. It must have dropped off the hooks into the bomb bay, and when they opened the doors it dropped out. Too bad it didn't blow them up. I hit the deck. There were some empty gasoline drums lying right there. The bombs started coming. They worked their way up the field: CARUMPH, CARUMPH. They kept getting closer. I just knew if the next didn't get me, if it landed over my head, I've got it made. And sure enough, man: CAROOOM! It's over my head. . . .

"I got up after all the damned bombs had dropped, and . . .there was nothing but smoke and fire all over the place. Two or three P-40s were burning. And the tents were gone. I heard the Zeros coming down, diving on the field. I had to get out of there.

"The field was on fire. They had dropped white phosphorus, and the grass was burning. There was lots of smoke. The quickest exit was to get in the smoke and run off the edge of the field, which I did. I ran off the field and ran into a Chinese guard post on the corner, a regular dugout. Then here came these Japs down strafing our aircraft, and this Chinese guard was just sitting in there. He wouldn't shoot at the airplanes or anything.

"I knew there was a .50-caliber machine-gun pit seventy-five to a hundred yards down from there, a twin .50. I thought if I could just get down there I could at least get some of these guys. So between passes of these planes, I ran to this place where the Chinese had been digging earth out, making mud out of it to put on the extension of our runway. There was a series of notches where they'd been digging, about three and a half feet deep. Every time a plane would come by I'd duck down in there. I got about half way to this .50, and this Jap came over in his strafing run. They'd pull the damned throttle back and then squeeze the trigger. The planes were Hamps— square-wingtipped Zeros—and they were painted just like a Lucky Strike green cigarette package. This one guy came by and looked me right in the eye. Then he whipped that airplane up in a turn, and I knew what he had in his mind. I was duck soup. I got up and ran my ass back to that dugout, and I just made it.

"When everything was all said and done . . . I went back onto the field. Our Chinese interpreter was sitting there peeling skin off his arm. He'd been hit by that phosphorus. He rolled over and died. At this tent I had laid alongside of, on the uphill side three frag bombs had hit side by side. Two went off and one was a dud. The door to the tent exited to the right. These three armament men had come out of that tent, and they were all lying there, dead. I remember seeing Eskridge's sheepskin jacket. Whatever they packed those frag bombs with had gone through him like a shotgun. The back of his jacket was turned inside out in about twelve places. And the other guys were dead.

"By this time, the Japs were gone and people were coming down from the hostel to survey the damage. The doctor came down, and this kid, Lynch, was wearing these one-piece fatigues. The doc looked at him, and the whole front of his coveralls was bloody around the belly. But there was no hole in his coveralls. The doc opened his coveralls up, and there were his guts lying there. And lying right in there was the end of one of these frag bombs, a threaded end about two inches across. It had come through from his back and laid him open but didn't have enough force left to come through the front.

"The doc started to walk away. He said Lynch was dead. Old Lynch opened his eyes and said, 'Like hell I am.' So they picked him up and laid him on a six-by truck and hauled him up to the mess hall. Laid him on a table. He died there."[6]

In all, five enlisted men were killed: Staff Sgt. Allen C. Eskridge, Sgt. Raymond A. Lynch, Sgt. Forest R. Shoemaker, Pvt. Oscar J. Brown, and Pvt. Frederick D. Hall. Five others, including Sergeant Lee, were wounded, along with the squadron's mascot dog, George. In addition, five P-40s were destroyed and eighteen were damaged. The 74th's survivors immediately got busy trying to prepare for what might come next.

The first jobs were to put out the fires and evaluate the damage. Four P-40s were found to be in quickly repairable condition, and these were placed on alert status that afternoon. The gas truck had been damaged, so the men rolled fifty-five-gallon drums of fuel from the storage dump to the flight line, where hand pumps were used for refueling. Everyone pitched in, including the pilots and orderly room personnel. The sheet metal specialist was particularly busy as nearly all the Sharks had shrapnel holes and rips in them to be patched. By the end of the fourth day, seventeen P-40s were back on flight status.[7]

Word of the attack flashed quickly to Kunming. General Chennault was in the United States for a conference with President Franklin Roosevelt, so the message went to Brig. Gen. Edgar Glenn, acting commander. Glenn had only been in China about a month, so he leaned heavily on Col. Casey Vincent, who was serving as his chief of staff, for advice. Vincent recommended pulling the 16th and 75th squadrons back from the east to protect Yunnanyi and Kunming, and Glenn agreed. Vincent was convinced that the Japanese would attempt additional attacks in honor of the emperor's birthday, which was coming up on April 29. The 16th left Kweilin immediately and arrived in Yunnanyi at about 4:00 P.M. that same day.[8]

The move came as a surprise to Col. Bruce Holloway, commander of the 23rd Fighter Group. Holloway had been busy himself on April 26 but in a place far removed from Yunnanyi. His day started at Lingling, where he was directing the 23rd's East China operations, but he had spent most of it in the cockpit of a P-40 on a long-range recon mission.

Holloway's destination was Shinchiku Airdrome on the northeast coast of the island of Formosa (now Taiwan). Nearly six hundred miles from Lingling, the flight would require refueling stops coming and going. Shinchiku was a major Japanese base, a key stop on their air route between the home islands and the Philippines. It was an appealing target for the Fourteenth Air Force, and Holloway wanted to take a look at it in hopes of launching an attack.

Colonel Holloway borrowed the 150-gallon drop tank off a new P-40M that 1/Lt. James L. Lee of the 75th had recently ferried up from India, and he also borrowed a Mae West life vest that Lee had brought with him from Panama.[9] The colonel chose to stage through Kienow, a remote airstrip in a Chinese-controlled pocket of Fukien Province. Kienow was 360 miles east of Hengyang, too far away from the Hump route to keep it supplied for full operations and too close to the Japanese at Foochow to protect it. A few Chinese troops manned the base for emergency service, and the Japanese bombed them regularly. On the way back he would stop for gas at Kanchow, another remote base but considerably closer to Lingling.

According to Holloway, he "got up a 4 o'clock again. Started checking the weather, and by 7 o'clock it looked good enough to the east to try and get over there and do a little looking around. I went by myself because I didn't know the country. The weather was not too good, and I didn't want to risk losing more than one plane in the event I got lost or the weather socked in completely. I refueled at Hengyang and went on to Kienow. It was very hazy and heavy broken [cloud cover] to overcast [solid cloud cover] most of this stretch. I found Kienow without too much trouble, but they had only about 2,000 feet of field available. They were still filling recent bomb holes on one end. I got down OK and managed to get her stopped a few feet from the bomb holes. Nobody spoke English, and everybody was excited to see me. It took 30 minutes to get serviced—all they had was five-gallon cans and a funnel. They filled the cans from drums, and the whole process was pretty laborious. I decided not to try to use Kienow for my proposed offense tomorrow for the reasons of this poor servicing and the limited amount of field available.

"I took off from there for Formosa at 10 o'clock, went south for awhile to avoid Foochow, then headed across the channel. The weather over the channel was CAVU [clear air, visibility unlimited], so I climbed to 20,000 feet on the way across. When I got to the island, however, there was a solid overcast at about 1,500 feet, so I went on down and got underneath. I couldn't find Shinchiku right away, so I went up the coast to the estuary and turned in to Taihoku. Saw a big radio installation at the mouth of the estuary. I looked over the field and saw about 13 twin-engine bombers and one transport, a lot of new construction work and a lot of small boats in the harbor. I messed around there a little while longer, then headed down the railroad toward Shinchiku.

"Just before reaching Shinchiku I ran across a passenger train going north and was about to go down and shoot it up when I saw a formation of nine planes headed right for me. I dropped my belly tank, ducked in the overcast, and flew along for a minute or so before I ran out of clouds. Then I saw that these were bombers and they showed no sign of having seen me. By this time I had my neck on a swivel looking for pursuits, but never did see any—it was getting sort of lonesome. I took a quick look at Shinchiku Airdrome and started back across the channel, climbing slightly and wishing there were more clouds. I saw another formation of seven bombers going up the channel but didn't get up enough courage to tackle them by myself. What a hunting ground—I couldn't wait to get back the next day with enough to mow them all down.

"I had gotten back to about 4,000 feet and was about 20 miles out to sea when I spotted a single bomber headed for the mainland. He was at about 3,000 feet, so I pulled in behind him and opened up. He didn't shoot back. He caught fire immediately and started down. I didn't watch him crash but went on toward the mainland, expecting about 20 pursuits to jump me any minute. But apparently there weren't any. I didn't see any single-engine planes all day. I went on to Kanchow (385 miles) and the weather had improved. From there

I went to Hengyang, and heard that all of the 75th at Lingling and the 16th at Kweilin had been suddenly ordered to Kunming by the 14th AF. I went on to Lingling, picked up my bag, and on to Kweilin. There I found out what had happened [at Yunnanyi]. . . . It was too late for me to get to Kunming before dark, so I went to bed. Nothing bothered us during the night."[10]

Colonel Holloway's roundabout route had taken him nearly fourteen hundred miles, a long day's work in an airplane that cruised at less than three hundred miles per hour. He flew to Kunming the next day and went on to Yunnanyi the morning of April 28 to take charge of the cleanup and repair operations there. His plans for a raid against Formosa were put aside for the time being. Casey Vincent was right: The Japanese were coming back.

As a matter of fact, Japanese bombers from Burma were on their way to Kunming at about the same time Holloway was flying down to Yunnanyi on April 28. As a result, he missed the action that day. But the 75th Fighter Squadron, under the tenacious Lt. Col. Johnny Alison, got plenty.

The day started much as April 26 had, with a one-ball alert going up in the morning at Kunming. A small patrol from the 76th was launched, while the rest of the pilots waited for further word on the advancing Japanese force. Word came at 11:15 A.M., but it was bad news: A large Japanese force of twenty-one bombers and about the same number of fighters was just five minutes southwest of the field. It was the first time that Japanese bombers had attacked Kunming since December 20, 1941, when the AVG scored four kills in its first combat of the war. Pilots of the 75th and 76th squadrons raced to their planes and took off as fast as they could. Colonel Casey Vincent just barely got off the ground in his P-40 before bombs started hitting the field. He, like most of the 76th's pilots, climbed toward the attackers but was unable to close on them.

One member of the 76th did get to attack. First Lieutenant Byron H. Gilmore was on patrol at twenty-eight thousand feet when the Japanese aircraft came into view below him. He immediately dived into the middle of a bomber formation but got caught up in the turbulence caused by their propellers and lost control of his P-40. Gilmore's plane was flipped upside down, and the bombers scattered to avoid hitting him. By the time Gilmore regained control of his plane, the bombers were long gone, but he had done his job. The bombers in the flight he attacked dropped their loads wide of the target and did not damage the field at Kunming.[11]

Other bombers did aim with better accuracy. A string of bombs hit the north end of the field and walked its way down the runway. The last bombs wrecked the control tower, operations building, and an armament shack. In the tower, Staff Sgt. Bernard Melman was directing the scrambling P-40s. He had chosen to stay in the tower when the alert sounded to help get the planes launched. A bomb struck right next to the structure and shredded it, knocking out the radios, but fortunately Melman was not hit. The plucky sergeant then ran to the alternate control room to continue directing the Sharks. He later was awarded the Silver Star for bravery shown that day.[12]

Another lucky guy was enlisted man "Rascal" McCauley of the 75th. He had the misfortune of being in the latrine with his pants down at the time of the bombing. According to squadron lore, McCauley could not decide what to do, so he hesitated. The explosions came and went so fast that he never had to make the decision whether to dive into the pit beneath him. He hitched up his trousers and walked out without a scratch.[13]

Others were not so lucky. The bomb that hit the operations building killed several men, including the newly arrived operations officer of the Fourteenth Air Force, Col. Don Lyon, and Lt. George Robertson of the 11th Bomb Squadron, a former 23rd Fighter Group pilot. Others who died were Staff Sgt. Harold Harwell of the 74th, and Pvts. Donald Goldsmith, Robert Graham, and Charles Tompkins of the 75th. Eleven men were wounded, including the boss, Brig. Gen. Edgar Glenn, who was hit in the back by a piece of shrapnel. Another stick of bombs landed on a Chinese village near the field and killed several hundred people.

While all this was going on, Lieutenant Colonel Alison was leading his 75th Fighter Squadron at full throttle on a course that he hoped would allow him to catch up with the Japanese on their return flight to Burma. It was a long shot, but Alison's battle judgment again proved flawless. His nine Sharks attacked the Japanese about one hundred miles southwest of Kunming near the Mekong River.

One of the pilots flying with him was Capt. Hollis M. ("Blacky") Blackstone. He gave the following account:

"We were sitting around the alert shack when one of the Chinese soldiers came tearing by hollering, 'Jing Bao!' Well, we ran to where our P-40s were tied down, cranked up our engines, and by the time our crews had dropped the tie-downs we put on full throttle and took off straight across the field with bombs dropping around us. I cleared the fence at the end of the field, banked left, and saw one of the Mitchell bombers on his takeoff roll when a bomb made a crater right in front of them. The explosion that followed left damned little of that airplane.

"I swung around, and my buddy, Capt. John Hampshire, and I joined up. Shortly afterwards, Lt. Col. Johnny Alison, our c.o., spotted the Japs and gave us a heading. From that bearing I knew they were heading for Lashio, Burma. Hamp and I spotted two of our fighters milling around, and we waggled our wings for them to join up. I picked out Lt. Joe Griffin, and I believe Hamp got Lt. Mack Mitchell. After awhile we could see a black line across the horizon. This turned out to be 21 Jap bombers in perfect vee formation. A little later we saw, like a swarm of bees, three umbrellas of Jap fighters with one honcho way above—35 fighters in all.

"Johnny Alison made the first attack and downed one of them, if I recall it right. By that time the four of us had caught up. Then all hell broke loose. We had started out with an altitude advantage and tore into the melee, our .50 calibers open and pieces flying from one of the Zeros and smoke from the other. But right then we saw eight Zeros diving on us and had to take evasive action. We did that with a steep banking dive, pulling away from the bombers' line of flight and realizing the Zeros would only follow us so far and then get back to their protective escort of the bombers. We regained altitude and hit again.

"I can't recall how many firing passes I made, but I shot down at least one more Jap plane. During this time we were joined by two more of our fighters, Maj. Ed Goss with Lt. Roger Pryor on his wing. Joe and I spotted six or eight Zeros and dived on them, our .50s blazing. Immediately some of them started a steep climb while the others dived. The one I was chasing burst into flames. While watching him go down and looking for Joe, whom I had lost contact with, I saw some more Japs coming after me but finally managed to elude them.

"I got some altitude again. Ahead and below me I spotted a buddy I assumed to be Joe [it was] hot after a Jap with his guns blazing. Just then what he didn't see was two Japs coming after him. I dove after them, blasted one, then saw two rips appear across the top of my left wing and my aileron shatter. My control stick was vibrating badly, I was low on gas and about out of ammo. I figured it was time to get the hell out of there if I could. Well, I made it. And the beautiful and amazing part of it was that we didn't lose a plane in spite of the great odds against us."[14]

In the dogfight, the Shark pilots claimed eleven victories and eight probables. One kill was credited to 1/Lt. Charles DuBois of the 76th, his sixth, and the rest went to the 75th. Captain Blackstone was credited with two kills and a probable. Major Edmund R. Goss, who had transferred to the 75th in January after six months of combat in the 16th, scored one confirmed kill and a probable. The victory brought this Floridian's total to five, earning him ace status and a Distinguished Flying Cross. Lieutenant Colonel Alison got one fighter confirmed and one probable. Several of the P-40s were damaged, including Colonel Holloway's personal plane, which Alison was flying. But Blackstone was right; everyone got home safely.

High man again was Capt. John Hampshire, with two fighters and one bomber destroyed, plus two fighters and one bomber probably destroyed. This brought Hampshire's total to 11 confirmed kills, by far tops in the CBI theater at that time. The popular Oregonian's star was shining brightly, but in a few days it would flash—and then blink out.

It happened May 2. The 75th had moved back to Lingling on April 30 when Col. Casey Vincent, filling in for the wounded General Glenn, decided the crisis in the Kunming-Yunnanyi area was over. He was anxious to resume operations on the eastern front, and besides, they were almost out of gasoline at Kunming.

At 9:00 A.M. on May 2 the warning net reported thirty to forty enemy fighters in the Lingling area, and Lt. Col. John Alison scrambled sixteen Sharks to challenge them. Two Japanese fighters quickly went down in flames near the field, one of them credited to Captain Hampshire, and 1/Lt. Joe Griffin shot down another about thirty miles northwest of Hengyang as it was fleeing for home. Then came word that a formation of Japanese fighters was strafing the Chinese-held city of Changsha, just up the river above Hengyang. Lieutenant Colonel Alison led his P-40s in that direction.

In a sky full of clouds, Alison caught up with his prey. The P-40s dived under a thunderhead to attack seven enemy fighters, and a wild melee ensued. When it was all over, six more Japanese planes had been shot down, including another one for Alison, his fifth, and yet another for Captain Hampshire. Unfortunately, Hamp had gone down, too.

Badly wounded in the stomach, Hampshire landed his P-40 wheels-up in the Hsiang River just north of Changsha. A Chinese Army command post relayed word to Lingling. The 75th's flight surgeon, Capt. Ray Spritzler, told Lieutenant Colonel Alison that he wanted to fly up to Changsha and see if he could help his friend John Hampshire. Lieutenant Griffin, just back from the air battle, volunteered to fly Spritzler up to Changsha in the baggage compartment of a P-43. Spritzler planned to bail out of the baggage compartment and parachute into Changsha. Against his better judgment, Alison said OK.

Griffin and Spritzler had barely cleared the horizon at Lingling when the Chinese at Changsha sent another message: Hampshire had died of his wounds. Alison tried to raise Griffin on the radio to recall him but failed to reach him because of interference from the stormy weather. Meanwhile, the weather worsened and darkness fell. Griffin was unable to reach Changsha, but luck was with Spritzler and him. He found an unmanned airstrip near a Chinese village and put the P-43 down there. They returned to Lingling the next morning, much to the relief of their squadron-mates in the 75th and especially Lt. Col. Johnny Alison.[15]

Still, Capt. John Hampshire, the first great ace of the 23rd Fighter Group, was dead. It was a tremendous shock to the squadron. His record of thirteen confirmed victories would stand for nearly six months, through the most ferocious fighting yet in the skies over China.

9

Thrust and Parry

One by one, the new, heavily loaded U.S. bombers rumbled down the runway at Kunming, gathered speed, and lifted off into the sky. It was the morning of May 4, 1943, the beginning of another phase in the air war over China.

Previously, the only bombers available to the Fourteenth Air Force were in a single squadron of twin-engine B-25 Mitchells. Now it also had B-24D Liberators of the newly arrived 308th Bomb Group (Heavy). The Liberators were bigger, with four engines and a long, thin wing mounted high on a deep fuselage. Their advanced design also gave the Fourteenth Air Force a powerful offensive capability for the first time. Their bomb load was nearly double that of the B-25s, they carried nine heavy machine guns for defense, and they were capable of flying at high altitude.

The B-24's most important capability, however, was its range. Carrying a normal bomb load of five thousand pounds, a Liberator could fly 2,850 miles. With these planes, the Americans would be able to strike targets deep in Japanese-held territory and threaten enemy shipping in the South and East China seas. Attacking the Japanese home islands themselves was not out of the question.

As the sixteen B-24s climbed out of Kunming, they took their places in formation and headed south toward Indo-China. Soon they joined up with nine B-25s of the 11th Bomb Squadron and nineteen Shark escorts from the 76th Fighter Squadron led by Col. Bruce Holloway. They formed the largest force mounted by the Fourteenth Air Force to date. The big formation followed the Red River south from Lao Kay, just below the border, to Hanoi in nasty weather. At Hanoi the B-24s turned off to the southeast. Their target was Samah Bay, across the Gulf of Tonkin on the southern coast of Hainan Island. This port area was a key link in Japan's line of communica-

111

tion with its occupied territory in Southeast Asia. Until now, it was far enough from the Fourteenth's air bases in China to avoid attack but not any more.

The shorter-range B-25s and P-40s could not make it to Samah Bay, so they continued to the port of Haiphong, attacked through the clouds, and returned to Kunming uneventfully. The B-24s found Samah Bay and attacked the airfield, docks, and other facilities. They encountered only light antiaircraft fire, but one B-24 did go down near Lao Kay on the return flight.

All in all, it was a highly effective, if not terribly exciting, mission, with one exception. Captain Bill Miller, operations officer of the 76th Fighter Squadron, got off late from Kunming and could not catch up with the rest of the squadron. He did find the B-24s near Haiphong; however, the bombers' inexperienced gunners opened fire on Miller when they spotted him. He was expecting that reaction and did not approach within gun range. After a short time following the B-24s, Miller turned away and headed back toward China, following a railroad line. On the way he shot up two locomotives. One of them was pulling some cars, and the whole train wrecked when the locomotive blew up. Miller just barely dodged the flying pieces and returned safely to Kunming.

The May 4 mission was an auspicious debut for the 308th Bomb Group. The B-24 aircrews would go on to compile an outstanding combat record, though they never did realize the dream of attacking Japan itself. One of the group's problems was supply. The B-24 was a gas-guzzler, and the Hump transports could barely supply enough to keep the P-40s and B-25s in the air. So the 308th crews had to carry their own fuel over the Hump, using bomb bay tanks to turn their B-24s into tankers. Once they had stockpiled enough fuel in China, they would run a mission. Then they would have to go back across the Hump for more gas before they could strike again.

At this time, Kunming had enough gas to mount one more B-24 mission. The Fourteenth Air Force executive officer, Col. Casey Vincent, wasted no time in putting it together. The targets would be the White Cloud and Tien Ho airdromes at Canton. The B-24s would fly there directly from Kunming, while the B-25s of the 11th Bomb Squadron would stage through Kweilin. The twenty-four escort fighters would be drawn from the 75th Fighter Squadron at Lingling and the 16th Fighter Squadron, which returned to Kweilin from Yunnanyi on May 6.

The mission went off according to plan on May 8, with the formation joining up over Wuchow and approaching the target from the west. Lieutenant Colonel Alison led the 75th's Sharks, and Colonel Vincent was Alison's wingman in "Peggy II," his personal P-40K. Major Harry Pike, squadron commander, led the 16th. The attack caught the Japanese by surprise, as the bombers attacked the Japanese airfields without interference from enemy fighters. One B-25, piloted by Capt. Douglas Weaver, blew up right over the city as its bomb bay doors were opening. Apparently a fragmentation cluster detonated prematurely, destroying the aircraft and killing the entire crew. The rest of the bombing run was extremely accurate, causing heavy damage to both targets.

Japanese fighters could be seen scrambling from the airfields during the attack, so the P-40s stayed around to hold them off while the bombers withdrew from the area. A wild twenty-minute air battle ensued, in which the Shark pilots claimed thirteen Oscars and Nates destroyed and five more probables. Top scorers were 1/Lts. Lauren Barnebey of the 16th and Robert L. Tempest of the 75th, with two each. Among the others scoring single kills were Colonel Vincent; Lieutenant Colonel Alison; 1/Lt. Melvin Kimball of the 16th, back from his short visit to the Burmese jungle; and 1/Lt. James W. Little, who scored his fifth victory and joined the 75th's growing list of aces. The only Shark pilot who did not come home was Lt. Joe Griffin of the 75th. He had to belly-land near Kweilin when he ran out of gas, and then he walked home from there.

On May 11, Col. Bruce Holloway, commander of the 23rd Fighter Group, got a request from his boss, Col. Casey Vincent, to rotate his squadrons. Morale was sagging in the 74th and 76th because of the lack of action, and Vincent thought moving them up to East China for a while would do them good.

The 74th's fighters flew out of Yunnanyi on May 13, stopping at Chanyi for a few days while the ground crews proceeded to Kweilin and prepared the base for them. The 16th Fighter Squadron departed Kweilin on May 12, leaving a P-40 and a P-43 behind for repairs. By May 14, Major Pike's squadron was ready for operations at Yunnanyi. The monsoon season soon took hold in southwest China, however, and the 16th had a fairly quiet summer ahead of mostly weather recons and occasional offensive sweeps into Burma.

The 76th Squadron moved out of Kunming on May 11, leaving a small detachment behind under the command of Capt. Lee P. Manbeck. The 76th was going to Lingling and trading places with the 75th. Major Grant Mahony, the 76th's CO, was particularly pleased about the move. At the time Mahony had four confirmed victories to his credit, and he knew that he soon would be sent back to the States. He wanted to score a fifth before he completed his tour, and moving up to Lingling appeared to increase his chances of doing so. The 76th found Lingling a pleasant base, with a hostel that seemed like a country club and had excellent food. Under the command of Maj. Edmund R. Goss after Lieutenant Colonel Alison was assigned to group headquarters, the 75th was less pleased about the trade. The men felt they had been pulled out of the fight just when it was getting good.

As it turned out, Major Mahony got his fifth victory on May 23 during a fighter sweep to Ichang in which he also destroyed two enemy fighters on the ground. By then he and the rest of the 76th's pilots knew that by moving out of Kunming they had missed the biggest air battle yet to take place over China. Action just seemed to follow the 75th that spring, no matter where the squadron went.

Perhaps in response to the B-24s' damaging missions against Hainan Island and Canton, the Japanese ordered a strong force up from Burma to attack Kunming on May 15. The crack 64th Air Regiment sent twenty-three of its Ki-43 Oscars up from the old AVG base at Toungoo, Burma, to provide direct escort for thirty Ki-48 Lily bombers.[1] They approached the target in mid-morning.

Colonel Vincent had received a direct order from his boss, Brigadier General Glenn, to stay on the ground, so Vincent could only stand by and watch as Col. Bruce Holloway led a patrol of P-40s off at 9:10 A.M. to look for the approaching Japanese. Holloway, leading Maj. Roland Wilcox and 1/Lt. Charles Crysler, climbed rapidly to the southeast. They were at twenty-three thousand feet and about sixty miles from the base when he saw the approaching formation headed straight for Kunming.

Later Holloway wrote, "I have never seen so many airplanes in my life. . . . They were high. The bombers at 26,000 in perfect formation and the Zeros from 27,000 to 30,000 milling around like mosquitoes. I started yelling in the dope and telling Goss to get as high as he could with everything he had. This was the force that the Japs had mustered for their threatened annihilation of the 14th Air Force.

"We pulled in behind them and started climbing. We gained on them slowly. By the time we got to the field we had 28,000 feet, and I decided enough margin to safely attack. About this time they dropped their bombs. They all apparently dropped on their leader, because there were an awful lot of bombs in a very concentrated pattern. They missed the field almost entirely—this made us feel mighty good when we saw where they hit. A small Chinese village was absolutely demolished, though. A few bombs did hit on the end of the field, however, and one of them set a B-24 on fire; another blew a lot of holes in a B-25, but it can be repaired. Two P-40s of the 75th dived head-on into the bombers just before they dropped their bombs—I think this rattled the lead bombardier and spoiled his aim.

"About the time the bombs dropped, we went in for our first attack. Two flights of the 75th were in position and did likewise. Two other flights of the 75th were climbing and at this time were only at about 10,000 feet; they never did get in the fight and I haven't been able to fathom where the tie-up was. Anyhow, we barged in. Wilcox got a Zero immediately, and so did Crysler. They both went straight down into the lake. I picked out a Zero but don't know whether I got him or not—think I did. Our surprise was gone, so we pulled out, climbed back up to 27,000 feet.

"The enemies made a low turn to the left, and we went in again. By this time we had about 15 P-40s in the fight and it was getting mixed up pretty good. The bombers were keeping perfect formation, but pretty soon there were a couple of stragglers (probably crippled). It didn't take us long to get these. Somebody polished off one of them, and I moved in behind the other and blew him all to hell. He caught fire, spun to the right about three turns, and exploded. This was at about 25,000 feet.

"We kept working on the Zeros, which were pretty well broken up and headed for home in a scattered, demoralized fashion. I saw somebody chasing one, so I joined him. We chased him lower and lower, coordinating our attacks until he was finally flying right on the ground. He successfully dodged us about six times, but finally we got him cornered in the end of a valley. Lieutenant Little closed in on him from the left, and I came in almost directly behind. He pulled sharply right, and I got him with a full 90-degree deflection shot. He pulled up, flipped over, and went straight into the ground—made a pretty fire.

"By this time I didn't see any more Japs, but the net was telling about a second wave coming in. I climbed back to 25,000 feet over the field and ordered Lombard [74th Squadron commander], who was standing by at Chanyi waiting to go east, to send three of his flights down immediately. Little left me because his guns were not working, so I was lonely again. I stayed over the field with headquarters and a few of the 75th until the red flights [the 74th's Squadron color was red] arrived from Chanyi, then I ordered all whites [75th's color] to Yangkai for a drink. [Yangkai was an auxiliary field, where the P-40s could refuel.] We went up there, and there was quite a traffic jam. Major O'Brien, c.o. of the B-24 squadron there, gave us marvelous service. We stayed about an hour. I listened to the situation over their tower radio, and it sounded like things were dying out. Kunming was pronounced clear, so we went back and landed about 12:30. No more waves came in.

"No Americans were hurt in the bombing. The count for today was 15 confirmed and eight probables. One P-40 got shot up a little, but everybody got back OK—so the score was nothing to fifteen in our favor, probably more."[2]

In fact, the score was a little higher. Captain Dallas Clinger of the 74th was able to make contact at the end of the fight, scoring one Oscar confirmed and another probable before returning to Chanyi. Clinger's victory was the first scored by the 74th for the year 1943 and was his personal fifth, adding his name to the 23rd's roster of aces.

The battle of May 15, 1943, marked the end of the Japanese spring air assault on the Fourteenth's bases in Yunnan Province. Enemy bombers would not return until September, and when they did, the 75th would be waiting to pounce on them again.

★ ★ ★ ★

On May 5, 1943, Japanese ground forces had moved out of Hankow to open the ground offensive that Tokyo had been planning since the previous December. They proceeded in a two-pronged attack: one force headed west up the Yangtze River in hopes of capturing the Chinese capital at Chungking while the other force moved south down the Hsiang River from Tungting Lake, planning to capture the U.S. air bases that had been causing so much trouble for the past year.

Some now doubt how serious the Japanese were about achieving these objectives, but the operation nevertheless forced Chinese ground troops into action by mid-May, and the 23rd Fighter Group was called on to give them support. The bulk of this work fell, naturally enough, to the 74th and 76th squadrons in the east. A new command was formed, the East China Task Force, with Col. Casey Vincent in command. On May 28, he moved from Kunming to Kweilin to set the force. Before long, the 23rd Fighter Group headquarters would move to Kweilin as well.

The 74th Fighter Squadron flew out of Chanyi at 9:00 A.M. on May 19 and landed at Kweilin at 10:30 A.M. The pilots spent the day settling in. The following morning, Capt. Dallas Clinger and 1/Lt. Paul Bell flew a recon mission to Tungting Lake, the big body of open water between Changsha and Hankow that the Japanese were using as a supply route for their advancing ground forces. From then on, weather permitting, the 74th would fly a mission at least once every day.

On May 23, Capt. John Lombard led two flights of his 74th Squadron up to Hengyang and operated from that advance base. It was coming under pressure as the Japanese pushed closer to Changsha. A typical day there was May 28, when the aggressive Lombard led two dive-bombing missions against the railroad yards at Yochow, a major supply center near Hankow. On this first mission, the P-40s encountered light flak as they plastered a warehouse and railroad sidings with their bombs. When they returned in the afternoon, 1/Lt. Teddy Shapou scored a direct hit on a turntable at the roundhouse that had a locomotive sitting on it.

Then on May 30, twelve Sharks of the 74th flew an offensive recon mission along the tracks between Yochow and Hankow, and along the Yangtze River from Yochow to Shashi, north of Tungting Lake. Lieutenant Paul Bell spotted a Japanese plane on a small field at Shashi and destroyed it. Then the Sharks found a large river freighter and a launch and strafed them thoroughly. Three locomotives exploded under fire from the P-40s as well, and finally the Sharks sunk a large river steamer at Yochow. A mission to the same area the next day started a fire in warehouses next to the railroad that was visible for ten miles. On that same flight, the pilots noted that the destroyed locomotives from the previous day had not been moved. And so it went for the 74th throughout the summer.

The 76th had similar experiences while flying out of Lingling and Hengyang; however, bad luck and bad weather combined to give Major Mahony's squadron more trouble. On May 31, twelve Sharks got caught in bad weather while on a mission to Ichang, a city almost due north of Lingling on the Yangtze River. This area was at the point of the Japanese advance in the north. The assault flight destroyed three trains and several trucks and started oil fires in several places. When the weather soured, Capt. Bill Miller made a forced landing at Changsha, while Lt. Tom Clark ran out of gas and had to land his P-40 on the small airstrip at Enshih, about one hundred miles west of Ichang. Both pilots returned to their base when the weather improved.

The formation's top cover, meanwhile, got completely lost. All five pilots force-landed their planes close to each other near Itu, which was downriver from Ichang in a Japanese-held area. Chinese guerrillas reached the pilots—Capts. Robert Mayer and Jewell Mathews and Lts. Lawrence Durrell, George Dorman, and Sam Berman—before the Japanese did and spirited them out of the area. The Japanese chased them for thirty-six hours, and the Chinese had to stop twice to fight delaying actions while the pilots ran ahead. They finally arrived at Hengyang on June 15, all sporting Chinese fatigues and shaved heads.

Lieutenant Tom Clark of the 76th had an even more harrowing experience on a mission June 6. Major Mahony led six Sharks from Hengyang north to attack the Japanese airfield at Kingmen, slightly east of Ichang. The ground fire was very heavy over the target, and two Sharks were hit. Lieutenant Vernon Kramer was able to nurse his plane back toward Chihkiang and belly-land in a rice paddy not far from the airfield. Lieutenant Clark's plane suffered a direct hit right over the target. The other pilots on the mission thought Clark had been killed because his plane crashed so quickly, but he actually was able to bail out and land without injury.

Once on the ground, Lieutenant Clark got away from the Kingmen Airdrome and started walking south. In the next four days he covered seventy-five miles, moving at night and hiding during daylight, without any food. On the fourth day, he reached the mighty Yangtze River. Despite being dead tired and weak with hunger,

Clark decided to swim the river. He waited until nightfall and started swimming. An hour and a half later he reached the southern bank, completely exhausted. By that time, all his clothes were gone except his undershorts. He lay down in a mud hole and went to sleep.

Many men might never have awakened in similar circumstances, but Tom Clark did. Covered with black mud, he started walking again. It was his fifth day without eating. At one point, he spotted a lone Japanese soldier ahead, sitting along the side of a road. Clark stooped over, took on the shuffling gait of a coolie, and walked right past the soldier. The Japanese never gave him a second glance.

Not long after this encounter some Chinese guerrillas contacted Clark, fed him, and escorted him to Enshih. He arrived on June 20 and put a call through to the 76th. First Lieutenant John Stewart flew a P-43 up from Hengyang to bring Clark back to the squadron.[3]

A big change had taken place in the 76th while Clark was gone. Major Mahony had received long-awaited orders to the States and left on June 9. He was overdue for a rest, having spent nineteen months in the combat zone while flying in the Philippines, Java, and China. The 76th's new CO was Capt. Robert Costello, who previously had commanded the squadron's detachment at Hengyang. The Californian was already known as an excellent pilot, and he quickly proved adept at the administrative side of running the squadron as well.

By this time, the Japanese advance was all but over. The northern force got as far west as the Yangtze River gorges, but the combination of this natural barrier, a stiffening Chinese ground defense, and some effective attacks by the B-24s stationed farther west at Chengtu stopped the drive. The Japanese also withdrew from the approaches to Changsha after confiscating the region's rice crop. The withdrawal was fortunate for the 23rd Fighter Group, because the deteriorating weather in eastern China made continuing operations difficult.

Still, on June 10, the Japanese 3rd Air Division took another crack at the U.S. base at Hengyang. Sixteen Ki-48 Lily bombers of the 90th Air Regiment, escorted by eight Ki-43 Oscars of the 25th Air Regiment and nineteen more from the 33rd, carried out the attack from Hankow. Waiting for them were ten Sharks of the 74th Fighter Squadron.

The 74th made its attack right over the airfield and completely broke up the Japanese formation. Captain William R. Crooks scored the only confirmed victory, but there were four probables as well. Then while the Sharks were landing, a second wave of attackers was reported coming in. First Lieutenant Harlyn Vidovich climbed out of the landing pattern with the rest of the Sharks and was back at altitude in time to engage a flight of Oscars when they arrived. A full-blooded American Indian of the Paiute-Shoshone tribe, Vidovich had flown his first mission with the squadron on May 8. Today he shot up one Oscar but was unable to confirm that it was destroyed, thus earning credit for a probable. The Japanese pilots claimed five P-40s destroyed, but in fact none were lost.[4] In the eleven months since the 74th Fighter Squadron was activated, the June 10 action at Hengyang was its first full-scale air battle. Many more would follow and soon.

The warning net came alive again on June 14 at Hengyang. Japanese bombers were attacking the advance airfields at Suichuan and Kanchow. These fields, in a pocket of Chinese-held territory between Canton and Hankow, were rarely used now, but later they would take on a greater role in the 23rd's operations. For the moment, they offered Maj. John Lombard an opportunity to take on the Japanese once more. He led seven Sharks of the 74th off at noon in pursuit of the Japanese; but instead of heading southeast to the bombers' reported location, he flew due east toward Nanchang where the Japanese had a bomber base.

Lombard's gamble, helped by regular reports from the warning net, was a good one. The homeward-bound enemy formation came into view at 12:55 P.M., when the P-40s were about thirty miles from Nanchang. The Japanese bomber formation included fighters as well, but the odds did not slow Lombard down. He led his P-40s straight into the attack. They had a field day, shooting down seven Oscars, and just two Sharks were slightly damaged. Major Lombard scored one victory, his seventh and last. Captain Teddy Shapou and 1/Lt. Davis G. Anderson got two apiece.

Nobody thought of the 74th as the School Squadron any more. They were equal partners in the 23rd Fighter Group's air war against the Japanese. But the heavy fighting took a toll on the pilots, as Bill Hawkins described below:

"North of Hengyang is Tungting Lake. It's a low, swampy place, a big rice-growing area. That spring the Japs made a big push in there, and our job was to go up and strafe. They had gunboats on the rivers for protection. Lots of the area was flooded, with just the roads between the rice paddies above water to travel on. The Japanese troops would see us approaching, and every one of them would put his rifle up and starting shooting at us.

"During one of those strafing attacks, I got hit just forward of the fire wall. A solid round went right through the airplane, bottom to top. Fortunately it didn't hit anything vital, and it didn't explode. But it sure scared the hell out of me.

"The forty millimeters they were using on the gunboats you could hear exploding above our engine noise, and you could feel the shrapnel hit the plane. It seemed like every mission we'd lose some guys.

Let me tell you: That's when your sporting blood turns to horse piss in a hurry.

"During the three- to four-week period, there were three thousand to four thousand Jap troops killed. But we sure paid for it.

"Some books give the idea that you [a combat unit] are keeping track of the scores like a football game. That's not the way it was. I don't say the guys were cowards, but everyone was fearful. We showed it one way or another. A guy would have to be a flaming idiot not to count the guys who got shot down. It happened.

"At Kweilin when we were flying every day, I knew I had to come to some kind of peace with myself. I couldn't keep going around in a sweat. Finally I decided that I was going to make them die for their country; I wasn't going to die for mine.

"After making that psychological change, things went better for me. I shot down some planes, sank some ships. In this game of air combat, about 90 percent of it is to stay calm, cool, and collected. It's so easy to say and so difficult to do. It's the difference between a veteran and a novice—when you can divide your attention and still function. It's just something you can do after a while."[5]

As the end of June 1943 approached, the weather grew steadily worse. In Yunnan Province, the 16th and 75th squadrons grew restless from the lack of action. At Yunnanyi, Major Pike scrambled all twenty operational P-40s in the 16th Squadron on June 22 for a practice mission just to keep the pilots occupied. The 75th sent a detachment to Kweilin late in the month to bolster the airfield's dwindling force of Sharks. Only one fight took place over Kweilin, on June 25, for Kweilin's weather was just as bad as it was farther west.

On June 30, Maj. John Lombard of the 74th set out from Hengyang on a weather recon to the north. Colonel Vincent hoped to run a bombing mission to Ichang and Tungting Lake later in the day, and he needed accurate data on the weather conditions. Lombard took off at first light, but he never came back. Caught in worsening sky conditions, he apparently tried to squeeze through under the clouds near Yiyang, but he crashed into a mountainside and died. When the Chinese recovered his body from the wreckage, they also found the .45-caliber automatic pistol he wore on combat missions. Lombard had hit the ground so hard that the barrel of the gun was bent almost in two. It was a sad end for this gallant and well-respected ace, a veteran of seventy-five missions during nearly a full year in combat.[6]

There was little opportunity to celebrate the 23rd Fighter Group's first birthday and America's Independence Day when they arrived July 4. It rained so hard at Kweilin that the hostel nearly flooded—hardly a day for picnics, softball, or flying P-40s. Still, the men of the

23rd could feel proud of their unit's accomplishments. To date, their score in aerial combat was 171 confirmed victories, 70 probables, and 24 damaged.

In addition, the recent Japanese offensive had honed the 23rd's skills in ground attack, making the group a true fighter-bomber outfit long before such a role found official sanction among the military planners in Washington, D.C. The 23rd was gaining legendary status approaching that of its predecessor, the AVG. As soon as the weather would permit, the men of the 23rd Fighter Group would begin to enhance the legend.

10

Buildup

When General Chennault returned to China from his trip to the Trident Conference in June 1943, he visited his forward bases to check on conditions and confer with his commanders. He brought good news from Washington: A further buildup of the Fourteenth Air Force was in the works.

The general was convinced that the recently ended Japanese advance proved his theory that the Chinese Army could hold its territory against the Japanese if given sufficient U.S. air support. That was the prevailing view in Washington as well, and new air units were being committed to China as soon as the supply lines could support them. Work began on new airfields at Kweilin, and improvements were scheduled for the facilities at Lingling, Hengyang, and elsewhere as well.

With the 308th Bomb Group's B-24s in place at Kunming and Chengtu, and with the 11th Bomb Squadron at full strength, General Chennault was ready to increase the pressure on the Japanese. He planned on using his bomber force to attack enemy lines of communication and supply throughout the region—from the Yangtze River at Hankow to the West River at Canton and especially in the open waters of the South China Sea.

The general's first step was to move the 11th Bomb Squadron from Kunming to Kweilin, thus freeing up space at Kunming for new units that would be arriving soon and putting the 11th's B-25s closer to the eastern front. The flight crews were familiar with Kweilin, having been deployed to the base numerous times in the past year. Now the entire squadron, including administrative and maintenance sections, would call Hostel 1 at Kweilin home. The men completed the move by mid-July.

Under Chennault's new scheme, the 23rd Fighter Group would continue to play a key role. One word described the unit—*versatile*. The pilots of the 23rd used their P-40s to perform virtually every duty required of warplanes: running reconnaissance missions, dive-bombing, skip bombing, strafing, escorting bombers, and always intercepting enemy raiders announced by the *jing bao* pole. They even delivered the mail in their rugged Sharks.

Two changes in squadron commands occurred in early July. On the second, Maj. Hal Pike transferred from the 16th Fighter Squadron to 23rd Fighter Group headquarters, where he took on the duties of executive officer. Command of the 16th went to Capt. Bob Liles. At this time, however, Liles had a full year of combat behind him, including three confirmed victories, and other pilots who had arrived in China with him were getting orders home. Chennault needed solid leaders to run each of his squadrons, and he asked Liles to extend his overseas tour. As it turned out, Liles stayed in China for another year. His stint as CO of the 16th was longer than that of any other fighter squadron commander in China throughout the war. For the time being, the Burma front continued to be quiet for the 16th Fighter Squadron. Liles kept his pilots busy running recon missions in the Lashio area and practicing skip bombing.

The 74th Fighter Squadron got a new commanding officer on July 7. John Lombard was replaced by Maj. Norval C. Bonawitz. The rugged outdoorsman from Missoula, Montana, had been serving in group headquarters and flying missions since March. On July 11, Major Bonawitz flew his first mission with his new squadron, a weather recon to Canton.

Bad weather continued to hamper operations in eastern China through most of July, but it cleared enough for an escort mission to Canton on the seventh. Colonel Casey Vincent netted two victories when eight Oscars came up to intercept the formation. The B-25s claimed near-misses on three vessels moored at Whampoa Dock, but the results of the bombing were not observed.

On July 20, Col. Bruce Holloway led a flight of six Sharks from the 76th Fighter Squadron out of Hengyang and flew a sweep of the Yangtze River from Yoyang to Hankow. According to Holloway, "We left about 1100. We went up the Hsiang [River] under the overcast, and after passing Changsha the weather began to clear up. We sashayed around Yoyang to miss the AA [antiaircraft artillery], then started down the river. I stayed top cover with my element to direct the attacks, and [1/Lt. James M. ("Willie")] Williams and [1/Lt. John S.] Stewart proceeded to work on the boats with their elements. The first one we found was docked at Sinti. It was a big barge with a 60-foot tug tied to it. They really worked it over, making about four passes apiece, and the timing was beautiful. The barge was loaded with drums, but they must have been empty as they didn't burn. They ruptured the boiler and tore the guts out of the tug.

"We then went on down the river and found a big steamer on a feeder stream about 35 miles downstream from Sinti. They worked on it in similar fashion, exploded the boiler and set it on fire. I watched all this from about 3,000 feet and it sure looked pretty—especially the incendiary bullets hitting the decks. We cruised on down toward Hankow and found another steamer at the big bend in the river about 30 miles south of Hankow. It was going full steam upstream and putting out lots of smoke. They really gave it the works and must have killed the pilot immediately, because it headed for the south shore, ran full speed into the bank at about a 30-degree angle, capsized and started burning.

"These boys were then out of ammunition, so we swung over to the railroad and started locomotive hunting. Williams and Stewart stayed up for me, while I went after the locomotives with my element. We got the first one at Puchi. It was in the yard and flanked with steel cars, a little hard to get. I made two longitudinal runs without much success and on the third pass came in from a 60-degree frontal run. This gave me a small clearing between the cars and the locomotive. It worked, and the boiler let go with a beautiful display. We went on down the track and found another locomotive about 30 miles from the first. I made one pass directly from broadside as there were no obstructions, and got the boiler. They really blew up. I also got a water tank on the same pass—it was right behind the locomotive (about 30,000 gallons).

"Slightly down the track there was another water tank (camouflaged) so I made a sieve out of it. We kept going down the track and almost ran into Yoyang. They opened up on us with all their anti-aircraft; their altitude was OK but their range was short. We turned off, ducked down a little, and headed for home. I called the Japs at Yoyang, who were probably monitoring our radio frequency, and told them their range was short—hope they heard me."[1]

★ ★ ★ ★

On an otherwise unremarkable day in July 1943, five twin-engine aircraft appeared over Kunming Airfield, having just flown across the Hump from India. They entered the landing pattern, broke away in smart fashion, and put down on the main runway. Their sleek, twin-boom design made them immediately recognizable as Lockheed Lightnings, but these were not more of the F-4 photo recon versions that had been flying in China since the previous autumn. These were brand-new P-38Gs, considered at that time to be the best operational fighter aircraft in the U.S. arsenal.

The five fighters and their pilots were the advance element of a full squadron of P-38s on its way to China. The pilots all had previous combat experience in the Mediterranean theater. Boasting long-range and high-altitude performance equal to the F-4s, their planes far exceeded the P-40's capabilities. In addition, the P-38Gs carried heavy armament, with four .50-caliber machine guns and one twenty-millimeter cannon grouped in the nose.

The P-38's only drawback, as General Chennault saw it, was that its twin engines used too much of his precious gasoline. The pilots of the 23rd Fighter Group did not worry so much about that, though. They just knew that the P-38 could outperform their old Sharks, and they were anxious to get their hands on one of the new planes. Few of them, however, got the opportunity. Within a few weeks, the full complement of P-38s would be operating out of Lingling with their own pilots as the 449th Fighter Squadron. It was the first additional fighter outfit assigned to China in more than a year, and it would be the only P-38 squadron ever sent there.

Captain Elmer Richardson of the 75th Fighter Squadron led the P-38s to Kweilin on July 23. Their arrival was fortuitous, because the East China Task Force had come under heavy attack that day at Lingling and Hengyang.

July 23 actually marked the opening shots in what the Japanese planned as their next major air offensive to annihilate the U.S. air forces in eastern China. But as in the past, their expectations far exceeded their ability to do the job. In fact, from July 23 through July 30, pilots of the 23rd Fighter Group were credited with no fewer than fifty-four confirmed victories, plus many more probables and damageds, while losing only three pilots and six planes of their own. Even considering the possibility of overclaiming by the American pilots, the victory ratio was in the range of nine to one. More important, the ability of the East China Task Force to wage war was undiminished by the Japanese offensive.

One of the pilots who remembered the July fighting well was 1/Lt. John S. Stewart of the 76th Fighter Squadron. At the time, he was assigned as a flight commander in the 76th's detachment at Hengyang. His good buddy, 1/Lt. Willie Williams, led the 76th's other flight at Hengyang, and the two pilots shared a room in the hostel near the field. These two pilots, who had flown with Colonel Holloway on the strafing mission of July 20, were anxious for action. Both had served in Panama prior to arriving in China the previous fall and had flown plenty of missions since, but neither had had an opportunity to shoot down any enemy airplanes. They were eager to change that.

About 5:45 A.M. on July 23, a Chinese attendant came into the hostel at Hengyang, woke Williams, and reported a one-ball alert. Williams woke up the pilots in his flight, and they drove the half-mile to the airfield in the unit's tired Ford station wagon (probably the same car Sgt. Dick Lee had hidden during the bombing raid of September 6, 1942). A little while later, Stewart was awakened by the sound of Williams's flight taking off. He got up, dressed hurriedly, and gathered his own pilots. Soon, the Ford returned to take them to their planes.

The Japanese took a roundabout route from Hankow, hoping to hit Lingling and Hengyang simultaneously. Stewart led his flight off from Hengyang and climbed to twenty-eight thousand feet, listening for sighting reports on his radio. He linked up with Williams's flight at altitude, but within moments, Stewart began seeing spots. His oxygen system had malfunctioned. While he still had his wits about him, Stewart descended to twenty thousand feet, and there, right in front of him, he found the Japanese bomber formation.

Stewart quickly lined up behind the nearest bomber and let go with a burst of fire. The bomber crumpled and nosed over in a death dive. Tracers arced toward Stewart from the other bombers, but he bored in on a second target and promptly shot it down, too. Then he attacked a third plane and hit it but had to break off when his own Shark shuddered under the impact of enemy gunfire. Knowing the P-40 was badly hit, Stewart headed back to Hengyang and prepared to land. It was then that he found out the landing gear would not come down. He elected to belly-land the plane and brought it in with minimal damage. He dived for a trench to take cover but found, to his disgust, that it doubled as a latrine, so he quickly took cover elsewhere. Later, mechanics counted 167 holes in his plane.

While Stewart had been shooting up the bombers, Williams's flight took on the escort fighters. Williams accounted for one confirmed and a probable, while 2/Lt. Richard J. ("Dick") Templeton shot down another.

Stewart had not been on the ground long at Hengyang when another wave of enemy bombers came in. They hit the field hard, gouging some big holes in the runway, but did not damage any airplanes or cause any casualties. When the field was clear, Stewart found one P-40 that was gassed up and ready to go. The radio reported yet another formation bearing down on Lingling, so Stewart fired up the P-40 and took off, heading into the fight. He arrived in time to link up with a flight out of Lingling led by Capt. Marvin Lubner. Together, they took on a formation of Ki-43 Oscars near the field. Three enemy planes went down in the fight. One each was credited to Lubner and Stewart and the last to 1/Lt. Morton

Sher, who poured an especially long burst into his victim and took some ribbing for it from his buddies later.

The 76th's main force at Lingling also had a successful engagement during the morning raid. Captain Lee P. Manbeck was credited with shooting down two fighters and a bomber, plus another probable bomber. One pilot, Lieutenant Johnson, received a slight head injury after getting shot up and crash-landing.

The 74th Fighter Squadron at Kweilin also got into the day's action. The 74th scrambled eighteen Sharks in the morning. They were flying at ten thousand feet when they reached Lingling and were jumped from above by the Japanese escort fighters. First Lieutenant Jess T. Garrett's plane was shot down, but he parachuted safely. The 74th was credited with three confirmed kills, two probables, and two damaged during two engagements. The victories went to Lts. Tom Bennett, Truman Jeffreys, and Cheng Tun-Yung, one of the Chinese exchange pilots.

Rounding out the action were three of the "wheels" of the East China Task Force. Colonel Vincent shot down a bomber for his fifth victory, and Lt. Col. Samuel ("Tex") Knowles, his executive officer, got another. Colonel Bruce Holloway also shot down a fighter for his ninth victory.

There was little time, however, to celebrate the day's successes. The pilots and ground crews were tired and expected action again the next day. The lights went out early in the hostels at Kweilin, Lingling, and Hengyang. And it is a good thing they did, because the warning net came alive first thing the next morning.

On July 24, the Japanese struck from the north and south. First to see action was the 76th Squadron at Lingling and Hengyang. The net picked up a large enemy formation coming south from Hankow at 9:30 A.M. and tracked it toward Lingling. Captain Bill Miller led a patrol of Sharks from Lingling and placed them in perfect position to attack when Japanese aircraft came into view about 10:15 A.M.

Miller was able to avoid the enemy escort fighters and make his first pass at the bomber formation from the rear. Three bombers went down immediately, with two credited to Miller and one to 1/Lt. Willie Williams. When the escorting Oscar fighters tried to intercede, the P-40 pilots turned on them. The remaining bombers dropped their loads harmlessly onto some nearby rice paddies and headed for home. First Lieutenant Bill Distefano shot down two Oscars, and 1/Lt. Bruce G. Boylan got another before the skies cleared of enemy aircraft. All of the 76th's pilots landed safely.

Also in that scrap were six Sharks from the 74th Squadron, which had been sent up from Kweilin with Major Bonawitz leading. Bonawitz received credit for two bombers destroyed, but his P-40 was shot up in the scrap and he landed wheels up at Lingling. In the rough landing, he banged his face against the gun sight in the cockpit and got a nasty gash across the top of his nose. Another member of the flight, 2/Lt. George R. Barnes (not the same George Barnes who flew with the 16th Fighter Squadron), was shot down and killed.

Meanwhile, the rest of the 74th Squadron fought a fierce engagement that morning with eight Oscars from Canton that flew up to scout Kweilin. Also taking part were the new P-38 pilots who had arrived at Kweilin the previous afternoon.

Bill Hawkins of the 74th recalled that day's events: "The P-38 pilots were new to our tactics. One of our pilots, Walter A. Smith, was assigned to lead them because he'd been a P-38 pilot.

"We'd been having *jing bao*s all day. Finally we had a big one, and we all went scrambling off. I was getting in my airplane and I looked up and here comes the group commander [Col. Bruce Holloway], a big old long-legged guy, running toward his P-40. It was the last one left on the field. So I took off and turned right around over the field to give him top cover taking off, because control said the Japs were right over us.

"The P-38s were already up, and Smitty made a turn to the south toward the direction the Japs were coming from. He got shot down right off the end of the runway. I saw his P-38 go in—SPLAT. I didn't see him bail out, but apparently he did. I swung around to give Colonel Holloway protection and then flew over to where the P-38 had gone down. There were two Japs right there, so I made a turn to swing in behind them.

"I was really close in behind this one Zero. I started shooting, and I was hitting him. I don't know what made me do it, but I looked up in my mirror and here's this other Zero behind me shooting, and he started hitting me in the tail.

"I popped the stick forward—I was only five hundred to six hundred feet above the ground—and then did some wild gyrations and rolled out. I just missed the ground by twenty or thirty feet. I was trying my best to get away, and I did it. But I'd taken off in such a hurry that I didn't have a map with me, so here I was—lost. I kept milling around until I finally found the field and landed. I got five or six hits in my tail on that one. And I got a confirmed kill on that Zero because he went down just a short distance away."[2]

Lieutenant Smith had indeed bailed out of his P-38 before it crashed, but he was badly burned on the face and hands, as well as suffering shrapnel wounds. He was rushed to the Kweilin hospital by the Chinese who found him. Another of the P-38 pilots, 1/Lt. Lewden Enslen, was credited with one fighter destroyed. Moreover, he was the first P-38 pilot to shoot down an enemy aircraft in the China-Burma-India theater.

Of the eight fighters attacking Kweilin, only one got away from the defending Sharks and Lightnings. One of the kills was credited to Colonel Holloway. This victory was Holloway's tenth, making him the 23rd's first active double ace since Captain Hampshire. Holloway recorded, "Our nine or ten P-40s had about six or seven thousand feet and were just about on an even keel with the Zeros, who were still hanging around and just flying individually. Things started popping pretty good then, and bullets were flying all over the place. I made a head-on run with one, but he ducked under pretty steep and I don't think I got him.

"A couple of Zeros then made runs at me but I ducked around a cloud, gave one the slip, and managed to get on the other one's tail. But just as I was about to line him up another P-40 cut in front of me, so I just sat there and watched. This P-40 only had one gun working, and he couldn't get the Zero—didn't hit him much for some reason, but we kept barreling along 1, 2, 3 in tandem with the Zero's engine smoking in traditional wide-open fashion. The other P-40 [Lt. Robert M. Cage] finally pulled out, the Zero pulled up steeply to the left, and I set him afire with a short burst at the left wing root. The pilot bailed out and his parachute and clothing burned all the way to the ground. The Chinese picked him up, I found out, but he died shortly afterwards."[3]

The Japanese did not return in the afternoon, and that gave the ground crews of the 74th and 76th time to service and repair the Sharks for whatever the next day would bring. As it turned out, the Japanese played it safe with their Hankow bomber force on July 25. They did attack at mid-morning, but their targets were the undefended outlying bases at Chihkiang and Shaoyang. The 23rd's Sharks did not attempt to intercept them. Instead, after the bombers turned for home, a formation of B-25s took off from Hengyang with an escort of nine Sharks and headed for the enemy airfield at Hankow. The Sharks did not encounter any antiaircraft fire or any intercepting fighters; their mission went smoothly. The bombers reportedly blew up several buildings and aircraft on the enemy field.

Colonel Holloway figured out when the B-25 mission would be returning to Hengyang and sent flights of Sharks from Kweilin and Lingling to cover the field in case Japanese fighters tried to catch the bombers in their landing pattern. It was a wise move, because fifteen Oscars showed up as well. Again, the P-40 pilots got the upper hand. Four Japanese fighters fell, credited to pilots of the 75th Squadron who had just been sent east from Kunming that morning. The B-25s diverted to their permanent base at Kweilin, refueled, rearmed, and then flew back to Hengyang in preparation for the next day's operations. In a hairy operation at dusk, the bomber pilots landed after dodging the multiple hazards of thick dust clouds, bomb holes, and two wrecked P-40s around the runway.

Everyone was ready for a strike on Hankow first thing the next morning, Sunday, July 26. Five B-25s departed Hengyang at 5:00 A.M., along with their escorts led by Capt. Elmer Richardson of the 75th Squadron. Again, the bombers arrived over the target unmolested and encountered little or no antiaircraft fire as they dropped their bombs. The airfield was well covered, with several parked airplanes destroyed.

The mission got rougher after that, as about fifty enemy fighters rose to intercept the Americans. One batch of Oscars dived out of the sun and eluded the Sharks momentarily to attack the B-25s. Not one of the bombers was shot down, but several sustained damage. Richardson and his P-40s pounced on the enemy fighters as they were recovering from their attack on the B-25s. He shot down two of them, and three other pilots got one apiece. On the other side of the ledger, Lt. Lee Hung-Lin, one of the Chinese exchange pilots, was last seen diving out of the fight with two Oscars on his tail. Reportedly, he later force-landed safely in Chinese-held territory. As the B-25s ran for home, the fight went on for 115 miles before the Japanese fighters broke off the engagement. The U.S. force put down at Hengyang just before 8:00 A.M.

A second B-25 mission planned for the afternoon was canceled because the force at Hengyang had just three bombers in commission. These planes were sent to the relative safety of Kweilin so they would be available for a planned raid against Hong Kong the next day. Also participating in this mission would be six P-40s of the 16th Squadron that had been sent from Yunnanyi to beef up the eastern forces. By this time, the Japanese aerial offensive was obviously losing steam, but the 23rd also had lost some planes and pilots. Fortunately, the Burma front was still quiet, so General Chennault felt he could thin his fighter force at Yunnanyi safely to continue operating at full strength in the east.

The mission to Hong Kong on July 27 was uneventful. Unfortunately, the B-25s missed their primary target, a big transport ship that was anchored off Stonecutter's Island. A small scrap later in the day near Canton resulted in a claim for one probable against the loss of one P-40 flown by Lt. Bob Wilson of the 16th, who walked home two days later. Lieutenant Colonel Hal Pike led the escorts the following day, July 28, on another bombing mission against Hong Kong. Again they encountered no opposition over the busy harbor. The warning net was so quiet that afternoon that Colonel Vincent put his units on maintenance status. This gave them another opportunity to prepare the aircraft for other operations, both offensive and defensive. That work paid off the next morning.

On July 29, the mission orders came straight from the Old Man. General Chennault was sending his B-24 heavy bombers from Kunming on a strike against Hong Kong, and he wanted Colonel Vincent to send a force from Kweilin to join them. No B-25s were available for operations, so Vincent sent a mixed formation of P-40s and P-38s to meet the B-24s and escort them over the target.

Colonel Holloway led the fighters, which consisted of fourteen P-40s and three P-38s. They rendezvoused with the eighteen B-24s perfectly over Wuchow at 11:50 A.M. and escorted them the rest of the way in. The P-38s took top-cover position at twenty-five thousand feet, with the P-40s at twenty-three thousand feet and the bombers at twenty-one thousand feet.

In clear skies over Hong Kong, the bombers split into three formations and hit dock areas as well as ships at anchor. They remained split during withdrawal, so Holloway had to split his fighters as well to provide cover for them.

Holloway remembered, "About this time somebody yelled 'Zeros!' I started weaving violently but never did see any. Spurgin [2/Lt. James E. Spurgin Jr. of the 74th], leading the second element of my flight, said one of them went along right over me looking over the situation for about a minute or two. Finally he looked like he was going to commit himself, so Spurgin and Lee [Lt. George W. Lee of the 74th] tried to get him. Spurgin managed to make a head-on pass and hit him, but he doesn't know whether he got him or not. Another Zero got on a P-38's tail but a P-40 shot him off. Another P-38 got on a Zero's tail but overshot him in a dive before he was able to get a good burst in. Nobody saw more than two Zeros, so there must have been very few there. There was a lot of AA but it was pretty inaccurate.

"I had been out of oxygen for about a half hour and was pretty groggy, so after I got lost from the rest of the flight I dropped down to 12,000 feet and started to Canton. Canton looked deserted. I didn't get jumped, so I started home by Wuchow. Smith [Lt. Lawrence W. Smith, 74th], my wingman, had engine trouble over the target so he went up the Canton-Hankow Railroad and landed OK at Chenhsien. . . . Helms [2/Lt. Earl E. Helms, 449th] in a P-38 got lost and I talked to him a long time trying to get info on his position by his descriptions of the terrain. He finally landed near Lingling unhurt and with moderate damage to the P-38. The B-24s went back to Kunming—six landed at Kweilin, one got stuck and then unstuck, and then all six took off for Kunming—and the rest of us came back here [to Kweilin]."[4]

While Colonel Holloway's force was hitting Hong Kong, the Japanese from Hankow were paying Hengyang another visit. Captain Bill Grosvenor of the 75th led the defending force of Sharks, only four of which were able to engage the enemy formation. Captain Aaron Liepe of the 16th destroyed one Oscar, and Captain Grosvenor shot up one bomber before his own aircraft was damaged and he had to break off. He landed at Hengyang with a flat tire and ground-looped his plane but was uninjured. In the meantime, the Sharks' small but aggressive attack threw off the aim of the Japanese bombers. They missed the airfield, but a few bombs fell on the railroad yards nearby, killing several hundred Chinese civilians. The Japanese would return to try again the next morning.

The Japanese attack on Hengyang the morning of July 30 was the last gasp of their staggering 3rd Air Division at Hankow. The raid was designed to confuse the warning net and the defending fighters, but it failed, just as others had in the past. The main force consisted of bombers and escort fighters, while a diversionary formation of nine Oscars swung wide to the west and then turned south toward Hengyang. The warning net tracked both formations accurately. Thus, when 1/Lt. Charlie Gordon of the 75th led the Shark defenders off from Hengyang, he knew just what to look for and where, and he found them.

The courses of the two Japanese formations converged before they reached the target, and by that time Gordon had his Sharks in position so he could see all of them coming. Gordon feinted at the smaller fighter force, which took the bait and committed toward the P-40s. The Sharks then turned sharply into an attack on the bomber force and tore right through their formation, firing all the way. Again, the P-40 pilots threw off the bombers' aim, and the bombs exploded harmlessly away from the airfield.

In the fight, Lt. W. S. Epperson of the 75th lost the tail off his P-40 and went spinning to his death. First Lieutenant Howard H. Krippner of the 76th also was shot down, but he bailed out safely and returned to duty. The P-40s had another field day, shooting down four bombers and three fighters and claiming six probables. The credits were well spread out, as pilots of every squadron except the 74th were able to turn in claims. First Lieutenant Thomas H. McMillan III of the 76th probably had the easiest kill of the day. A Japanese fighter flew right in front of him and just stayed there, as if he were trying to get shot down. McMillan obliged him with a long burst that sent the enemy plane down in flames. He did not even turn on his gun sight.

The fight of July 30 finished the Japanese air offensive in China for the time being. They simply could not sustain the losses that the 23rd had been handing them for the past eight days. U.S. records credit pilots of the 23rd Fighter Group with fifty-four victories from July 23 through July 30. Gunners on the B-24 and B-25 bombers also claimed kills during the period. Air battles being what they are and without Japanese records for the period, it is impossible to determine exactly how many Japanese planes were lost. But it is safe to say that the Americans of the East China Task Force took the measure of the Japanese in the eight-day exchange.

★ ★ ★ ★

The last day of July 1943 was so quiet it was almost spooky for the men of the 23rd Fighter Group. Not a single report of enemy air activity showed up on the net: no observation flights, no attacks on undefended bases in Fukien or Chekiang provinces; nothing. Then it started to rain, and not a single combat mission took place in China for nearly two weeks.

That did not mean, however, that the bases occupied by the 23rd Fighter Group were inactive. On August 7, the remainder of the P-38 outfit, designated the 449th Fighter Squadron, arrived at Kunming and was attached to the 23rd for operations. This was the same arrangement that the 16th Fighter Squadron had been operating under for more than a year, though technically the 16th remained a unit of the 51st Fighter Group in India. The 449th did not have a permanent group assignment.

On August 10, Col. Casey Vincent received intelligence information that the Japanese were gearing up at Hankow to renew their air offensive against his eastern bases. The weather remained awful, but he decided to make preparations in case it broke. On the fourteenth, he moved the 449th to Lingling to operate as a full squadron. Major Ed Goss, commander of the 75th and an experienced combat hand, would act as temporary CO of the 449th during this breaking-in period until its own commander, Capt. Sam Palmer, gained enough experience in the combat area to take charge. While the 449th moved in at Lingling, the 76th Fighter Squadron moved to Hengyang. Now Major Costello's full squadron would operate from this easternmost base along with the two flights led by Captains Williams and Stewart. The ground contingent of the 76th gave high marks to their new home, which had more facilities and a better hostel than they had had at Lingling.

Far to the west at Yunnanyi, Maj. Bob Liles and his 16th Squadron continued to hold the line with recon missions into Burma and occasional dive-bombing attacks when the weather permitted. The most successful one took place on August 14, when Capt. Clyde Slocumb led four Sharks to the town of Lungling and bombed its installations, starting big fires.

At Kunming, the high point of mid-August for the 75th Fighter Squadron was the celebration of Chinese Aviation Day on the fourteenth. The Chinese on the base hosted a big banquet for the squadron, which gave high marks for the food. The officers adjourned to a party afterward, while the enlisted men watched a movie.

On August 16, the weather in the east broke enough for Maj. Bob Costello and his wingman, Lt. Bob Colbert, to fly to Hankow and scout around. On the way home, a couple of Ki-27 Nates tried to intercept them near Yochow. The Shark pilots put their noses down and ran for home. The clouds closed back in until August 19, and on that day the 16th Fighter Squadron's detachment at Hengyang ran two more recon missions to the Ichang-Hankow area. The pace was picking up, and on the next day, it broke into an outright sprint.

11

Summer Offensive

Early in the morning, Thursday, August 20, 1943, the air raid warning net came to life at Kweilin for the first time in three weeks. Nine enemy aircraft were reported heading toward the base at 7:00 A.M., and Col. Bruce Holloway scrambled a flight of his P-40s to intercept them. The Sharks did not make contact with the Japanese, however, as the enemy formation turned back toward Hankow before reaching Kweilin. The disappointed P-40 pilots returned to their mountain-ringed base and landed, but they had not been on the ground long when another report of approaching enemy aircraft came in. This was a definite change from the dull pattern that had prevailed since the end of July.

Colonel Holloway and Maj. Norval Bonawitz led fourteen P-40s of the 74th Fighter Squadron aloft from Kweilin, and at about 9:15 A.M. the twenty-plus Japanese raiders came into view. Immediately the Americans saw that the Japanese were trying new tactics. For one thing, they were flying a fighter sweep. Without bombers for the Japanese fighters to protect, the fighters were free to maneuver as the situation dictated. For another, they were high enough—thirty thousand to thirty-five thousand feet—that the P-40s could not reach them. And finally, these were the new Ki-44 Tojo fighters, which possessed better speed and diving performance than the more common Ki-43 Oscars that the Shark pilots were accustomed to encountering. Holloway's Sharks were in for a tough time.

Ironically, the Japanese employed the very same tactics that General Chennault had been drilling into his fighter pilots since 1941: Maintain your height advantage, dive to the attack, and then zoom away to regain altitude; and do not try to turn with your opponent. Colonel Holloway and his formation were forced to cruise along several thousand feet below the Tojos and wait for them to initiate the action. Occasionally, a flight of Tojos would dive down in a slashing attack, try to pick off a P-40 straggling on the edge of Holloway's formation, and then zoom up and away from the Sharks. Within a few minutes two P-40s went down, taking flight leader Capt. Truman O. Jeffreys and one of the Chinese pilots, Lt. Mao Y. K., to their deaths.

Captain Arthur W. Cruikshank Jr. managed to catch two of the Tojos and shoot them down. Colonel Holloway tried to chase another one that was attacking Major Bonawitz, but the enemy pilot broke off his run and pulled into a climb that carried him right out of Holloway's firing range. The enemy fighters, probably of the 85th Air Regiment, broke off the engagement at will when their fuel supply dictated it. In addition to the battle over Kweilin, there had been alerts at Lingling and Hengyang as well but without action.

There was no time to brood over the losses when the Sharks landed. The P-40s were quickly refueled and rearmed while the pilots were briefed so they could escort six B-25s of the 11th Bomb Squadron south to Canton. Again, Holloway and Bonawitz would lead the fighters, but this time there would be only ten of them.

The bombers' target was the Tien Ho Airdrome, a major enemy base near the city. The B-25s approached unmolested, but just as they arrived over the target, a flock of enemy fighters dived on them head-on. None of the bombers were badly hit, and the angle of the enemy attack gave the 74th's Sharks the opening they needed to pounce on the Japanese defenders. A dogfight erupted among the fighters while the B-25s made their escape. In the fight, Captain Cruikshank shot down another fighter, his third of the day, and Colonel Holloway, 1/Lt. Fennard Herring, and 1/Lt. Samuel P. M. Kinsey each got one, too. It was impossible to observe the results of the bombing in all the action, but the bombs appeared to have fallen in the revetment and hangar areas.

All U.S. planes returned to Kweilin unharmed. By that time, the wreck of Captain Jeffreys' plane had been located, and the grisly news returned: Jeffreys had died of a bullet wound to his head. Despite the success of the Canton mission, the day's events hit the 74th Squadron hard. It was one thing to see a buddy go down in a normal dogfight, but to watch someone get picked off like target practice was different. These new enemy fighters were going to be trouble.

One thing was certain: The air battle over eastern China had resumed. It seems doubtful anyone in the Fourteenth Air Force was aware of it, but on August 20, the Japanese had initiated the second phase of their summer air offensive. To the U.S. pilots and ground crews, the past three weeks had just been a short lull in a long war. During the first phase of their offensive, the Japanese had used bombing attacks to chase the Fourteenth's units out of their eastern bases, but the tactic failed miserably. Not only had the Japanese lost more than fifty aircraft, the U.S. forces were stronger than ever. In phase two, the Japanese would use mostly fighters in air-to-air combat and strafing to try to do the job. They renewed the pattern of flying large formations between Canton and Hankow while striking the U.S. bases between them. Their routes varied. Sometimes they would feint toward Kweilin to the west; other times they would run a more direct route north or south. If the U.S. fighters got close enough to intercept, the Japanese would engage. Otherwise, they could knew the Americans were burning up precious aviation gas while responding to them, even if they did not fight.

The Americans of Col. Casey Vincent's East China Task Force went about their business as they had before. One of Vincent's favorite tactics was to hit Japanese formations as they were returning to their bases after attacking him. The 23rd Fighter Group continued its varied role, which included air defense, bomber escort, ground attack, and reconnaissance missions. Its supply situation had improved a little, so if the enemy attacked, the Sharks would respond; if they did not attack and flying weather was good enough, the Sharks would find some other way to cause trouble for the Japanese. And on many days they did both. August 20 had been such a day, and August 21 would be another.

Big doings were on Colonel Vincent's agenda for that Sunday. He had put quite a bit of effort into planning an August 20 bombing mission against Hankow that would involve the B-24 Liberators of the 308th Bomb Group. The strike had been delayed one day, so this would be it. Similar to the July run against Canton, the mission would involve B-25 Mitchells and escorting fighters linking up with the heavy bombers en route to the target.

According to Vincent's plan, the B-24s would fly over Hengyang at 11:30 A.M. and rendezvous with their fighter escort there. The escort would consist of P-40s from Hengyang and P-38s from Lingling. It did not work out that way, however, thanks in part to the Japanese.

Colonel Holloway flew up to Hengyang from Kweilin, with a stop at Lingling, first thing in the morning. He wanted to check on plans for the escort mission, but he had no sooner landed at Hengyang than the warning net flashed word of a Japanese formation heading north from Canton. Holloway ordered Maj. Bob Costello of the 76th to take twelve Sharks midway between Lingling and Hengyang, while the colonel led a similar formation right over the field.

One of the pilots in Holloway's bunch was 1/Lt. Harvey G. Elling. A member of the 16th Fighter Squadron's detachment at Hengyang, "Nightmare" Elling had been flying in China since June. Of the

August 21 scramble, he recalled, "It seemed as if 21 August would be hot, sticky and dusty just like the day before. The Japs had come to Hengyang the day before, but we did not make contact. It had been a fighter sweep of a large number. The warning net had plots again of a large formation headed our way. We took off and started climbing with hopes of getting the top position. I was about the last P-40 in the formation. Maybe this would be the day we could hit them from above and out of the sun.

"We climbed and listened to the plots being broadcast by the warning net. They were coming in for the ball—no doubt about it. We were turning to the north from southwest of Hengyang, and the plots put them right on us. Suddenly from out of the sun and above they dived right into our formation. We each had one belly tank and they carried two, all of which were released at the same time. The air was filled with Japs, tanks and P-40s, most of which were just ahead of me.

"There was suddenly a wall of twisting smoke tracers on both sides of my canopy, and a quick glance back said I was in trouble. I looked into a large radial engine between short wings and smoking cannons. This was time to survive by using our proven evasion maneuver, which consisted of jamming the control stick forward and right full travel. At the same time, full power was applied and down you would go in a cross-controlled dive that makes the P-40 very difficult to follow or to shoot at with any degree of success. It is not a pleasant maneuver for the pilot because of redout, dirt rising in the cockpit, and [sic] oxygen mask on top of the head because of negative gravity forces.

"This dive was intended to reach the usual three hundred indicated, followed by a hard pull out and up. This would usually cause the Jap to break off. I did all the right things, only to look back and see the Jap with the big engine right on my tail, shooting as if he had lived for just this moment. Such a dive meant giving up thousands of feet of precious altitude, but I obviously had no option but to repeat the process and try to do better. The other option was to become a flag on the side of my tormentor's aircraft, because P-40s could not hope to turn with the Japs. The second dive produced the same results as the first and left me with only enough altitude for a last dive to the ground. This I did in a twisting, cross-controlled plunge for the hills, now far south and west of Hengyang.

"I leveled out on the deck and looked back at that large radial engine and those wings spitting smoke. I was making my P-40 a very difficult target, but this could not last. The Jap was flying a better machine than I was. Again I looked back, maybe to see the end of the chase, when the Jap suddenly turned back from where he had come. I saw the outline of his aircraft and recognized that this was not the usual Zeke or Oscar, which we had until now been combating. I returned to Hengyang for debriefing not as a conquering hero, but very glad to be back. The Jap either ran out of cannon shells or had too little fuel left, or both. . . .

"Shortly after this date, information came to us of a new fast and heavily armed fighter which could outperform the P-40 due to its large engine and sturdy elliptical wings. It was called the Tojo. I had seen it!"[1]

While Lieutenant Elling had a scare on the mission, the rest of the Sharks were heavily engaged as well. Major Costello's flight made contact with the Ki-44 Tojos at twenty-two thousand feet, and 2/Lt. Dick Templeton flamed one almost immediately. First Lieutenant Bob Colbert got one a few minutes later, as did 1/Lt. Willie Williams. The P-40 flown by 1/Lt. Donald Hedrick of the 76th was shot up badly, but Hedrick managed to bail out and parachute down safely. The P-38s from Lingling also got into a scrap, claiming one destroyed and three probables, with the victory credited to 1/Lt. Willard Bolton.

After the initial skirmish, Colonel Holloway led a small flight of Sharks north, hoping to catch the Japanese fighters on their way to Hankow. Near Hankow, he and his wingman, Lieutenant Williams, each shot down stragglers. They returned to Hengyang, landing about 11:10 A.M.

The rendezvous with the 308th's B-24s was scheduled for 11:30 A.M., so a mad scramble ensued at Hengyang to get the P-40s refueled and serviced in time to join up. Holloway had six Sharks ready to go on time, but the B-24s took a different route to the target and never showed up at Hengyang. The big bombers attacked Hankow without escort and lost two of their number to the intercepting Ki-43 Oscars and Ki-44 Tojos. Meanwhile, the mission's B-25s arrived over Hengyang at noon, so the Sharks escorted them to Hankow behind the B-24s. Only two intercepting fighters came up to meet them, and they ran for cover before the Sharks could reach them.

The next two days passed with only inconsequential *jing baos* on the eastern front. On August 23, two pilots of the 74th flew a weather recon down to Canton but saw nothing out of the ordinary to report.

Meanwhile, the Japanese at Hankow had a new idea. They sent a bomber formation with heavy escort to attack the Chinese capital at Chungking on the morning of August 24. The route to and from the target sent them north of the U.S. bases, which allowed them to avoid serious aerial opposition. They did not lose any aircraft on the mission, but how much damage they did to the Chinese is also questionable.

Colonel Vincent had made plans of his own for August 24, but they did not involve trying to avoid the enemy. He planned another rendezvous mission to Hankow with B-24s, B-25s, and fighters. This time, everyone got it right.

Sixteen Sharks from the 16th, 74th, and 76th squadrons took off from Hengyang at 11:10 A.M. with Colonel Holloway leading. If ever there was a military commander who led from the front, it was the tall Tennesseean. Any time the 23rd Fighter Group was headed for action, Holloway wanted to be in on it. His P-40s rendezvoused with six B-24s and seven B-25s over the field, then turned north toward Hankow. About thirty miles south of the target, the B-25s altered course to the right, according to plan. They would swing wide of the target and approach from the east, while the B-24s bored straight in to hit the enemy air bases at Hankow and Wuchang on the same bombing run. Holloway took ten Sharks with him to provide cover for the B-25s. Captain Art Cruikshank of the 74th led the other six Sharks as they covered the B-24s.

One of the pilots in Cruikshank's flight was Lt. Harvey Elling of the 16th, who had experienced his close call with a Tojo earlier in the week. Again, Elling recalled, "we formed what protection was possible with the small number of fighters, and came into the target area. . . . Hankow was an impressive area to see from our mid-twenty thousand foot level. I could see the large metropolitan area fronting a vast ship dock complex. Then I saw the numerous airfields north of the city, and saw many fighters climbing rapidly from them. Then came the anti-aircraft bursts—it was obvious we were to be given the full treatment. I now got the full meaning of the nickname of this area, Tin Pan Alley!

"Swarms of fighters were coming up rapidly and would soon be attacking. I wished I were not such a greenhorn and that we were attacking in greater numbers, but speculation gets little time in combat. As I turned to look at the bombers, I noticed one was not in close formation with the others. I turned to look again, and that bomber became a large, black cloud—instantly. He had taken a flak hit in the open bomb bay. There were no parachutes.

"Now the Japs were all around us and above us. I saw some start to dive at the bombers as my element leader, Capt. [John] Stewart of the 76th Squadron, turned in to attack a Jap. We turned left toward the bombers as Capt. Stewart dived on this first target. He fired a long burst and pulled left, which gave me a go at it. I pulled up over Stewart as he moved back in for the kill. The instant he fired, the Jap blew up, and I saw Japs moving into position on my rear. I pulled hard to the right and down, followed by a hard climbing left turn which seemed for the moment to clear the action to my rear. I looked up and saw a Jap cross closely from right to left, the direction

I was turning. I didn't know where he came from, but he was an instantaneous target that got the full attention of my six .50 caliber guns. This was more than enough to make him an uncontrolled flamer headed down.

"I realized I was separated from the other P-40s, in fact I could not see the bombers in the haze. Moving toward where I thought they would be, I recall having seen many Japs who also must have been looking for the center of the action. One was below me and left, so I started to close on him. I had to fire too far out, as he started to climb as if he had seen me. He absorbed a lot of ammo as he turned hard left and down. Too much time had been spent already, and I was still alone. I started for Changsha and Hengyang while there was still fuel to get home."[2]

Elling was not the only member of the B-24 escort to get a confirmed kill. Captains Cruikshank and Stewart got two kills apiece and added their names to the 23rd's roster of aces. Stewart was especially exuberant when he hopped down from his P-40 after the mission. Cruikshank also had reason to celebrate because he was the 74th's first homegrown ace. His predecessors—Ajax Baumler, John Lombard, and Dallas Clinger—had all scored most of their victories before joining the 74th. Also scoring twice was 1/Lt. Bill Hawkins of the 74th.

While all the action was going on over Hankow, Colonel Holloway and his Sharks covered the B-25s as they bombed Wuchang Airdrome. There were scattered sightings of enemy fighters in the area, but Holloway held his escorts close to the bombers. One foolish Japanese pilot made a head-on pass at Holloway, who was able to blast the enemy plane out of the sky without even breaking formation.

Later, when the formation was about one hundred miles south of Wuchang and on its way home, a flight of three B-24s came into view, being hounded by a single Japanese fighter. Holloway led his section over to assist and wound up right on the tail of the fighter—a "perfect sitter," as he called it. Holloway moved over and let his wingman, 2/Lt. Francis Beck of the 16th, make the kill.

It was a bad day for the B-24s, as they lost two of their seven planes and sustained damage on most of the others. The 308th's operations officer, a Major Foster, suffered a head wound and died at Hengyang that night. But they hit their targets accurately, and the total tally of victories was ten, plus more probables claimed. When Colonel Holloway landed at Hengyang, he found Casey Vincent waiting for him with plans for two missions to Hong Kong the next day.

Both of Vincent's bombing missions got to Hong Kong on August 25, and in the first, the B-25s did quite a lot of damage to shipping at

Whampoa Docks. However, the bombers missed their targets on the second try. No enemy aerial opposition was encountered on either mission, probably because only a small detachment of naval aircraft was stationed at Kai Tak Airdrome at the time. Not one to waste good flying weather, Vincent put more missions on for August 26.

The first strike of August 26 was supposed to hit the Hankow area from Hengyang, but due to bad weather to the north, Vincent changed the target to Tien Ho Airdrome at Canton. Major Robert Costello led ten Sharks of the 76th, along with two pilots from the 16th. The weather was not much better over the target than what was reported up north, but the mission ran as planned.

One of the pilots on the mission, Captain Williams of the 76th, became an ace that day. In a letter he wrote, "I guess the enemy didn't get a lot of warning because as we approached the target I could see Zeros still taking off from the air base. I was impressed with their fast rate of climb. When they were climbing, we had the altitude and speed advantage.

"I was able to shoot down one Zero and hit another one. In our aerial combat, our flights became separated. Then came the second part of the fight that was the most satisfying to me of any mission. The Japanese had some new fighters in the air. They were larger and faster than what I had seen before. One got on my tail. I dived and turned left, which would normally shake the Zeros that I had seen before. This one stayed with me, but could not lead me [when both aircraft are turning in a fight, the attacker must turn tighter than the aircraft in front of him in order to lead the target enough to hit it] enough to shoot me down.

"There were some clouds. I turned and flew instruments in the clouds for a while. When I came out, this new fighter—called the Tojo—was not around. I was in the process of joining up with the bombers and heading back when I saw a P-40 behind and below me with a Zero on his tail. I could see the white tracers from the Zero just pumping into the P-40. I guess the P-40's hydraulic system had been severed because one wheel had fallen down. It was a pitiful sight.

"I turned back, rolled over, and fired way ahead of the Zero. I knew I was out of range but hoped the Zero pilot would see my tracers. He did see them and pulled straight up. Climbing was the thing for a Jap to do, only this time I had altitude on him. When he got to the top of the climb I was almost in formation with him. All I had to do was pull the trigger and let those six .50 calibers do the rest. He rolled over with black smoke pouring out of the airplane and went into the ground.

"The P-40 was piloted by Lt. Robert Sweeney. Sweeney belly-land-ed the P-40 on a sandbar and was not injured. His airplane was really full of holes. He landed just on our side of enemy lines. The Zero went down very close to where Sweeney landed. Sweeney reported that the Chinese thought that he had been in a dogfight with the Jap and that they thought the two of them had shot each other down. Sweeney said the Chinese gave him a party to remember."[3]

Sweeney returned to Hengyang in a few days and resumed flying. He served a full and eventful tour with the 76th, becoming known for his aggressive ground attack style, but that was all thanks to the quick actions of Captain Williams on August 26. Joining Williams on the 76th's growing list of aces that day was another old hand in the squadron, Capt. Marvin Lubner. He would soon complete his combat tour and return to the States, but China had not seen the last of him. Lubner returned to the 23rd Fighter Group in 1945 and ended the war as a squadron commander.

The second mission on August 26 went down to Hong Kong, with P-40s from the 74th Squadron and P-38s of the 449th escorting B-24s to the target. Colonel Vincent disobeyed the orders barring him from flying combat and went along as leader of the seven Sharks.

Apparently, the Japanese had reinforced their fighter defenses following the previous day's raid, because eight interceptors rose to meet the U.S. formation. In the fight, Vincent shot down one enemy fighter and probably another, while 2/Lt. Altheus B. Jarmon also received credit for a victory.

★ ★ ★ ★

The aerial victories of August 26 were the last of the month, but missions continued when weather allowed. The 23rd Fighter Group was flying more than bomber escort missions, however. Ground attack missions were the order of the day on August 27. On one of them, Capt. Howard Krippner of the 76th was killed while strafing trucks near Yoyang. His plane was seen to take a hit on the first pass, and he crashed headlong into the side of a hill.

Then came August 30, one of the most destructive days yet recorded by the 23rd Fighter Group, though not a single enemy plane was destroyed. All the damage was done to the Japanese on the ground and at sea. Colonel Holloway sent out three effective strikes against river and rail traffic in the Hankow area.

Meanwhile, Colonel Vincent had something special up his sleeve at Kweilin: the first skip-bombing mission ever flown by Sharks against shipping targets. Bill Hawkins of the 74th took part in the mission and another that followed a few days later. He recalled, "One of the things General Chennault wanted to start working on was the shipping down in the South China Sea. The P-40 was equipped so you could hang one bomb or belly tank under the fuselage, but not both. But they had enough room behind that rack for another belly tank, so the crew chiefs rigged up a second shackle so you could carry a bomb under the fuselage with a seventy-five-gallon bamboo tank right behind it. We had to crank the tail wheel down to get as much clearance as possible, but even if you would scrape a hole in the tank you'd still get some gas out of it before it drained.

"[On August 30] we made a sweep over the sea near Hong Kong. Andy Anderson and another pilot [Capt. Paul Bell] had bombs, and I led the top cover of two [with Lt. Thomas P. Bennett].

"So we took off and went out over the sea. We didn't even have Mae Wests in case we went down in the water. We had just about given up and were heading back when we spotted three transports and a destroyer. Andy said he'd take the first transport, and [Bell] the second one. Then the destroyer started shooting at us.

"I broke off and made a strafing pass at the destroyer. The damned thing blew up right in front of me! It went flying in all directions. Andy and Bell were successful—one ship sunk and the other was beached, we found out from recon later. I thought that was an outstanding mission."

General Chennault agreed. He sent Lieutenant Anderson a personal commendation letter as soon as he saw the combat report crediting Anderson with sinking the freighter. Three days later, Lieutenant Hawkins carried a bomb. As he remembered, "On [September 2] we were supposed to bomb Hong Kong—the Kowloon docks. Our P-40s would give the B-25s top cover, and while all this was going on, myself and another pilot were to take five-hundred-pound bombs and skip bomb a ship in the harbor. There was supposed to be four of us with bombs and two for top cover. Well, when we rigged up the bombs and belly tanks, it took a lot of fooling around. The rest of the mission took off but my P-40 was still not ready. Andy Anderson was flying that day. He said he'd go ahead without me, and I said 'Oh no, I'm going.' We got off about a half hour late.

"I could hear a fight going on over the radio as we approached Hong Kong. I wasn't too optimistic about going in there under the Zeros, but the die was cast. We had practiced skip bombing at Kweilin. You really had to get right up to the target to hit it.

"I was determined I was going to hit this tanker. Boy, it was a big old monster. There was Andy out there beside me. He hadn't remembered to turn his generator switch on, so his radio and guns weren't working. When we were approaching, finally he got them turned on. I flew right up to the ship. It was like flying up to a ten-story building. God Almighty, here's this huge thing in front of me. It's like running up to the base of a cliff.

"I dropped my bomb and hauled back on the stick. I just barely missed flying through the damned thing. Andy saw the bomb hit just a few feet from the tanker, so we knew it went in. There was a seven-

or eight-second delay on the fuse. That allows quite a bit of time for getting away from the bomb blast, so we headed toward the docks and then back west toward our base.

"I saw some fireboats trying to put out fires in the big tanks on the docks that had been hit by the B-25s. So I started strafing them as I went across. Then lo and behold, there were a couple of Zeros.

"We didn't have enough gas to go all the way back to Kweilin, much less get in a fight with these guys. We had small auxiliary fields all over China, and we planned to refuel at one of them. Two Zeros latched on to us. By that time, thunderstorms had built up out of Hong Kong. We tried flying through them and around them, but we couldn't slow down because every time we'd make a turn, those Japs were there, a little closer.

"They followed us for maybe forty minutes. Finally I found this little auxiliary field and told Andy I'd go down to land. If the Japs came in and strafed me, he'd know to keep going. If they didn't, he could follow me in. By then I was low on gas and really had to land. It was such a short field that I had to ground loop at the end to get the P-40 stopped.

"I jumped out of the plane and ran to a ditch to take cover. I could see Andy coming in behind me. Then the two Japs turned around and left. They probably saw the thunderstorms building up fast and figured they had a poor chance of getting through them and back to Hong Kong.

"Auxiliary fields had gas stored in five-gallon cans. They'd break them open with a can opener, then pour them into the planes through a filler with a chamois. It was a laborious thing to get fueled up. By the time we were ready to go, it was getting near the end of the day. Andy's airplane wouldn't start right away. I got going and went back to Kweilin, and then he followed a little later.

"That was an adventuresome day. They took pictures of the raid, so I got that ship confirmed—a ten-thousand-ton tanker."[4]

★ ★ ★ ★

For all intents and purposes, phase two of the Japanese summer offensive against the Fourteenth Air Force ended in the last days of August. The U.S. fighter squadrons at Kweilin, Lingling, and Hengyang continued to get occasional alerts of approaching enemy aircraft in September, but each time the Japanese aircraft avoided combat and returned to Hankow or Canton. They did, however, continue to attack safer targets such as the unoccupied airfields at Kienow and Wanhsien, where they would not be subject to the attentions of the 23rd Fighter Group's P-40s and P-38s.

The Japanese officially called off phase two on September 8. They shifted the 3rd Air Division's fighters and bombers out of the Hankow area south to Canton and Indo-China, where they hoped to take advantage of better flying weather in the coming weeks. By the time they made the move, however, the Japanese ranks were thinner by several airplanes. Pilots of the 23rd claimed five enemy aircraft destroyed and two probables during the first eight days of September in the counteroffensive of the East China Task Force.

Meanwhile, changes were happening at Kweilin. Colonel Casey Vincent got a long-awaited break from the action on September 4, when General Chennault sent him to Washington, D.C. Vincent was happy for the chance to spend some time with his wife and young daughters, but his official reasons for going stateside were to hand-deliver a letter from Chennault to President Roosevelt and to lobby the War Department. Chennault wanted them to equip the fighter squadrons in China with a new aircraft, the superlative North American P-51 Mustang.

Vincent would be gone for two months. During his absence, Col. Bruce Holloway would command the East China Task Force, which now was called the Forward Echelon. Also, Vincent's deputy and operations officer, Lt. Col. Tex Knowles, was sent back to Kunming to prepare for taking command of a new fighter group coming to China. His replacement was Col. "Rosy" Grubbs.

By this time, Col. Bruce Holloway had been on overseas assignment for nineteen months. He had spent almost all of that time in combat and was the Fourteenth Air Force's leading ace with thirteen confirmed victories, scored while flying 106 missions. He had led the 23rd Fighter Group through a period of tremendous growth and success, and he was due for a rest. General Chennault relieved him of command of the 23rd Fighter Group so Holloway could devote full time to leading the Forward Echelon and be taken off combat status. The Old Man wanted to make sure he could send Holloway home in one piece as soon as Casey Vincent returned from Washington.

Of all the fine commanders the 23rd Fighter Group had during World War II, none had more respect from his men, or more ability, or went further in their Air Force careers than Bruce Holloway. When he finally retired from the military in 1972, he was a four-star general who had served as commander in chief of the Strategic Air Command and vice chief of staff of the U.S. Air Force. He subsequently held positions in the National Aeronautics and Space Administration and the United States Strategic Institute. At this writing, the quiet "gentleman general," as one of his pilots referred to him, is enjoying a busy retirement in Florida.

Taking Holloway's place as commander of the 23rd Fighter Group was Lt. Col. Norval Bonawitz, the well-seasoned combat leader of the 74th Fighter Squadron. He officially took over command of the group on September 16, the day after the group executive officer, Lt. Col. Hal Pike, was shot down near Wuchang and taken prisoner. Suddenly the 23rd Fighter Group was short of bodies at the top. The 74th Fighter Squadron's new CO was Capt. William R. Crooks, the former squadron operations officer. Crooks was one of the original School Squadron pilots and would complete his tour within a few weeks. He had just scored his second victory September 4 on an escort mission over Canton.

★ ★ ★ ★

In the afternoon of September 9, 1943, a twin-engine Japanese transport plane lifted off from Kagi Airdrome on the island of Formosa and headed west across the South China Sea toward Canton. Aboard the plane was Lt. Gen. Moritaka Nakasono, commanding officer of the 3rd Air Division, Japanese Army Air Force, and the ranking Japanese air force officer in China. Also among the passengers were his intelligence officer and operations officer.

The general and his subordinates were in the process of moving the 3rd Division's command post from Hankow, where it had been located since July, to Canton in preparation for the opening of phase three of the summer offensive against the Fourteenth Air Force. They were not destined to complete the move.

At 2:00 P.M. that same day, four P-38s of the 449th Fighter Squadron set out from Lingling toward Canton. The big fighters, led by Capt. Lewden Enslen, each carried two five-hundred-pound bombs under their bellies for a dive-bombing attack on the Whampoa Docks.

The Lightning pilots spotted several enemy fighters as they arrived over the city, but they easily evaded them and pushed over into their dives. The Japanese fighters chased them down in attack dives but never managed to close the distance. The bombs fell from the P-38s and caused big explosions among the warehouses on the docks.

The P-38s pulled out from their dives cleanly and cleared their tails of the Japanese fighters. Then one of the pilots, 2/Lt. Billie M. Beardsley, spotted a twin-engine transport plane off to his left a few miles southeast of the city. He and his wingman detoured in its direction, and once Beardsley confirmed it was a Japanese plane, he lined up his guns on it and opened fire. The plane began to burn and then crashed in the Pearl River. All aboard the plane, including General Nakasono, were killed.[5]

Lieutenant Beardsley had no way of knowing it, but he had just put the enemy's plans for phase three in complete disarray. A new commanding officer for the 3rd Air Division, Lt. Gen. Takuma Shimoyama, arrived in Canton a few days later, but the final phase of the summer offensive would prove even less effective than the first two. In fact, the Japanese only completed one attack on a

Fourteenth Air Force airfield during the entire month-long campaign, and when they did, it created a field day for the defenders of the 16th and 75th fighter squadrons.

The 75th had spent an extremely quiet summer at Kunming, with just a few escort and strafing missions to the Hanoi area to show for it. The only other events of note were Major Goss's return August 27 from his temporary assignment leading the 449th and the death of 1/Lt. Bob Maxent at Chanyi on September 5, when he spun in his P-40 during a mail flight. By the last day of summer, the 75th had not placed a claim for an enemy aircraft in seven weeks. That dry spell would end September 20.

September 20 also found the 16th Fighter Squadron in an odd situation. After spending most of the summer at Yunnanyi, Major Liles's outfit had been ordered to move to Kweilin on September 7. The squadron already had a detachment at Hengyang, and it would be leaving some P-40s behind at Yunnanyi for air defense. On the last day of the summer, the 16th's main force was at Chengkung, an auxiliary field about fifteen miles south of Kunming, during a stopover en route to the new assignment. Any successful fighter pilot knows that a big part of his success is due to being in the right place at the right time. On the morning of September 20, that is where the 16th Fighter Squadron was.

The warning net signaled the first report of enemy aircraft approaching Kunming while the pilots of the 75th were eating breakfast. They bolted their meals, grabbed their gear, and ran to their P-40s. The same warning reached the 16th Squadron at nearby Chengkung, and Major Liles led seven Sharks off around 8:00 A.M. The Japanese formation—Ki-21 Sally bombers and Ki-43 Oscar fighters of the 8th Air Brigade—was approaching from Indo-China, so the 16th would engage first.

One of the 16th's pilots who took part in the scramble was 1/Lt. William B. Evans. He described the action:

"We took off from Chengkung as a flight of seven aircraft led by Bob Liles, he with four aircraft and me with three. Upon becoming airborne, my engine rpm [revolutions per minute] went wild, and I had to return to base and land with a runaway prop. I taxied to the parking area, and without shutting off my engine my crew chief determined that my prop trouble was caused by a popped out breaker switch behind the pilot's seat which was not accessible in flight.

"He reset the breaker, and I took off again, climbing at full power to rejoin our formation, which had been circling the lakes south of Kunming 50–60 miles at approximately 24,000–26,000 feet. I rejoined our formation in the number seven position, or as tail-end Charlie. Just about the time I was able to rejoin our formation, we saw the inbound Japanese aircraft below and to the south flying at

19,000–21,000 [feet] headed due north toward Kunming. There were approximately 30–35 bombers and the same number of fighters. . . . The bombers were in a large Vee-type formation in flights of three or four aircraft. Their escorting fighters were 800–1,200 feet above and to the left, right and rear of the bombers, making a series of loops in formation.

"We immediately dropped our external belly tanks and made a diving pass against the bombers on their one o'clock position. On our fight pass I almost collided head-on with a flaming Zero shot down by Liles that was going in the opposite direction. I could almost see the expression on the Jap pilot's face as he went by. He was leaning forward as if he had been hit.

"We made three or four passes, and after our attack we were immediately jumped on by the Zeroes. Then shortly afterwards we got scattered fending off the attacking Zeroes. I didn't see the bomber that I was credited with go down, but I do know that I got some hits. We were all too busy about that time to follow all of the action. I believe everyone in the flight was credited with one or more aircraft.

"The bombers proceeded to Kunming without most of their escort, which at that time were keeping us busy, apparently assuming that our seven aircraft was the only American aerial opposition. When they arrived over Kunming they were hit hard by the 75th Squadron."[6]

Indeed, the Japanese bombers were hit hard by the 75th. Captains Matthew M. ("Charlie") Gordon, William Grosvenor, and Roger C. Pryor led the P-40s down out of the sun, and they shattered the bomber formation. Only a few bombs hit the airfield, causing minor damage but no casualties. Meanwhile, the 75th's pilots were credited with shooting down twelve aircraft, along with claiming several other probables and some damaged. Grosvenor and Pryor got two kills apiece. Gordon added one to his score to reach five and join the roster of aces. Only one P-40 from the two squadrons failed to return. It was piloted by 1/Lt. Lyndon R. ("Deacon") Lewis of the 75th, who filed the following report when he returned to base five days later.

"During the fight my ship was hit in the wing, leaving a large hole. I noticed that I only had a little gas left but figured it would be enough for another pass at the bombers. I climbed to a position over the bombers and came in out of the sun to make my final pass. A Zero came in on my tail, and I figured it was about time I was leaving those parts and dived into a cloud.

"After losing the Zero in the clouds I decided to head for home and set my course. After flying this course for awhile I again changed it and soon discovered I was lost. I circled for a few minutes and decided to belly-land. In bringing the ship down, the wing that had a hole in it gave way and the ship cartwheeled when it hit the ground. After landing I cleared the ship as quickly as possible. Chinese carried all of my baggage to the nearest Chinese Army post, three miles up the valley.

"I told the Chinese official in the little Chinese language I knew with pictures and map where I wanted to go. They brought me some rice to eat and after eating made me go back to the plane and get everything that was loose out of it. I was still trying to get started back to Kunming, but they would not let me leave until morning. All that afternoon I was being stared at. To help pass the time away, I did a few tricks for the Chinese boys. As it was now quite late, the soldiers made the kids leave so I could eat and get some sleep. About 10 minutes after the boys had left, two of them returned and wanted to see me. The Chinese soldiers let them in, and each had an egg to give me. I had just finished some rice and meat that had spoiled my appetite, but I had to eat those eggs before I could go to sleep. I boiled them myself."[7]

Lieutenant Lewis left the camp the following morning with an escort of soldiers. Traveling on foot and by donkey, he spent the next four days making his way toward Kunming. On the fourth day, he reached a village where missionaries lived, and he was able to send word to Kunming of his whereabouts. A six-hour jeep ride on September 25 completed his journey to Kunming, and he soon was back in combat with the 75th.

The interception at Kunming on September 20 effectively ended the Japanese summer offensive against the Fourteenth Air Force. According to Japanese records reviewed after the war, they lost forty-eight aircraft during the campaign. More important, they failed completely at reaching their objective of destroying the U.S. air forces in China. On October 8, the campaign was declared over. The 3rd Air Division moved its headquarters and aircraft from Canton and Indo-China back to the Hankow area, where they would try to rebuild their depleted squadrons.[8]

The rest of the month passed quietly for the 23rd Fighter Group, with the 74th Fighter Squadron flying uneventful escort missions on September 21, 22, and 30. Big changes were ahead, however. The Fourteenth Air Force was continuing to grow, and General Chennault was developing new ideas for bringing his increased firepower to bear against the Japanese.

12

Raid on Shinchiku

The Yangtze River is the third longest river in the world. Flowing west to east through the middle of China, it provides a natural highway linking coastal areas to the interior. The Japanese invaders made maximum use of the Yangtze in the late 1930s as they pushed westward to the industrial city of Hankow, and they continued to use the river to keep supplies and equipment flowing to their occupation forces for years thereafter.

By late 1943, however, the Japanese were finding it increasingly hazardous to ship goods on the Yangtze because of the danger of air attack from the Fourteenth Air Force's Forward Echelon. Fighters of the 23rd Fighter Group scouted from Tungting Lake eastward along the river almost daily, looking for targets and attacking almost anything that moved. The Japanese response was to arm larger vessels with machine guns and light cannons for self-protection, and they also deployed antiaircraft guns at key points along the banks of the river.

Engine noise, along with the hiss of churning water, made it difficult for boat crews to hear approaching aircraft. On September 10, 1943, a 175-foot supply boat was traveling on the Yangtze near Kiukiang, about 90 miles east of Hankow. The crew was watchful, but they were caught by surprise when four P-40s of the 76th Fighter Squadron suddenly popped over a hill and appeared right in front of the boat, lining up to strafe it. In the lead Shark was 1/Lt. Willie Williams. Through his gun sight, Williams watched the men on deck scramble for their guns. Then he pressed the trigger and watched the slugs from his six .50s kick up high spouts of water as they walked right up to the boat and then enveloped it in flying lead. By the time the four Sharks finished their first pass, all of the boat's guns were silent.

Williams led the Sharks in for another pass. This time, they aimed at the boat's waterline. Again, the slugs ripped into the boat, and it began to take on water. Then Williams made a mistake. Despite his better judgment, gained during nearly a year of flying combat missions, Williams decided to go in for a third run at the boat. He knew that he increased his chances of getting hit if he made too many passes on the same target, but this time it seemed a safe bet. It was not.

As Williams passed over the stricken boat on his last run, he could see men firing at him from the shore. Then he felts their bullets striking his aircraft. Instantly, the temperature gauge in the cockpit began to rise. Williams knew his engine's cooling system had been severed. He was in trouble.

Williams turned away from the river and headed toward friendly territory. His engine continued to run for only four minutes. Then it froze solid, leaving Williams with no choice but to bail out of the plane. Luckily for him, the four-minute flight had carried him far enough away from the river that friendly Chinese were able to reach him after he bailed out. By the end of September, he had made his way back to the squadron at Hengyang.

Williams was ordered to Kunming to debrief the commanders on his experiences walking back from the mission; that was standard procedure. While in Kunming, he was summoned to General Chennault's office for a conference.

Willie Williams had been in China since the previous October. First assigned to the 74th Squadron, he was transferred to the 76th in January 1943. The sandy-haired Texan was an excellent, very aggressive pilot. He made the most of his opportunities for air-to-air combat, scoring six confirmed kills, two probables, and one damaged during a five-week stretch in July and August. He certainly had done enough in China to earn a trip home, but the Old Man had a deal for him.

At that time, the 23rd Fighter Group was in the middle of a major changeover. Many of the pilots had been in the theater for a year or more and were due for rotation to the United States. Some, such as Jack Best of the 16th, had already left China; Bill Hawkins of the 74th and others would be leaving soon. The units still needed experienced, competent pilots to fill key leadership roles, however, to avoid a drop in combat effectiveness. Chennault's deal for Williams was simple. The 76th's CO, Bob Costello, was due to complete his tour in a couple of weeks. If Williams would agree to stay on for an extended tour, Chennault would give him command of the 76th Squadron.

Williams never hesitated. He accepted the offer eagerly, along with a promotion to captain. As part of the deal, he also agreed to pass on a similar offer to his friend and fellow flight commander in the 76th, John Stewart. Williams's attitude toward commanding a squadron was typical of most leaders who served in the 23rd Fighter Group throughout the war. Williams said, "I had never had any training to be a squadron commander, but I did have some excellent help. Prior to becoming squadron commander I was a flight leader, where I felt responsible for my flight. Now, all of a sudden I felt a responsibility for all flights of the squadron.

"Discipline was no problem: We all knew our mission and became a close unit—we still are. I felt that my objective was to motivate pilots to fly and fight—and that I should lead the squadron to do the most damage to the enemy and with the utmost safety of our squadron personnel."[1] As events would prove, Williams met his objective and then some.

John Stewart would not get command of a squadron, at least not right away, but his job would be every bit as big a challenge. The air base at Suichuan was being upgraded for full-time operations, and Stewart would take charge of its forces. At first, these would consist of two flights from the 76th Fighter Squadron. Later, F-5 recon aircraft, P-38s, and B-25s also would come under Stewart's command at the advance base, which was located about 125 miles east of Hengyang in Hunan Province.

The Suichuan base would have immense tactical value immediately. Its location not only put it directly between the two Japanese strongholds at Hankow and Canton, but it also put U.S. planes within striking range of several more ports on the coast of China, as well as the shipping lanes in the Formosa Strait. Chennault had even bigger plans for Suichuan. He wanted to base heavy bombers there, with the eventual goal of attacking mainland Japan.

For the time being, however, Suichuan would be the domain of Stewart's Sharks. The new captain received orders October 3, 1943, to proceed to the base with his small force of eight pilots and planes plus thirteen enlisted men for support. Their primary duty would be air defense for nearby cities such as Kukong that were subject to regular bombings by the Japanese. The Sharks also would provide air cover for the construction work that was progressing on their base. They did not have to wait long for action to start.

One pilot who moved to Suichuan was 2/Lt. Richard J. Templeton of the 76th. He recalled, "Soon after arriving we began receiving plots from the Chinese warning net of Japanese aircraft approaching from the south. So we had to take off again, and though we never made any contact, the Japs approached the field several times and then turned back, keeping us airborne until it was dark. The field had no runway lights, so some of the ground personnel and their Chinese helpers went to the nearby village and gathered up all the lanterns they could find. They then had the Chinese stand at the edge of the runway holding the lanterns.

"We recovered all the aircraft without damage, but I remember after landing and watching the row of lanterns on the left side for guidance, suddenly the aircraft was bouncing over a really rough surface. Some of the people holding the lanterns had become worried about their closeness to the landing aircraft and began moving back from the edge of the runway. I had followed them off the runway. Fortunately, the plane was not damaged."

Three days later, early in the morning of October 6, Stewart's Sharks were back in action at Suichuan. Again, Templeton remembered, "we received plots of large numbers of Japanese aircraft approaching from the south. The 76th detachment took off and had sufficient time to climb to an altitude of about 20,000. The flight of eight P-40s was hit by numerous Zeros, dropping from above us as usual, and was pretty well split up, but managed to confirm one Zero [by 1/Lt. Judson Bullard] and a probable.

"I was chased down to bomber altitude by several of them, and finally was able to spot the bomber formation, which had already dropped their [sic] bombs from a low altitude and was heading home. I caught up with the bombers about 20 miles from the field at about 2,000 feet and made three passes, confirming one bomber and damaging two others.

"I had noticed a flight of four Zeros about 5,000 feet above the bombers, but apparently they didn't see me until I was making my third pass. Then they came raining down. I was able to elude them by getting on the deck and flying down in some gullies and between some trees. My plane was pretty well shot up, with the hydraulic system out and one tire flat, but after pumping down the gear I was able to land safely. That P-40 was one rugged bird."[2]

That skirmish resulted in claims of two confirmed victories, one probable, and three damaged. Although it was not a big score, the Japanese gave the base at Suichuan a wide berth for nearly two months before attacking again. For his part, Templeton would continue flying with the 76th Squadron through September 1944, destroying four Japanese aircraft and earning a Distinguished Flying Cross and several other medals in the course of seventy-four combat missions.

★ ★ ★ ★

One of the reasons the 76th Fighter Squadron was able to send a detachment to Suichuan was that the fighter strength of the Fourteenth Air Force was growing again. While Stewart's men were getting settled at their new base, two full fighter squadrons—the 25th and 26th—moved to Yunnanyi and Kunming.

These squadrons transferred from the Tenth Air Force in India, along with the 51st Fighter Group headquarters, in early October. The 51st's squadrons had been flying combat missions over Burma for nearly a year from bases in the Assam Valley. When they came to China, they boosted the P-40 strength by forty-seven; however, many of these planes were as well used as the ones already flying in China.

The 25th's P-40s flew across the Hump in late September and were in Kunming on October 1 to fly with the 75th Fighter Squadron on an escort mission to Haiphong. This was not a particularly successful day, for the 75th lost three pilots. Two were Chinese fliers who were attached to the squadron for combat duty. The third man, 1/Lt. Henry Wood, was shot down when ten Oscars jumped the Sharks over the target area. He spent the rest of the war as a prisoner of the Japanese. On the plus side, Capt. Bill Grosvenor shot down one of the Japanese interceptors and became the 75th's newest ace.

When the 51st Fighter Group arrived in Kunming, it assumed responsibility for protecting China's side of the Hump route. Command of the group went to Lt. Col. Tex Knowles, who had formerly served as Colonel Vincent's executive officer in the Forward Echelon. Knowles sent the 25th down to Yunnanyi when the 26th arrived at Kunming on October 9. The 16th Fighter Squadron, which had been attached to China for operations with the 23rd Fighter Group since July 1942, was returned to its parent group, the 51st, on October 19. That same day the 449th Fighter Squadron was assigned to the 51st. For the time being, the 16th stayed at Hengyang and the 449th at Lingling. Later, the 16th would move to Chengkung, an auxiliary base near Kunming, and the 449th would take up station with its P-38s at Suichuan for a time before transferring west to the Kunming area in 1944.

In any case, all squadrons of the 51st Fighter Group would continue to work closely with their counterparts in the 23rd. It was not unusual for the 51st's squadrons to detach pilots for temporary duty with the 23rd, and vice versa, when the tactical situation dictated it.

The 23rd Fighter Group now consisted of just three squadrons. They would be concentrated on the bases east of Kunming. Kweilin would serve as the 23rd's headquarters, and the 75th Fighter Squadron also moved there on October 11. With the new base came a new squadron commander for the 75th, though he was no stranger in the outfit. Major Elmer Richardson, a Texan and one of the squadron's original Panama pilots, assumed command October 9. Also at Kweilin, the 74th Fighter Squadron's CO, Captain Crooks, had finished his tour. Crooks was replaced by Capt. Paul N. Bell, a Pennsylvanian who had been flying in the 74th for nearly a year and had one ground kill to his credit.

The 23rd's three new squadron commanders had very little opportunity to show what they could do during most of October, as weather shut down virtually all combat operations from October 9 through the beginning of November. That was just as well in Captain Bell's case, as he fell sick on October 23 and had to turn over command of the 74th to 1/Lt. Lynn F. Jones for five days. All commanders used this quiet period to send pilots to India on ferry missions. This gave the pilots a short break from the routine in China and also kept the supply of new aircraft flowing.

Meanwhile, ground crews took this opportunity to perform much-needed maintenance on any well-worn Sharks that were not being replaced. By this time, the bulk of the planes were P-40Ks and P-40Ms, though a few P-40Es remained. In the 76th, four secondhand P-40Ks that had arrived late in the summer still carried the desert camouflage and markings from their combat flights with the 57th Fighter Group in North Africa. One of them even had three small swastikas painted on it, signifying the German planes its previous pilot shot down during the desert campaign.

The P-40M was slightly different. It was Curtiss-Wright's first attempt to build a lighter version of the P-40, and it carried only four machine guns in place of the usual six. A new model just beginning to arrive in China, the P-40N, took the weight savings a little further but brought the armament back to six guns. Pilots noticed little improvement in the new models' performance, however. If anything, the P-40K was considered a bit faster in level flight.

One of the new pilots who arrived in late 1943 was 2/Lt. Robert L. Milks of the 74th Fighter Squadron. Milks, then twenty years old, had been assigned to the squadron in early October. He recalled the P-40N's idiosyncrasies and one of his first missions in a story he wrote for his children in 1988.

"On Nov. 16, 1943, I was assigned a mission to escort B-24s to bomb Kowloon docks at Hong Kong. . . . Our P-40s carried 75-gallon external tanks. We flew to targets using the belly tanks until combat started, then dropped them and fought on internal tanks. So far, all was well; however, just as we reached Hong Kong my belly tank ran dry and I didn't catch it in time. My P-40's engine quit just as the Jap Zeros jumped us. That's when my tale begins and nearly ended.

"I fell out of formation and started losing altitude—the formation was at about 17,000 feet. I pulled everything that would pull, pushed everything that would push, and turned everything that would turn. The engine would not restart. Losing altitude all the time, I determined to bail out at 1,000 feet. At 2,000, I pushed the prop control forward and the engine caught.

"Although life looked brighter, ahead all hell broke loose in the air battle being fought. I was fairly brave, but not totally foolish. I wasn't going to stick my nose into that, yelling, 'Hey, fellows, wait for me!' I turned around.

"Although a junior wingman, I didn't have to navigate going to the target. I had charted our course on my maps. All I had to do, in theory, was to fly reciprocal headings and I would be 'home free.' It didn't exactly work out that way. In China, we flew a combination of dead reckoning and pilotage. The only electronic navigational aid in southeast China then was a radio range at Kweilin; it didn't work. I had to fly below the clouds or chance descending through the clouds into our Kweilin air base, which was located among the picturesque Kweilin mountains. We learned to recognize these distinctive peaks as 'ice-cream-cone' mountains. They resembled ice cream cones inverted on a table. The only other true landmark was a railroad. The only railroad in southeast China ran south from Hankow, on the Yangtze River, to Hengyang, where it divided. One leg ran through Kweilin to Nanning—ours. The other ran to Canton—the Japs'.

"I flew my reciprocal headings northwest, dodging in and out of clouds, for enough time—I thought, but wasn't sure because we had no weather wind information—to reach our railroad. But I didn't see it. I figured I had overflown it and turned back east to find it. I spotted a railroad, but didn't know whether I was north or south of Kweilin. I felt safe of Jap interception of a radio call, so I called our Kweilin air raid warning net and told them I was on the railroad. They advised me that the warning net had reported a single aircraft on the railroad north of Kweilin. They told me to follow the railroad south. I did. However, the aircraft on our railroad turned out to be a transport plane. I was on the wrong railroad flying south toward the Jap base at Canton.

"At Kweilin, we had two airfields [later three]; at Canton the Japs had two airfields. I approached the first airfield flying at 2,000 feet at 180 mph to conserve gas. Although I was new, things didn't look right. The mountains didn't look right. As I flew over the air base, little black clouds started appearing around me—anti-aircraft flak— and I saw water ahead. There was no large body of water at Kweilin! I was no longer lost. I knew where I was. I pushed the throttle full-forward and hit the deck. I had seen enough of Canton!

"I checked my gas gauges, and they read 20 gallons of gas left— and I was going 'full bore.' I headed west up the West River. I knew I wasn't going far, but I figured one minute in the air could mean one day walking in the mountains, if I bailed out. I looked back and saw no Japs following, so I throttled back. The P-40 would climb at 180 airspeed and not lose speed. I always thought I would bail out rather than belly-land in China because there were usually only two choices to land in: mountains or rice paddies, both conducive to a short life span. However, the West River was a wide river with many sandbars. I decided I could land on one of them safely. Also, I wanted the eight-day clock from the instrument panel. I climbed and picked out sandbar after sandbar, hoping to go as far from Canton as possible. I reached 12,000 feet.

"We carried a printed list with code-name call signs for all of our bases and prominent places in South China. I knew from my map and call signs that we had an emergency airfield at Wuchow on the south bank. I was heading for it. I called Kweilin and gave the code name for Wuchow. There was one small problem; the call signs were changed routinely. I had an obsolete list.

"The emergency airfield at Wuchow was just that—a grass field. Being near Canton, the Japs used it for bombing practice. It often had potholes in it.

"At 12,000 feet altitude I looked ahead and saw a good-sized city on the north bank of the river with a field nestled in a half-moon-shaped hill on the south bank. I figured it had to be Wuchow. All of my gas gauges indicated zero. I was on a 'wing and a prayer'—and believe me I was praying. My mind was made up. Bomb holes or no bomb holes, I was going into that field!

"I lowered my landing gear at 12,000 feet and started a 'falling leaf' maneuver to go down. I was going straight in—no circling or reconnoitering. I had my hand on the gear handle. If overshooting, I would pull the handle and collapse the landing gear. I had to get in. I couldn't afford the gas to go around and try again. By the grace of God, I made it.

"The field was covered with grass about a foot high, which probably helped me to stop in a short field. It could be a problem on take-off. Tough Chinese soldiers converged on the plane. I jumped out, yelling 'Megwa, Megwa' [American, American]. They answered with the international language, they smiled. The soldiers didn't speak English, and I didn't speak Chinese, but I pulled out my 'pointee-tal-kee' booklet (of American and Chinese phrases) and with gestures I managed to tell them I needed gas. Gen. Chennault maintained 55-gallon drums of gasoline at emergency fields around China. Wuchow was one. The soldiers rolled out the drums and hand-poured the gas through a funnel into the airplane.

"While they were refueling the airplane, they signaled for me to follow them to a cave in the hillside surrounding the field. Inside the cave they had a vertical plotting board with a map of China. On the map they had placed little red flags indicating that Jap airplanes were coming up the river. I had to get out fast! (It later developed that the flags were for my own flight up the river.) There was one small problem—getting the P-40 started.

"Curtiss-Wright, manufacturer of the P-40, had gotten a brilliant idea. To make the P-40 lighter so it could go higher and fight the Jap Zero, they made certain modifications to the P-40N-5 model, the type I was flying that day. They took out part of the armor plate, replaced the gyro instruments with electrical instruments, bolted the seat in a fixed position (it couldn't be raised or lowered by the pilot) and took out the starter. The airplane had to be hand-cranked from the outside while the pilot remained in the cockpit. My problem now was how to teach a peasant Chinese soldier how to crank the airplane before the Japs caught me on the ground. Again, the good Lord was with me.

"From the town of Wuchow, across the river, came a young Chinese-American lieutenant, C. K. Wong. Wong had been sent by Gen. Chennault on a special mission to Wuchow. There were no roads from American bases, so Wong must have taken several days coming down river to reach Wuchow. To save time, Wong wanted to ride back to Kweilin with me. I explained that I was new to China and had just gotten lost and wound up over a Jap air base, but if he wanted to come he could. Wong was in a quandary—several days roughing it going upriver by boat or foot, or tempting fate with me. I was ahead either way, because he would crank the P-40. Wong was young, brave, and/or foolish—he chose to go with me.

"Wong cranked the airplane. I was able to get the engine to catch, and any water in the gas was minimal if at all. We were nearly home free. The P-40 was built for one person, but as most single-seat fighters it had a baggage compartment with a small door between the cockpit and the tail. The door opening was about 15 to 18 inches square. Inside the compartment, it could hold a B-4 bag (canvas suitcase) in addition to the bulky parts of our radio equipment and battery. Wong became more knowledgeable than I about the space and called it 'the battery compartment.' The door could only be opened from the outside.

"After cranking the airplane, Wong opened the baggage compartment door and climbed in. We were fortunate that I had jettisoned the belly tank over Hong Kong, because it might have given [us] trouble in the tall grass on takeoff. With maximum power, we took off and headed for Kweilin.

"Navigation in China in 1943 was a challenge for every flight. We carried a sheet of paper with magnetic headings from airfield to airfield on one side and distances on the other side. With this sheet and magnetic heading and distance known, Wong and I flew safely back to Kweilin.

"I reported to [Lt. Luke] Kissick, our intelligence officer, for debriefing on my mission. Kissick covered my 'boo-boos' in the official mission report and issued me my mission chit. We received two ounces of medicinal whiskey for each combat mission. Since I wasn't old enough to (and didn't) drink, I gave my mission whiskey to others. I just kissed the 'Good Earth' after each mission and thanked the Lord."[3]

That was not the end of the story, though. Bob Milks received a telephone call in January 1988 at his North Carolina home from none other than C. K. Wong in Pennsylvania. The two men had not seen each other since they parted on the field at Kweilin on November 16, 1943. Their conversation led to the composition of this account, which later was published in the *Jing Bao Journal*, the official newsletter of the Fourteenth Air Force Association. Milks added as a postscript that he had neglected to mention to Wong that internal starters were fitted to the P-40Ns not long after this incident.

★ ★ ★ ★

What the 23rd's pilots really wanted was not an upgraded version of the P-40 but a new plane, the North American P-51 Mustang. This sleek fighter originally was designed for export to Great Britain. When the U.S. Army Air Force realized the potential of the new plane's performance, however, it also made arrangements to equip its units with the Mustang. The first versions of the Mustang used essentially the same Allison engine that propelled the P-40, so they, too, were limited to medium- and low-level operations. Even so, their performance at any given level was far superior to that of the P-40 due in great measure to the new laminar flow design of the P-51's wing. Also, the P-51's maximum speed was about 390 miles per hour, some 40 miles per hour faster than the fastest P-40. Furthermore, the Mustangs also had a better climb performance and about 100 miles of additional range. The range advantage could be extended by attaching two drop tanks under the wings.

So with great anticipation the 76th Fighter Squadron received word in early October that it soon would reequip with new P-51As. Ground crews were given maintenance manuals to study, and pilots sought out any information they could find about the Mustang's flight characteristics. The first new planes arrived at Kunming on October 17, and by the end of that week, fifteen of them were on hand. Soon they were moved up to Lingling, where a transition school of sorts was set up. Maintenance crews busied themselves by painting the obligatory shark mouths on the new planes' noses, though the smooth line of their lower cowling did not lend itself particularly well to the design. As time permitted, pilots of the 76th came from Hengyang and Suichuan to check out on the new planes.

The new fighters were in very short supply, and there was no assurance that more of them would be available any time soon. Because of this, the Forward Echelon was leery of basing the P-51s at Hengyang, where they would face greater exposure to enemy air attack. Soon after Col. Casey Vincent returned from Washington on November 2, 1943, he decided that the 76th and 75th squadrons should trade places so that the P-51s could be based at Kweilin, a little farther out of harm's way. The 75th transferred up to Hengyang to join the 16th Squadron on November 18, while the 76th moved down to Kweilin with the 74th. Except for the eight Sharks based at Suichuan and under Captain Stewart's command, the 76th left its remaining P-40s in the hands of the 16th.

The arrival of these first P-51s with their longer range opened some new possibilities for the 23rd Fighter Group. But another development at the same time had a similar impact: "Tex" was back. After a year in the States, Col. David L. Hill had returned to China. As Hill recalled, "I returned to China in the latter part of October '43. There were many more people there, and headquarters had expanded to beat hell. The 308th Bomb Group had heavies there. We also had a B-25 group. We only had the 11th Bomb Squadron of B-25s in '42. I came back with Bill Fisher, who took over that 308th.

"I never will forget, when we landed [at Kunming] we walked over to Chennault's headquarters. Chennault greeted us and immediately went over to the board and started telling Fisher, . . . 'Bill, you're going to have the 308th Bomb Group. Tex, you're going to have the 23rd Fighter Group.' And then he said, 'We're getting ready to start bombing Japan from here.' He started right in. Fisher had never been in that part of the world. He was sitting there blinking. We were going to stage out of some fields in the east. We could have done it once maybe. But without escort there was no way you could sustain it. The B-29s found that out later the hard way."[4]

Colonel Fisher never did get his B-24s over Japan, but he would command the 308th with distinction. Meanwhile, Colonel Hill flew from Kunming over to Kweilin and assumed command of the 23rd Fighter Group on November 4. Norval Bonawitz stayed on in group headquarters as executive officer. Before long the two of them and their boss, Casey Vincent, cooked up a mission plan that would put the capabilities of the new P-51s to good use. The target would be Shinchiku Airdrome on the island of Formosa, the same place that Col. Bruce Holloway had scouted several months earlier in his daring solo recon mission.

Hill recalled how the Formosa mission developed. He said, "It was something that was absolutely secret. Bruce Holloway had done some recce over there. I saw Bruce when I was coming in, and he was on his way back to the States. He told me, 'Man, Tex, they've

really got a lot of airplanes over there if you can just get to them.'
Casey Vincent and I dreamed up a way to do it with what we had.
We took everything in China to make that trip."[5]

★ ★ ★ ★

On November 24, 1943, the Forward Echelon dispatched an F-5
Lightning photo recon aircraft from Suichuan to check out the
Japanese airfield at Shinchiku. When the plane arrived over
Formosa, its pilot turned onto his photo run, took his pictures, and
then ran for home. The F-5s had been taking pictures over Formosa
for several months, but this time was different. Vincent and Hill had
put together a strike force consisting of fourteen B-25s, eight P-38s,
and eight P-51s. If the photos showed sufficient aircraft on
Shinchiku to warrant an attack, the mission would go the next day—
even if it was Thanksgiving Day.

When the F-5 returned to Suichuan, the cameras were quickly
unloaded and their film processed. The pictures showed Japanese
aircraft by the dozens. In fact, Hill recalled the count of 100
bombers and 112 fighters, parked all over the place. The mission
was on.

At Kweilin, eight P-51As of the 76th Fighter Squadron were alerted immediately for a 2:00 P.M. flight to Suichuan. The pilots did not
know where they were going from Suichuan, but they knew something big was up when they were issued Mae West life preservers,
the first they had seen since arriving in China. Colonel Hill led the
eight Mustangs off at 2:15 P.M., and they arrived at Suichuan an
hour and a half later. That same afternoon, the P-38s from Lingling
and B-25s from Kweilin also flew to Suichuan. The pilots went to
bed early, because they knew reveille was at 4:00 A.M. on
Thanksgiving Day.

The pilots learned about their target at an extensive briefing at 8:30
the next morning. The route to Shinchiku would take them 424 miles
out and about the same distance back, plus whatever maneuvering
might be necessary during the attack and a possible aerial engagement. Nearly 100 miles each way would be over the waters of the
Formosa Strait. Upon leaving Suichuan, the planes would take an initial heading northeast, as if they were going to Tungting Lake, and
then turn southeast toward Formosa. They were to approach the
island at low level to avoid radar detection, climb to one thousand feet
just southwest of Shinchiku, and proceed with the attack from there.
The P-38s would provide top cover, with the P-51s as close escorts to
the B-25s. Six of the bombers were from the 2nd Bomb Squadron of
the Chinese-American Composite Wing, which had just arrived at
Kweilin and would be flying their first ever mission. The other eight B-
25s were from the veteran 11th Bomb Squadron.

According to the plan, the P-38s would escort the B-25s directly to the target, engage any interceptors, and then strafe the field. The B-25s would follow them in and drop parachute-mounted fragmentation bomb clusters on one side of the field, while the P-51s would follow and strafe the other side as well as the dispersal areas. If any fighters went down in the strait on the way home, the last B-25 was to circle back and drop the pilot a life raft. The crews also had the name of a missionary to contact in a coastal town south of Foochow if they went down over the mainland near the coast.

Colonel Hill would be the mission leader as well as leader of the P-51 escorts. Captain John Stewart, Suichuan detachment commander, convinced one of the junior P-51 pilots in the formation, Lt. Joe Hiner, to give up his seat so Stewart could go. Other P-51 pilots were Capts. Willie Williams and Lee Manbeck, plus Lts. Donald Hedrick, Bob Colbert, Richard O. ("Rick") Olney, and Dale Bell—all of the 76th.

Takeoffs began at 9:30 A.M., and they had to be done in single file because of soggy field conditions. The last plane was off by 10:00 A.M., and the pilots settled down for their long run to the target. Captain Manbeck had not gone far when he encountered a problem with his hydraulic system. He was the only pilot to abort the mission. The twenty-nine–plane formation stuck closely to its flight plan, and the navigation was absolutely accurate. The aircraft crossed the coast of Formosa at about noon and began their run north to the target.

Shortly, someone called in a twin-engine enemy aircraft approaching down the coastline. Colonel Hill dispatched a flight of the P-38s to go after it, and 1/Lt. Robert Schultz shot down the plane quickly. The P-38s were returning to their station when Hill spotted some enemy fighters taking off from the airfield ahead. A few seconds later, the P-38s found themselves among a fighter pilot's dream—a formation of enemy bombers strung out in the landing pattern for their air base. A short but decisive air battle ensued.

The P-38s had a field day, destroying eleven bombers, while the B-25s swept across Shinchiku. Down below, ground crews waiting to service the incoming aircraft ran for their lives as the B-25s dropped their deadly loads. Meanwhile, Colonel Hill's flight engaged the few Oscar interceptors that managed to get airborne. Hill shot down one that chandelled in front of him while it tried to get on the last B-25's tail. Lieutenant Bell sent another fighter down blazing a few seconds later. Then Hill led his P-51s in for a strafing run, and the flight destroyed several more aircraft on the ground. The B-25s and P-38s also did considerable damage to aircraft and facilities on the airdrome.

No U.S. aircraft were lost on the mission, but two P-51 pilots had frightening moments. Ironically, the first was Captain Stewart, who was flying his first mission in a Mustang. He dropped his wing tanks just before going down on his strafing pass but forgot to turn on the switch to his internal fuel tanks. His engine died immediately, and his plane glided across the field silently as he scrambled frantically to find the fuel switch. He got the engine restarted just in time to take aim at a bomber parked on the field's edge and fire a burst that blew it up.[6]

Colonel Hill had the second scare as he was pulling up from his strafing pass. He was just forming up for the flight home when an explosion rocked his plane. His heart jumped, and he shot a glance over his shoulder to try to spot the enemy plane that must surely be behind him. Nothing was there, and he realized that a round of ammunition had cooked off in one of his hot wing guns. No harm was done, except to his nerves, and he led the formation back to Suichuan without further excitement.

"It was a risky mission," Hill recalled many years later. "We could have lost everybody. But we pulled off a perfect mission."[7]

A photo recon Lightning arrived over Shinchiku at high altitude about fifteen minutes after the attack and took pictures of the carnage below. Those photos, in addition to some taken during the attack from the B-25s, helped confirm the following claims by the P-51 pilots: Hill, one confirmed in the air with one confirmed and one probable on the ground; Williams, one confirmed and one damaged on the ground; Stewart, one confirmed on the ground; Bell, one confirmed in the air; Colbert, one confirmed on the ground; and Hedrick, one probable and one damaged on the ground. The only damage they sustained occurred when Lieutenant Olney had a rough landing at Suichuan and damaged the propeller on his plane. The P-51s returned to Kweilin the next day.

Accolades poured in to Colonel Vincent's office in Kweilin over the next few days from as far away as India. The mission was a complete success. Not only had it inflicted specific damage on Japanese aircraft and installations at Shinchiku, but it also had strategic value. No longer could the Japanese assume that Formosa was out of reach from enemy air attack. They would have to bolster their air defenses on the island, using aircraft and men they badly needed to oppose the Allied advances in the South Pacific.

13

Defending the Rice Bowl

While the Thanksgiving Day 1943 raid on Shinchiku Airdrome was a great success, it was really a sideshow to the main event in China at that time. On November 13, units of the Japanese Eleventh Army had left their camps in the Hankow area and headed toward the Chinese-held city of Changteh on the west side of Tungting Lake. This was the beginning of what came to be known as the "Rice Bowl Offensive."

The operation was aptly nicknamed, as the primary goal of the Japanese troops was to relieve Chinese farmers of their crops in the rice-rich Tungting Lake region. The Japanese needed the rice to feed their own forces in China and elsewhere in Asia, a far more important goal to them than keeping mere Chinese alive. A side benefit of the advance was that it would engage Chinese ground forces and prevent them from transferring to Burma, where an Allied ground campaign was imminent.

The Japanese crossed the Yangtze River near Shihshow, north of the lake, and headed for the city of Lichow. Almost immediately, the 23rd Fighter Group was called on to support the Chinese troops under attack from the Japanese. The 74th and 75th squadrons carried out most of the missions—patrols over Changteh, attacks on Japanese communications and supply efforts, and strikes against enemy airfields in the Hankow region. A favorite target was the railroad line from Yochow at the mouth of Tungting Lake all the way to Wuchang.

A typical mission took place November 20, when the 75th Fighter Squadron dispatched twenty Sharks to reconnoiter the Ling Ho

River and strafe any worthwhile targets. They caught a cavalry unit, which was common among Japanese forces in China at that time, and strafed the men and horses thoroughly. Estimated casualties were one hundred men and twenty horses. Then they strafed another cavalry formation, with estimated casualties at forty more men and fifteen horses. Next, the Sharks fired on two small riverboats; then a small town suspected of housing Japanese troops, with two fires reported; and finally, three more boats before the Sharks returned to Hengyang safely.

The very next day, twelve Sharks from the 75th reported sinking or damaging no fewer than fifty small boats on one mission and did so again later in the day. In the second attack, the pilots could see that the Japanese were using the boats to ferry troops across a river. November 22 brought four more missions for the 75th; the 23rd, another pair.

Late in the month, Japanese forces reached the outskirts of Changteh. There, Chinese resistance stiffened, and a seventeen-day siege ensued. Starting on November 28, the 75th added air-dropping supplies to its list of mission profiles, when P-40s dropped belly tanks loaded with ammunition and food to the Chinese defenders at Changteh. The first try in the morning was scrubbed due to bad weather over the city; but in the afternoon, several Sharks got through. They dropped their tanks and then patrolled before returning to their base 140 miles south. These missions continued throughout the siege.

And so it went for the 75th at Hengyang. The 74th sent a detachment of nine Sharks there on December 3, and both squadrons flew multiple missions nearly every day for the next three weeks. Finally the Chinese defenders at Changteh were able to break the siege, and the Japanese troops withdrew to their former positions near Hankow in late December.

★ ★ ★ ★

Aerial combat resumed with a vengeance during the Changteh siege. It started on the first day of December, and by the end of the month, the 23rd Fighter Group had rolled up its highest monthly victory total of the war. In the course of flying 962 combat sorties, forty-four aerial kills and eight additional ground kills were confirmed by the 23rd's pilots. The cost was considerable, however, as twelve aircraft were lost in combat and four pilots killed.

The first air battle came on December 1, when ten P-51As of the 76th Fighter Squadron were assigned to escort B-24s attacking Canton and Hong Kong. Led by Colonel Hill, the Mustangs flew out of Kweilin a little past noon. The aircraft proceeded to Canton unmolested by enemy fighters or ground fire; however, four of the Mustangs were forced to run back because of mechanical problems.

They did not know it at the time, but Capt. Willie Williams, the popular commander of the 76th, and 1/Lt. Bob Colbert were flying their final missions of the war that day. Williams described his experience in a debriefing conducted seventeen days after the mission.

"We never had over 10,000 feet until just before we got to the target. Then Col. Hill started climbing. We got strung out there, but over the target I was beside Col. Hill (at about 22,000 feet). The others were a little far back.

"Just over Hong Kong, the colonel's element turned north. He probably didn't know I moved up. I saw Zeros coming in behind us (from above and to the left) and said so over the radio. I also heard someone yell "Zeroes!" What I should have done was shoot my guns. Anyway, [1/Lts. Dale] Bell and [Harry G.] Zavakos dove a little, and Colbert and I started weaving, trying to hold them back.

"I waited, thinking that Col. Hill was waiting until they got almost there, but he did nothing and then it was too late. We had already made the bombing run and were over the bay when they jumped us. I never saw more than five [enemy fighters] and they were all Tojos.

"Colbert knew they were back there, but he stayed with me. Finally they came in too close and Colbert got hit in the cooler. I fired a burst at the Zero that hit him, then dove and turned a little to sea. Colonel Hill and Wilson [Hill's wingman, Flight Officer (FO) Bob Wilson of the 16th Fighter Squadron] continued on.

"After a rapid spiral to about 17,000 feet I started to climb back up. My engine got rough, and a glance at the instruments told me I'd lost all oil pressure. I couldn't do anything after that but fly west. I couldn't figure which one shot me down. I guess I saw them all but the one that hit me. Heading west over the bay, my manifold pressure dropped to 20 inches and just after that she quit altogether. I continued to glide in the same direction and called over the radio, 'This is Willie. I've been shot down and am not over the lines.'

"Down to 1,000 feet, I slowed it up to 120 mph and started over the right side [of the cockpit] with my head down. The plane rolled with me, and I couldn't get out. I got back in, righted the ship and lost more altitude in so doing. The ship had stalled, and I nosed it down to pick up to 200 mph. I then pulled up to 300 feet but was too low to bail out so I picked out a large rice paddy [just north of Macao] and refastened my safety belt while gliding down to it.

"After I bellied in, I got out and started to burn the ship. I could see no bullet holes in the ship, but I couldn't see the underside. To burn the ship I unscrewed both gas tank caps and dipped dry rice straws into the gasoline and spread them out along the wings and fuselage. Then I used my handkerchief to spread more gasoline and finally struck a match to it. Seeing my beautiful ship go up in flames sure hurt me."

As had been the case when he was shot down in September, Williams was lucky enough to contact Chinese guerrillas almost immediately. They dressed him in Chinese clothes, put him in a sampan, and started him on the long journey that took him to Liuchow and eventually back to Kweilin on December 17. There, during his debriefing at group headquarters, Williams was asked if he carried a gun with him on the mission. He replied, "No sir, I didn't. I feel this way about carrying a gun. I think that if I met a small group of people they would be Chinese because a small group of Japs would be wiped out or quickly gotten rid of (by the Chinese). A large number of Japs would probably get me anyway. To shoot Chinese would be equally serious. If I had a gun and they wanted it, I would give it to them."[1]

Lieutenant Colbert rode a train into Kweilin a few days behind Captain Williams. He, too, had been shot down by the Tojos, but he had managed to bail out of his Mustang. Like Williams had, Colbert made contact with friendly Chinese. His plight was a little different, however, because he parachuted into an area east of the railroad line linking Canton and Hong Kong. He was deep in Japanese territory and needed to cross the rail line to get out. To make matters worse, Colbert's leg had been wounded when his P-51 was shot up. After several close scrapes with the Japanese troops who were searching for him, Colbert and his Chinese escorts managed to cross the railroad track at night and proceed into friendly territory.

For the December 1 mission, the plus side of the column showed just one Tojo damaged, with credit going to Colonel Hill. It cost the 76th two lost P-51s and Williams and Colbert. The Fourteenth Air Force's policy at that time removed from combat status any pilot who escaped from enemy-held territory. This was done to protect the Chinese who had aided their escapes. If a pilot were to go down again and be captured, he might reveal information about his earlier escape that would result in Japanese reprisals against the Chinese involved. Williams and Colbert were sent over the Hump and across India to Karachi, where they would spend three months as instructors in the operational training unit before getting their orders home. Captain John Stewart had taken over as temporary squadron commander of the 76th when Williams went down, and he got the job permanently when Williams left.

Another result of the December 1 mission was a feeling of respect for the Tojo's performance by one Col. Tex Hill. Recalling the fight and its aftermath, Hill said, "I was shot up pretty good, too. When I got back, I told Chennault about it. I said, 'I don't think we can beat these new Japs in the air.' He said, 'Don't worry about it. Just hit 'em on the ground.'

"That's the way Chennault was. He knew exactly what he was doing. And he told us right. One of his favorite sayings was, 'If you want to teach a dog to do a trick, first be smarter than the dog.' He was always thinking positive."[2]

In the months ahead, Hill would find more opportunities to catch Japanese fighters on the ground. For the rest of December 1943, however, air combat was the order of the day.

Perhaps in response to the Hong Kong raid, the Japanese mounted an attack against Suichuan December 2. The net reported enemy aircraft throughout the morning, and fighters were scrambled twice at Kweilin without making contact. The Japanese arrived over Suichuan around noon, and Sharks from Captain Stewart's command were waiting for them. In the air battle that followed, two P-40Ks went down, but their pilots, Elmore P. Bullock and Max Noftsger, escaped injury. Confirmed victories were awarded to Lieutenant Noftsger and Lt. Vernon Kramer, while Stewart damaged one fighter and Capt. Eugene McGuire got a probable and a damaged. Alerts continued at Suichuan throughout the month, but most of these were nuisance raids at night until after Christmas.

The 74th and 75th squadrons were the next to tangle with Japanese aircraft. Both squadrons had several contacts on December 4. On a morning patrol north to Changteh, Lt. Wallace Cousins of the 74th was shot down when six Tojos jumped his formation. Cousins survived the encounter and returned to the 74th later in the month. Then on an escort hop to Changteh in the afternoon, sixteen Japanese fighters intercepted and shot down Capt. Paul Bell, CO of the 74th. He managed to bail out of his P-40 but broke his leg in the jump. He was sent home not long after walking in from Matshihtang, and Capt. Eugene Lundy was chosen to replace him as commander of the squadron. Several pilots, including Captain Bell, claimed probables and damageds during the day, but no victories were confirmed for the 74th.

The 75th also met resistance over Changteh on December 4. In an attack on the airfield, pilots claimed two probables and two damaged for no losses. The next day, eight Sharks of the 75th were jumped by twenty Ki-43 Oscars during a strafing mission. No P-40s were lost, but Lt. Vern Tanner had his hydraulic system shot out and had to belly-land his plane. Lieutenant Earl Green also was hit, and his plane was on fire when he landed at Hengyang.

This was at the height of the fighting around Changteh, and missions continued there for several more days. Three pilots of the 74th—Capt. Harlyn S. Vidovich, 1/Lt. Lawrence W. Smith, and 1/Lt. William O. Morin—got confirmed kills on December 5 and 6. The squadron also added two probables and seven damaged to its score-

board in ten missions to Changteh. Then on December 10, the
Japanese made a serious counterattack against the 23rd Fighter
Group.

The moon was full on the night of December 9–10, and the
Japanese took advantage of it. Beginning at 3:00 A.M., bombers from
Hankow arrived over the bases at Hengyang, Kweilin, and Lingling,
dropping an occasional bomb and causing the sleeping pilots to
abandon their beds and run for the slit trenches. The nuisance
attacks kept up until dawn, when the real fireworks began.

The first big raid of the day was called in around 5:00 A.M., and
twenty-one Sharks of the 74th and 75th squadrons scrambled from
Hengyang on short notice. Lieutenant Bob Cage of the 74th, taking
off in the early morning gloom, had just cleared the runway when he
clipped another P-40 that was taxiing out. Cage crashed off the end
of the runway, but neither he nor the pilot of the other Shark was
injured. Meanwhile, 1/Lt. Altheus B. Jarmon, a seasoned and popular pilot in the 74th, ran over a piece of shrapnel and blew a tire on
his P-40 while taxiing out to take off. He shut down the plane,
jumped out, and ran for a trench as the bombs began to fall.
Unfortunately, a fragmentation bomb fell in the trench with him,
and he was killed when it exploded.

One of the pilots who did manage to take off was 2/Lt. Charles E.
("Smoky") Cook Jr., a relatively new member of the 74th. He was flying a P-40N-1, squadron number 27. Cook kept a diary during his
tour in China, and he recorded the following about his December 10
mission.

"We took off in darkness with three waves [of] Japs coming in.
Several ships cracked up taking off. I made a pass at six Zeros at
15,000 feet, damaged one, and two Zeros got on my tail. My canopy
blew off, so I had to leave the fight and landed at Lingling. My tire
blew out on landing. Another raid hit Lingling, but I had to stay on
the ground. My plane was strafed as they bombed the field. I
watched from a hill."[3]

In all, the 74th recorded one probable and three damaged in the
morning fight. The 75th pilots had more luck, both good and bad.
Four of its Sharks engaged seven Oscars at nineteen thousand feet
while the first wave of Japanese bombers was making its run over
the field from two thousand feet. It was a new tactic for the Japanese
to bomb from low level, perhaps adopted because their bombardiers'
aim from higher altitudes was generally bad. When the third wave of
bombers swept over the field, 1/Lt. Deacon Lewis was ready for
them. He made a diving head-on pass on the bombers from the
south and flamed a Ki-48 Lily right over the field. The smoking
bomber pulled up, did a wingover, and nose-dived into the ground
about two hundred yards from the hostel. Lewis tried to take aim at

a second bomber, but his speed was too great and he overran it. By that time, the escorts were all over him and his guns were nearly out of ammunition. He dived out of the fight, followed the river down to Lingling, and landed there.

Other bombers were destroyed by Lts. Jesse Gray and Wiltz ("Flash") Segura, but 1/Lt. Robert Beauchamp was killed in the fight. He tried to bail out of his burning P-40K near the field but was too low. His parachute only partially opened, and Beauchamp fell to his death. Segura ran out of gas returning to base and had to land his Shark on a road. The plane nosed over on its landing run, but Segura was unhurt.

The Lingling raid came in at 1:00 P.M. and consisted of eleven Ki-21 Sally bombers escorted by nine Oscar fighters. The 74th Squadron pilots who had landed there with Cook in the morning scrambled to meet the raid, and a sharp fight followed. Lieutenant Sam Kinsey shot down one Oscar about fifteen miles northeast of the field and damaged two others. All the P-40s returned safely, but several others parked on the field, including Cook's, were badly damaged in the enemy attack.

The Japanese never did attack Kweilin on December 10, but the 76th Fighter Squadron was busy there anyway. The squadron scrambled five times during the day in response to net reports, but each time the enemy aircraft turned away before the 76th could catch them.

The 76th had moved virtually all of its planes out of Suichuan on December 7, so when the Japanese raided the base on December 11, they did not find much of a target. When word reached Hengyang that the enemy was hitting Suichuan, Maj. Elmer Richardson scrambled nine Sharks of the 74th and 75th to go after them. Richardson, battle-wise commander of the 75th, knew they could not get to Suichuan fast enough to catch the Japanese there, so he took a gamble. Richardson figured the enemy aircraft had come from Nanchang, the Japanese stronghold south of Poyang Lake in Kiangsi Province. Richardson set a northeasterly course and proceeded directly to Nanchang.

When Richardson's Sharks arrived, they found a perfect setup. The Japanese aircraft were in their landing pattern—slow, low on fuel, and extremely vulnerable to attack. Richardson led the Sharks straight into the middle of them, and they had a field day. Within minutes, they shot down seven Japanese fighters. Then the Sharks went down and strafed the airfield at Nanchang, destroying several more planes in the process.

Two of the aerial victories were credited to Maj. Witold A. Urbanowicz. He was a Polish officer who had come to China "on leave" following a highly successful combat tour with the Royal Air

Force. Urbanowicz was credited with seventeen victories during 1940 and 1941 while flying in England, and then he was assigned to Washington, D.C., as the assistant Polish air attaché. The RAF would not let him return to combat status, so he wangled an assignment to China, ostensibly to observe General Chennault's fighter tactics. Urbanowicz observed them more closely than his superiors expected by getting himself assigned to combat duty with the 75th Fighter Squadron. He flew with the squadron throughout the winter of 1943–44 but did not have further opportunities to engage enemy aircraft after December. Urbanowicz chose to stay in the United States following the war and eventually became a U.S. citizen.[4]

The Japanese had taken substantial losses on December 10 and 11, but they were not finished trying to destroy the Forward Echelon. According to their intelligence, the raids of the past two days had been highly successful. In fact, they believed forty-one U.S. aircraft, including at least twenty-three P-40s, had been destroyed. Hoping to finish the job, the Japanese sent heavy raids down from Hankow again on December 12. Had they known how small the actual American losses were—three P-40s, one B-25, and one B-24— the Japanese might have reconsidered continuing the campaign for another day.

The warning net started giving plots on enemy raids early in the morning on December 12, but the first ones proved false alarms. Then in the mid-morning, as the haze was beginning to burn off, the squadrons at Hengyang got the order to scramble. The 74th, led by Capt. Eugene Lundy, made contact right over the hostel. Lundy managed to get behind one Oscar and shoot it down, but then his engine was hit and he had to bail out.

The 74th's CO cleared his falling aircraft, pulled the rip cord on his parachute, and began his slow descent to earth. Then Lundy heard the roar of an aircraft engine and looked around to see, to his horror, that an Oscar was taking aim at him while he hung helplessly below his parachute. The Oscar bored in close and opened fire. Through either luck or the Japanese pilot's poor aim, not one bullet struck Lundy. The Oscar flew off toward Nanchang, and Lundy completed his parachute ride without further incident. He returned to the squadron later in the day. Two other members of his flight, 1/Lts. Fred Meyer and Bob Milks, also got confirmed kills during the scrap.

While Lundy's flight was engaged over the field, another flight of the 74th set out in pursuit of the Japanese. Led by Capt. Lynn F. Jones, this flight repeated Major Richardson's success of the previous day by heading directly to the Japanese base at Nanchang. The Sharks caught the enemy planes near Nanchang, and Jones shot down an Oscar. It was his fifth victory, which added his name to the 23rd's growing list of aces. Two probables and three damaged also were awarded to the pilots in Jones's flight.

Also scrambling at Hengyang that morning was the 75th Fighter Squadron with Major Richardson leading. The Sharks met two flights of Ki-48 Lily bombers at two thousand feet that were covered by about thirty Ki-43 Oscars stacked up to about ten thousand feet. The twelve Sharks made their first attack over the field and then chased the Japanese off to the northeast. During this engagement, one of the more remarkable kills ever recorded by the 23rd Fighter Group took place.

Second Lieutenant Donald S. Lopez, a replacement pilot who had only been with the squadron for a few weeks, was flying in the number three slot as wingman to the leader of White Flight, 1/Lt. Jim Anning. Flying an old P-40K named "Duchess" that was normally assigned to 1/Lt. Leonard Aylesworth, Lopez followed his leader closely as the 75th gained altitude on the scramble. They had reached fifteen thousand feet when Anning spotted the Oscar escorts, dropped his belly tank, and winged over in a dive. Lopez followed, though at this point he had not yet spotted the enemy fighters himself.

The Sharks came down in a screaming dive, and Lieutenant Anning nailed an Oscar in the first pass. Lopez picked up the Oscars in time to snap off a burst at one of them before he plunged through their formation and began hauling back on his stick to recover. In the process, Lopez lost sight of Anning in the haze, but as he was circling to regain altitude, he spotted an Oscar chasing another P-40. They were quite a distance away, but Lopez decided to join the chase.

Lopez closed in behind the Oscar, but then the enemy pilot spotted him and whipped around in a tight turn to make a head-on pass at Lopez. The P-40 and the Oscar closed the distance between them rapidly, and both pilots opened fire. Lopez could see his bullets flashing as they struck the front of the Oscar's radial engine, and then the two planes were right on top of each other. The Oscar pilot flipped into a vertical right turn in an attempt to avoid collision, but he was too late. Lopez felt a jolt, and his plane yawed heavily to the left. The two fighters had collided. Lopez glanced over his shoulder and saw the Oscar whirling away in a crazy dive, minus its left wing. His own left wing was mangled; the wingtip and pitot tube were gone and the end of the aileron shredded. He tested the controls and found to his surprise that the old Shark was still flying more or less normally. His airspeed indicator would not work without the pitot tube, but that did not present a problem either.

Lopez flew around in the haze trying to figure out where he was and eventually met up with Anning again. He returned to Hengyang for a safe landing. Lopez recalled that Aylesworth had a few jocular remarks to make about the young pilot's combat style when he saw the damage to "Duchess"; however, the old P-40 flew again with a new wing.[5]

Lopez's victory originally was credited as a probable but later was confirmed. It was one of nine kills by the 75th that day, and 1/Lt. Curtis L. Scoville was high man with two confirmed. On the ledger's negative side, 2/Lt. John A. Beaty was killed. Beaty, the number four man in Anning's flight, was on his first combat mission. His plane was hit during the initial pass through the Oscars. The ground crews watched helplessly from the airfield as Beaty's plane fell in a flat spin and crashed in the southern section of the city of Hengyang. Another pilot, 2/Lt. Frank McEnteer, was wounded in the shoulder and eye but made a successful landing, while 2/Lt. Richard ("Dick") Jones made a forced landing near the railroad tracks north of Hengyang and rode the train back to base.

The Japanese may have thought they hurt the U.S. forces in eastern China with the December 10–12 raids, but they also knew how badly their own forces had suffered in the fighting. That, combined with the persisting ground fog and haze over the Forward Echelon's bases that gave their bombardiers fits, forced the Japanese to call off the daylight assaults for the time being.

On December 13, the 23rd Fighter Group went right back on the offensive. The Japanese ground offensive at Changteh had almost run its course by this time, so the 74th Squadron sent eight P-40s to escort bombers to Lichow, a supply center near Tungting Lake. No enemy fighters responded, but on the return flight, one of the pilots spotted about thirty sampans on the lake near the city of Nanhsiang. That afternoon, eight Sharks of the 75th and eight fighters from the 51st Fighter Group went back and strafed them. The Sharks encountered heavy ground fire from Nanhsiang, but they all returned safely to Hengyang. The 74th flew similar missions on December 14, 15, 16, 18, 20, and 21 to keep pressure on the retreating Japanese ground forces.

Meanwhile, the 75th flew another outstanding mission on December 15, when Major Richardson led eight of his own Sharks and eight from the 26th Fighter Squadron of the 51st Group on a strafing attack against the major enemy air base at Paliuchi. This base, just north of Tungting Lake and not far from the Yangtze River, would receive a lot of attention from the Sharks in the coming months. On this day, Richardson's P-40s made their approach north of the field and achieved complete surprise. After the first pass, they circled around the base and made a second run from west to east. Major Richardson, Capt. Don Glover, and 1/Lt. Joe Brown each destroyed a bomber, and several other bombers were damaged. In addition, a line of gasoline trucks was set afire near a revetment, and one pilot peppered a radio station, probably damaging extensively the equipment inside. Again, no enemy fighters attempted to intervene, and everyone got home safely. On the next day, Major Richardson went right back to Paliuchi and did the same thing all over again. This time there were fewer aircraft on the field, but Richardson confirmed another bomber destroyed, as did Lt. James Vurgaropulos. On this mission, heavy ground fire arced up at the passing Sharks from pillboxes and gun pits on the field, but again all planes returned to Hengyang safely. The fighters attempted a third strike against Paliuchi on December 17, but they ran into bad weather on their way to the target and had to abandon the mission.

On December 19, the warning net began to note signs of the Japanese Imperial Air Force coming back to life in the Hankow area. Over the next few days, all three squadrons of the 23rd scrambled on alerts, but the Japanese aircraft failed to approach and no contact was made. Night raids also resumed, but again the ground haze and fog helped shield the bases. Japanese engines could be heard above the field, and occasionally bombs would explode in the distance.

Finally, the 76th Fighter Squadron scrambled two P-51As on the morning of December 22 to chase a Japanese recon aircraft that reportedly was approaching the field. First Lieutenant Henry Farris, the flight leader, and 2/Lt. Daniel Schaible climbed to twenty-eight thousand feet and spotted a Ki-46 Dinah coming toward them. The Mustang pilots pressed their attack in a head-on pass, and the Dinah went down on fire. Farris got credit for the victory.

While the weather was causing problems in eastern China, Japanese air forces in Burma mounted heavy raids against Yunnanyi and Kunming on December 18, 19, and 22. The squadrons of the 51st Fighter Group ably countered the attacks. In fact, Major Liles of the 16th Squadron, who had served so long in the 23rd Fighter Group before his squadron's transfer, shot down an Oscar on December 18 for his fifth kill and became the 51st's first ace. In all, the 51st recorded thirty-four victories during the three days of fighting.

Meanwhile, Col. Casey Vincent was anxiously awaiting a break in the weather so he could resume offensive operations against targets in the Canton–Hong Kong region. His chance came on December 23. That day he sent P-40s and P-51As of the 74th and 76th squadrons to escort B-24s of the 308th Bomb Group to Canton. They were intercepted by about fifteen enemy fighters over the target, and the P-40s attacked while the P-51As held their position with the bombers. The Sharks hit the Ki-44 Tojos from above and behind, though several of the enemy fighters were able to make runs at the B-24s. Confirmed kills were credited to 1/Lt. Vern Kramer of the

76th, 1/Lt. Richard Mauritson of the 74th, and Flight Officer Wilson, one of the 16th Fighter Squadron pilots who were on temporary duty at Hengyang at that time.

Unfortunately, the bombers hit the wrong target, dumping their loads on the empty White Cloud Airdrome instead of Tien Ho. The B-24 crews got overexcited during the mission and jammed up the radio communications. This almost had tragic results, as Lt. Wallace Cousins of the 74th got lost on the way home and had trouble getting a fix from Hengyang through all the chatter on his radio. He made it home safely after some frustrating moments trying to figure out where he was.

Vincent sent the B-24s back to Canton on December 24 with similar results. This time, they bombed an auxiliary field instead of Tien Ho. Again, Japanese fighters intercepted, but this time there were many more of them. The Shark pilots claimed just one probable, by Capt. Lee Manbeck of the 76th, and a couple of Oscars damaged. Two Sharks failed to return from the mission. Lieutenant Virgil A. Butler of the 74th made a forced landing at Chaoping on the way home, and 2/Lt. Harry Zavakos of the 76th crash-landed out of gas. Zavakos filed the following report when he returned to the squadron:

"There were only three P-40s in our flight, and two of them turned back due to engine trouble. I joined up with another flight of P-40s, and there was another P-40 who joined on my wing.

"When we were just about on the target, someone said on the radio, 'Zeros, at just about every hour of the clock!' I didn't see any, but when I turned around I saw my wingman drop his belly tank, and I did the same. Then I saw him go straight down and smoking, so I knew there were some Zeros nearby. I spotted one a thousand feet below me and back a short distance. I watched him for awhile, then decided to make a pass on him, go out some distance, and come back making another pass and still stay with the bombers. All our other fighters were pulled out, because I didn't see any others around.

"I made my pass, went out a short way (but not far enough), turned, and made another tight pass. The Jap flipped on my tail and started pumping away. I dove out but my engine started running rough, and I ran out of gas on one tank so I changed tanks and dove out again. My engine was still coughing and acting up, and this Zero was closing in on me. I was now on the deck and had everything forward, but my engine was still acting up. I thought my engine would quit, so I unfastened my safety belt, just in case. He must have thought I was on fire. I pulled away from him and started heading home.

A Chinese soldier runs up a two-ball alert on the *jing bao* pole at Kweilin. The effectiveness of the 23rd Fighter Group's air defense in China depended on a complex air-raid warning system consisting of ground observers reporting to a control center that in turn alerted air bases of impending attacks. One ball meant enemy aircraft had been spotted, two balls indicated enemy aircraft were approaching the base, and three balls meant an attack was imminent. *Molesworth collection*

Colonel David L. ("Tex") Hill, the tall officer standing at right, welcomes Chinese leader Generalissimo Chiang Kai-shek to Kweilin on February 5, 1944. The aircraft in the background is a C-47 transport. At the time, Colonel Hill was commander of the 23rd Fighter Group, which was headquartered at Kweilin. *Molesworth collection*

The first aircraft assigned to the 23rd Fighter Group were hand-me-down P-40s left over when the American Volunteer Group (AVG) disbanded in July 1942. This one, assigned to the 75th Fighter Squadron at Hengyang, still carries the Chinese serial number P-8194 on its tail. While with the AVG, this aircraft was assigned to Squadron Leader Bob Neale, the unit's top-scoring ace. Note the white fuselage band marking, which the 75th inherited from the 1st Pursuit Squadron, AVG. The plane also displays the AVG "flying tiger" insignia, as well as the 1st Pursuit Squadron's "Adam and Eve" green apple marking. *Don Hyatt*

Ex-AVG P-40E, number 131, of the 76th Fighter Squadron patrols near Kweilin during the summer of 1942. The fuselage band aft of the number is blue. Note the pilot is flying with the canopy open, and either a bomb or a drop tank has been released from the shackles under the centerline of the fuselage. *Bill Johnston*

First Lieutenant Jack Best of the 16th Fighter Squadron poses at Kunming with his P-40E, number 13, which he took over from Maj. Harry B. ("Hal") Young in the fall of 1942. Later, the plane was renumbered 27 and named "Fogarty Fagin III." It is painted in dark earth and tan camouflage, which was applied to most of the 16th's P-40Es. The color of the propeller spinner is unknown. *Jack Best*

First Lieutenant George Barnes of the 16th Fighter Squadron watches while his crew chief, Staff Sergeant Smith, works on their P-40E, number 24. Note the fuel filler cap is open behind Barnes's leg. Photo taken at Hengyang, September 1942. *George Barnes*

Pilots of the 16th Fighter Squadron gather outside the alert shack at Kweilin, November 1942. From left, Lts. Llewelyn Couch, John Lombard, Bernard Dyrland, unidentified, L. F. ("Chip") Myers, Clyde Slocumb, and possibly L. E. Hay. Lombard later would command the 74th Fighter Squadron, and Slocumb the 75th. *George Barnes*

Key officers of the China Air Task Force (CATF) display a "flying tiger" banner presented by the Chinese to Maj. Gen. Claire Chennault, CATF commander, at Kunming in early 1943. They are, from left, Col. Clinton D. ("Casey") Vincent, CATF operations and executive officer; Maj. Albert ("Ajax") Baumler, 74th Fighter Squadron commander; Lt. Col. Bruce K. Holloway (kneeling), 23rd Fighter Group commander; Lt. Col. Henry F. Strickland, CATF adjutant; and Chennault. *Bruce K. Holloway*

Major Hal Pike of the 16th Fighter Squadron shot down this Japanese Ki-48 Lily bomber near Kweilin on November 23, 1942. The bomber, assigned to the 90th Air Regiment at Hankow, had two yellow bands painted vertically around the rear of its fuselage. *George W. Hazlett*

This Republic P-43A Lancer was assigned to the 76th Fighter Squadron at Kunming in the fall of 1942. Several of these fighters were "loaned" to the 23rd Fighter Group by the Chinese Air Force, hence the Chinese serial number P-1237 on the tail. The Lancer performed well, but its leaky fuel tanks and lack of armor protection for the pilot made it a dangerous aircraft to fly in combat. *George Spencer*

This Japanese A6M Zero fighter was captured by the Chinese in late 1942 and rebuilt by mechanics of the 23rd Fighter Group under the direction of Staff Sgt. Gerhard Neumann. Here, Maj. Ajax Baumler of the 74th Fighter Squadron taxis the plane out for a test flight prior to its shipment to the States for evaluation. Unfortunately, the plane was damaged during shipment and never flew again. *Leon Klesman*

Wing guns of the fighters were aimed so their fire converged at a point several hundred yards in front of the plane. Here, P-40K number 174 of the 75th Fighter Squadron has its guns bore-sighted, probably at Kunming. Note how the plane's tail is propped on the bed of a truck so the guns will be pointed horizontally. Note also the patches of dark olive paint applied to the tail and rear fuselage of the plane. *Bill Harris*

Captain Bob Liles of the 16th Fighter Squadron poses with his new P-40K-5, "Duke," probably at Chanyi in February or March 1943. Liles continued to fly this plane, serial number 42-9912, for more than a year. His crew chief, Sgt. Floyd Avrett, later painted a diving eagle on both sides of the rudder and the number 400 on the fin. *George Barnes*

Captain John Hampshire of the 75th Fighter Squadron was the 23rd Fighter Group's leading ace with thirteen confirmed victories when he was shot down and killed during a dogfight over Changsha on May 2, 1943. He is pictured here, probably in early 1943, in his P-40K-1, serial number 42-45732. *Jack Cook*

Captain Bill Hawkins flew this P-40K throughout his tour in China with the 74th Fighter Squadron, 1942–43. Here, he points out several of the patched bullet holes in its fuselage. This picture probably was taken at Kweilin in September 1943. *Bill Hawkins*

Captain J. M. "Willie" Williams, an ace with six confirmed victories, commanded the 76th Fighter Squadron during autumn 1943. He was shot down twice and walked back to safety both times. Photo taken at Lingling, May 1943. *John Stewart*

Major Elmer ("Rich") Richardson flew this P-40K, number 171, "Evelyn II," while flying with the 23rd Fighter Group in 1943. One of the original Panama pilots assigned to the 23rd Fighter Group, Richardson commanded the 75th from October 1943 through March 1944 and was an eight-victory ace. *Elmer Richardson*

This P-40N-1, number 41, of the 74th Fighter Squadron had its landing gear collapse during a landing at Kweilin in the spring of 1944 and lost its propeller. The second aircraft in the line of parked P-40s is "War Weary," P-40K number 47 of the 74th. *John Wheeler*

Captain John S. Stewart was the top-scoring ace of the 76th Fighter Squadron, with nine confirmed victories. He commanded the task force at Suichuan in the autumn of 1943 and assumed command of the full squadron in December of that year. He returned to the States in May 1944 after two full years of overseas duty. Note the 23rd Fighter Group patch on Stewart's flight jacket. *Dick Templeton*

The last wartime commander of the 118th Tactical Recon Squadron was Capt. Marvin Lubner, shown here with his P-51K, "Barfly," number 199. Lubner was an ace, with six confirmed victories scored while flying in the 76th Fighter Squadron during his first tour in China, 1942–43. *Marvin Lubner*

Second Lieutenant John W. Wheeler of the 74th Fighter Squadron sits on alert in the cockpit of a P-40N at Kweilin in the spring of 1944. The aircraft behind him also are P-40Ns, numbers 28 and 37. *John Wheeler*

Replacement pilots received operational training on war-weary fighters at Karachi, India, prior to being assigned to combat squadrons in China. Second Lieutenant Jerome P. Ellis flew "Zola," a P-51A Mustang retired by the 76th Fighter Squadron, at Karachi in the summer of 1944. Ellis later flew his combat tour with the 76th. *Jerome Ellis*

Lieutenants Don Lopez (*left*) and Dick Jones of the 75th Fighter Squadron discuss their mission of July 5, 1944, during which Lopez barely avoided being shot down by a Japanese fighter that surprised him near Changsha. Damage to the left aileron of his P-40N is visible between the pilots. Note the armorer on top of the wing removing a belt of .50-caliber bullets from the ammunition bay. *Ed Bollen*

Lieutenant Colonel Charles E. Griffith, a veteran of the campaign in the Aleutian Islands during 1942–43, came to China in mid-1944 to command the 76th Fighter Squadron. "Griff," as his pilots called him, was killed when he crashed a P-51 Mustang while stunting with another pilot over Luliang air base on December 18, 1944. Note the 76th Fighter Squadron patch on his flight jacket. *Don Scott*

Colonel Ed Rector, CO of the 23rd Fighter Group, pins a medal on Lt. Col. John C. Herbst of the 74th Fighter Squadron. The ceremony probably took place at Luliang in February 1945, just before Herbst left China at the end of his combat tour. *Leon Klesman*

Major Donald L. Quigley was the commanding officer (CO) of the 75th Fighter Squadron when he was shot down and captured north of Hengyang on August 10, 1944. He remained a prisoner of the Japanese for the rest of the war. Quigley, a five-victory ace, is seated here on his assigned airplane, P-40N number 175, named "Rene the Queen" after his wife. The P-40N behind him is named "Dipsey Doodle." *Don Quigley*

Nakajima Ki-43 Oscars were the Japanese fighters most often encountered by the 23rd Fighter Group during World War II. This Oscar I was captured and repainted in Chinese Air Force markings at Kweilin in the autumn of 1944. Note the crude telescope gun sight and two-bladed propeller, identifying this as an early-model Ki-43. *Everett Hyatt*

The 118th Tactical Reconnaissance Squadron joined the 23rd Fighter Group in June 1944. In mid-November the squadron moved to Suichuan, where this picture of the 118th's pilots was taken. Top row (*from left*): Roy Christenson, Lynn Decker, Hiram Bushong, Frank Palmer, Maurice Wells, Bert Petersen, John Egan, Harold Tollett, Everson Pearsall, Carlton Covey, Claude Jackson, and Fred Lanphier. Front row: John Carpenter, Russ Williams, Nimrod Long, Samuel Bowen, Edward McComas (CO), Ray Crowell, Pete Petris, Max Parnell, and Billy Guy. The Mustang behind them was number 600, "Miss Revenge," an F-6C photo ship assigned to Major McComas. Note the round camera port on the lower fuselage. *Berthold Petersen*

Lieutenants Fred Richardson (*left*) and Rusty Packard (*right*) of the 118th Tactical Recon Squadron pose in spring 1945 with the P-51C they shared, number 591, and the crew chief who kept it flying, Sergeant Moyle. The plane was named "Martha" on the left side of the nose and "Billie" plus "Still—Who Cares" on the right. Note the distinctive black lightning squadron markings. *Russell Packard*

Major John C. ("Pappy") Herbst, top ace and CO of the 74th Fighter Squadron, flew P-51B 43-7060 through most of the squadron's guerrilla operations at Kanchow, 1944–45. "Tommy's Dad," named for Herbst's son, was number 40 and displayed eighteen Japanese flags plus one German swastika to signify Herbst's final score of victories. The small lettering under the windshield, barely visible in this picture, reads: (*top line*) PILOT—MAJ. "PAPPY" J.C. HERBST, (*bottom line*) CREW CHIEF—T/SGT. B. SHIPMAN. The serial number was painted on the tail. *Barney Fudge*

The Japanese-occupied river town of Paoching comes under attack by the 76th Fighter Squadron on May 9, 1945, during the battle for Chihkiang. This was the first mission in which the 76th dropped napalm fire bombs, and their effectiveness is obvious from the large amount of smoke seen rising from the center of town. *Russell Packard*

Captain Barney Fudge of the 74th Fighter Squadron flew this handsome P-51K-1 Mustang, "Oklahoma Kid," during the final months of the war. The nose was painted solid black, standard squadron marking for this period. The small lettering under the windshield reads: (*top line*) PILOT—CAPT. B. FUDGE, (*bottom line*) C/C—ART HOLBIEN. The serial number of this fighter was 44-11459. *Barney Fudge*

Lieutenant Leroy Price of the 118th Tactical Recon Squadron survived this fire at Laohwangping. On July 23, 1945, a cluster of parafrag bombs on his P-51 failed to release during a mission, and Price tried to land with it still attached. The landing jarred the cluster loose, and two bombs exploded, setting the plane's gas tanks on fire. Price ground-looped the plane and jumped to safety but was badly burned in the process. Note the propeller is turning in this picture, indicating the engine was still running when the photo was snapped. *Ivan Ball*

"I flew my heading for about 15 minutes, then I heard some ping-ing. I thought my engine was acting up again, but then I saw some tracer and knew there was [an enemy fighter] back there. I made a sharp turn and pushed everything forward again, and this time I made sure I got rid of him. Incidentally, this was a very hazy day and visibility was very poor.

"I started for home again. I noticed I was getting low on gas, so I flew my heading until I switched to my reserve tank. Then I changed my heading to due west. I flew this heading for quite some time so control could get a plot on me, or maybe I would intercept the rail-road tracks. I called control and asked them if they had any plots on me, and they said no. I only had 12 gallons of gas left, so I circled a town and fired my guns and called control again. Still they had no plots on me. After a few minutes they called me and told me to circle another town. I went south and circled another town and fired my guns and still no plots on me.

"I called control again and said I would have to belly in. Just then the warning light came on. I had already picked a spot [to land], but I looked down and remembered my safety belt wasn't fastened. I had a heck of a time fastening it, because it was stuck under the seat, but finally I got it. By then I was right over the spot I had picked, and high. I used a little flaps and wasn't going down fast enough, so I slipped her down to the deck. I didn't want to go around, so I slammed her onto the ground. I hit once, twice, and then rolled over on my back. I pulled myself out of the ship shaken up quite a bit; I came out with a few bruises and a couple of cuts.

"There were a couple of Chinese around, but they didn't come out to the ship, they stayed up on a hill. I picked up my chute and walked toward them. I showed them my flag, and they came down. Then I went to work on them with the Pointee-Talkee; told them to guard the plane.

"They took me to a Chinese military home and got me a room. I asked them if there was a telephone around and they said no. The next day they took me out to the plane, and they had concealed it very well. I imagine it would have been very hard to see from the air. The trip back home was a long, tiresome ride in riverboats upstream."[6]

Zavakos returned to action with the 76th and shot down an enemy fighter in March 1944. Later he developed a reputation as the most skillful dive-bombing pilot in the squadron.

Colonel Vincent decided the B-24s had used up enough of his pre-cious fuel for questionable results, so he sent them back to western China. Christmas 1943 was a day off for the men of the 23rd Fighter Group. The 76th had a party to welcome Captain Williams and

Lieutenant Colbert, who had just returned after being shot down December 1. The 74th was back together at Kweilin, its Hengyang detachment having returned the previous day. The squadron and group headquarters personnel had a big Christmas dinner. And at Hengyang, Chinese officials brought gifts of gratitude from all over Hunan Province to the airfield and presented them to the men of the 75th Fighter Squadron.

On the day after Christmas, the 76th Fighter Squadron picked up everything and moved its entire operation to Suichuan air base. The Japanese intelligence system noted the move, however, and the warning net began to report enemy aircraft activity first thing in the morning of December 27. Captain John Stewart, CO of the 76th, led a mixed formation of P-51As and P-40s early in the morning after a report of enemy aircraft approaching from the south. The Japanese only came as far as Kukong before turning around, so the 76th was unable to make contact, and Stewart led his fighters home to refuel. It was a common occurrence in China, though every American squadron commander tried his best to avoid wasting precious gasoline on these wild goose chases.

Two balls went up on the *jing bao* pole again at about 11:30 A.M., and Stewart scrambled his planes once more. As commander of the air units at Suichuan, Stewart determined how the gasoline would be used, and as CO of the 76th, he was responsible for providing air defense for the base. He was being very careful not to let his precious Mustangs get caught on the ground, especially not on their first full day on the job.

Stewart's planes, which numbered seven P-51As and seven P-40s, were airborne by 11:45 A.M. They climbed rapidly to gain as much altitude as possible before the enemy formation arrived, but this time the new Japanese low-level bombing tactics worked against the Americans. With Stewart and his boys bouncing the fighter escorts at twelve thousand feet, the Japanese bombers swept over the base from the south nearly on the deck and dropped their bombs with unusual accuracy from fifteen hundred feet. Colonel Casey Vincent was on the airfield that day and watched helplessly as the string of bombs fell from the sky and exploded in a direct line toward him. Fortunately, the bombs bracketed him and fell on either side, leaving the Forward Echelon's commander unharmed but thoroughly shaken.

One bomb wrecked the pilots' alert shack and burned everything inside, including all of Lt. Glen Beneda's clothes and Lt. Stephen Bonner's prized camera. A B-25 parked in a revetment close by was hit and began to burn. Also in the revetment were thirty-six drums of gasoline and a P-51A Mustang. Lieutenant Elmore P. Bullock had scrambled in the plane earlier, but after its canopy came unfastened in flight, he brought the Mustang in for an emergency landing, taxied it into the supposed safety of the revetment, and shut it down. He jumped from the cockpit and into the closest slit trench just as the enemy bombs began to fall.

Within moments, a bomb landed in the revetment, setting the B-25 and several drums of gas on fire. Staff Sergeant Robert S. Yarano of Cleveland, Ohio, who had been watching from another slit trench, ran to the revetment in hopes of saving any undamaged equipment from the fire. When he saw that Bullock's Mustang was intact, Yarano gathered several nearby Chinese coolies to help him push it out of the shelter. When they had pushed the fighter to the entrance of the revetment, Yarano hopped into the cockpit and started the engine, hoping to taxi the Mustang away. Yarano was not familiar with the new fighters, however, and could not get it moving.

Lieutenant Bullock saw what Yarano was trying to do and came running. He took Yarano's place in the cockpit and taxied the Mustang to safety, passing under the burning bomber's wing in the process. Two minutes later the B-25 and several bombs erupted in a tremendous explosion, but by that time the Mustang was out of harm's way. Bullock and Yarano both were awarded the Soldier's Medal for their bravery in saving the Mustang.

While all this was happening on the airfield, Stewart's fighters were having a tremendous battle with the Japanese escort fighters above. Twelve of the thirteen pilots filed claims after the mission, resulting in credit for five kills, and only one pilot—2/Lt. Robert L. Schaeffer—failed to return. Schaeffer filed the following report later:

"I was in a P-40, squadron number 112, rolling straight down on a Zero's tail when I felt the engine jump, looked down at my manifold pressure gauge, which started dropping, and realized I was hit. So I dove away to the east on the deck. Tried to use the throttle and prop controls, but both were useless.

"The fight was still going on over the field, and as I had only 20 inches Hg [mercury—the measure of the engine's manifold pressure] showing, decided I would have to sit down someplace else. I picked out a sandbar along the river, cut the engine with the mixture control, pumped down full flaps, and bellied in. I overshot a bit and bounced off an eight-foot bank onto another sandbar. After making sure there were no Zeros around to strafe me, I called YK9 [Suichuan operations] for about five minutes on my radio, the receiver of which still worked. I got no results, so I quit and looked up to see a Chinese boy about 12, hiding a knife behind him that was almost as big as he.

"I jumped out of the cockpit, waved my flag, and shouted 'Megwa,' at which he stopped and saluted me. About that time several Chinese came across the river and walked over to me. I tried to use my Pointee-Talkee but didn't get anywhere. They wanted me to go with them, so I gathered up my chute and everything loose in the plane and went to a sampan which carried me across the river. We grounded about 10 feet from the shore, and an old man carried me piggy-back to the sandbar. When he sat me down, everyone clapped and cheered. A boy about 15 came forward and asked me in English what country I was from. I said, 'America,' which he repeated. That started more clapping and cheering.

"Several boys grabbed me by the arm and almost dragged me along a trail to the Changsi Middle School. Several teachers, all of whom spoke some English, met me and took me to the principal's office. I assured them I was not hurt, washed up, and insisted that they call YK9 and tell them I was OK. They said it was not possible to call direct, but that they would notify authorities as soon as possible. I told them I wanted to start for home immediately, but they said I must rest and that a messenger was coming from YK9 to take me back."

The friendly Chinese finally convinced Lieutenant Schaeffer to spend the night with them at the school. He returned to Suichuan the next day.

While Lieutenant Schaeffer was on the road back to Suichuan December 28, Captain Stewart led a flight of four P-51As on an uneventful mission north. It was supposed to be an escort for bombers, but the planes became separated in thick haze, and Stewart brought the Mustangs home after a sweep along the Yangtze River. Back at Suichuan, a lone Japanese recon ship made a high-altitude run over the base about 10:00 A.M. Captain Lee Manbeck took off in pursuit but was unable to catch up with the snooper.

Action continued at Suichuan on December 29, but this day was marked by tragedy, not triumph. Another escort mission was planned for four Mustangs, this time with 1/Lt. Stephen Bonner leading. A line of planes was parked along the runway as the Mustangs took off, and Bonner and his wingman cleared them without any problem. The second element was not so fortunate. Captain Manbeck took off, but his wingman, 1/Lt. Bruce G. Boylan, lost control and crashed into the line of parked planes. Boylan's plane, full of fuel for the mission, burst into flames. There was no fire-fighting equipment available at Suichuan, and the best that anyone could do was to push nearby planes away so the flames would not spread to them. The men had no way to save Boylan, and it was small consolation when the flight surgeon, Capt. Robert Merrill, said later that the pilot had been killed on impact and did not suffer in the flames. In all, one P-51 and two P-40s were destroyed and two more P-40s were damaged in the accident. The subsequent mission was uneventful.

The Japanese added to the misery at Suichuan early the next morning. It was just 6:45 A.M. on December 30 when eight enemy fighters roared over the field at low level, their guns blazing in a strafing attack. The strafers set up in a pattern of lazy eights over the revetments while twelve escort fighters circled at higher altitude for protection. A mixed formation of two Sharks and six Mustangs had taken off a few minutes before the raiders appeared, and the U.S. pilots were able to engage the top cover.

Meanwhile on the field, Staff Sgt. George H. Spencer ran to the southern end of the runway, where a water-cooled .50-caliber machine gun was mounted in a fortified pit. Spencer, a crew chief, started tracking the Japanese fighters as they passed. One plane pulled up steeply from its strafing run, and Spencer opened up on it with just the right amount of lead. He fired two bursts, totaling about 150 rounds, before his gun jammed. Spencer could not see any damage to the plane as it flew off, but some mechanics who were taking shelter on the far side of the field saw the plane nose into the ground and blow up northwest of the base. Spencer was recommended for a Silver Star in recognition of his bravery and marksmanship.

Also firing at the enemy planes from the ground that day was 2/Lt. Rick Olney, a pilot. He got off a couple of shots with his pistol but apparently did not hit anything.

In the air battle, the 76th's pilots got four kills without losing any of their own planes. One of the successful pilots was 2/Lt. Bob Schaeffer, exacting a little revenge for having been shot down three days earlier. Other victories were credited to 1/Lts. William Butler, Donald Hedrick, and Dick Templeton. On the negative side, the strafers managed to destroy one B-25 and one F-5 Lightning on the field and badly damage another B-25 and a C-47 that had landed at Suichuan on one engine the previous day.

★ ★ ★ ★

So ended combat for the 23rd Fighter Group in 1943. One other notable event took place in late December that would have a major impact on the future conduct of the war in China.

On December 23, 1943, the Fourteenth Air Force reorganized its combat forces to operate under the command of individual wings. The Chinese-American Composite Wing had several squadrons of P-40s and one squadron of B-25s already operating out of Kweilin, and more squadrons were training in Karachi for eventual operations in northern China. West of longitude line 108, the 69th Composite Wing would control air operations from its headquarters in

Kunming. And in eastern China, the 68th Composite Wing would direct operations from Kweilin.

The 23rd Fighter Group and the 11th Bomb Squadron were assigned to the 68th Wing, and that suited the personnel of both units just fine. They knew their wing commander—a great leader and a hot combat pilot—would treat them right. He was Col. Casey Vincent.

14

Quiet Before the Storm

New Year's Day 1944 began with the quiet misery of hangovers for many men of the 23rd Fighter Group. The weather cooperated for once, as low clouds and rain kept aircraft on the ground throughout eastern China all day. The respite from operations turned into tedium, however, when the bad weather stretched on through the first week of the new year.

In the operations shacks at Kweilin, Hengyang, and Suichuan the pilots played chess or cards, reread old magazines and books, talked, or dozed. When it was not raining, they would set up a net outside and play volleyball. At Hengyang and Kweilin, they could go to town on their days off. That was not much of an option at Suichuan, where the local Chinese community was just a small town.

In the hangars, a big project was under way. Bendix radio compasses were being shipped to the bases for installation in the group's aircraft. These devices were navigational aids that allowed pilots to take a "fix" from a ground transmitter to determine their location and the proper heading back to their base. Sporadic deliveries of the compasses delayed the retrofits, and it was decided to put the first ones in the planes assigned to squadron commanders and flight leaders. Of the fifty-three P-40s and P-51As assigned to the group on January 1, 1944, only ten received the new gear during the month. The project continued through April, by which time new fighters were being assigned to the group with radio compasses already installed.

Another maintenance problem noted at this time had to do with the tires on the group's P-40s. Many of these tires were recapped six-plies, which worked fine on smooth runways back in the United States, but out in China, the coarse gravel runways shredded these tires in no time. After four P-40Ks suffered blowouts in the same month, Lt. Ken LaTourelle, assistant engineering officer of the 74th, issued an urgent request for supplies of eight- or ten-ply tires for his squadron's P-40s.

The first flights of 1944 took place on January 6, when the 75th sent out a sweep from Hengyang up toward Tungting Lake and the 76th flew a practice flight at Suichuan. Then on January 9, nine P-40s of the 75th flew a river sweep on the Yangtze from Hankow eastward fifty miles to Kiukiang. They shot up six steamboats and numerous smaller craft, causing an estimated thirty to forty casualties. All of the Sharks returned safely to Hengyang. It turned out to be the 75th Squadron's most productive mission of the eight it flew in January.

Action continued the next day at Suichuan. Captain John Stewart led eight P-51As to Kienchang to make the 76th's first attempt at dive-bombing with their Mustangs. The target was a railroad bridge. The P-51A Mustang was equipped with two hard points, one under each wing, to which drop tanks or bombs could be attached. Stewart winged over and led his planes toward the bridge, released his bombs, and pulled the stick back to recover from his dive. The rest of his flight followed, and after all the bombs dropped, the bridge was still standing. Two bombs hit the railroad tracks just south of the bridge, but none of them hit the bridge itself. It was a disappointing start, but the Mustangs soon would prove themselves fine dive-bombers as well as superlative fighters.

To extract a measure of satisfaction from the mission, Captain Stewart led his Mustangs down the railroad line until they found a troop train to strafe. On the squadron commander's first pass, his gunfire tore into the engine's boiler and it exploded, stopping the train. After that the train was a sitting duck, and the Mustangs strafed it thoroughly, causing many casualties among the Japanese troops on board.

Another mission went off from Suichuan on the afternoon of January 10. This time, eight P-40s would escort three B-25s of the 11th Bomb Squadron on a Yangtze River sweep toward Kiukiang. The original flight plan called for the bombers to go all the way down the river to Wuhu, a distance of more than four hundred miles from Suichuan. This would have stretched the range of the P-40s to their very limit, with no reserve available for air combat should the Japanese attempt to intercept. At the last minute, the plan was changed. Now the mission would go directly to Anking and pick up the river there, turn southwest, and fly back to Kiukiang up the river. The Shark pilots were much relieved by the change in plans.

The P-40s were led by Capt. Richard A. Mauritson of the 74th, one of several pilots from that squadron who had been sent to Suichuan to fly with the 76th. The formation stayed low, though it meant flying in thick haze. As the planes approached Kiukiang, the bombers spotted several Japanese fighters climbing toward them. The Ki-43 Oscars were still climbing when Mauritson's Sharks jumped them from three thousand feet. The Sharks prevented the Oscars from making a single pass at the B-25s. First Lieutenant George Lee of the 74th got one confirmed kill and one damaged, 1/Lt. Henry Farris of the 76th got a probable, while Lts. Bob Schaeffer and George Lunsford of the 76th each damaged one Oscar. These were the 23rd Fighter Group's first claims of 1944; hundreds more would follow. One B-25 went down over Kiukiang, but it had been hit by ground fire from a gunboat it attacked on the river, not by the intercepting Oscars.

The Japanese responded to the resumption of U.S. air operations on the night of January 10. Flying in two-plane strikes, enemy bombers made seven attacks on Suichuan throughout the night, dropping fragmentation clusters each time. One P-51 received slight damage, but other than that the only thing the Americans lost was sleep.

The pilots at Suichuan were wide awake and ready for action on the morning of January 11 when the warning net reported a raid coming in from the north. Perhaps the Japanese thought the fighters at Suichuan had been wiped out by the night bombings. If so, they got a rude surprise. Captain Stewart led a mixed formation of four P-51As and eight P-40s off at about 7:30 A.M. He led the Mustang flight, while 1/Lts. Stephen Bonner and George Lee led the two P-40 flights.

Captain Stewart spotted the enemy formation, which consisted of three Ki-48 Lily bombers and a dozen escorting Oscars above them, approaching the field at ten thousand feet. He went straight for the bombers and sliced through them in a high-speed pass. The bombers dropped their loads prematurely and turned away from the target to run for home.

Before Stewart could turn his Mustangs around for another pass, Bonner's P-40 flight hit the bombers. Bonner picked out the Lily on the right and set its engine on fire with his first burst. The plane did not go down, though, so Bonner took up position on its tail and continued to pound .50-caliber slugs into it. Meanwhile, 1/Lt. Rick Olney took the bomber on the left. He let fly with a devastating burst of gunfire that apparently hit the bomber's cockpit. The plane nosed right over and went straight down to crash near the airfield, all in plain sight of the ground crews who cheered like fans at a football game when they saw it fall. Olney, a spirited guy with a good sense of humor, had been growing a mustache for several months and vowed that he would shave it off as soon as he scored his first confirmed kill. There was no doubt that the pilot would be using his razor as soon as he landed.

While all this was going on, Captain Stewart led his Mustang flight in for a second pass. He picked up the third bomber, which now was to the left of Bonner's victim, and poured fire into it until it dropped off in a death dive. This was Stewart's eighth victory. Now Bonner's Lily was the only one left. He continued to fire away until finally it, too, dropped off in a long dive and crashed near Taiho. Strangely, the Oscar escorts never intervened. One of them was damaged by 1/Lt. Irving Saunders, but the rest just turned around and went home. That was the end of air-to-air combat for nearly two weeks, as the weather closed back in and severely limited further operations.

That month the 74th Fighter Squadron in Kweilin flew just one mission, an escort to Hong Kong on January 23. Led by Col. Tex Hill and flown with the newly arrived 3rd Fighter Group of the Chinese-American Composite Wing, they targeted Kai Tak Airdrome on the mainland side of Hong Kong Harbor. One intercepting Oscar was shot down, as was a P-40 flown by 2/Lt. Chester Denny. He returned to the squadron, however, and went on to have an outstanding combat tour with the 74th, scoring three aerial victories and eight more on the ground.

The big blow to the 74th came five days earlier, when five pilots left Kunming in new P-40Ns with the mission of ferrying them to Kweilin. Their leader was Capt. Harlyn S. Vidovich, a highly experienced pilot. They did not arrive in Kweilin, and their fate was a mystery for more than a week until one of the pilots who survived was found and told their story. Apparently, the P-40 pilots had become trapped in the clouds and spun in. Two managed to parachute to safety, but Captain Vidovich, 1/Lt. Lawrence W. Smith, and 2/Lt. Walter C. Washer were killed. Smith was another seasoned veteran of the 74th, and Washer was a replacement pilot who was on his way to join the 76th at Suichuan.

★ ★ ★ ★

Early in February, General Chennault made a quick inspection trip to his easternmost bases. He arrived at Kweilin on February 3, then took off the next day in a transport with Col. Casey Vincent as tour director and went to Suichuan. This base was key to his plans for the future, because it was being built up to accommodate B-29 Superfortress bombers and support missions for directly bombing Japan. Pentagon planners believed the big Boeing bombers, which were still in testing at the time, would have sufficient range and firepower to attack Japan without the need of an escort.

Chennault found the base shaping up nicely. It had a long runway in operation and more under construction. The alert shacks were neat, and the men were even showing movies in the mess hall. All that Suichuan needed now was a big supply of gasoline and some B-29s to burn it up on the way to Japan. But there was reason to worry as well. Undeniably, Suichuan's location between Hankow and Canton made the base vulnerable to enemy air attack. And starting in January, intelligence sources had begun to report a buildup of Japanese ground forces in the Nanchang area, below Poyang Lake. Nanchang was a short run down the railroad tracks from Kiukiang, making it a simple task for the Japanese to transport men and equipment from the river port down to the edge of Chinese-held territory. From there, it was a straight run down the Kan River to Suichuan if the Japanese ever decided to capture the base.

Chennault also visited at the bases being expanded near Suichuan at Kanchow and Namyung before flying back to Kweilin in soupy weather. A few days later, he ordered the 449th Fighter Squadron to move from Lingling to Suichuan. That would put the long-range P-51A and P-38 fighters at the same base and make room at Lingling for another P-40 squadron of the Chinese-American Composite Wing. Now, more than ever, the fighters at Suichuan would focus their attentions on pounding the Japanese in the Kiukiang-Nanchang area.

The first such mission of the month took place on February 7, when Capt. John Stewart led four P-51As and four P-40s of the 76th for another try at bombing the Kienchang railroad bridge, which they had missed in January. This time, they used the P-40s for the assault flight, with the Mustangs for top cover. The Sharks, led by Lt. Ed Burbank, came in low to skip their bombs off the river surface, and Lt. Max Noftsger got a direct hit on the south end of the span. The other three bombs were optimistically described as "near-misses."

When the P-40s pulled up from their runs, Captain Stewart led the formation up the river to Keian, where his Mustangs strafed Japanese barracks and a storage area while the P-40s provided top cover. One of the pilots in the Mustang flight was Capt. Kenneth E. George, a newcomer to the squadron who had flown a previous tour in P-39s in the Aleutian Islands. George was leading the second element on its first pass when he felt his Mustang shudder under the impact of ground fire. He completed his run and pulled up to follow Stewart up the railroad line, but then his wingman called to report that he could see George's aircraft trailing oil or coolant behind it.

George watched his gauges closely, and soon the telltale needle on the temperature gauge began to swing around. He could feel the cockpit starting to heat up as well, so he swung out of the formation and set a course of 200 degrees to head for Suichuan. His course took him along a mountain range, and he flew close to the mountains so that he could hide in the hills in case he went down. Before long, the oil pressure gauge gave George more bad news, and then the engine began to smoke. He was too low to clear the mountains or to bail out, so he cut the engine and began looking for somewhere to land the plane. The ground below him was crisscrossed with dikes, so he chose instead to belly-land the Mustang on a hillside.

At the last moment, George saw that instead he was landing on top of a dike. The plane skidded along, dropped off the dike into a gully, and jolted along from side to side. George's shoulder straps were tight, but he bounced around quite a bit inside the cockpit. He was able to brace his forearm in front of his head, saving his face from striking the gun sight. Bruised and battered, he climbed from the cockpit to find his smoking Mustang a total wreck, with one wing crumpled and the engine torn completely out of its fuselage mounts. George avoided the first group of people he saw approaching the wreck, not sure if they were friend or foe. Later in the day, he was contacted by Chinese guerrillas. The days that followed included several skirmishes with Japanese troops, but George reached the Chinese-held town of Kian near the end of the month and was transported back to Suichuan on February 25 to resume flying.

The 76th lost another pilot three days after George, but this one did not come back. Major Lee Manbeck, who had been overseas for thirty-one months and had just received a promotion, was shot up near Kiukiang on February 10 when Oscars intercepted a combined formation of P-51s and P-38s. Manbeck bailed out, and Lt. Henry Farris reported seeing his empty parachute on the ground a few minutes later, so everyone figured Manbeck had landed in good condition.

After the mission returned to base, a report came in that an American had been seen at Kian, a town about one hour's flying time north of Suichuan. Manbeck's roommate and close friend, Lt. Stephen Bonner, got permission to fly to an auxiliary field near Kian and try to find the missing major. Bonner spent two days in the area interviewing local authorities, but he turned up nothing. Sometime later intelligence sources reported that the badly injured Manbeck had been taken prisoner. He never came home from the war, however; his fate remains unknown.[1]

The night after Manbeck was lost, an event took place at Suichuan that gave the morale of the 76th personnel a real boost. Vernon J. Kramer, who at that time was the operations officer of the squadron, wrote, "We had been bombed several nights prior to this, and during our evening meal we received word from the Chinese net that engine noise, Jap bomber or bombers, was headed our way. Either John Stewart or myself suggested that we try to intercept the bombers.

Captain Bill Smith took his jeep down to the north end of the runway and turned his lights on to help guide us down the runway. The weather was clear with about a half moon, so it was bright.

"About 7:30 P.M. we took off, John first as we had decided he would cruise at 3,000 feet and I would hold at 2,000 feet so we would not collide or shoot each other down. After we took off, I circled south of the runway as the Japs always came in from the south and headed north to their home base, Hankow. I could see clearly any aircraft above me, but looking down it was very black as there were no lights below except a very few bonfires. Therefore, I would not be able to pick up an aircraft flying under me. However, there was a small river flowing east to west just south of the airfield and it reflected moonlight, so I could see an aircraft flying below me there.

"I was flying east along the river when I spotted the Jap bomber below me. I knew it wasn't John, as it had twin tails, so I attacked it from the left rear. When I thought I was in range I fired a burst from the P-40's six .50 caliber guns. Much to my surprise, I became blinded by the tracers and momentarily went on instruments. Also to my surprise, the Jap bomber kept on going with apparently no hits. I recovered from my shock of firing guns in the dark and closed back in on the bomber. By that time, the tail gunner apparently saw me and began firing.

"I focused my gun sight on the left engine, giving it a good blast, and then moved the sight to the cockpit of the bomber. The plane caught fire and went down. We landed without further incident. I went to the downed bomber the next day, looking for a sword, but no luck. However, I did pick up a pistol, a cylinder head and a piece of sheet metal as souvenirs. I believe this is one of the few successful night encounters of the war in China."[2]

Indeed, it was the first successful night interception since Johnny Alison and Ajax Baumler did it back in July 1942. Kramer's target went down in full view of the men on the ground at Suichuan and crashed with its bomb load still on board. A tremendous explosion lit up the night sky as the men cheered. Then another enemy bomber buzzed low over the field and dropped its bombs as its gunners fired wildly. The gunners in the machine-gun pits around the field blazed away as well, but the plane escaped into the darkness.

Suichuan was spared the enemy's attention on February 11, but the Japanese came back the next day with a formation of Oscars and Tojos. Captain John Stewart sent up everything he had against them—P-40s, P-51s, and P-38s. The Lightnings of the 449th and Stewart's flight of Mustangs caught the enemy formation at twenty thousand feet between Kanchow and Suichuan. They attacked together, and then Stewart saw one green Oscar peel away from the formation, heading south. Stewart followed in a slight dive and pulled up to a position just below the Japanese fighter and only about fifty feet behind. Apparently, the enemy pilot had failed to spot the Mustang closing in on him. Stewart fired a deadly burst from his four .50-caliber guns, and the Oscar immediately caught fire and dived into the ground. This was Stewart's ninth and last confirmed victory. It made him the all-time highest scoring ace of the 76th Fighter Squadron.

While Stewart was busy shooting down the Oscar, Lts. Elmore Bullock and John Celani both got shots at enemy fighters as well. Bullock hit his target, a Tojo, heavily near the root of the left wing. It flipped over and dived away smoking considerably, and Bullock was credited with a probable kill. The fight was not all one-sided, however. Lieutenant William Butler, a promising new pilot in the squadron who already had one confirmed victory, was shot down and killed. Still, with Stewart's victory and six more claimed by the 449th's P-38s, the Japanese had taken another beating. They did not risk another attack on Suichuan for the rest of the month.

While Suichuan was getting all the enemy's attention, the pilots at Kweilin and Hengyang were able to do some offensive work during February—fuel supplies and weather permitting, of course. The 75th Fighter Squadron concentrated its efforts on knocking down a steel truss railroad bridge at Puchi. The bridge was a key point in the line between Hankow and Tungting Lake, and knocking it down would sever the rail line at least until repairs could be made. Twelve Sharks carrying five-hundred-pound bombs attacked the bridge on February 7, scoring several near-misses but failing to damage the span. Then sixteen Sharks went back on February 27 and hit the bridge several times with one-thousand-pound bombs. Damage was reported to both approaches, and one span was destroyed. The 75th also found some action in the air near Kiukiang on February 24, resulting in one Oscar shot down by 1/Lt. James Folmar and six others damaged.

At Kweilin on February 11, Maj. Barry Melloan led six Sharks from the 74th Fighter Squadron, along with P-40s from the Chinese-American Composite Wing, on an escort of B-25s that were to attack Kai Tak Airdrome, Hong Kong. Melloan was a new arrival in the squadron and was preparing to assume command of the 74th when Captain Lundy completed his tour. The 74th was flying top cover at twenty-one thousand feet near the target when ten Oscars jumped them from above. The enemy pilots aggressively pressed their attacks until the formation crossed back into friendly territory. Lieutenants George Lee and Robert Gibeault turned into the attack and fired on the top section of Japanese fighters. Lee, flying a P-40M, shot down two of them before he was hit himself and had to bail out. At about the same time, Lt. Oren Bates also was shot down.

Fortunately, the two pilots escaped capture, although Lee suffered a bullet wound in the leg. They returned to Kweilin on February 19.[3]

This was the only exciting mission of the month for the 74th, but it was not the only interesting flying at Kweilin. On February 5, two officers had arrived from the States on temporary assignment to the squadron. Captain William Black and Lt. Paul Brown brought with them a supply of bazooka-like tubes that could be mounted under the wings of P-40s and used to fire aerial M-9 rockets at ground targets. This was the first stop in China for the officers, and eventually many P-40 squadrons would add the rockets to their arsenal of weapons. A rocketry range was set up near Kweilin, and the pilots spent much of the month practicing rocket attacks on ground targets. These early rockets were a mixed blessing, for they packed a terrific punch but also were somewhat erratic.

John W. Wheeler joined the 74th as a replacement at about the same time the rockets were introduced. He remembered, "Most of the pilots were very young. I was 20 when I got to China and 21 when I got out in 1945. I think very few were older than 22 or 23. . . . I had about 500 hours of intensive flying training when I got to China, about 200 hours in P-40s and mostly mock aerial combat, gunnery, rat racing, and low flying. A goodly number got killed in accidents along the way, but the rest of us were first class pilots when we got there. I used to feel that the few married men were over-cautious and more accident-prone because of it, but most of us were really good.

"About [then], some special bazookas showed up at Kweilin. We thought it was the first time rockets had been used in combat by fighter planes. They were triple tubes, about six inches [in] diameter, and we carried them [in] one cluster under each wing. They made a nice explosion when they hit, but I only used them on one mission and they petered out pretty quickly. I think it was hard to get an accurate shot. They were an awful drag, too, and we seldom dropped belly tanks or bazooka tubes except in emergency because everything was too hard to replace."[4]

The 74th first used the rockets in combat on March 3, when Major Melloan led eight Sharks to Hainan Island off the southern coast of China. The mission was code-named "Gadget Mystery,"[5] and the target was Chiungshan Airdrome on the north end of the island near the city of Haikou. The rocket-loaded Sharks, flying in conjunction with P-40s of the CACW for top cover and B-25s of the 11th Bomb Squadron, made a low-level approach over the water to avoid detection. They completely surprised the enemy.

Fifty planes were parked on the airfield, and Major Melloan led his P-40s at fifty feet to one hundred feet altitude for the attack. Firing rockets and strafing, the Sharks destroyed four aircraft and damaged four others. They also strafed a radar station and fired rockets into two hangars, setting them on fire. The rockets also scored several hits on barracks buildings. Ground fire was sporadic and inaccurate; all Sharks returned undamaged. Credit for ground kills went to Melloan for two and to Lts. Bill Morin and Ted Adams for one each.

After this, rocket use would increase slowly as accuracy of the weapons improved and supplies became more reliable. Later models of the P-51 delivered in 1945 featured zero-length rocket racks, which eliminated the performance penalty caused by the bazooka tubes.

March 4 also was a significant and successful day for the 76th Squadron at Suichuan. Four B-25s flew in from Kweilin that morning and landed in the fog. Once the bombers were reloaded, they took off with four P-51As for escort and headed for the Yangtze River port of Wuhu. This was the same target that had been scrubbed several weeks earlier because the squadron's P-40s lacked sufficient range to reach it safely. The Mustangs could reach it, however, and 1/Lt. Donald Hedrick led them off at 10:40 A.M. The mission would be the farthest foray down the Yangtze to date in the war.

The formation reached Wuhu unchallenged and began working its way west up the river. Flying at low level, the bombers attacked two cargo vessels, and then someone called in four silver Oscars swooping down to attack. Hedrick turned his Mustangs to meet the enemy fighters head-on before they could reach the bombers. First Lieutenant Harry Zavakos made his pass from slightly above and hit one of the Oscars with a full burst of fire. It fell off into a dive and crashed into the river. Hedrick made several passes, damaging one Oscar before taking some hits himself. The fight ended as quickly as it began, but when the Mustangs reformed, First Lieutenant Bullock was nowhere around. Ten days later, Bullock walked into Suichuan to report that he had been shot down during the fight. It was the second time in four months that Bullock had been forced to bail out and then walk home from a mission.

While Hedrick's flight was out on the March 4 mission, Lts. Ed Burbank, Max Noftsger, and Dick Templeton landed at Suichuan in three new P-40N-15s. After their two-week ferry mission to India, their fellow pilots in the 76th were glad to see them return, but they were disappointed to see the ferry pilots' Sharks. The squadron expected replacement Mustangs—specifically, the new P-51B models—not just more retread P-51As. The men's disappointment mellowed a bit when the ferry pilots revealed they had also brought twelve bottles of Black and White Scotch whiskey, plus a supply of new phonograph records, with them. The ferry pilots also assured their friends that what they had had heard about the P-51s coming to the squadron was true. More important, the new Mustangs were in Kunming being modified by the air service group there, and the planes would be delivered as soon as they were ready.

The introduction of the P-51B Mustang in China was big news, because the plane had a substantial performance edge over anything else flying in the Far East. It could fly as high, as fast, and as far as a Lightning or better—its top speed was about 440 miles per hour—but it also had maneuverability and fuel economy similar to a P-40. It climbed and dived well to boot. This version of the Mustang had flown its first combat missions from England in December 1943, and already it was the escort fighter of choice in the Eighth Air Force. With Mustangs to protect them from Luftwaffe interceptors, the bombers of the "Mighty Eighth" would literally obliterate the cities of Germany within a year.

What turned a good fighter design like the P-51A into a great one like the P-51B? All it took was the right engine. In place of the ubiquitous Allison power plant, the P-51B had a potent Merlin engine similar to those used in the legendary British Spitfires. License-built in the United States by Packard, the engine was an in-line V-12 design with similar displacement to the Allison V-1710 series, but it was fitted with a two-stage supercharger that allowed it to continue delivering power at altitudes in excess of thirty thousand feet.

If the P-51B had a shortcoming, it was in the armament. Like the A-model, it mounted just four .50-caliber machine guns in the wings. The thin design of the wing also made for cramped gun bays, so the guns tended to jam when fired during high-G maneuvers. This problem eventually was remedied by installing motors to help feed shells into the guns. Later P-51 models mounted six guns, but these would not arrive in China for another year.

Modifications on the first new Mustangs were completed March 14, and Lts. Max Noftsger and Irving Saunders were sent to Kunming to pick them up. Meanwhile, five other pilots from the squadron left for India to ferry more P-51Bs to China. Things were definitely looking up for the 76th Fighter Squadron and just in time. The squadron's supply of P-51As was continuing to dwindle.

After Lieutenant Bullock lost his Mustang on March 4, it was less than a week before another one went down. On March 10, three Mustang pilots were assigned to fly to a small island off the coastal city of Foochow and strafe a cable station. Captain Ken George, having recently returned from his crash in the Kiukiang area, led the flight southeastward on the long haul toward Foochow. With him were Capt. Eugene McGuire and Lt. Ed Burbank. Unbeknownst to them, a strong wind had blown their Mustangs southward, far off course. This was first time that fighters had ventured in this direction since the Formosa raid on the previous Thanksgiving, so the pilots did not expect to recognize the territory beneath them.

George's flight reached the coast near Amoy, an area that looks similar to Foochow from the air, and found an island that matched the description given during their briefing. They strafed some buildings that looked like they might be the target, then headed westward along the coast and strafed some oil tanks. Finally, they circled over an airfield for awhile in hopes of stirring up some response, but the field appeared to be deserted, so they took up a course designed to send them back to Suichuan.

The Mustangs flew for a while but were unable to make radio contact with anyone. George's wing tanks had failed to jettison when he tried to drop them, forcing him to use a higher power setting to overcome the drag they created. Eventually George began to get low on gas. He belly-landed his plane near the town of Linhsien, well south of Suichuan, and suffered minor cuts on his face. Friendly Chinese quickly took him to safety. Captain George returned to the base later in the month.

When McGuire and Burbank began to run low on gas, they found a tiny glider field with a twelve-hundred-foot runway and put their Mustangs down there. They were toasted that evening by the Chinese station personnel while gasoline and ammunition were being trucked south from the auxiliary field at Namyung. The next afternoon, the two pilots gunned their fighters down the short airstrip and headed north for the hour's flight home to Suichuan. During their debriefing by the 76th's intelligence officer, the two pilots agreed that a P-51A could remain in the air for seven hours if it was (a) equipped with twin fifty-gallon drop tanks, (b) flown at settings of twenty-two inches to twenty-three inches of manifold pressure and 2050 revolutions per minute, and (c) its fuel-air mixture was set on "auto lean." They knew this was true, because they had done it.

The weather socked in Suichuan during the middle of March, but action resumed later in the month. Two missions attacking the enemy at Nanchang occurred on March 28 and 29. The first one did quite a bit of damage to facilities on Nanchang's airfield, but no one noted any enemy activity or Japanese aircraft in the air or on the ground.

The next day, the target was Nanchang's railroad station. Fifteen P-40s and four P-51s took off at 6:45 A.M. and proceeded to the target at six thousand feet. Three flights of P-40s approached the station from the northwest, made their bomb runs in string formation, pulled off, and rendezvoused northeast of town for the trip to Suichuan. They saw a few bursts of flak, but it was not accurate. One pilot, Capt. Ed Collis, decided to make a pass over the Nanchang Airdrome. He came down the runway on the deck and fired into a group of people who appeared to be rebuilding the control tower. Collis was a fairly new member of the 76th, having joined the squadron in December 1943 after wangling a transfer from his job as a transport pilot in India. He was intent on making the most of his opportunity to fly fighters.

While Collis was strafing, the top-cover flight of Mustangs was fending off an attack by about fifteen Japanese fighters that apparently had been on patrol in the area. The Mustang pilots made no claims, and Lt. Harry Zavakos was wounded slightly, but they were able to keep the enemy fighters at bay while the Sharks did their work. On the way home, one of the P-40 pilots spotted a Japanese fighter at two thousand feet chasing a P-51 flown by Lt. Wendell Stoneham. A Shark pilot, Lt. Jack Green, closed in, but the enemy pilot spotted him and broke away in a climb. Green pulled his nose up and opened fire. Hits sparkled all over the green and brown fighter. It continued climbing for a moment and then fell off in a dive, trailing fire and crashing with a big explosion. It was the first kill for Green, who had only been in the squadron for a month.

The pilots gave their combat debriefings in their usual high spirits after the mission. Combined with the mission of the previous day, clearly they had done a great deal of damage at Nanchang. It was only logical to expect the Japanese to retaliate. The following day, 1/Lt. Rick Olney wrote this vivid account of the tension at Suichuan on March 30:

> The air in the alert shack this morning is filled with a certain tenseness. All the pilots are half-expecting a raid, a sort of return visit to be paid by the Japs in reprisal for our raids of yesterday. Some of the boys are reading the "Roundup," last month's "Newsweek," some old comic strips; some are studying "Impact" and other intelligence bulletins. Some are playing cards and checkers. None of them look comfortable, kind of perched on the edge or leaning against the wall, but swinging their foot or drumming their fingers against anything they can touch.
>
> One of the checker players, nibbling at his fingernails, absentmindedly makes the wrong move. His opponent sees it quickly enough, jumps two men and gets a king. Then from a half-smoked cigarette he lights a fresh one, grinding the other out under his heel. I notice there are half a dozen butts in the same place.
>
> A first lieutenant is lighting his pipe just as the phone rings once. That's Radio calling. The air is brittle, the pilots expectant, every muscle taut and ready to take the fighters to their planes. But it's not a plot, the Japs are not airborne yet. Only a few words of telephone

conversation are necessary to make the boys sit back and relax a little. The butterflies in my own stomach seem to subside, and I watch
the pipe smoker lick the match burn on his finger, then strike another.

I don't wonder how the boys feel when they expect an aerial fight.
I know![6]

The scene Olney described happened day after day at airfields all
over China. On this day, the Japanese never did come, but of course
on many others they did.

In a sense, too, Olney's scene described the overall feeling in the
Fourteenth Air Force at that time. From General Chennault all the
way down to the lowliest buck private, the men knew through intelligence and observation that the Japanese were building up for something big in China. They had been stockpiling supplies and moving
troops into the Hankow area since the first of the year. In February,
their aerial forces in China were redesignated from the 3rd Air
Division to the Fifth Air Army. The strength of the individual
Japanese air units, greatly diminished after their disastrous drub-
bing by the Americans in December, was being replenished with
deliveries of up to fifty aircraft a month. Reconnaissance flights by
the high-flying Japanese Ki-46 Dinahs continued whenever the
weather cleared enough to give them a peek at the U.S. air bases.

The Japanese were gearing up for a big push, and everyone in the
Fourteenth Air Force knew it was coming soon. But for the time
being, rain clouds were the most important factor in the China air
war throughout April 1944. Capt. Jones C. Laughlin, new flight surgeon of the 75th Fighter Squadron, had joined the unit in Hengyang
on March 29. He wrote the following description of life there during
his first month:

From Lingling to Hengyang the transports flew about 200 feet above
the river and about the same distance below the soup, which was a
solid overcast. For the next month [April] the soup hung on the chim-
ney tops or lay on the ground, or it rained. During the first part of
April we ran out of powdered milk for coffee at breakfast (we have
coffee only one meal a day), and later in the month we had no coffee.
We received mail only once, and that was by ground delivery. The
weather was so bad that the birds could not see to fly in the soup,
which constantly precipitated and slowly dropped in a fine spray or
more like descending fog. The birds sat under bushes on the ground
and hopped around to catch bugs and worms.

The temperature was low, but the air was so wet that all body heat
was quickly lost. It was necessary to wear a leather coat and wool
pants, overshoes and carry an umbrella to keep warm and dry. The

green mold grew on all bricks except those walked on. Shoes were covered with green mold in a few days' time, and the zippers on fleece-lined winter flying suits corroded quickly. This type of weather persisted all month. The visibility was limited to a few hundred yards, and it was dark inside the buildings during the day. A type of melancholia prevailed the atmosphere, and sick call ran 20 to 30 men each morning out of 150 enlisted men. . . . Many came to sick call to get out of going down to the [flight] line at 5 A.M. in the rain and cold. . . .

At this time the 75th Fighter Squadron was occupying Hostel 1 at Hengyang, which made it a short distance to town. A new hostel had just been completed. This was a mile on the other side of the field, which made it three or four miles from town. Most of the pilots and enlisted men did not want to move, as Hostel 1 was so convenient to the town by sampan [river boat] across the river. The hostel was a two-story, brick "U"-shaped building that before the war housed a Chinese girls' school. The rooms were large, but the downstairs rooms were dark in the daytime, and mosquitoes were active around the clock. The hostel was lousy with bedbugs, but the plumbing facilities were the best in China. We had hot and cold showers, and eight stateside commodes with flush bowls that worked. . . .

The new hostel was clean, and free of bed bugs, and new mosquito screening was on the windows. All things were good in general except that no water was in the tank at the new hostel. S.O.S. [Services of Supply, which was in charge of base facilities] had built the hostel so high up on the hill overlooking the river that the pump system would not elevate the water.

While the squadron was deciding (about 50–50 pro and con) on the moving proposition, the Japs came over one night and laid a string of bombs across the hostel in which we were living. A bomb dropped in one of the wings and destroyed about 40 bunks. This settled the question, and we moved. It was around the last part of April or around the first of May, and the weather cleared and the war started. . . .[7]

15

Ichi-Go

The war in China changed completely on April 17, 1944. On that day, Japanese troops poured across the Yellow River at Kaifeng and headed south through Honan Province toward Hankow, about 250 miles away. At the same time, Japanese troops headed north out of Hankow intending to link up with the southbound force. This was the first phase of Operation Ichi-Go ("Number One"), which would soon become the biggest Japanese land offensive of World War II.

The objective of Ichi-Go's opening phase was to complete the railroad link between Hankow and Peiping. Although the Japanese held both cities, the Chinese controlled the rail line through Honan Province; thus, the Japanese could not use it to move men and equipment south to support the upcoming main thrust of the offensive.

Once the rail link was secure, the Japanese planned to move south out of the Tungting Lake region and take another crack at capturing Changsha. They had tried to do this three times before and failed, but this time, they were determined to succeed. Changsha was just an interim objective, however. The Japanese intended to keep pushing south all the way to Indo-China, swallowing up the Fourteenth Air Force's air bases in eastern China in the process.

The purpose behind Ichi-Go was threefold. First, the Japanese wanted to create an alternate land route for moving raw materials from Southeast Asia to Japan, because shipping in the South China Sea was being increasingly badgered by U.S. air attacks from China and submarine attacks by the U.S. Navy. The railroad tracks were already in place between Hanoi and the seaports of northern China; all the Japanese needed was to control them. Second, since they had been unable to destroy the U.S. air forces flying in China, the Japanese wanted to remove the U.S. air bases in eastern China and the threat they posed. That threat included the possibility that B-29s from Suichuan and Kweilin would soon commence raids against Japan itself. Finally, the Japanese hoped that a successful offensive would force the Chinese government to drop out of the war, thus freeing up Japanese forces for battle elsewhere.

Ichi-Go was a bold plan, but it was a well-designed and well-timed operation. General Shunroku Hada, the Japanese military commander in China, knew that his forces were superior in fighting quality and equipment—if not overall numbers—to the Chinese troops they would face. He also knew that the political support for the Nationalist Chinese government was very weak in Honan Province, where the people had been suffering through a prolonged famine. And he knew that General Chennault's Fourteenth Air Force, though stronger in numbers than ever before, continued to be dogged by supply problems.[1] A final factor was the weather: If Hada's troops could gain momentum while Chennault's planes were stuck on the ground, the offensive would be hard to stop later when the skies cleared.

The first phase of Ichi-Go had little impact on the 23rd Fighter Group because all the action was hundreds of miles north of its bases. For the first few days even Col. Casey Vincent, commander of the 68th Composite Wing, had little information about what was happening. In fact, the first effect of Ichi-Go was a slight improvement in the crowded conditions at Kweilin, because the 3rd Fighter Group and 2nd Bomb Squadron of the Chinese-American Composite Wing were moved north to air bases in eastern Szechwan Province as soon as the thrust of the Honan offensive was recognized. From the Szechwan bases, the CACW pilots would fly the first missions opposing Ichi-Go.

Before long the Japanese battle plan became apparent. As soon as the weather broke, Colonel Vincent sent a strong force of fifty-four bombers and fighters to the Hankow area in hopes of destroying Japanese supplies before the second phase of Ichi-Go started. The mission was set for May 6, 1944, and Col. Tex Hill would lead the fighter escorts.

Vincent and Hill briefed pilots at Hengyang and Lingling. The 76th Fighter Squadron sent sixteen P-51s to Lingling to meet up with P-38s of the 449th Fighter Squadron, and then the combined force rendezvoused with P-40s of the 75th and the bombers over Hengyang. Visibility was poor, with heavy haze and scattered clouds, but most of the formation stayed together on the run up to Hankow. About ten minutes before they reached the target, a supply area just off the edge of the main Hankow airdrome, several Oscars popped out of the clouds. They made a head-on pass at a flight of Mustangs led by Maj. Charles E. Griffith. A former college wrestler from Rhode Island, Griffith had recently joined the 76th and would assume command May 17 after Maj. John Stewart went back to the States. Originally, Capt. Ken George had been slated for the command, but he was taken off combat status after walking out from enemy territory in March. Just like George, Griffith had flown a previous combat tour in the Aleutian Islands. Flying P-39 Airacobras out of Adak with the 42nd Fighter Squadron, Griffith had led the first strafing attack against Kiska Island on September 14, 1942.

Griffith's Mustangs tangled with the Oscars for a few moments and got the worst of it, but the bombers went unchallenged and caused heavy damage to the target. Lieutenant Glen Beneda was shot down, the first combat loss of a P-51B in China, and everyone thought he was dead. He walked out two months later, however, after being rescued by Chinese Communist guerrillas. Lieutenant Wendell Stoneham's hydraulic system was punctured, but he made a successful landing at Hengyang. Griffith's Mustangs made no claims for damage to the enemy.

The P-38s also engaged some Oscars on the mission, but Colonel Hill had the only confirmed kill. This was Tex Hill's last victory of the war, giving him a total of 14.75 confirmed (sharing one victory with another pilot), one probable, and five damaged. At that time, his victory total was tops in the Fourteenth Air Force by far.

The May 6 mission was a good, if not spectacular, start to the campaign to blunt the Japanese offensive. But as far as Tex Hill was concerned, the effort was too little, too late. He aired his frustration:

"They had moved the B-29s into the Chengtu area, and they were put under the 20th Air Force, but the operational control was directly under Hap Arnold [commanding general of the U.S. Army Air Force]. The reason for that was they didn't want Chennault or the Generalissimo to get their hands on them.

"In order to launch any kind of offensive, at some point you have to concentrate a hell of a lot of matériel in one place. The Japanese jump-off place was Yochow, which is up in the Hankow area. We had it located, and request was made to put a saturation raid [by the B-29s] on that jumping off point, and they refused. They said this was a strategic air force, and they were not going to put it on a tactical target. So the result was, the Japs were able to come on down and launch their offensive.

"Later, after the offensive got under way, I think they used the B-29s one time. But by then it was too late. We put the B-24s on it, but we only had that one 308th Bomb Group of heavies, and there just wasn't enough to do any good. But the B-29s could have stopped it right in its tracks; it never would have gotten off the ground."[2]

While the 23rd Fighter Group was flexing its muscles in advance of Ichi-Go, the Japanese Fifth Air Army was trying to do the same thing. Its assignment during April and May was to secure air superiority over the Hengyang and Suichuan areas so that the Americans would be unable to disrupt the buildup for the offensive. Why the Japanese high command thought this was possible now, when similar efforts to subdue the 23rd Fighter Group had failed repeatedly in the past, is unknown.

Nevertheless, the Japanese tried. On May 3, the 75th Fighter Squadron lost a P-40N that was hit by bomb fragments during a raid at Hengyang. Then on May 11 and 12, the Japanese sent out strong missions to attack the Suichuan area.

The first strike against Suichuan came late in the afternoon of the eleventh, when about thirty-five Oscars were reported heading toward the nearby town of Namyung. Most of the 76th Fighter Squadron's P-51s were on temporary duty at northern bases, but a small force of three P-40s and two P-51s scrambled to meet the attack. Captain Ed Collis took the lead in a Shark. The P-40s attacked together, closing in behind a vee formation of Oscars. The Oscars saw them coming and dropped their wing tanks, but Collis still was able to get a good burst into the tail of one of them. The plane went down smoking, and Collis later spotted a fire on the ground where it hit.

Another pilot flying with Collis was Lt. Bill Watt. He recalled the fight this way: "We in the P-40s sighted about 12 Oscars flying about 1,000 feet below us. We dove down and succeeded in each of us killing an Oscar. As I remember, there wasn't much to it. I just picked off one of the Oscars and got the hell out of there. We made it back to Suichuan without being intercepted by the Jap planes flying top cover."[3]

The Japanese came back to Suichuan twice early in the morning of May 12 and twice more during the day. Captain Collis attempted a night interception after the first raid by a single bomber destroyed a B-25 on the field. He got off several bursts at a Ki-48 Lily bomber before losing it in the darkness.

The air raid warning net failed, and at about 6:30 A.M., a mixed formation of six Lilys and thirty Oscars reached Suichuan without being intercepted. Three P-40s and three P-51s of the 76th, along with Sharks of the Chinese-American 5th Fighter Group, scrambled late and were still climbing when the Japanese formation arrived over the base. The bombers flew past the field, turned, and made their bomb runs while heading north. Ground control called out their position to the fighters as a flight of Oscars came over the base on a strafing run.

Lieutenant Stephen Bonner, leading the 76th's P-40s, dived toward the base. He was unable to spot the bombers, but he picked up the Oscars and made a head-on pass at one of them, getting good strikes on its engine before the two planes passed. The Oscar limped out of sight as Bonner turned his attention to another target. He made this attack from above and behind the second Oscar. This time he saw many hits in the wing root and in the forward fuselage. The Oscar went down, trailing heavy smoke and fire, and ground observers confirmed it as destroyed. This victory made Bonner an ace with five kills and the top scorer in the squadron when Major Stewart left.

Other kills were recorded by two of the P-51 pilots, Capt. Lester K. Murray and 1/Lt. Charles Gibson. Murray had just joined the squadron that week to serve as operations officer, but he was no novice. He was a veteran of fifty missions in Burma, scoring two victories flying P-51As with the 1st Air Commando Group.

One P-40 was lost in the fight. The hydraulic system in 1/Lt. Irving Saunders's plane was shot out, and he had to make a belly landing. The plane caught on fire and burned, but Saunders was able to get out uninjured.

That afternoon another big formation of enemy raiders approached Suichuan. This time, only three P-51s were available from the 76th, plus several P-40Ns from the CACW squadron. Captain Murray led the Mustangs again, but just as he reached the Japanese bombers, his engine began throwing out white smoke. Thinking he had been hit, Murray dived out and made an emergency landing. Lieutenant Gibson also tried to close with the bombers, but the Oscar escorts cut him off. He had a busy few minutes turning circles with them and eventually got clear, but he was unable to make any claims.

Lieutenant Wendell Stoneham was the only pilot to close with the bombers. He caught them traveling north after they had made their bomb runs over the base, and he dived on the trailing group of five Lilys. They closed in a tight formation so their top gunners could concentrate their return fire on the Mustang, but Stoneham ducked below their line of sight and made a climbing pass from underneath the last bomber on the left. His first burst hit the plane's left engine, and then he hit it in the fuselage. The plane caught on fire and was trailing a long plume of flames when it fell out of formation and crashed. The smoke from its explosion could be seen from the airfield. Stoneham made similar attacks on two more bombers, setting one of them on fire. He claimed one a probable and the other as damaged.

For the Japanese, this strike was the most effective of the day. One string of bombs fell directly across the revetment area on the base, destroying three P-38s and damaging three B-25s and three P-40s. It also was the last major bombing attack the Japanese made against Suichuan that summer. The base was nearly out of gas, and Colonel Vincent pulled his B-25s out of there that same day. The next morning, Colonel Hill led the 76th's main force of twelve P-51s back to Suichuan from their temporary assignment at Liangshan. On their way, the Mustangs dive-bombed a barracks and storage area at Shayang near Tungting Lake. Bad weather followed the Mustangs to Suichuan, and the 76th was idle for the better part of May.

While the 76th Fighter Squadron had been kept busy tangling with enemy aircraft during early May, the 74th was usually inactive at Kweilin. The 75th Squadron, however, was piling up missions and hours at Hengyang. In the first thirteen days of the month, the 75th flew eleven offensive missions, both ground attack and bomber escort, and fifteen local alerts. It was a tremendous leap from the lull in April and much appreciated by most of the pilots, including the new squadron commander, Maj. Philip C. Loofbourrow. This quiet 1940 graduate of West Point had assumed command of the 75th in March, when Major Richardson transferred to group headquarters prior to going home.

The 75th's pilots really wanted a chance to do battle with the Japanese air force; the squadron had not recorded a confirmed kill in nearly two months. On May 14, they got their chance with an early morning escort mission to Yochow. Major Loofbourrow led eight Sharks off from Hengyang at 6:15 A.M., and they covered a flight of B-25s to the target. Northeast of Yochow they spotted a string of fifty trucks, obviously part of the enemy supply effort. The Sharks pounced and thoroughly shot up the trucks. While climbing to a safer altitude after the strafing, one of the pilots spotted twelve to fourteen Oscars heading their way. Major Loofbourrow turned into them, and a furious fight ensued. Once more, the 75th got the best of it. Lieutenants James Vurgaropulos and James Folmar each scored single confirmed kills, while probables went to Capt. John D. Long and Lt. Francis ("Army") Armstrong. Seven damaged claims also were recorded. The only damage to the Sharks was suffered by Major Loofbourrow's plane, which was hit in the left stabilizer and fuselage. Loofbourrow sustained superficial flesh wounds on the arm and leg but returned to base safely with the rest of the Sharks. The flight surgeon, Captain Laughlin, patched up the major, and Loofbourrow led another mission that afternoon.

Three days later, the 75th had another run-in with enemy aircraft, and again the Shark pilots got the better of it. First Lieutenant Oswin H. ("Moose") Elker, noted in the squadron for his impressive handlebar mustache, had vivid memories of this fight. He recalled that "all but two of our available P-40s had gone on a mission north into Japanese-held territory. Lieutenant Vern Tanner and I were to stay at the field at Hengyang for field defense. Later, as the mission was returning, we heard via the telephone network that some distance behind our returning planes was a large group of planes heading south. We knew these must be Japs trying to catch our returning mission either after landing or in the air, low on gas.

"Our returning planes were diverted to Lingling to refuel, and Tanner and I got into the air and reached for altitude, which was limited by a solid overcast at 4,000 feet. Very shortly, the Japs came into view. Our personnel on the ground counted somewhere between 35 and 40 planes. As they reached the field they got into what we called their 'squirrel cage' formation, in which some circled in one direction and some in the opposite direction. Some looped and some rolled. The purpose of this tactic was to give them good visibility in all directions against attack from any angle. More than anything else, it resembled a bee swarm.

"As they came below us, Tanner and I attacked those that came within our range. The attacked Japs always headed into the squirrel cage where, due to the diverse maneuvers of their comrades, there would always be one of them to attack the pursuer. I made my attacks short and got back into the overcast to lose my pursuers, of which there were always several. After a quick turn in the overcast I'd come back down, and with so many planes in the air there was a good chance I would sometimes come back down behind one within range. I would usually get in one good burst before I'd have tracers coming over my shoulder and would have to get back into the overcast.

"One time up in the clouds I made an S-turn to get into position for emerging to look for another target. As I made the last turn in the 'S' a dark blob passed directly in front of me and in the same split second I got a tremendous jolt, which was the prop wash of the Zero that had followed me into the cloud cover and whose tail I must have just barely missed. In my subsequent trips into the clouds I made no more S-turns.

"By this time the Japs knew they had failed to catch our planes on the ground and were heading back north, still in the squirrel cage formation. I continued my cat and mouse game and was able to get one Zero smoking heavily and go into a spiral descent. In three instances I saw pieces fly from my targets, and in one case there was a big puff of smoke from under his cowling, but no flames.

"One time when I dropped down to look for a target I came almost wing to wing with a Zero. We were always under the assumption that all Japanese had typical slant eyes, but when this guy suddenly saw me so close his eyes were ROUND. This was possibly the shortest formation flight ever recorded.

"Quite often when I dropped out of the overcast I would not be in position to get a shot at anything, and as the Japs converged on me I'd go back up. With all the hostile planes in the air I wasn't about to try to keep my cripples in sight in order to make any confirmations. I turned in the heavy smoker as a probable and the four solid hits as damaged. My probable was later confirmed as it fell close to the field. I had been able to take potshots at this formation while staying above them and heading north with them for a distance of about 100 miles, at which point the overcast ended. I headed back with no ammo left and quite a few holes in my plane to attest to the encounters.

"After the very first contact with the enemy, Tanner and I didn't see each other again until I landed, which must have been about an hour later though it seemed much longer. Tanner was badly shot up and had belly-landed. He also reported a probable, which was not recorded by the squadron; however, later the Chinese reported several plane crashes farther from the field along the route the Japanese had taken on their way north."[4]

Moose Elker continued to fly with the 75th for many months. He was shot down later in May and again in July, but he was able to walk out to safety both times. Then in August, Elker and Technical Sgt. Don Van Cleve earned the Soldier's Medal for pulling Lt. Robert Miller out of his burning P-40 after Miller crash-landed in a rice paddy and was knocked unconscious.

★ ★ ★ ★

On the same day Elker was battling the squirrel cage over Hengyang, Japanese troops in Honan Province completed their operation to link the Peiping-Hankow railroad line. Nine days later, on May 26, 1944, the main phase of Ichi-Go began. The Japanese Eleventh Army, with some 60,000 assault troops in a force nearing 250,000, crossed the Yangtze River near Yochow and headed south toward Changsha. Chinese resistance was light at first but stiffened as the invasion crept closer to the city, where Gen. Hsueh Yueh was in command of nearly 150,000 defenders.

Immediately, the pace and profile of missions flown by the 23rd Fighter Group changed. Now, in addition to striking at supply lines and defending their bases as before, the pilots would begin making attacks on Japanese troop concentrations, either in the field or while in transit to the front. With more action also came greater risks, as enemy air activity was increasing as well. The 75th Fighter Squadron lost two pilots on the first day of the offensive. Lieutenant Warren Smedley went down during a dogfight over the enemy's forward air base at Kingmen. Lieutenant Marvin Balderson, who also was shot up during the fight, crash-landed his P-40 on a street in Changsha. Captain Laughlin, the 75th's flight surgeon, flew to Changsha in a C-47 and parachuted into the city, hoping to save Balderson's life. Laughlin found the pilot already dead when he arrived. Laughlin boarded a boat the next morning and headed down the Hsiang River, just ahead of the advancing Japanese, arriving in Hengyang two weeks later. The doctor was awarded the Soldier's Medal for his efforts to save Balderson.

In all, the 75th lost seven Sharks from May 26 through May 29. That left the air base at Hengyang critically short of aircraft at a time when it was seriously threatened, so Colonel Vincent moved the 76th from Suichuan to join the 75th on May 31. The gasoline supply was very low at Suichuan anyway, so fighters there would only have been available for air defense. In addition, intelligence sources were reporting that the Japanese also were massing troops in the Canton area for a possible push northward to link up with the Hankow forces. Suichuan, with its lovely long runway and big revetment areas, would have to be left undefended for the time being.

By this time, the squadrons were flying multiple missions each day. The 75th flew seven missions on June 1. One of them was particularly memorable for the squadron commander. More than forty years later, Phil Loofbourrow wrote the following description:

"We were on a mission to dive-bomb a warehouse area in some Japanese occupied town [Pingkiang]. The mission was made up of a couple of flights of P-40s from the 75th Fighter Squadron and one or two flights from a Chinese-American fighter [the CACW] squadron that was operating with us. When we arrived at the target, I rolled into the dive and started down. I had barely got lined up on the target when a Japanese two-seater reconnaissance airplane, which I identified as an Ida, crossed through the middle of my gun sight. I considered briefly whether or not to jettison my bomb and go after the airplane, and decided to hang on to the bomb and complete the bomb run because that's what we were there for.

"I released the bomb at somewhere between 2,000 and 800 feet and in recovering from the dive found myself overrunning the Japanese airplane too fast to make a proper gunnery run on him. I started shooting behind him and pulled a burst through him as I recovered. I went over the top and never saw him again. I saw no hits because I was probably going 250 miles an hour faster than he was.

"When I got home and landed, I was filling out the mission log (Form One) when Bob Van Ausdall, who had been leading the Chinese-American flight behind me, ran over to my airplane and congratulated me on the kill, which he had seen hit the ground."

Loofbourrow, who later that year would be named commander of the 23rd Fighter Group, had this to say about the P-40: "The majority of our activity in the spring and summer of 1944 was against the Japanese ground forces, and the Japanese infantrymen shot down more of our airplanes than did the Japanese fighter pilots. For this type of activity the P-40 probably did better than the P-51 Mustang, because the rear-mounted radiator in the P-51 gave the rifleman a vulnerable target going away from him. Anyone trying to hit a P-40 radiator had to stand up and face six .50-caliber machine guns coming at him. Against the fighters, of course, the P-51 was superior because it had about a 100 mph advantage in speed.

"I flew the P-40 for 3½ years in the States, Iceland, India, and China. I have taken it off from grass, mud, mixed clay and rock, concrete, and a carrier deck, and the airplane never let me down. It did what it was designed to do and a lot of things the designer never dreamed of. I liked it."[5]

On June 1, while Loofbourrow was flying combat missions, Col. Casey Vincent took off in a C-64 utility aircraft from Hengyang and flew up near Changsha for a visit with Gen. Hsueh Yueh. On the way, he saw thousands of refugees streaming south. The Chinese commanding general expressed confidence that he could hold the city once more, but Vincent had his doubts as he returned to Hengyang. Three days later, Vincent drafted a strong letter to General Chennault, pleading for more gas and ammunition because he felt they were in danger of the Japanese capturing all of eastern China. Unfortunately, Vincent's assessment would prove accurate.

Seeking to get maximum utilization from his fighters, on June 3, Vincent moved the 74th Fighter Squadron from Kweilin up to Hengyang and moved the 76th's Mustangs out to Lingling. The 75th Fighter Squadron was nearly out of planes by now, and a week later, it joined the 76th at Lingling. June 9 was a big day, with nine missions flown including five by the 74th. The squadron's new commander, Maj. Arthur W. Cruikshank Jr., led three of them. One of the original School Squadron pilots and an ace, Cruikshank had recently returned to China for a second combat tour. Within the month, he would score two victories, be shot down twice, and then be pulled out of combat.

June 9 also was a big day for Casey Vincent, although he did not know it at the time. That day orders were cut in Washington, D.C., promoting Vincent to the rank of brigadier general. What made it all the more significant was the fact that Vincent was just twenty-nine years old. One of Vincent's biggest fans was Tex Hill, who remembered his former boss this way: "At that time, the 23rd was under the 68th Composite Wing, and Casey was the commander. I was his deputy, plus group commander of the 23rd. It was his entire responsibility [to manage the air units]. Here's this little guy, 29 years old, with the whole burden of the China war on his shoulders.

"Casey was one of the greatest officers I've ever been around. He was strong, smart, just a hell of a good man. He was never recognized for what he did. He handled it well in China. But you could tell in his diary that he felt like he'd been left hanging."[6]

Irony has a way of reaching out and slapping combatants in the face during a war. On June 15, 1944, at 4:16 P.M., the first of seventy-five Boeing B-29 Superfortresses took off from their bases in an area around Chengtu, China, and set course to the east. Their target was the Imperial Iron and Steel Works at Yawata on the island of Kyushu, Japan. On this night, U.S. aircraft would make their first attack on the Japanese lands since the famous Doolittle raid in the spring of 1942.[7]

Again, one of the primary reasons that the Japanese embarked on Ichi-Go was to prevent just such an air attack by B-29s. On this same day, Japanese troops bypassed the city of Changsha, China, effectively accomplishing the first objective of the Ichi-Go offensive and placing the air base at Hengyang in extreme jeopardy. To make matters worse, the B-29s did insignificant damage to their target in Japan and burned up many thousands of gallons of fuel that the 23rd Fighter Group's fighters desperately needed to continue their operations against Ichi-Go.

With a heavy heart, Casey Vincent ordered the 74th Fighter Squadron to vacate Hengyang on June 16 and return to Kweilin. Pilot Charlie Cook noted in his diary that day that the squadron's strength was down to "just eight planes left in flying condition, and only three of them fit for combat; the rest are too shot up."[8]

On June 20 the Japanese reached the gates of Hengyang city. All U.S. units had been evacuated from the base, and the following night Vincent ordered it demolished. The fresh, new hostel went up in flames, along with the other buildings on the base, and heavy bombs buried in the runway were detonated to blast big craters in the landing surface. By morning, the base that had been the scene of so many of the 23rd Fighter Group's greatest triumphs, dating all the way back to its first day in action, was nothing but smoking rubble. It was a scene that would be repeated more times than anyone in the 23rd Fighter Group wanted to consider. From now on, the order of the day would be, as Vincent sadly noted in his diary, to "fire and fall back."

★ ★ ★ ★

With the air base at Hengyang gone, Lingling and Kweilin became the primary airfields for the 23rd Fighter Group. The one positive note was that the Chinese Army's defense had stiffened near Hengyang. The troops at Hengshan, twenty-five miles north of the city, held a strong defensive position and were refusing to give up.

From June 17 through June 25, the 68th Composite Wing threw the full weight of its firepower into supporting the Chinese at Hengshan. The weather stank, with a low overcast hampering visibility, but mission after mission went out anyway. The majority of these strikes were river sweeps designed to catch the Japanese hauling men and supplies down the Hsiang River to bolster their frontline troops. In nine days, the pilots of the 23rd Fighter Group flew 538 sorties. The group lost just one aircraft, when Lt. David Rust of the 75th experienced engine failure in his P-40N and had to belly-land ten miles north of Lingling.

The bad weather was a significant factor in the 23rd's low loss rate, because Japanese fighters at the Hankow airfields were having more trouble getting airborne than the Americans were. And when they finally did make contact with the Sharks and Mustangs, the Japanese got the worst of it again. The 76th scored three victories without any losses on June 17 and 18. The next contact was not until June 25, when Major Cruikshank led a mixed formation from the 74th and 75th out of Lingling on an offensive sweep up the river from Hengyang. Cruikshank was credited with two of the three confirmed kills that day. Lieutenant Robert S. Peterson, a pilot in the 75th, flew that mission. He recalled it this way:

"I was flying the wing of Lt. Vurgaropulos in an eight-ship flight. We were carrying parafrags [small fragmentation bombs with parachutes attached to them] and a full load of .50-caliber. We met nine Oscars and six Hamps [probably Tojos], who had been escorting a flight of Val dive-bombers [probably Army Ki-51 Sonias]. The Vals ran, with the Jap fighters between us and the Vals. I was glued to Vurgaropulos, this being my first contact with Jap fighters. We dove on a Hamp, and when Vurgaropulos scored hits on him, he turned across my sights and I got in a good burst. As we were outnumbered, we dove away without seeing the Hamp hit the ground. We claimed a probable, sharing half each.

"While this action was going on, the weather had moved in between us and Lingling. We had become separated from the others, so Vurgie told me to join up on his right wing and we would follow the Hsiang River back to Lingling. It was a typical monsoon rain. He took the left bank and I took the right. The river twisted and turned between high banks. The rain was so heavy I could hardly see Vurgie's plane; water was coming in around the canopy. At that moment the plane shuddered and I saw wire draped over and around the nose and canopy. I had run through the telephone lines that crossed the river. On landing, the wire was strung out for 1,200 feet behind me."[9]

Bob Peterson went on to complete ninety-four combat missions. He shot down two enemy fighters in August and September, and dive-bombed the major Japanese airfield at Paliuchi the following January to score several more confirmed on the ground. He retired with the rank of major general after thirty-eight years of flying on active duty and in the Air Force Reserve. First Lieutenant James C. Vurgaropulos was killed four days after the June 25 mission. His P-40 crashed into a building during a strafing run over Changsha.

Despite the furious air support Casey Vincent's fighters and bombers provided, the Chinese finally folded at Hengshan and retreated back into the city of Hengyang. But to everyone's surprise, the Chinese held Hengyang under a state of siege for nearly six weeks. As Tex Hill described it, "The Chinese Army had the worst of it. We used B-25s and C-47s to drop supplies to them at Hengyang. It was just like the Alamo. When the Japs finally came in, they slaughtered all of them."[10]

With Hengyang surrounded, the Japanese now were free to continue their drive down the Hsiang River valley. The next U.S. air base along the way was Lingling, which became untenable immediately. Not only were the Japanese ground forces only days away from capturing the field, but General Chennault's longtime trump card, the air raid warning net, was falling apart in the Tungting Lake area. Without sufficient notice of incoming enemy air raids, the 23rd Fighter Group could easily be caught on the ground at Lingling now. The squadrons fell back again on June 26, with the 75th going to Kweilin and the 76th farther south to Liuchow. Kweilin was getting crowded again, for the 74th Fighter Squadron already was there and a new squadron had just arrived.

★ ★ ★ ★

The 23rd Fighter Group's new squadron was not a fighter outfit per se. It was the 118th Tactical Reconnaissance (Tac Recon) Squadron. The 23rd's commander, Col. Tex Hill, was not one to quibble over details, however. As far as he was concerned, the 118th was just another fighter squadron, with the slight advantage that it also was equipped and trained to take aerial pictures.

The 118th Squadron dated all the way back to World War I. Formed in 1917 as the 118th Aero Squadron, it served in France as a supply unit during the war and then was reformed as the 118th Observation Squadron, a unit of the Connecticut National Guard, in 1923. The squadron was inducted into federal service in February 1941, flew antisubmarine patrols off the Atlantic Coast in 1942, and began retraining in tactical reconnaissance early in 1943 before shipping out to India. The 118th arrived in China with its new P-40Ns during the middle of June 1944 and set up shop at Kweilin. These special Sharks had an aerial camera mounted in each one. One of the 118th's pilots, Ronald M. Phillips, described tactical recon operations as follows:

"Tactical recon fighters were identical to all others—guns, bombs, tanks and all—plus they carried a 52-pound camera in the back that was operated remotely from the cockpit. The tactical recon pilot was specially trained, usually at Key Field in Meridian, Miss. Training was nearly all to become skilled in low-level flight and picture taking. The object was to fly the combat mission in regular formation, drop out of formation, and while the rest kept top cover, fly over the intended target very low for a pre-raid picture. Then you'd join the flight for the raid, do the damage intended, and drop out again for 'after-raid' photos before joining up to return to base. Many recon flights varied in their actual mission, however."[11]

Commanding the 118th was a wiry young officer from Kansas, Maj. Edward O. McComas. Like most of the squadron's pilots, he was highly experienced in the air after long months of training. All they needed was a little practical combat experience, which they picked up quickly. By the end of June, the 118th's pilots had flown sixty-four sorties, and the unit was fully capable of taking its place beside the veteran squadrons of the 23rd Fighter Group.

16

Fire and Fall Back

On June 27, 1944, a plane landed at Kweilin's Erh Tong Airfield and taxied over to the operations shack that the 74th Fighter Squadron called home. The officer who stepped down from the plane was a small, slim man with the tan face and squinting eyes of a veteran aviator. He looked too old to be a fighter pilot, though. Heck, he was even graying at the temples.

This man was Capt. John C. Herbst, arriving to assume command of the 74th. His predecessor, Maj. Art Cruikshank, had been shot down the previous day on a strafing mission. The men were receptive to a change in leadership, however, as Major Cruikshank had not endeared himself to them during his month in command. If the young pilots of the 74th had any doubts about their new boss, they would forget them quickly. Herbst was quiet, precise, and very protective of his pilots. Before long they would be calling him "Pappy"— and doing so with genuine affection and respect.

Herbst had been handpicked for the job by none other than Col. Tex Hill, the group commander, and Hill knew a real fighter pilot when he saw one. Hill recalled meeting Herbst in Florida while Hill was stationed at Eglin Field between his first and second tours in China. Hill remarked, "I had a guy down there at Eglin named Pappy Herbst. He was in Arctic-Desert-Tropic, but he was assigned to me for flying to get his time. One Sunday we were out at the beach and here comes this P-51. The '51 was new then. We had a lot of test gear on it. So here comes this '51, and the damned guy rolls it right on the water. Then he put on a hell of a show. I was just amazed. But then it dawned on me: Who is that? God Almighty, he's not supposed to have that airplane. I got back to the base, and it was old Pappy Herbst.

"Well, I knew doggoned well that I had to do something, so I went in to see Colonel Morse [Winslow ("Winnie") Morse was Hill's boss at the time, and he later served in China as commander of the Chinese-American Composite Wing]. I told him, 'You know, we've got this guy. We've got to do something. I recommend that we ground him for about 30 days [which amounted to a slap on the wrist].

"Later on, when I came back to China, I was up there visiting Winnie [probably at Peishiyi] and this transport lands. Here's old Pappy Herbst getting off. I said, 'What the hell are you doing here?' He said he was reporting in to General Morse. I said, 'Wait a minute. I'm short as hell of squadron commanders. Don't report in. Let me see if I can get you over here with me.'

"So I went in to Morse and said, 'You remember that damned eight ball we had down at Eglin when we had to ground him?' Well, if there was anything that Winnie Morse was allergic to, it was an eight ball. So he said, 'Hell, you can have him.' Pappy got on the plane and went back to Kweilin, and I gave him the 74th Fighter Squadron. He was a hell of a guy; just top-notch. He was just wise— low profile, but a hell of a good pilot."[1]

Pappy Herbst was already thirty years old, a father, and an experienced civilian pilot when the war started. Early in the war he ferried aircraft from Canada to England, and he reportedly had an opportunity to get into combat in England for a time, shooting down one German aircraft. He spent his first month in China flying with the 76th Fighter Squadron and scored his first victory against the Japanese with that outfit. And when the 23rd Fighter Group tallied its confirmed aerial victories at the end of the war, Herbst's name came out on top with a total of eighteen, and that did not include the Luftwaffe kill.

Herbst took command of the 74th at a time when the pilots and ground crews were reeling under the pressure of heavy operations. Entries for this period taken from the diary of 74th pilot Charlie Cook reveal the hectic pace.

"June 27: Two missions today totaling nine hours' flying. First was a patrol over AX2 [code name for Lingling]. Second, seven of us escorted B-25s up in the lake district. 180 [degree turn] in enemy territory. Hit by Ack Ack [antiaircraft artillery] coming back. Twelve Zeros jumped us. Jones's flight left, leaving [Robert] Woodward, [Chester] Denny and myself. I got one probable and Denny got one damaged.

"June 28: Day off. 118th Squadron lost two men, but believe one is OK.

"June 29: Flew 10 hours today. Vurgaropulos killed this morning while strafing; we were giving him top cover. [Lieutenant Thomas] Aston killed this afternoon while we were taking off on a mission. His motor quit. We went on a third mission to Hengyang. Seven of us intercepted 20 Zeros; I was leading one flight and [Ted] Adams another. After climbing to their level, I made a head-on pass with one and set him on fire for my first confirmed Zero; his wingman put some 20 mm holes through my wing. I saw a pilot in a parachute but didn't know who it was so I didn't strafe it. Turned out to be a Jap that [Stanley] Trecartin shot down.

"July 1: I have flown seven missions and 25 hours of combat in the last 72. Just about worn out at the moment. Cruikshank is back and OK. He bailed out in enemy territory and walked out; going back to the States. 'Pappy' Herbst our c.o. now; a very good one it looks like.

"July 5: Flew my 50th mission today. We went NE [northeast] of Sinshih and caught a supply dump loaded with tanks, armored trucks, men, horses, ammunition and gas. We set a lot of it on fire and all picked up holes on the first pass: heavy ground fire and Ack Ack. Sixteen Zeros jumped us, but top cover took care of them."[2]

And so the summer went for pilots such as Cook, as the 23rd Fighter Group pounded out mission after mission against the Ichi-Go offensive. A typical day's flying started with a weather recon up the Hsiang River valley from Kweilin first thing in the morning. These recons were necessary now that the warning net was no longer available to provide such information. Once an up-to-date picture of the weather conditions was in hand, the squadrons could send out missions. Some were escorts of B-25s that were assigned to bomb stationary targets such as railroad yards, airfields, and supply dumps; but most of the fighter flights were offensive sweeps or search-and-destroy missions.

A typical sweep involved two flights of four fighters each. If the target area was not too far away, the planes could attack with high-explosive bombs, rockets, parachute-mounted fragmentation bombs, or a combination; and of course, with their machine guns. The farther away the targets, the more gas the fighters needed. So for long-range missions, drop tanks were fitted to the wing racks and the attack work was limited to strafing. Once the planes reached the target area, one flight would drop down to low level and attack while the other hovered overhead on top cover and provided protection against Japanese fighters. When the first flight finished dropping its loads, it would trade places with the top cover so that the second flight could also unload its ordnance on the target. During July, an average mission lasted about three and a half hours. It was not unusual for the squadrons to send out as many as five or six missions in a day.

The Japanese fighter units were very active during this period as well. The original battle plans for Ichi-Go called for Japanese fighters and bombers to concentrate primarily on cooperating with the ground forces by attacking Chinese defensive positions and supply efforts. They were instructed to avoid combat whenever possible. The heavy attacks by Casey Vincent's fighters and bombers against the Japanese lines of communication and supply were hampering the ground offensive, forcing the Japanese commanders to change their plans. They now assigned their fighters to patrol the supply lines and attempt to ward off U.S. air attacks. Each pilot of the 25th Air Regiment who flew Ki-43 Oscars flew between 80 and 120 hours of combat time during July alone. Also, a provisional unit, the 6th Air Regiment, was moved to the captured airfields at Changsha, Hsiangtan, and later Hengyang to fly ground support missions. The 6th was equipped primarily with obsolete ground cooperation aircraft such as the Ki-51 Sonia, a two-seat, single-engine light bomber with fixed landing gear.

★ ★ ★ ★

With all of these Japanese aircraft committed to the Ichi-Go offensive, inevitably air-to-air encounters picked up. Pilots of the 23rd Fighter Group recorded claims every day from July 5 through July 15, and they probably would have continued the string longer had not the weather interrupted operations on July 16.

The mission for the 75th Fighter Squadron on July 5 was to escort B-25s to Tungcheng, a supply center about forty miles east of Tungting Lake. Eight P-40s took off at 6:30 A.M. from Kweilin with Maj. Donald L. Quigley leading. When Major Loofbourrow was transferred to group headquarters in June, Quigley became the 75th's new CO. Quigley got his initial combat experience over Burma while assigned to the 80th Fighter Group and had been flying with the 75th for several months. Major Quigley only had two permanently assigned 75th pilots with him: Lt. Don Lopez, who led the second flight of four, and Lt. Joshua ("Chief") Sanford. The other pilots were on temporary duty at Kweilin to bolster the 23rd's strength and also to gain combat experience. Four of these pilots were from the 33rd Fighter Group, a P-47 outfit assigned to Chengkung in western China to provide air defense for its B-29 bases. The last pilot was from the 51st Fighter Group in Kunming.

The formation proceeded northeast, and just past Lingling the weather cleared. About that time, one of the pilots from the 33rd reported a rough engine and turned for home. The farther they went, the more alert the seven remaining pilots became for signs of enemy opposition. Heads swiveled and eyes strained to pick out the tiny dots in the distance that might grow into a flock of Oscars or Tojos.

Just north of Hengyang, Lieutenant Lopez spotted them: twelve Oscars coming in for a bounce. Major Quigley had just enough time to call the bombers and advise them to clear the area before whipping his Shark around in a steep turn and lining up for a head-on pass with the Japanese interceptors. He picked out an Oscar that was slightly below him and opened fire. The enemy plane staggered under the blows from Quigley's guns, and then the two planes passed. Quigley rolled over on his back and observed the Oscar dive straight down and crash. By now, aircraft were all over the sky, and the major had no trouble picking up another target. This time he attacked from the rear and set his target on fire, but he had to break off and so claimed it as a probable. He also damaged two more Oscars before the fight ended.

Lopez, meanwhile, had opened the fight with a long-range shot at an Oscar below him. The maneuverable enemy plane clawed into a tight turn to the left, which the U.S. pilots referred to as a "flip," and Lopez could not follow. He turned his attention to another Oscar, which was turning below him to the right. Lopez followed the turn, pulling so much lead on his target that it dropped out of sight behind the big engine cowling on the front of his Shark. He opened fire with a short burst, eased off the turn to observe the results, and repeated the process with a longer burst. When he eased out of this turn, Lopez saw what he had hoped to see: The Oscar was on fire, with flames blazing from the wing roots and engine cowling. It went down as Lopez cleared his tail. By this time his wingman, Lt. Albert Haynes of the 51st Fighter Group, was out of sight. Lopez later saw a parachute going down, and that proved to be Haynes.

Lopez picked up some battle damage early in the fight, but it might have been worse. Lieutenant Sanford and his wingman, Lt. Art Heine of the 33rd, spotted two Oscars on his tail. Heine pulled in behind the one that was hitting Lopez and opened fire. This Oscar caught on fire and nosed into the ground. Sanford shot up the other Oscar with a long burst from 150 yards. It flipped over in a spiral to the right but did not catch on fire. Sanford picked out another target and was hitting it when yet another Oscar got on his tail. This Oscar hit Sanford's Shark with a good burst into the fuselage and cockpit area. Sanford was wounded in the foot and broke off immediately. He flew home as far as Lingling, where he belly-landed his Shark.

Later that same day the 76th Fighter Squadron sent out eight P-51s on an escort mission to Lukow. Over the target, four Oscars jumped a two-plane element of Mustangs and shot one down that was flown by a 51st Fighter Group pilot. The P-51 pilots salvoed their bombs, and then four of them spotted twenty Oscars and went down to attack. The Japanese fighters scattered, but one of them stayed around to fight it out. The Japanese pilot took on the four Mustangs alone for five minutes, turning and diving with such skill that the U.S. pilots never got a good shot at him. Finally, the four Mustangs ran out of ammunition, and the Oscar dived away unscathed. When the pilots returned to base and talked about the mission, they agreed that they had been outfought by a Japanese flier of rare ability. They immediately dubbed him the "Kiukiang Ace." It is not known if this pilot was ever encountered again, but from then on the pilots of the 76th kept a sharp eye out for him whenever their missions took them to the Kiukiang-Nanchang area.

Scraps like these occurred day after day. On July 7, 1/Lt. Oran S. Watts shot down two Oscars at Anking for the first confirmed victories of the 118th Tac Recon Squadron. The future ace scored again on July 14, as the new squadron's combat hours piled up quickly. On July 24, the 118th sent out six missions, totaling thirty-three sorties. The first mission of the day was an eight-Shark sweep against targets of opportunity in the Hengyang area. One pilot who remembered it well was Lt. George H. ("Spider") Greene. He wrote, "We were led by Major Ira Jones, our operations officer. I was an element leader and had a pilot named Richard Stutzman on my right wing. Jonesy spotted a Jap patrol of six Oscars at 9 o'clock low. We dropped our parafrags and external tanks and immediately began climbing.

"I made a pass at the leader of the Jap formation and fired, noticing hits on his fuselage and canopy. At the same time I heard machine gun fire and believed I was being fired on, so I broke off contact and dove out of the fray. It later proved that the fire I heard was coming from Stutzman's guns. It seems he went on in and made a pass with me in formation. Lucky we didn't both get killed."[3]

When July ended and the statistics were tallied, they made impressive reading. Pilots of the 23rd Fighter Group had flown 1,712 sorties for 6,503 combat hours. They had destroyed twenty-seven enemy aircraft in aerial combat and five more on the ground. The price had been heavy, however. One pilot—1/Lt. Richard D. Mullineaux of the 74th—was killed, and twenty-four P-40s and P-51s were destroyed in combat and accidents.

The month came to a close with a night alert at Kweilin on July 31, and two fighters took off to chase the enemy raiders. Piloting the P-51 was Col. Tex Hill. In the other plane, a P-40, was Hill's boss, Brig. Gen. Casey Vincent. There is no way to know what might have happened if Vincent had made contact with the enemy, as he was under strict orders from General Chennault to avoid combat flying. As it turned out, all Vincent saw in the darkness below him was a line of lights that appeared to be pointing the way to Erh Tong Airfield. He dropped down to strafe them before returning to the field.

★ ★ ★ ★

The Chinese defenders of Hengyang held out for forty-four days. During that time, the 23rd Fighter Group pounded their Japanese attackers mercilessly from the air. The Chinese government, however, steadfastly refused to send reinforcements to Gen. Hsueh Yueh, whom Generalissimo Chiang Kai-shek considered untrustworthy. Without fresh troops, and with the meager supplies and ammunition that the Fourteenth Air Force could deliver by air drops, the city was doomed. The end came on August 8, 1944. The tattered remains of Hsueh's army pulled back to a line seventy miles northeast of Kweilin, leaving the air base at Lingling basically undefended.

The fall of Hengyang also had implications for the air base at Liuchow, present home of the 76th Fighter Squadron. The long-expected push out of Canton by the Japanese 23rd Army had commenced in late July with the object of seizing the railroad link north to Hengyang and then capturing the city. Now, with Hengyang already in Japanese hands, the priorities changed. The rail line could be taken anytime. Instead, the 23rd Army turned left and headed along the West River toward the new air base at Tanchuk and, beyond it, Liuchow. Meanwhile, the Japanese ground forces in the Hengyang area halted for several weeks to regroup and replenish their supplies before continuing their drive down the Hsiang River toward Lingling and Kweilin.

Air operations of the 23rd Fighter Group continued without respite in August. The squadrons spent the first week concentrating on enemy truck convoys that were supplying the siege forces at Hengyang. Casey Vincent recorded in his diary that his planes destroyed or badly damaged nearly three hundred trucks on the first day of the month alone.

Encounters with Japanese fighters also continued. A typical fight took place August 6, when the 74th Fighter Squadron sent eight P-40Ns to Hengyang for an early morning strike against the trucks. Pilot Charlie Cook wrote the following account:

"My recall of this is better than of other events due purely to my stupidity in handling the attack. Pappy [Herbst], Ted [Adams, Cook's close friend], and I were leading three flights north at 12–14,000 feet when we spotted a large gaggle of Zeros above and north of us. I spotted six Japs strafing below us and called Pappy, who instructed me to take my wingman down and engage.

"We firewalled it down and naturally shot past the Vals [probably Ki-51 Sonias] without making a hit. Then we returned, and at about 500 feet I had a direct burst and flamed one. At that time, black smoke belched out of the stacks and my engine detonated badly. Looking back, I saw two Vals tossing orange balls at me. Suddenly I had become the hunted and they the hunters!

"I realized my mistake and jammed the fuel mixture from 'lean'— for altitude—to 'rich.' The engine cleared partially and smoke ceased, but they were able to chase me into friendly territory. I recovered at Lingling while the others got back to Kweilin after a successful dogfight. Lesson learned: Eagerness overpowered good judgment."[4]

Adams shot down one fighter during the scrap, but the big scorer was Pappy Herbst, who got two. These were his fourth and fifth victories, making him the 74th's newest ace.

The 75th Fighter Squadron's CO also joined the roster of aces in August, one day before Herbst made it, but Maj. Don Quigley did not have a chance to enjoy his new status for long. He wrote the following account of his August 10 mission and its aftermath for the 75th Fighter Squadron's alumni newsletter.

My story started on the first strafing run just south of the bend in the Hsiang River—Dog Dog 2-4 [the location on the target maps]. We came in from the west and, of course, I knew it was a hot spot. I guess now I started too close to the bend in the river and was dead meat for a machine gun nest, as I found out later. The black smoke started pouring back and I knew I was in trouble. I rolled the canopy back with immediate thoughts of getting out, but had to close it again while unbuckling because of smoke and flames being sucked in. I must have jumped out from 600 to 800 feet and hit the ground standing up. The only thought was—get out of the chute and take off, which I did. But it wasn't 10 minutes later I could see soldiers with rifles closing in from a circle around me like a fox hunt.

They had me cold, and after taking the butts of rifles a while and being stripped of my watch and insignia, I was marched off to an old farmhouse nearby. The Japs had taken it over for housing, etc. and I was tied up in the lean-to that was a water buffalo shed, and easy to tell. I spent the night there tied hand and foot to a post, with my own personal guard. The mosquitoes were driving me nuts, and in the middle of the night a Jap came around and put a net over my head. I think it was out of my chute pack.

I stayed there the next day and that night was walked up to the river and went across to the north side on the outboard motor-driven raft they used to haul one truck at a time across the river to the south. I can't understand why we didn't run a few two-man missions up there at night and strafe and bomb that place but good. If we could have sunk that raft, which they tied up and camouflaged during the day, their truck traffic south may have been slowed considerably.

I spent the next night in a building near the landing strip on the north side of the bend. They allowed me to sleep on a spring bed with an old mattress on it and a blood-covered sheet—we must have hurt someone real bad.

The next morning early they walked me down to the field and they put me in an airplane—the back seat with a guard cramped in with me—and off to Yochow with a short stopover and then to Hankow. Had a 20-minute ride into town from the field and was put in a five-foot by five-foot cell in the basement of a local jail filled with Chinese in the other cells. Leaving the field I saw an old P-40, maybe an A or B, sitting on a ramp.

About 10 days later I was told to turn my back to the aisle and stay that way. I heard some hobnail boots coming down the cement aisle and quickly turned my head to see a pair of stockinged feet and khaki pants go by with a guard. Of course, I knew it was a fellow airman. Some five or six days later, the Chinaman diagonally across from me caught my attention and threw a wad of paper across the aisle. I reached out through the four-inch by four-inch wood posts that were used as bars on the cells, picked it up and unfolded a scrap of paper plus a pencil. On it was a message—"I'm Don Watts from Marion, Ohio." HOLY SMOLY, that's where I'm from. Out of how many thousands of GIs in China at any one time would this happen? I wrote my name on the paper and said I was from Marion, Ohio, and that I had gone to school with a Florine Watts. A few days later the paper came back saying, "Yes, that's my sister!" Then and there I could place this fellow because his sister had married a friend of mine.

Don Watts was a crew chief on a C-47. He fell out of his plane over Hengyang one night when the city was surrounded and the ATC [Air Transport Command] had a couple of C-47s drop ammunition and medical supplies by kicking out bales with chutes attached, flying low over town. Watts got his foot tangled up in the rice rope and was pulled out with a bale. He told me later that on the first pass he didn't have his chute on but decided to do so while the plane was maneuvering for a second pass. The Japs got him after chasing him around the edge of town for a few hours. He was bayoneted three times in the process.

In about three or four weeks we were taken out together and placed in a second-story room of another building and kept there until December. While there a couple of B-29s bombed the rail yards close by us; an incendiary landed in the streets about 75 yards from our building and the concussion knocked the plaster off the ceiling of the room we were in. Ol' Watts was under the bed.

In late December we joined several other pilots and crewmen and were placed on a river steamer bound for Shanghai. They traveled only at night and tied up in Nanking. We were taken off and marched through the streets to the local hoosegow to spend the day and boarded again that evening to proceed to Shanghai.

There were about 1,200 of us in the camp there, Marines and civilian personnel off Wake Island mostly. The whole camp was moved in May 1945 by train—boxcars—to Nanking and north to Peiping. We spent a month in Peiping in a large warehouse and were then moved again to Mukden and down through Korea to Pusan, where we were deloused and shipped over to Japan.

We went to Tokyo by rail—boy, things were burned out for miles by the fire-bombing that had gone on—and on north to the island of Hokkaido. All prisoners were dropped off along the way at various places, and only 12 of us—the "Diddled Dozen"—went on to Sapporo, Hokkaido. We were there until September 1945, when a C-46 flew in to pick us up and fly us to Okinawa and on to Manila. Re-uniformed in Manila and checked out, we 12—being Air Force and flying personnel—tried to wangle a flight back to the States, but no luck. We boarded a slow boat for Frisco and finally made it back to home soil.[5]

Quigley was not the only member of the "Diddled Dozen" from the 23rd Fighter Group. Lieutenant Jim Taylor, also of the 75th Fighter Squadron, was shot down in a P-51 in November and met up with Major Quigley on December 28, 1944, during the trip down the Yangtze. They were together through the rest of the war.

★ ★ ★ ★

The heavy operations were taking a toll on the aircraft and men of the 23rd Fighter Group. By the middle of August, Gen. Casey Vincent begged the Fourteenth Air Force headquarters at Kunming to send him more pilots and aircraft. The temporary duty pilots from western China simply were not enough to fill the gaps.

The 23rd lost thirty aircraft during August 1944. By far, most of them were destroyed by enemy ground fire. Only one, a P-51B, was destroyed in the Japanese night bombings that were a regular hazard now. Another five crashed due to engine failure, showing the extreme wear and tear that the aircraft were taking. The in-commission rate for aircraft that month was just 68 percent, compared with 81 percent in June, and the total number of aircraft available for operations at the end of the month was forty-eight, down five from August 1. Among the replacement aircraft received during the month were two obsolete P-40K-5s and one even older P-40K-1.

The biggest single blow to aircraft and pilots occurred August 6. A three-plane flight of P-40Ns from the 118th Tac Recon Squadron got caught in low overcast at Kweilin while returning from a strafing mission. All three aircraft spun in and crashed, killing Capt. Robert E. Gee, a popular and talented flight leader, and Lts. Robert G. O'Brien and Ernest W. Swanson. In all, six pilots in the group were killed during August while two others, Major Quigley and Lt. Gordon F. Bennett of the 74th, were taken prisoner. No fewer than seventeen other pilots went down on missions and were in various stages of finding their way back to their bases during the month.

One new pilot who arrived at about this time and was assigned to the 75th Fighter Squadron was 2/Lt. Mervin Beard. He recalled his introduction to his new group commander. According to Beard, "Colonel Tex Hill had me report to him the second day I was on base. I'll never forget that experience. I wasn't sure he had a uniform on, and his adjutant was getting ready to take off on some mission. He had his shaving kit with him, and Col. Hill said, 'You won't need that where you're going.'

"Colonel Hill put one foot on top of a two-drawer file cabinet and just sort of talked about the war in China and what he expected of a fighter pilot. He was serious and yet friendly and somewhat awesome. I have reported to quite a few commanding officers, but this was by far the most unique experience I ever had."[6]

Brigadier General Vincent sent Colonel Hill to Kunming on August 18 to lobby for replacement pilots and airplanes for his fighter group. When General Chennault paid a visit to Kweilin the following week, Vincent noted in his diary that the boss "didn't have much to say."[7]

Supplies continued to be a problem as well. For example, the 76th Fighter Squadron flew missions out of its base at Liuchow early in August, mostly carrying two five-hundred-pound bombs on each Mustang to targets in the Hengyang area. Then, after a period of intense operations, the base ran out of these bombs completely. In order to use the Mustangs more efficiently, the 76th moved its planes up to Erh Tong Airfield at Kweilin to share space with the 118th Squadron.

And then, just as the 23rd Fighter Group was gasping for breath—figuratively, if not literally—the Japanese Eleventh Army began to move again, pushing down the river toward Lingling and Kweilin. The Lingling air base was in danger immediately, because no Chinese forces were in place to defend it. General Hsueh made his plans to stand and fight at Chuanhsien, about seventy miles northeast of Kweilin, but that was well south of Lingling. In any case, the airfield at Lingling had already been stripped of any permanent units and was used only for emergency stops and for staging to refuel on long-range strikes beyond Hankow.

With the Japanese moving south at a rapid rate, bridges became a primary target for the 76th Fighter Squadron's Mustangs. The best way a pilot can destroy a bridge is to drop a bomb right on top of it. The P-51 was especially well suited for dive-bombing bridges because it was easy to trim in a dive, whereas the P-40 had a tendency to roll. Lieutenant Harry Zavakos continued to shine as the 76th's top bridge-buster. He became so good at hitting them, in fact, that whenever he led a flight it was assigned two targets: one for him and one for the other three pilots.

On September 7, the Japanese captured the town and airfield at Lingling. Once a safe haven for the fighters of the 23rd, now they would become a target. With Lingling gone and the Japanese still moving, Brigadier General Vincent had to face the fact that his 68th Composite Wing probably was going to lose Kweilin soon. This posed a much bigger problem than losing Lingling, because Kweilin now had three bases: two for fighters and one for bombers. They hosted tactical fighter and bomber squadrons, the wing and group headquarters, and facilities for heavy aircraft maintenance. Thus, while the strategic implications of losing Kweilin were enormous, the logistics of clearing out were hugely problematic, too. Keeping with the Fourteenth Air Force's policy of leaving as little as possible of its bases for the enemy, everything had to go.

Vincent split all his units into "essential" and "nonessential" elements. In this context, essential referred to the business of getting airplanes ready to fly and flying them. Essential ground personnel such as mechanics, armorers, and radio technicians would stay at forward bases with the pilots as long as possible.

The evacuation of Kweilin was under way by September 9. Administrative functions began moving to a new base at Luliang, just forty miles east of Kunming. The 23rd Fighter Group's aircraft continued to fly from Kweilin, but all preparations were made to move out at a moment's notice. All of the squadrons would not necessarily be moving backward, however; Vincent had a small surprise in store for the Japanese. He moved the 74th Squadron to a base in the Chinese-held pocket of territory east of the Hankow-Canton railroad. The big airfield at Suichuan still was in Chinese hands, as was the smaller field a few miles south at Kanchow.

The 74th and 76th squadrons had been using Kanchow intermittently since July. Whenever sufficient gasoline and ammunition stockpiles there could support operations, flights of fighters moved in until the cupboard was bare again. Now Vincent felt that with his bases of operation shrinking, he would be able to keep a steady flow of gas and ammunition flowing into Kanchow by air transport. He sent word to Maj. John Herbst that this would be the 74th's new base.

The first squadron to leave Kweilin was the 76th. But instead of returning to its permanent base at Liuchow, the squadron went due south to Tanchuk. This small airfield was east of the city of Wuchow and was right in the path of the Japanese 23rd Army's advance up the West River. As a relatively new base, it had comfortable living quarters and good food for the men but lacked one important element—air raid warning. The warning net in the Canton region had broken down, just as the one in the Tungting Lake region had, and efforts to set up a primitive radar system at Tanchuk had not been very successful.

Still, the 76th was able to operate effectively from Tanchuk for several weeks. The P-51s pounded ground targets along the route of the Japanese advance on the West River, averaging four missions a day. This pace took a toll on the pilots and ground crews alike, as did the knowledge that a Japanese air attack might occur at any moment.

Before first light on the morning of September 14, the radar station at Tanchuk reported a flight of unidentified aircraft circling over the hills east of the base. The report aroused suspicion that the Japanese were waiting until sunrise for enough visibility to bomb more accurately than they had been lately at night. Lieutenant Bob Schaeffer, now one of the old hands in the squadron, volunteered to take off in the darkness so he would be in position to attack when the Japanese came in. He made his takeoff run guided by the flashing lights of a jeep parked at the end of the runway. Then as daylight broke, four more Mustangs took off to join Schaeffer, but they did not find any Japanese aircraft anywhere. The radar report apparently had been false.

Still, on the rare occasions when the Mustangs did run into Japanese aircraft, they hit the enemy hard. Later on the morning of September 14, the 76th sent out eleven Mustangs. Led by 1/Lt. Tom R. Wilson, the P-51s were to dive-bomb at Sanshui, a key town just west of Canton, and then sweep over the White Cloud Airdrome at Canton to see if they could stir up any Japanese opposition. Stir they did, as ten Tojos were spotted just as the P-51s were lining up for their bomb runs.

Pilot Bill Watt, who flew the mission, recalled, "As I remember, we had made our bombing run and were climbing back up to altitude when we were intercepted by some Jap Tojos. One of them made a head-on pass at me; both of us were shooting. The Jap broke away first, I followed and expended the rest of my ammunition at him. Debris came from his right wing root and the plane began to emit smoke as it was going down in what seemed to be a controlled dive. We were over enemy territory, so I elected to go home rather than stick around and see if he made it or not, as there were several Tojos in the air above me."[8]

During the scrap, Lieutenant Wilson and Lt. Richard L. Anderson each got confirmed kills, while Lt. Bob Schaeffer got a probable to go along with that of Bill Watt. Three other Japanese planes were reported as damaged. Though the squadron flew a record number of missions during the month of September, its pilots recorded only one other air-to-air claim during the month—a Tojo damaged by Lt. Bill Eldridge on September 18.

By the middle of the month, Japanese ground forces had surrounded the city of Wuchow. This made it too dangerous for the 76th to continue operating at Tanchuk. As the squadron's intelligence officer, 1/Lt. Ed Paine, wrote in his account of this period, the men feared each night when they went to sleep that they might wake to find a new houseboy named Yamamoto. The 76th packed its bags and flew back to Liuchow.

Likewise, the end came at Kweilin on September 14, 1944. Major General Chennault and his boss, China-Burma-India theater commander Lt. Gen. Joseph Stilwell, flew in for a brief last look before demolition started. Fortunately, the weather cooperated and the transport aircraft were able to fly out the remaining personnel and equipment, along with the two "big wheels."

Of the last days, September 14 and 15, at Kweilin, Tex Hill recalled, "During base evacuations, we'd move the nonessential people out and leave one crew to destroy the base, even at Kweilin. Casey and I were there to the last. We flew out in the 'Silver Slipper' [Vincent's B-25]. On the last night, there was no security. Lots of refugees were around, and of course wherever they were, you had a chance of Jap fifth columnists. They [the demolition crew] dug holes in the runway and buried 1,000-pound bombs to blow it up.

"We moved everything out ahead of time. We could hear gunfire all night that last night. Casey and I tried to figure out how to booby-trap the toilet in our quarters. It was the only one on the base, so we knew some Jap general would be sitting on it soon."[9]

Vincent and Hill got up at 4:00 A.M. on September 15, had a quick breakfast and a last look around, then took off at 5:30 A.M. They circled over the city and inspected the demolition work at the air bases, which had gone according to plan. Heavy clouds of smoke and dust rose from each base. Then they set course to the southwest and followed the Hsiang River down to Liuchow, where Vincent would set up his new headquarters for the 68th Composite Wing.

Along with wing and group headquarters, Liuchow would now support the 76th and 118th squadrons and the 11th Bomb Squadron. The next seven weeks would prove the most intense period of operations during the entire war for the 76th and 118th, as they threw everything they had into the effort to slow the Japanese advance.

The situation was a little different for the 75th. This squadron was sent up to Chihkiang when Kweilin was evacuated. The Chihkiang base, about 140 miles north of Kweilin, was the home of the 5th Fighter Group, Chinese-American Composite Wing. Its four squadrons had been operating there all summer. Chihkiang was an ideal location for hitting targets in the Tungting Lake and Hankow areas, and it also was in striking distance of the Ichi-Go forces advancing on Kweilin.

The 75th was now under the command of Maj. A. T. House Jr., who took over after Major Quigley went down in August. House was a highly experienced combat veteran, having flown a full tour on P-40s with the 49th Fighter Group in Australia and New Guinea during 1942 and 1943. His score stood at four confirmed victories. Some of the 75th's pilots soon began to wonder if House's tour in the South Pacific had taken a bigger toll on their new commander than he let on. From August 15 through the end of that busy month, he flew just two sweeps and two dive-bombing missions. In September, when the squadron flew eighty-eight missions, Major House only flew on six days. In fact, after two intense days of operations on September 3 and 4 at Kweilin, the commander did not fly another combat mission until September 23, and then he flew just two recons and a local alert the rest of the month. When October came, he did not fly a single mission.

Although the new CO was a disappointment, the 75th did have some bright spots during this period. For one, the squadron finally began to get some Mustangs to supplant its dwindling supply of P-40s. The new planes were all P-51B-10 and C-7 models, which were essentially identical. The important feature on these Mustangs was the eighty-five-gallon gas tank behind the pilot's seat. This tank boosted the aircraft's range considerably, even in comparison with the earlier P-51Bs.

Another improvement was that the location of the 75th's new base enabled the squadron to engage in some good air-to-air encounters with the Japanese that the squadrons at Liuchow were missing. The first one, a sweep to Changsha and Shaoyang, came on September 16. This would also be the 75th's first offensive mission flying P-51s, though there were only two of them in the ten-plane formation.

One of the P-40 pilots flying that day was Lt. Louis W. Weber. He recorded his frustration over a missed opportunity: "This was one of the ones I would like to have over, since I missed a cinch victory. I was flying a wing position, number two or number four. The Zeros had been called out and I was on one in a hard right turn. My shots were flashing on his [aircraft's] skin when I flipped over the top.

"I came out in a steep dive and spotted a Zero with a P-40 in trail. I overtook them because of my angle of closure and waited for the other man to shoot him down. What I did not know was that the Zero was already leaving the other P-40, which had no closure on him. I waited too long, and he saw me and left me as well. The pilot in the second P-40 was John D. Rosenbaum.

"We chased him for about 10 miles in level flight at low altitude, but since he did not turn we couldn't close on him. At the initial contact in this fight my 75-gallon drop tank was a bit reluctant to let go, but I was clean on the first engagement and would have claimed a victory, but I could find no gun camera film of it. Rosenbaum could not understand why I didn't just shoot down the Zero he had been chasing."[10]

In all, the 75th filed six damage claims for the mission, including Weber's Zero, and 1/Lt. Jesse B. Gray got credit for one probable.

One of the P-51 pilots, Lt. Don Lopez, experienced the Mustang's characteristic jamming problem when he fired at an Oscar in a high-G turn. He got a few hits, and then the guns went silent.

The 75th was back in combat with Japanese fighters on September 21 and 22. On the first of these missions, 1/Lt. Bob Peterson led twelve Sharks of the 75th out of Chihkiang with sixteen P-40s of the CACW. The formation proceeded east at ninety-five hundred feet under a thin overcast to Ninsiang, where the CACW P-40s bombed while the 75th provided top cover. Then the roles were reversed, and the 75th's Sharks led the way to Sinshih. As Lieutenant Peterson wrote later, "The mission was briefed through an interpreter. . . . My bombs, a pair of 500-pound demos, started a huge explosion and fire. As I was pulling out of my bomb run the usual jolt of adrenaline came with the call, 'Zeros!' No one bothered to say in which direction or height they were. Everyone within radio range assumed that they were on their tail. Having been caught on the deck before, I found it a bit hairy to hear that Zeros were in the area.

"It was balls to the wall and head on a swivel until you were clear and could locate the Zeros. I climbed up as close to the engagement as possible without exposing my flight to attack. I bored in on one of the Jap planes head-on and commenced firing. The Zero began burning and spiraled into the ground."[11]

Peterson also got off a seventy-degree deflection shot at another Tojo and damaged it later in the fight. But while he had been climbing up to engage, the top cover already was involved in a tremendous scrap. The leader of the 75th's second flight, 1/Lt. Forrest F. Parham, attacked first. He climbed up above a flight of eight Tojos that was preparing to drop down on some other Sharks and then dived down behind one of them and opened fire. Parham saw hits flashing in the Tojo's nose area before the plane slow-rolled and dropped into a dive. Parham was hot on his tail; in fact, Parham was too hot. He got in several more bursts at the Tojo but then found himself overrunning the target. Parham passed so close that he clipped off his Shark's radio aerial mast on the way past. The Tojo dropped away streaming vapor behind it, and Parham claimed it as damaged.

Before long airplanes were twisting and turning all over the sky. A pilot on temporary assignment from the 81st Fighter Group at Chengtu, Lt. William T. Griswold, watched an enemy fighter spiral down out of the fight and then begin to climb back up. He dived in behind the Tojo and opened fire from about two hundred yards away. Flames belched from under the cowling of the Japanese fighter as it rolled over and dived into the ground. In all the 75th scored two confirmed, two probables, and five damaged in the fight. The CACW pilots submitted additional claims for six confirmed.

The next day's scrap, which took place over Sintsiang, was even more successful. Captains Dick Jones, Chief Sanford, and Flash Segura scored single victories, and 2/Lt. Gordon E. Willis got two confirmed kills. This was the end of the 75th's scoring for more than a month; however, things would pick up after the squadron got a new commanding officer.

★ ★ ★ ★

While the 75th Fighter Squadron under an unpopular commanding officer was struggling to keep its chin up and its planes in the air, and as the 76th and 118th squadrons were practically stacking up while operating from the overcrowded base at Liuchow, the 74th was facing an entirely different situation. This squadron, now stationed alone hundreds of miles east at Kanchow, was racing to keep up with its aggressive, gray-haired commander. Major Pappy Herbst was busy inventing a whole new way to wage an air war.

17

Guerrilla Operations

Kanchow was a nice place to be stationed in the fall of 1944, as long as the men did not dwell on the fact that they could not go very far in any direction without running into the Japanese. The airfield originally was designed to accommodate medium bombers, so it was reasonably spacious and had good revetment areas. Like most airfields in China, it had a magnificent runway built by hand and made of crushed rock.

The hostel area was about a mile and a half from the airfield; that was far enough away to make it an unlikely target for enemy bombs. The modern redbrick barracks were situated in a fold in the hills overlooking the scenic Kan River. Officers lived two to a room in two buildings that even featured toilets that flushed, a rarity in China at the time. Mess hall and recreation facilities were in the same compound.

But the physical setup was not what made Kanchow important to the 74th Fighter Squadron. For Maj. Pappy Herbst and his men, it was Kanchow's location. From this base, the 74th Fighter Squadron could hit targets not available to any other outfit in the 23rd Fighter Group. The Japanese Ichi-Go offensive had been pushing steadily westward from Hengyang and Canton throughout the summer of 1944, but the Chinese still held a large pocket of territory in southeastern China's Kiangsi and Fukien provinces. And in that pocket was the city of Kanhsien, home of Kanchow Airfield.

Throughout August, the 74th Fighter Squadron split its aircraft so that half flew out of Kweilin and half from Kanchow, which was nearly three hundred miles to the east. While the Kweilin detachment flew missions in support of Kweilin's defense, the pilots at Kanchow struck at the advancing Japanese from the rear. They hit targets along the Hsiang River from Changsha to Lingling. They pounded traffic along the Yangtze River to the north and the West River to the south. And they also flew missions to more distant targets where the Japanese were not expecting them.

One of the first long-range strikes was a sweep led by Major Herbst to Amoy Island on August 8. Just off China's coast and opposite the center of Formosa, this island was a refueling point for Japanese ships traveling in the South and East China seas. It also had a Japanese airfield. Herbst's Sharks checked the harbor area and attacked the airfield, destroying four enemy planes on the ground. On August 16, the Sharks went far to the east on the Yangtze River to attack Wuhu and Anking, and on August, 21 they swept the airfield at Kinwha, which was close to the port city of Hangchow. In order to reach Kinwha, Herbst's P-40s required a refueling stop at Kienow, the emergency strip that Col. Bruce Holloway had used when he made the initial recon of Formosa back in the spring of 1943.

Until the evacuation of Kweilin, Major Herbst stayed in constant motion to keep track of the two halves of his squadron. The pilots at Kweilin were doing vital, exhausting work, but the Kanchow detachment needed his leadership as well, so he flew back and forth between the two bases regularly. Early in September, he flew the 74th's first assigned P-51 to Kanchow. The Mustang's arrival was greeted with enthusiasm, because the pilots knew what they could do with its tremendous range and performance capabilities from their forward base.

Major Herbst scored the first Mustang victories of the 74th Fighter Squadron on September 3, when he accompanied a flight of P-40s bombing railroad facilities at Lishui. According to the combat report, Herbst left the P-40s and flew northeast along the Hangchow-Kinwha rail line alone, looking for a railroad bridge that he could skip bomb. He found the bridge, but it took him three passes to shake the bombs off his wing racks, and then they overshot the target. As he pulled up from this third bomb run, he spotted two single-engine aircraft that he identified as "Vals" (again probably Ki-51 Sonias of the 6th Air Regiment) coming out of the clouds in formation at two thousand feet altitude.

Herbst worked his way around behind the pair without being spotted. His first burst of fire exploded one of the Sonias, and the other one flipped away in a tight turn, trying to escape. Herbst chased the plane down to treetop level, where the Japanese pilot began a series of steep turns, apparently trying to cause the Mustang to spin in and also to give his rear gunner a clear shot at Herbst. The gunner missed the Mustang, but Herbst fired back and chewed up the Sonia's rudder. Next, the Japanese pilot tried to land his damaged plane in a field, but it flipped over when it hit the ground.

Herbst, now with just the two inboard guns firing, strafed the Sonia and then headed home to report his sixth and seventh victories.

Two days later Herbst took off from Kanchow in the P-51 bound for Kweilin, where he planned to have the jamming problem on its outboard guns fixed. He encountered bad weather right away and skirted north toward Chaling, east of Hengyang, to avoid it. There he spotted two eight-plane flights of Oscars milling around at ten thousand feet. Characteristically, Herbst did not run for safety; he looked for a way to attack. He began to climb, with the intention of attacking the tail-end Charlie on one of the flights, but the Oscars saw him coming and turned into the lone Mustang. Herbst attacked nose-to-nose with the lead Oscar and saw it begin to trail smoke as it flashed past. Then his windshield and canopy shattered as gunfire from another Oscar ripped Herbst's P-51. Flying glass cut his face, but otherwise Herbst and his plane were OK. Now the second flight attacked, and again Herbst made a pass on the leader. He saw this plane begin to smoke, too, but then he broke off the engagement due to his jammed guns and his hampered vision. He returned to Kanchow, rather than try to reach Kweilin, and filed a claim for his eighth victory.

Herbst certainly was not the only pilot in the 74th who was fighting during September. The full squadron reunited at Kanchow after Kweilin's evacuation during the middle of the month, and more Mustangs began to arrive. Operations picked up accordingly.

On September 16 four Sharks were dive-bombing near Nanchang with two P-51s for top cover when seven Ki-44 Tojos bounced the P-40s. The flight leader, 1/Lt. Chester N. Denny, fired on a Tojo that was attacking another P-40 and got good hits in its cowling and wing root before breaking off. The Mustang top cover never saw the Tojos.

Also that day, Major Herbst took Maj. Philip G. Chapman out for an "orientation" to squadron operations. The new major was slated to take over command of the 74th after Herbst finished. They were bombing a bridge near Kinwha when the engine in Chapman's P-51 was hit and he had to bail out. According to Herbst's report, he watched Chapman land safely and continued on toward Kinwha. He spotted a train and strafed it before reaching the airfield. There he encountered an Oscar at two thousand feet and shot it down. Back at Kanchow, victory flag number nine went on the side of Herbst's P-51, which was named "Tommy's Dad" in honor of his son.

The 74th's men had taken to calling their unit the "Guerrilla Squadron" in honor of their unique situation. It was quite a step up from the old School Squadron moniker. The Guerrillas' most successful mission of September came on the twenty-eighth. First Lieutenant James A. Crawford led four P-40s and two P-51s back to

Amoy Island on a low-level raid against Hoshan airfield, with a nearby seaplane base as a secondary target. Intelligence sources had indicated a buildup of Japanese aircraft there the previous day, and Herbst did not want to miss such an opportunity.

As the formation approached Hoshan, the Mustangs zoomed to five thousand feet to provide top cover and spot targets for Lieutenant Crawford's attack flight. There were plenty of them, all parked in revetments. The P-40s set up an irregular pattern of bomb runs to throw off enemy antiaircraft gunners and went after the planes. Ground fire was heavy, with Crawford and Lt. Bob Martin picking up hits in the wings, but the Sharks took a heavy toll with seven Japanese fighters destroyed. Crawford, Martin, and Lt. Ira Binkley destroyed two apiece, and Lt. Bill Fandl got one. After the Sharks pulled off the target and headed home, the two Mustangs dropped down and strafed the docks at the seaplane base.

By this time, Major Herbst had piled up more than one hundred missions, which was considered the limit for pilots on combat status. He had only been in China for about six months, however, and was hardly ready to go home. Accordingly, Herbst was supposed to be grounded from further combat flying. When Major Chapman walked in from his "orientation" flight at the end of the month, he became the 74th's vice squadron commander, but Herbst stayed to run the show at Kanchow. As might be expected, he managed to keep on flying missions, although now he was technically doing so as an observer. That was one of the beauties of operating at Kanchow: Group headquarters was four hundred miles away at Liuchow, so the brass was not around to push the rules and regulations.

As October arrived, so did a full moon. That meant the Guerrilla Squadron could expect nightly visits from Japanese bombers based at Hankow. By this time, Capt. Charlie Cook was an old hand in the squadron and nearly at the end of his tour. He wrote the following about an event during this period.

"Three bombers were hitting us every clear night, so Pappy sent me (in a P-40) to Kian, which had a grass emergency strip, about 180 miles north of Kanchow on the Kan River. The bombers came down and up that way every clear night. I landed after dark with the help of one bonfire so the Jap spies—Chinese—would not see me and was met by Major Chou, who was the station master, and others. We went into town, and they insisted on some wine tasting.

"From a hostel second floor balcony we watched three bombers with running lights on heading south. We went back to the strip with plenty of time, and I took off with the help of another fire. After circling Kian for over thirty minutes beyond their estimated time of arrival, I headed back to Kanchow. The damned Japs spies had done their job and warned their friends of my presence, hence the bombers vectored a perfect rectangular route around Kian. Our Chinese net confirmed this fact."[1]

A week later, on October 14, a sampan arrived at Kanchow that had traveled down the river from Kian. It carried a package for Capt. Charlie Cook. Along with the package was the following note:

> Dear Captain Cook,
> We are sending you herewith two kinds of wine you like. Please accept them as a token of our gratitude for the kindness you have done us.
> We hope that you will shoot down all of the Jap planes and knock out all cornerers [sic] before long, and carry on the world in peace.
> Will you please give our kind regards to Mr. Cousins [Lt. Wallace Cousins] and Mr. Nick [Lt. Nick Gazibara].
> See [sic] again!
> Ever yours,
> Station Master Major K. Chou
> Engineer Captain C.H. Ching

Cook recalled that he and the rest of the Guerrillas enjoyed the wine very much. Several days later, and apparently not related to the wine, Cook began to suffer from back and leg pains. He was grounded and sent to the hospital, where he was diagnosed with jaundice and amoebic dysentery, common ailments for Americans in China during the war. His orders to return to the States arrived while he was in the hospital, and he left China in early November after completing a series of shots. He went on to serve a full career in the U.S. Air Force, retiring with the rank of colonel.

The second week of October brought some stiff air battles for the 74th Fighter Squadron. On the seventh, Lts. Chester Denny and Wallace Cousins got confirmed kills when their formation caught a flight of Oscars taking off at Kiukiang.

The next day, a skip-bombing mission on the Yangtze River near Hukow was jumped by Oscars. Lieutenant Tom Angel, flying top cover, dived in behind them and hit one Oscar with a burst from twenty degrees deflection. The Oscar caught on fire and crashed. Then Angel attacked another Oscar that was on the tail of his wing-man, Lt. Nick Gazibara, and damaged it. Gazibara also got a proba-ble, but then he broke off with a Tojo on his tail. The Tojo chased him for one hundred miles at low altitude and hit him in each wing. At one point, Gazibara flew so low that he clipped the top of a tree, but he finally shook off the Tojo. Gazibara landed wheels-up at Kanchow, washing out his P-40. Two hours later, he boarded a C-64 utility plane headed for Liuchow. His tour was over, and he was on his way home.

On October 9, Captain Cook led a skip-bombing mission up to the Yangtze River. This time the target area was Anking, which required a refueling stop at Nancheng. The fighters bombed shipping on the river and took a look at the Anking airfield, where they spotted twelve parked planes. The fighters made three passes in the face of light ground fire, destroying two bombers and eight fighters before returning home safely.

The weather got progressively worse during the week, but it was still good enough to send a mission off on October 10. Unfortunately, a P-40 flown by one of the squadron's new pilots, Lt. Thomas H. Upchurch, got caught in the weather and crashed into a mountain. Upchurch was killed on his first combat mission.

Weather limited flying for the rest of October, with just one other claim for a ground kill filed during the month. This turned out to be a time of transition for the squadron, however, with many experienced pilots leaving the units and their replacements arriving. One of those new men was Capt. Barney Fudge, who arrived in China after two years of duty as an instructor in fighter-replacement training units in Florida. He was assigned to the 74th on October 31 and arrived at Kanchow a few weeks later. In a letter to the sister of a fellow pilot, Capt. Louis Anderson, who was killed shortly after the war, Fudge recalled his early days in the squadron. According to Fudge, "Louis was already in China when I arrived. It was not until November 13 that I got to Kanchow. We had nice facilities at Kanchow where about 20 of us lived in each of two buildings with two men in each room, and I shared a room with Louis.

"Newcomers were kidded and called 'New Jokers,' but Louis was kind to me from the moment I arrived, and never looked down on me as some of the others did. . . . We got along fine as roommates.

"My most vivid memory of that period was that even with the mosquito nets over our beds, we would be awakened when a rat would join us on the bed with only the mosquito net separating us. Our squadron was composed of a great group of young men who got along well together and had a good time. . . . I know that I thought I was suffering tremendous hardships at that time, but now I can only think of the good fellowship and fun."[2]

Fudge's description of life in the 74th could just as well have been written about any of the squadrons in the 23rd Fighter Group. They were stationed at different locations, but otherwise they were much the same. The combination of young men, high-performance aircraft, and a high degree of danger drew the squadrons together like families. Many of the friendships formed in the heat of battle have lasted a lifetime.

While the 74th was busy pressuring the Japanese in new areas with new tactics, the 76th and 118th squadrons battled hard against the Ichi-Go offensive from Liuchow. Their air base was the last stop on the Hsiang River line; once it was lost, the Japanese would be able to sail past the 69th Composite Group's air base at Nanning in Kwangsi Province and into Indo-China. The squadrons' task was made all the more difficult because the Japanese were advancing from two directions, with the Twenty-third Army heading west from Tanchuk and the Eleventh Army closing in from the northeast.

The 76th, under the command of Maj. Charles Griffith, had a particularly difficult October. Flying nonstop missions to oppose the advancing Japanese, the squadron lost twenty-two aircraft, including four aircraft and two men on October 4 alone. Then on October 29 and 30, three P-51s and seven P-40s were lost in bad weather as they were flying from Liuchow to Luliang. Three Shark pilots were killed, and two of the Mustang pilots were missing and presumed dead.

In the meantime, on October 16, the 76th and 118th participated in one of the biggest missions put together to date—a strike on Hong Kong by B-24s and B-25s, with Sharks and Mustangs for escort.

Flying that day was Lt. H. L. Kirkpatrick, a 75th Squadron pilot on temporary duty with the 76th. He wrote. "The mission was very dicey for the P-40s—I was flying one of them—as we were at the limit of our range and an early drop of the external tank meant you would not get home. The B-24s were jumped by Zeros inbound to the target, so a fight already was under way before we arrived. The B-25s started their run to the deck from 15,000 feet and literally ran off and left us in the P-40s.

"We were right behind them as they were bombing and strafing the harbor. The B-25s' bombs were still exploding on the docks, and by the time we overflew the harbor, the AA was in full operation. It was quite a spectacular sight to see the coordinated attack as we were juking through the flak. We finally caught up with the B-25s again at about 10,000 feet. We were supposed to be their escort, but it was kind of like yelling, 'Wait for me; I am your leader!'"[3]

The 76th Fighter Squadron scored its last confirmed aerial victories of the war on October 17, though of course no one realized it or even would have guessed as much at the time. The 76th attacked Tien Ho Airdrome at Canton, with victories going to 1/Lt. William Eldridge and 2/Lt. Paul J. Smith.

The 118th had a better time of it at Liuchow, losing just one aircraft and no pilots during October. Luck plays a big role in the life of any combat outfit, and the 118th certainly got a bigger share of it that month than the 76th. On October 5, 1/Lt. Oran Watts got his fifth victory to become the 118th's first ace. The mission was an escort of B-25s to Sanshui, just west of Canton. The B-25s were able to hit their target and turn for home before a dozen or more Ki-44

Tojos were sighted and the 118th engaged. The 118th claimed four confirmed kills in the fight. Single victories went to the flight leader, Capt. Ray Darby; Lieutenant Watts; Lt. Henry F. Davis; and Lt. Jack Gocke, who was shot down and walked out later.

The 118th flew a similar escort mission to Sanshui on October 20, followed by a sweep over Hong Kong. This time the squadron commander, Maj. Edward McComas, was leading. Scoring his first confirmed victory just four days earlier, McComas got a probable kill on the mission, but 1/Lt. Jack Greene topped him, with one Tojo confirmed and another damaged. According to Greene, "We flew as a squadron that day. I had Lt. [John] Egan on my right wing, and in the maneuvering over Hong Kong I lost him. In trying to locate him and in the following action I got separated from my outfit.

"I immediately turned north, and in the process of trying to find my position I saw two Tojo-type aircraft beneath me. I climbed and then made a pass at them, hitting the wingman and setting him on fire, and damaging the leader. I broke contact and got out of there fast, as I was low on fuel and only had enough to make Liuchow."[4]

Greene's tour was almost over by this time. Though he had only started flying combat missions in June when the 118th arrived in China, he had already flown one hundred missions by November. Soon Greene, along with twelve other pilots in the squadron, received his orders to go home. By that time, Greene had dropped from his regular weight of 135 pounds down to 118 pounds, and the flight surgeon grounded him. He recovered quickly after returning to the United States and got married in December 1944. Like Charlie Cook and many other pilots who flew in the 23rd Fighter Group, Greene made a career of the Air Force after the war.

Despite all the best efforts of the 76th and 118th squadrons, Liuchow became untenable by early November 1944. The Japanese were continuing to advance, and the weather was getting progressively worse. Again, it was time to blow up a base and fall back. Brigadier General Vincent gave the order on the morning of November 7.

This time, luck was not with the 118th, however. Two of the squadron's new P-51s and a P-40 went down in bad weather on the flight out. Among those killed was 1/Lt. Henry E. ("Hink") Miehe. A senior flight leader, Miehe was noted in the squadron for his uncanny ability to spot potential ground targets such as supply dumps, truck convoys, and troop bivouacs that pilots flying with him did not see.

When the 76th Fighter Squadron pulled out of Liuchow, its planes and pilots were sent to Luliang to rejoin its rear echelon. Major Griffith sent out a couple of recon missions to observe Liuchow from Luliang, but he could see that it was too far removed from the front to be an effective base for operations. He lobbied for a new base, and late in the month, the squadron's planes and essential personnel were transferred to Tsingchen. It was a short, remote airstrip in the mountains near Kweiyang, about 250 miles northeast of Kunming. The Japanese in Liuchow seemed to be making an advance on Kweiyang, and the squadron figured it would get action there. The weather, however, did not cooperate. It snowed at Tsingchen on November 28, and the 76th's Mustangs stayed socked in well into December.

From Liuchow, the 118th went to Chengkung. This air base just south of Kunming was headquarters for the 51st Fighter Group and a major supply and repair depot. It did not have much combat action to offer the 118th, but it did have plenty of one thing the squadron wanted: paint. During their stay at Liuchow, the pilots had had long discussions about naming the squadron and how they might paint their aircraft to make them distinctive. This camaraderie appealed to their commander, Maj. Ed McComas. The pilots finally decided to call themselves the "Blue Lightning Squadron" and to paint their planes accordingly. When they got to Chengkung, however, they found the only color of paint available was black. It was close enough, they agreed, and the "Black Lightning Squadron" was born. Large black lightning bolts trimmed in yellow were painted down the sides of the Mustangs' fuselage with smaller lightning bolts on the tips of the wings and tail.

The Black Lightning Mustangs stood out among the other airplanes in China; even the once-menacing shark mouths and eyes on the remaining P-40s looked bland by comparison. The shark-mouth design did not adapt particularly well to the P-51's nose, and even the 76th Squadron dropped the shark-mouth tradition a few months after it got the new fighters. Naturally each of the other squadrons wanted a unified look, and they soon followed the 118th's lead. The 75th Fighter Squadron decided to paint the entire tails of its Mustangs black, and later the 76th painted large Indian heads on the vertical tails of its Mustangs. The 74th, cut off from the outside world at Kanchow, did not have excess paint for such purposes. When the squadron finally did get access to paint the following spring, it colored the entire noses of its P-51s black.

★ ★ ★ ★

Besides new paint jobs and air bases for the 23rd Fighter Group during the fall of 1944, leaders were also in transition. On October 15, Col. Tex Hill got his orders to go home after eleven months in the hot seat as the group's CO. Hill, widely recognized as the most outstanding fighter pilot and combat leader of the war in China, was getting a plum of an assignment back in the States. He would form and command the USAAF's first fighter group to be equipped with jet-powered aircraft. In the months to come, he would recruit many of his former 23rd pilots to serve in his jet outfit. Hill would leave active duty after the war but continue to fly in the National Guard while pursuing a successful business career in Texas. He retired from the Guard with the rank of brigadier general.

Taking Hill's place as commander of the 23rd was Lt. Col. Phil Loofbourrow. This twenty-eight-year-old Wisconsin native arrived in China in January 1944. After a stint as commander of the 75th Fighter Squadron, he had transferred to group headquarters in July. Loofbourrow had two confirmed kills to his credit and several damaged. Not as colorful or outgoing as Tex Hill (who was?), Loofbourrow nevertheless excelled in the job of group commander.

One of Loofbourrow's first tasks was not a pleasant one. A leadership problem in the 75th Fighter Squadron was just coming to a head, and it needed to be resolved. About the situation involving Maj. A. T. House, Hill said, House "was a major who came over late. Just about the time I was getting ready to leave, some pilots in the 75th came to me and told me he was running down the squadron. He wouldn't fly the missions. I was leaving, so I told Phil Loofbourrow about it and suggested he get rid of him [which he did].

"Casey had come over on the boat with House [returning from leave in the United States], and he saved him. He moved him up to the 68th Wing headquarters. Later on something else happened, and I never heard anything about him again."[5]

Fortunately for Loofbourrow, he had the perfect officer to take charge of the 75th Fighter Squadron, which had been foundering at Chihkiang for a month. Loofbourrow's choice was Maj. Clyde B. Slocumb Jr., a twenty-four-year-old Georgia boy who had flown a tour with the 16th Fighter Squadron in 1942–43. Now he was back in China with a new set of oak leaves and a strong desire to get into action again. He assumed command of the 75th on November 9, and the change became evident before sundown. The squadron's pilots flew four missions that day, the first ones they had flown all month.

The next morning, November 10, Major Slocumb led a flight of four Mustangs on a dive-bombing raid against a radar station at Yochow. While his flight was still out, another mission went off to Nanyo, led by Capt. Forrest Parham. The twelve Mustangs encountered seven Oscars over the town and shot down two of them, with another probable and three others damaged.

Then, that night Slocumb took on a mission that Brig. Gen. Casey Vincent had personally requested on September 22 during a visit to Chihkiang. Vincent wanted some searchlights knocked out at Hankow, and he had briefed pilots on how he wanted them to do it. Major House had sent one pilot out for an unsuccessful stab at it but never followed up.

Slocumb took off at 6:45 P.M., the first of three P-51s heading for individual targets. The searchlights went out when the planes approached the city, and they turned for home not knowing if they had been successful. Only Slocumb and Lt. Donald ("Skip") Stanfield returned; Capt. Joe Brown, the squadron's operations officer, got lost in the dark and finally bailed out west of Chihkiang.

If Major Slocumb's first two days in command were not proof enough that the 75th Fighter Squadron was back in the war, the next day cinched it. On November 11 at 7:00 A.M., sixteen P-51s lifted off from Chihkiang for a sweep along the Hsiang River valley. According to intelligence reports, the Japanese had moved numerous aircraft into the former U.S. bases there over the past few days. The 75th's four flights flew together as far as Lingling, where they split into two groups. Lieutenant Don Lopez led eight planes south to Kweilin while Capt. Stan Kelley led the rest north to Hengyang.

The intelligence reports were accurate, as the Japanese had been loading up the airfield at Hengyang for a week or more. Unfortunately, the Japanese were ready when Kelley's Mustangs approached Hengyang, and a strong enemy formation jumped them out of the clouds. Three P-51s went down almost immediately, but then the Mustangs began to get the upper hand. Lopez led his flights into the fight a few minutes later, and the outcome was assured. Lieutenant Mervin Beard flew in Kelley's flight that day and wrote this account:

"It was the first time I ever had a shot at a real enemy plane, and my first burst surprised me as we were in a tight turn. My tracers looked as though they were curving to the outside of the turn. In fact, I could swear that the barrels of my guns were bent.

"It didn't take me long to figure it out. He crossed in front of me, and this time I used some lead and got a hit. But he didn't go down. Unless he blows up in front of you, it is hard to know what happened when you are spending as much time looking behind you as ahead.

"I pulled up to get some altitude, and as I looked down I saw several planes go into the ground. I couldn't tell whose they were, but they were silver in color. I didn't have much time to think about it, as there were three Japs coming in on my tail, so I dove for the deck. I saw 500 mph on my airspeed indicator, and it was almost impossible to move the stick, but I finally got the plane going back up. It was a close one; the trees were getting pretty big.

"I had outrun them, but they were still coming so I turned into a bank of nearby clouds. As soon as I was sure that they didn't follow me into the clouds, I turned to 330 degrees and headed for home. I was alone, and I began to wonder what happened to everybody. I soon had other things to think about as my propeller was in high rpm, commonly known as 'running away.' I had no control of the pitch, so I slowed the plane to where I could just maintain my altitude and prayed I would make it back.

"I soon found a checkpoint I recognized and made the necessary correction to head into the field. When I attempted to put the wheels down I found I had no hydraulics, so I had to pump the wheels down by hand. I guess I landed with a teacup full of gas."[6]

Beard had been lucky, but luck was not with the three pilots who went down. One of them, 1/Lt. Robert P. Miller, was killed. Miller, a faithful diary keeper, was from the Boston area and had been in the squadron since June 7. He had escaped his crash landing at Lingling in August with minor injuries after Lieutenant Elker and Technical Sergeant Van Cleve saved him, and he just recently had begun flying with the squadron again after a long layoff.[7] Another pilot shot down on the Hengyang mission was Lt. Jim Taylor, previously mentioned as a prisoner of war and member of the "Diddled Dozen." The third pilot lost, Lt. Jack Gadberry, later walked out and returned to combat.

On the plus side, the squadron was awarded eight confirmed victories in the fight, and two pilots scored their fifth kills to become the last two aces of the 75th Fighter Squadron. They were 1/Lt. Don Lopez and Capt. Forrest Parham who, just as Major Herbst of the 74th, went by the nickname of "Pappy."

When the pilots got back to Chihkiang and Major Slocumb heard about the fight, he immediately put together another mission to attack the airfield at Hengyang and try to catch the Japanese on the ground. Lieutenant Lopez was assigned to lead the strike, because he was familiar with the area. Major Slocumb tagged along in a wingman slot. Only a few Oscars were found on the field, and Slocumb was credited with destroying one of them. But the 75th had done its job. After the war, the Japanese admitted pulling back their fighters from Hengyang to Paliuchi after the November 11 action because the field was too vulnerable to attack from Chihkiang.

By this time, the Japanese were beginning a half-hearted advance toward Kweiyang. The 75th Fighter Squadron turned to a steady series of road sweeps, tearing up enemy vehicles, troop formations, and even horses that were heading for the front. When the weather cleared at Tsingchen, the 76th joined the effort. The Chinese Army finally held, and the advance petered out in December.

★ ★ ★ ★

The 118th Tac Recon Squadron ended its short stay at Chengkung on November 12. The squadron's next stop would be Suichuan, the big base near Kanchow that the 76th had left the previous spring. The freshly painted Black Lightning Mustangs flew first to Chihkiang, where they refueled and picked up a flight of C-47 transports to escort on the long flight. At Suichuan, the 118th would get back into action as the 23rd Fighter Group's second "guerrilla" squadron.

During late November and early December, the 74th and 118th targeted Japanese supply lines in the Hsiang River valley and along the Yangtze. Both squadrons also were kept busy responding to air raid alerts over Kanchow and Suichuan, but enemy bombers never attacked the bases during daylight.

A typical offensive mission flown by the 118th took place on December 4. Four Mustangs went up to Kiukiang, which is on the Yangtze River at the north end of Poyang Lake. Lieutenant Berthold Peterson, one of the original 118th pilots to arrive in China, was leading. He recalled, "I was leading a flight of four to bomb and strafe shipping on the docks. We surprised a flight of 10 Oscars and dropped down on top of them. I hit the leader before they knew we were there. The second was hit as he turned away. He took a burst right in the cockpit and stalled, but was not seen to crash so was never confirmed. The third one in line attempted to get away by diving. I caught up easily and put in a burst from 50 yards away.

"I got two confirmed and one probable. Incidentally, that was the only time in all my missions that I saw an enemy plane."[8]

The three other pilots on the flight also scored during the scrap. First Lieutenants Richard Windsor and Maurice Wells each got one confirmed victory, and 1/Lt. Fred Lanphier got one probable.

Meanwhile, the 74th Fighter Squadron was working up plans for another long-range strike into new territory. This time the target would be the former capital of China, Nanking. This city was farther east on the Yangtze River than the guerrillas had ever ventured. More important, it had immense shipping facilities and two airfields that were believed to be packed with Japanese aircraft.

Sixteen P-51s left Kanchow on the morning of December 8 and flew to the remote field at Nancheng to refuel. The timing was not incidental. Pappy Herbst wanted to do something special to remind the Japanese that this was the third anniversary of the Pearl Harbor attack. The mission was special, all right, though Herbst himself did not fly that day. Led by 1/Lt. Ken LaTourelle, the Mustangs left Nancheng at 10:15 A.M., proceeded north to Wuhu as a diversion, and then followed the river northeast in a diving run into Nanking.

The eight Mustangs that were carrying bombs attacked a railroad ferry on the river and dock facilities. Four Oscars sneaked out from behind a mountain as the seventh dive-bomber began its run. By this time, the first bombers were climbing back to altitude, and they quickly dispatched the Oscars. Captain Robert E. Brown scored one confirmed destroyed and a probable.

The formation proceeded to Ming Ku Kung and Tai Chao Chan airdromes and found all sorts of airplanes parked on them. The top cover came down to join the strafing, and irregular patterns were set up over both fields to throw off the antiaircraft gunners. In the next few minutes, the marauding Mustang pilots burned up no fewer than eighteen Japanese aircraft on the two fields. High honors went to Lieutenant LaTourelle, who destroyed three and damaged two more in four passes. Eleven of the pilots destroyed at least one apiece.

Meanwhile, several Japanese fighters tried to attack the strafers and quickly found themselves under attack. Two of them went down under 1/Lt. John W. Bolyard's guns. His first victim was identified as a Kawasaki Ki-61 Tony, which was a streamlined, inline-engine fighter rarely encountered in China. Bolyard took him head-on at four thousand feet, but the Tony scissored underneath. The enemy pilot repeated the maneuver several times but then fell to the ground north of Tai Chao Chan.

Bolyard climbed up and over the field. Then he spotted a Ki-84 Frank flying south. The Frank was a high-performance fighter built by Nakajima, which also manufactured the Ki-43 Oscar and Ki-44 Tojo. It was considered the finest Japanese fighter developed during the war. All the performance capabilities in the world would not have saved the Frank that Bolyard spotted, however, because its pilot was not paying attention. Bolyard closed in right behind it and opened fire, and the plane burst into flames before spinning into the ground. The pilot never took any evasive action.

Single aerial kills also were confirmed for 1/Lts. Heston ("Tony") Cole and Wallace Cousins. Only one Mustang was lost. Lieutenant Frederick J. McGill's P-51 was hit in the propeller by ground fire during an attack on the ferry boats. He nursed the plane twenty miles away from Nanking and parachuted to safety.

On this same day the 118th flew a successful bombing mission to Hong Kong. That evening, Brig. Gen. Casey Vincent noted in his diary that the two outstanding missions on the anniversary of Pearl Harbor made a "nice present for the Old Man."[9]

★ ★ ★ ★

The Pearl Harbor Day entry was one of the last that Casey Vincent made in his wartime diary. Five days later he was on his way home to the States. Vincent was war-weary and homesick for his wife and children, but still full of fight. He hoped to get another combat assignment after taking leave, but the young general and fighter ace was kept stateside for the rest of the war. With such a brilliant start, it was only logical that Vincent would make the Air Force a career. His star continued to rise after the war, but his career was cut short by his untimely death in 1955.

Colonel Clayton Claassen, executive officer of the 68th Composite Wing, had arrived in Suichuan in late November to serve as commander of the wing's Forward Echelon. In early December, when

Brigadier General Vincent finally got his long-awaited orders home, Claassen assumed command of the 68th Composite Wing.

Lieutenant Colonel Phil Loofbourrow also was at the end of his combat tour. When he left on December 12, he turned over command of the 23rd Fighter Group to a man who was no stranger to the China air war, Col. Ed Rector. The former AVG and 76th Fighter Squadron ace had returned to China several months earlier and was assigned to wing headquarters. There, he had a chance to fly with several of the squadrons and get familiar with the changes that had occurred since his departure in December 1942. Rector would serve as commander of the 23rd Fighter Group for the remainder of the war.

Another officer who would play a key leadership role in the 23rd from this point on was Lt. Col. Charles H. ("Chuck") Older. Like Colonel Rector, Older had flown in the American Volunteer Group during 1941 and 1942. Older scored ten confirmed victories while flying in the AVG's 3rd Squadron. He had returned to China during the summer of 1944 and added another victory to his total on July 28. Now he would serve as deputy commander of the 23rd.

Rector and Older would see each other only rarely during the coming months, due to the far-flung locations of the group's units. The two men traded off duties between administration and operations. While one was in Luliang taking care of paperwork at group headquarters, the other would go out to a forward base to fly missions with a squadron.[10]

During December 1944, Lieutenant Colonel Older was in Suichuan, flying with the 118th. Rector made an inspection trip to Chihkiang and then continued east to Kanchow to meet Pappy Herbst and the 74th. It was from these guerrilla bases on December 18, 1944, that the two leaders participated in the most massive aerial attack ever mounted in China during World War II.

18

The Last Withdrawal

Ever since the B-29s of the Twentieth Air Force arrived at Chengtu back in May 1944, Maj. Gen. Claire Chennault had been lobbying Washington for a chance to use the bombers against the Ichi-Go offensive. His requests were denied time after time. Instead, the big bombers were sent out to attack more distant strategic targets in Manchuria, Burma, Indo-China, the Malay Peninsula, and southern Japan. After six months of operating from Chengtu, however, the B-29s were clearly not working out as planned. Chengtu's supply problems were too great, as was its distance to potential targets. The USAAF made plans to move the Superfortresses to new bases in the Mariana Islands of the western Pacific Ocean.

Chennault knew the B-29s would be leaving soon, and in December 1944, he made one last effort to get some use out of them. The target he envisioned was a worthwhile one: the Japanese supply lines feeding the Ichi-Go advance. His own 68th Composite Wing had battered them to the point of near collapse. The Hsiang River and the railroad line and roads running through the river valley were graveyards filled with the twisted wreckage of boats, bridges, trains, and trucks. Although this route was also hammered by air attacks from the guerrilla squadrons at Suichuan and Kanchow, supplies nonetheless continued to flow along the Yangtze River as far as Hankow. This meant just one thing to Chennault: Hankow was the choke point of the Japanese supply line. Its docks and warehouses were loaded with war-making materials that had nowhere to go. If the Old Man had his way, the only direction those supplies at Hankow would go was up in smoke.

For once, Washington saw it Chennault's way. An all-out B-29 raid against Hankow, using newly developed incendiary bombs, was arranged for December 18. But that was not all Chennault had in mind for Hankow. He planned a maximum effort by his own air forces to coincide with the B-29 strikes, and the 68th Composite Wing would play a key role. B-24s and B-25s of the Fourteenth Air Force would make coordinated attacks with the B-29s against supply depots and other targets in Hankow. Meanwhile, fighters of the 23rd and the Chinese-American Composite Wing would keep the Japanese interceptors away from the bombers. This involved not only escort missions but also attacks against the airfields around Hankow.

Three squadrons of the 23rd Fighter Group participated in the Hankow operation. First, the 75th sent off sixteen P-51s from Chihkiang to escort B-24s of the 308th Bomb Group that were assigned to bomb an airfield. The bombers made clean runs to the target and plastered the field without any opposition from enemy fighters. The Mustang pilots spotted Japanese fighters in the distance but did not engage them, and all returned to base safely.

It was a different story for the two guerrilla squadrons. The 74th sent off eighteen Mustangs from Kanchow, with Maj. Phil Chapman leading and the group commander, Col. Ed Rector, at the head of Red Flight. They topped off their gas tanks at Suichuan and escorted B-25s to Wuchang, which is across the river from Hankow. There the bombers attacked a satellite airfield half an hour after the B-29s' attack on the city. The attack was timed to catch the Japanese fighters landing to refuel, but while the Mustang pilots downed five Oscars, hardly any enemy fighters were seen on the field. Then the B-25s headed home as the Mustangs turned east to sweep the Yangtze River down to Kiukiang.

The Mustangs found a gold mine of parked airplanes on Erh Tao Kow Airdrome at Kiukiang. They burned ten planes and damaged quite a few more in the next few minutes, with Capt. Floyd Finberg getting credit for six destroyed.

One 74th pilot was not so fortunate. As 1/Lt. John Wheeler wrote, "My plane was disabled by ground fire, and I had to bail out southeast of Hankow, deep in nominally Jap territory. The first night I holed up in a remote mountain village that seemed safe from Japs. Before next morning I was located and contacted by a gang of American guerrillas who were running a whole underground Chinese army.

"There were six or eight Americans, mostly Navy enlisted men but also a Navy doctor and an officer. They had been there a long time and had quite an organization. They were hoping to salvage machine guns from my plane and we went to where it had crashed, but they were all bent. They had a radio and kept in touch with our forces in the Pacific Theatre. They got supplies occasionally by submarine on the coast between Shanghai and Hong Kong. They had American weapons and got shipments of freshly printed Chinese money from the coast. I saw a few of their Chinese soldiers, but they kept most of them pretty well dispersed.

"They told me about attacking the railroad along the Yangtze and ambushing Japs when they would go out in the country to capture the rice crop after harvest. We pilots had no idea there were Americans working behind Jap lines in China. I suppose that they were part of the O.S.S. [Office of Strategic Services], but we had never heard of the O.S.S. in those days.

"I stayed with them through Christmas and helped them eat their canned G.I. turkey. Then I walked back to the river below Kanchow and got a boat ride back from there. The Chinese had really done a job to make the mountain roads in that region impassable to the Japs. For miles and miles along the route I traveled, they had removed whole sections of the road every quarter mile or so. The dirt was actually taken away, and nothing was in sight to repair the gap with."[1]

The 118th Tac Recon Squadron took Lt. Col. Charles Older, deputy group commander, along on its Hankow mission. At 10:30 A.M., Lt. Col. Ed McComas led seventeen P-51s off from Suichuan with a similar assignment to that of the 74th: to escort B-25s to Wuchang. This mission's target was the main airfield there, and again the B-25s were able to bomb without problems. This airfield had plenty of aircraft parked on it, however, so the Mustangs escorted the bombers back toward Suichuan a safe distance before they strafed the field.

Four Oscars were sighted in the air as the 118th arrived to begin its strafing runs. Lieutenant Colonel Older caught up with one of them at four thousand feet and hit it with a telling burst in the cockpit and wing root area. He overshot his target, but his wingman, Lt. Everson Pearsall, saw the Oscar crash off the end of the field. A second confirmed kill went to 1/Lt. Carlton Covey, who hit an Oscar with a deflection shot and then watched as the enemy pilot bailed out. With the sky cleared of enemy interceptors, the 118th was free to strafe the field thoroughly. Seven more planes were destroyed in the face of light ground fire, and all planes returned safely to Suichuan.

The only squadron in the 23rd Fighter Group that did not take part in the Hankow attack was the 76th. The weather at Tsingchen closed in on December 10 and did not improve until January. The men could not even fly the mail in and out of Tsingchen for a while.

As it turned out, tragedy—not triumph—struck the 76th on December 18. The popular squadron commander, Lt. Col. Charles Griffith, was at Luliang and went up for a practice flight with

Lieutenant Hewitt. The two pilots were stunting in formation near the field when they lost control of their Mustangs while doing a roll. They crashed into the ground. Both men were killed. Maj. L. V. Teeter assumed command of the 76th the following day.

Admittedly, the 23rd Fighter Group did not play a central role in the December 18 assault on Hankow; the B-29s did. Their incendiary bombs started fires that burned large sections of the city. But any day that a fighter group can destroy twenty-four enemy airplanes is a successful one. In China, where Japanese air strength was dwindling, twenty-four victories was a bundle.

Early the next morning, December 19, Lieutenant Colonel Older took off alone in a P-51 from Suichuan heading back to Wuchang for another look at the airfields strafed the previous day. Near Hankow, he spotted a Ki-48 Lily bomber flying west at three thousand feet and pulled in behind it. When the range had closed sufficiently, he put a long burst into the bomber's left engine and wing. The plane nosed down and crashed ten miles northeast of the city. Older was still carrying his drop tanks, so when he reached the main Hankow airdrome he dived down and dropped them on the field while strafing a revetment. Four Oscars came up to chase him, and he managed to tack onto one of their tails and shoot the plane down in flames. It crashed just off the edge of the field as Older proceeded east to Wuchang. There he was jumped from above by ten to twelve more Oscars. Older whipped his Mustang around to face his attackers, and as they passed, he got in a good burst from twenty to twenty-five degrees deflection on one Oscar that was straggling at the back of the formation. It, too, crashed and burned for Older's third victory of the day. The remaining Oscars cleared the area, and Older returned to Suichuan without further interruptions.

While Older was busy at Hankow, Colonel Rector and Major Chapman of the 74th took two P-51Bs to Amoy Island for a recon and to familiarize Rector with the area. Perhaps the new group commander should have picked someone other than Chapman to show him around, as Chapman had been shot down on just such a flight back in September. This time, however, Rector was the unlucky one.

While flying low over the airfield on Quemoy Island, Rector felt small arms fire rattling against his plane, followed by a heavier thud. He looked out to see a big hole in his right wing, and then he felt his engine starting to miss. Soon his windshield was covered by a spray of oil, and Rector knew he was in trouble. He climbed up to eighteen hundred feet and prepared to bail out. The canopy release mechanism malfunctioned, but Rector finally was able to heave upward, push off the canopy with his shoulders, and bail out. He landed near Tungan and fortunately was contacted by friendly Chinese who led him to safety. Three weeks later when he returned to duty, Colonel Rector grounded all P-51Bs until their canopy release mechanisms could be inspected.[2]

December 19, 1944, also is listed as the day Lt. Col. Ed McComas scored his fifth and sixth confirmed victories to become the 118th squadron's second ace. The kills came on a midday mission to Hong Kong.

The guerrilla squadrons continued to pile up missions and victories through the end of the month, but they also lost an unusually high number of pilots. The 74th lost three from December 23 through December 27, while the 118th had four pilots killed in action between December 21 and 26. In addition, 1/Lt. Max Parnell of the 118th was shot down at Hong Kong on Christmas Eve and spent the rest of the war as a prisoner of the Japanese.

On December 23, the 118th sent sixteen P-51s to attack the Hankow-Wuchang ferry installations on the Yangtze River. The flight was intercepted by a strong force of Oscars, and as usual, the Mustangs came out on top with eight confirmed victories for one plane lost. But what made the fight extraordinary was that five of the kills were credited to one pilot—Lieutenant Colonel McComas. It was the highest aerial victory total ever recorded by one pilot on a single mission in the 23rd Fighter Group's history. The following combat report described the colonel's action:

> McComas, leading the cover flight, made several passes on the Wuchang airdrome, probably destroying one Lily and damaging one Oscar on the ground. As he pulled up off these passes he observed six Oscars above him. One Oscar tailed him and scored hits in his wing, but McComas dived away and then climbed to 7,000 feet and tailed one Oscar from astern. He fired a long burst at this Oscar and saw hits going in the wing root. The Jap pilot jettisoned his canopy and bailed out. One confirmed on this.
>
> Two more Oscars jumped McComas, so he headed southeast toward Kiukiang. He passed over Erh Tao Kow field and saw nine Oscars preparing to take off. He circled and made a west-to-east pass on two Oscars just as they cleared the runway on takeoff. He fired a good burst into one Oscar, and it flipped off and crashed into the other, and both crashed just east of the field. Two confirmed on this. McComas then motored up behind two other Oscars after they took off abreast. McComas closed to within 50 feet of them and fired a long burst into each. He observed them both to crash east of the field. Two confirmed on this.[3]

Lieutenant Colonel McComas scored once more the following day, bringing his total to fourteen confirmed and making him the leading ace in China at the time. This honor only lasted a few days before Lt. Col. Pappy Herbst of the 74th returned to the top of the list. He scored two victories, his fourteenth and fifteenth, on a sweep of the airfields at Canton on December 27. Herbst would add three more victories in January, but McComas scored no further kills.

These two pilots presented an interesting contrast. Herbst inspired far more universal admiration and respect from his fellow pilots than did McComas. While Herbst was quiet but approachable on the ground, some pilots thought McComas was a martinet, concerned primarily about his own record. Whatever their personalities, the fact remains that both were highly skilled fighter pilots, and they both commanded tremendously successful combat units.

The 74th added two more aces before the end of the year. When the squadron paid a return visit to Nanking on Christmas Day, Maj. Phil Chapman knocked down three Ki-61 Tonys and brought his total to six confirmed kills. He added a seventh on December 27, when the 74th destroyed eight Tojos over Canton. One of the victories went to 1/Lt. John W. Bolyard, making him an ace as well with a total of five confirmed.

★ ★ ★ ★

Christmas 1944 fell on a Sunday, and it passed quietly for most of the men of the 23rd Fighter Group. While the 74th Squadron sent a strong mission to Nanking, the 118th stood down to give the pilots a much-needed day of rest. The 76th remained socked in at Tsingchen, and the 75th flew just a single two-plane strike against ground targets at Paoching.

One of the enlisted men in the 75th, aircraft mechanic Staff Sgt. Art Goodworth, wrote a description of Christmas Day at Chihkiang in a letter to his parents. The following excerpt details the squadron's efforts to make life on a forward air base in China more bearable during the holiday season:

"Today, being Christmas, I got up in time for the breakfast of fried eggs, bacon and pancakes, usually four eggs each morning. Spent most of the morning sawing wood, helping to put a door in the front of our tent. It doesn't look too fancy but serves the purpose, saving us the trouble of tying and untying the flaps every morning and night.

"Dinner was a good meal of canned turkey, no bone, potatoes, beans, cranberry sauce, bread, jam, cocoa, mince pie, tangerines, walnuts and cashews, and open packs of cigarettes on the tables. One plate was sufficient, and it sure tasted good. In the afternoon I went over to the Red Cross tents that just opened up. In one tent there's a jukebox, Victrola and radio, nice chairs and a big Christmas tree. There were boxes under the tree, each containing a little notebook and pencil, package of chewing gum, playing cards, two packs of cigarettes, fig bar, and two packages of candy.

"I got one, and then after listening to music for awhile I went to the next tent. Here there were tables and chairs, a big table where you helped yourself to coffee with good cream, chocolate nut cake, cookies, two kinds of fudge and a mixture of candy. Two servings of that and I headed back to the tent.

"Time out for chow again, but I took out a turkey sandwich I had brought back at dinner time, ate that and some candy, and was full. They had duck for supper and the fellows said it was good. I had seen rows of ducks that night before in the mess storeroom, so I knew they weren't canned.

"It's the next day now, a cold morning, and the fellow I'm supposed to be helping hasn't come around so I don't know if he's going to work or not. . . . Two other fellows moved into our tent and last night, a couple of the one's friends came in slightly under the weather and didn't leave until 3 A.M. I was burned up, but it's the holiday season and so one just takes it and likes it. . . .

"Received lots of birthday and Christmas cards and have plenty of letters to answer, but think I'll wait until the first of the year. A new year coming up and I hope it's the last year of war but it doesn't look like it to me. We'll just have to sweat it out, that's all."[4]

★ ★ ★ ★

The new year of 1945 brought an additional threat for the guerrilla squadrons at Suichuan and Kanchow. The intense operations by the 74th and 118th during December were more than the Japanese were willing to endure, so the enemy launched a new ground offensive to capture the remaining U.S. air bases in eastern China. Again, the Japanese used a two-pronged advance. Units of the Eleventh Army moved south from Chaling, and the Twenty-third Army sent units north from Canton. And despite Gen. Hsueh Yueh's promises that his army would hold the bases at all costs, the Chinese ground forces offered weak resistance.

The general could not get much help from the 23rd Fighter Group, either. The weather socked in on New Year's Day, and neither the 74th Fighter Squadron at Kanchow nor the 118th Tac Recon Squadron at Suichuan could turn a prop until January 13. By then, the Japanese advance had gathered momentum. It was just a matter of time until both bases would have to be abandoned.

Colonel Ed Rector was not going to evacuate his guerrilla bases, however, without giving the Japanese something to remember from his 23rd Fighter Group. On January 15, he sent a strong mission of sixteen Mustangs from the 118th Tac Recon Squadron to skip bomb Hong Kong's harbor and strafe the Canton airfields. While the Mustang pilots did a lot of damage, they also lost four of their own. One of the pilots who went down, Maj. David A. Houck, had just joined the squadron and was slated to replace Lieutenant Colonel

McComas soon. Instead, Houck was captured and later executed by the Japanese.

The Hong Kong mission, and another the previous day by the 74th Fighter Squadron to Anking, turned out to be just preliminaries to the 23rd's main event. On January 16, a photo plane brought back pictures showing a big buildup of enemy aircraft at Shanghai's five airfields. Because U.S. forces were then invading the Philippine Islands, the 23rd's intelligence officers speculated the Japanese had flown the planes in from Luzon to keep them from being captured or destroyed.

Shanghai, the giant seaport near the mouth of the Yangtze River, was the farthest objective ever attempted by the guerrilla squadrons. It was well within range of Rector's Mustangs, though, and he was not about to waste what might be his final chance to hit this juicy target. He gathered a force of twenty P-51s from both squadrons and sent the planes east to refuel at Nanchang on the morning of January 17. They took off at 10:50 A.M., bound for Shanghai, two and half hours away. Lieutenant Colonel Chuck Older initially led eight Mustangs from the 118th Squadron, but three of them turned back with mechanical problems. Major Phil Chapman led the assault flights of the 74th Squadron, with Maj. Pappy Herbst on "observer" status in the 74th's top cover.

The flight approached from the east. Achieving complete surprise, Lieutenant Colonel Older and the 118th's pilots struck Tachang Airdrome from about ten thousand feet. Older was at two thousand feet on his first pass when he saw a Ki-51 Sonia flying in front of him. He gave it a quick burst, and it crashed east of the field. He completed his strafing pass, and then he saw two more Japanese aircraft flying together low and near the river. He pulled up on them quickly, fired at each one from behind, and watched them both fall away to crash into the river. Older made several more runs over the base, noting very light ground fire, and set several more planes on fire. First Lieutenant Raymond A. Trudeau destroyed another Sonia in the air, and the total number of ground kills awarded at Tachang Airdrome was eleven. All of the 118th's planes returned safely.

The 74th Fighter Squadron struck at Lunghwa and Hungjao airdromes and had even greater success, tallying no fewer than fifty-seven aircraft destroyed on the ground. In addition, Lieutenant Colonel Herbst shot down one of two Ki-44 Tojo fighters he spotted at seven thousand feet near the field.

One pilot in the 74th who remembered this mission well is John C. Conn, who was a first lieutenant at the time. He recounted, "This was probably the only mission where everything went according to plan. Even the weather was clear and sunny—only a few scattered clouds. This was a low-level strafing attack. They had the two airfields loaded with aircraft. Lunghwa was the fighter field and was the one hit by the flight I was in—Major Chapman, Lt. Wade Terry and myself.

"We approached Lunghwa from the southwest and when about five miles out and at about 5,000 feet we started a long, straight-in approach on the field. We came over the field on a northeasterly heading and started firing as soon as we were within range. The Jap fighters were lined up, wingtip-to-wingtip, along the east edge and north edge of the ramp, forming two rows at right angles to each other. We set up a traffic pattern over the airfield and just kept circling around and firing on each pass until we had destroyed all aircraft on the field. There were fires burning all over the ramp area where the aircraft were parked. Obviously the Japs were not expecting an attack and had not drained the fuel from their aircraft. They made a pretty sight, with huge columns of black smoke coming from the burning aircraft and fuel.

"We had very little or no opposition to our attack. On our first pass over the field we could see a huge swarm of Japs come running out of the two hangars located at the north end of the ramp. They managed to get a couple of aircraft started, and one even started to taxi out, but he never made it. The flight of P-51s that hit Hungjao had about the same experience: Jap planes all over the field, and most of them destroyed."[5]

John Conn was credited with seven aircraft destroyed on the ground that day. Top honors in the squadron went to Chapman and Terry, with ten apiece. The pilots who attacked Hungjao, led by 1/Lt. Ira Binkley, accounted for another thirty aircraft destroyed.

With seventy-three Japanese aircraft destroyed on the ground and in the air, the Shanghai raid was the most destructive single mission ever flown by the 23rd Fighter Group. The fact that everyone came home safely was icing on the cake.

The guerrilla squadrons stayed closer to home on January 18 and 19, flying numerous missions against the Japanese Army's advance on their bases. Then on January 20, the squadrons went back to Shanghai, hoping to mop up the leftovers from the previous strike. Woosung and Kiangwan—two airdromes that were not attacked in the January 17 raid—were the primary targets for the 74th Squadron's Mustangs. The 118th would revisit the other three.

The flight plan for the mission was nearly identical to the previous Shanghai strike, but the pilots flew under dissimilar circumstances. First, the leaders were changed. Captain Floyd Finberg of the 74th was the mission leader, and 1/Lt. Russ Williams led the 118th's contingent. Both were experienced flight leaders, however, and they had no trouble directing their pilots to Shanghai after staging through

Nancheng. The Mustangs carried full internal fuel loads, but they did not have bombs or drop tanks.

Next, conditions were not as favorable when the Mustangs arrived over the city. For one thing, a heavy layer of smoke hung over Shanghai, making visibility poor. More important, this time the Japanese defenses appeared to be alerted. Few intercepting fighters were encountered, but ground fire was very heavy. This consisted not only of machine guns and forty-millimeter cannons on the airfields but also support fire from emplacements in the city and from several vessels anchored in the river nearby.

Two pilots in the 74th's top cover, Lts. Ed Beethoven and James Harrison, spotted twin-engine Navy G4M "Betty" bombers flying near the target and shot them down. Meanwhile, Captain Finberg decided that the smoke was too heavy over Woosung and Kiangwan airdromes to make safe and successful strafing passes. He diverted the 74th to Hungjao and Tachang and led his eleven Mustangs down to attack.

Finberg's P-51s flashed across Hungjao first and made several strafing runs, destroying two bombers and damaging several others. Flight Officer Billy Seago, number four man in Finberg's flight, apparently was shot down and killed during one of these runs. He was last seen making a strafing run, but no one saw him or heard a radio call from him after that.

When the smoke from the burning planes mixed with the smoke already in the air, Finberg decided visibility was too poor to continue attacking Hungjao. He led his flight to Tachang and burned up three parked aircraft. Then Finberg was hit by a forty-millimeter shell and forced to break off for home. Lieutenant John Branz also picked up some machine-gun hits, and the Mustang flown by Lt. Cyril Huss had most of its rudder blown off. Huss flew his plane back as far as Nancheng, but it was too badly damaged to repair. The ground crews burned it when they evacuated the base a few days later.

The 118th pilots also had a tougher time on their second trip to Shanghai, though this time they inflicted heavier damage. During its run to Lunghwa Airdrome, the 118th's primary target, the flight led by Lieutenant Williams spotted several Japanese fighters. Williams peeled off the run to make a pass on an A6M "Zeke" navy fighter that was in the landing pattern. He hit the Zeke and it exploded, but as Williams flew past, his wing clipped the burning Zeke's wing, causing major damage to the Mustang. The Zeke fell to earth. It was Williams's fifth kill, making him the last ace of the 23rd Fighter Group. He nursed his damaged P-51 back to Suichuan and made a safe landing.

Meanwhile, the rest of Williams's flight was mixing it up with several Ki-43 Oscars. First Lieutenant James ("Earthquake McGoon") McGovern shot down two, with single kills going to 1/Lt. Melvin Scheer and 2/Lt. Frederick Lanphier. The aerial victories scored on January 20 were the last of the war for both the 74th and the 118th squadrons.

First Lieutenant Raymond A. Crowell led the 118th Tac Recon Squadron's first flight to strafe Lunghwa. He recalled the mission this way: "It was a search and destroy mission, really. I had a flight for strafing the airfield—four airplanes. We were going so damned fast when we made that first pass that about the only thing I could aim at was a hangar. So I did. Nothing happened, so we circled around, but I saw an airplane burning under me as I went over.

"We came back in and made another pass, this time not going quite so fast. As we were pulling up and leaving the area I looked over at my wingman, Lt. H. B. Tollett, maybe 250 feet away. All of a sudden his airplane started to burn from the prop to the tail. Everybody hollered, 'Get out,' and he did. His chute was opening as he went over the top of the aircraft.

"He landed safely on the ground. The story has it—I didn't see this, of course—that he landed within five miles of the airport in the middle of a field. He hid in a pigsty, and the Chinese Communists picked him up before the Japs could get to him. The Japs were on their way. I know that much because I took a shot at their trucks leaving the field.

"Tollett was months getting back, and I guess he was severely burned. His biggest problem was the handoff between the Communists and the Nationalists. The Communists wanted a receipt for him, and the Nationalists refused to sign. It was a couple of weeks before he could get loose of that and finally come back home.

"That was a long flight: five hours. Then on landing, one of the other men in my flight had had his airspeed shot out. He landed on my wing. I didn't land. He put her on the ground and I circled around and came back, almost out of fuel. Then I got a red light on my landing gear. I called the tower and asked them to check it. They checked it and said it looked down and locked. So I came in and landed.

"Thank goodness I made a very smooth landing because as I was rolling down the runway that right wing kept dropping and dropping and dropping. Finally there was nothing I could do. I couldn't pick it up with torque or anything. The wing dug in and she spun around. There were two interesting parts to that. One, the reason for the landing gear not coming down was that someone in the factory had left a rivet bucking bar in the wing, and it had slid down in front of the locking pin for the landing gear. Therefore, the gear wouldn't lock.

"The other thing: Two days later we evacuated the air base back to Chengkung. I flew the airplane that had dropped the wing. I couldn't get the landing gear up, so I flew that thing all the way back with the landing gear down. That was a long and a slow flight, but we saved the airplane."[6]

The 118th's total in ground kills for January 20 was eleven, with Crowell getting credit for one that was set on fire when he strafed the hangar. Top scorer was 1/Lt. Silven Kosa, with four Oscars and one Tess destroyed.

Besides Lieutenant Tollett, 2/Lt. Glenn Geyer failed to return. Flying only his seventh combat mission, Geyer was hit on his third pass over Lunghwa. He turned south, flew until his cockpit filled with smoke, and then bailed out about eleven miles south of Shanghai. Nationalist guerrillas quickly picked him up, but it took him more than three months to get out from behind enemy lines. He wrote this highlight of his experience after reaching safety:

"I had been living with the Chinese guerrillas for about 70 days when a ring-necked pheasant landed along a canal about 200 yards from our camp. The guerrilla general, Ting Si San, took his carbine rifle and tried to shoot the bird, but he missed and the bird flew a short distance down the canal; the general handed me the gun and indicated for me to try.

"I walked approximately 100 yards when the bird moved. Knowing I had no time left, I threw the rifle to my shoulder and fired. I cut the bird's throat, so we had pheasant for dinner.

"The best part of the story is I hadn't even had time to aim, and some of the guerrilla band thought I had shot from the hip. From that time on I was told no one wanted to challenge me to a shootout."[7]

★ ★ ★ ★

The January 20 mission marked the end of guerrilla operations by the 23rd Fighter Group at Kanchow and Suichuan. Local air raid alerts caused several uneventful scrambles on January 21, but the real threat to the bases came from the Japanese ground forces. Chinese resistance was crumbling. When the forecast for a week of bad weather arrived at Suichuan that day, Lieutenant Colonel Older gave the order to evacuate. He did not want to risk having the 118th Tac Recon Squadron's planes trapped there.

First Lieutenant Carl Colleps led a flight of five P-51s out of Suichuan at 2:00 P.M., and they landed at Luliang four hours later. The next morning, Lieutenant Colonel Older led the remaining nineteen Mustangs to Chengkung. The great base at Suichuan, once central to General Chennault's plans for bombing Japan, was blown up after transports flew the ground personnel and their equipment to safety.

Kanchow was a short hop from Suichuan and subject to the same weather forecast. Lieutenant Colonel Herbst gave the order to evacuate to Luliang January 23. One Mustang crashed on takeoff, killing 1/Lt. Nick Gazibara. Then four C-47s carrying out personnel and equipment ran into bad weather, and three of them crashed. Fortunately, the men on board were able to bail out safely, but Lieutenant Gazibara's body was lost in one of the planes.

Major Phil Chapman, Capt. Floyd Finberg, and Lts. John Branz and Wade Terry stayed behind at Kanchow with four P-51s and a skeleton crew to wait until the last possible moment to clear out. Weather and the ground situation got progressively worse through the following week. Finally, on February 4, Major Chapman led the four Mustangs and a C-47 out of Kanchow for the last time. A small crew stayed behind to blow up the base and then escaped to Changting, a remote field in Fukien Province that remained in Chinese hands.

One of the most exciting and productive periods in the history of the 23rd Fighter Group was over.

19

Final Victory

By the beginning of 1945 the old shark-mouth P-40s had nearly disappeared from the operational rosters of the 23rd Fighter Group. The few that remained were like P-40N number 181, the last Shark in the 75th Fighter Squadron. Used as a utility plane, it mostly carried mail and payroll between Luliang and Chihkiang. Old 181 could take a passenger, too, because the mechanics had removed the armor plate and decking under the canopy behind the pilot's seat and installed a second seat. Getting in and out of the cramped space was difficult, but that did not stop most ground-bound technicians and administrative personnel from going up for a flight whenever possible.

The 23rd Fighter Group was now strictly a P-51 outfit for operational purposes. The pilots had learned that the sleek Mustangs, with their great speed and range, were far superior to the P-40 in most aspects except armament. The four machine guns of the P-51Bs and Cs not only carried less punch than the P-40's six guns, but they also continued to jam. For instance, on January 16, 1945, two pilots of the 76th Fighter Squadron had the rare good fortune to catch a Japanese transport plane on the ground at Kweilin. They dived down for the easy kill, but when all eight guns in the two planes failed to fire, they had to return to Tsingchen empty-handed.

Now, even this problem was improving. The first P-51D and K model Mustangs began to arrive in the squadrons during January 1945 and boasted several improvements. For one thing, the armament was increased to six .50-caliber machine guns, and they were mounted differently inside the wings to reduce the jamming problems. More noticeable and almost as important was the change in the fuselage. The high upper decking behind the cockpit was cut down, and a streamlined bubble canopy was fitted to eliminate the earlier models' blind spot behind the pilot's head.

These modifications took the classic P-51 design to its peak and made it arguably the best piston-engine fighter aircraft of World War II. The P-51Ds had been flying out of England with the Eighth Air Force since May 1944, and by this time, they had clearly helped to break the back of the Germans' fighter defenses. Ironically, by the time these magnificent machines were introduced in China, the Japanese air forces already were shattered.

Air-to-air encounters with Japanese aircraft would become increasingly rare after January, as the Japanese moved what few aircraft remained in fighting condition back to the Shanghai-Nanking area for defensive and training purposes. That did not mean the action was over for the 23rd Fighter Group, however; ground attack missions of all kinds continued. The Mustang's performance was well suited to low-level work, as the plane was plenty fast, maneuverable, and capable of carrying a variety of weapons. Its Achilles' heel—the radiator placement below the wing—remained, but the pilots came to accept that vulnerability as the price they paid for the Mustang's high performance.

One of those P-51 pilots was Lt. Harold Bedient, who joined the 76th Fighter Squadron in January 1945. As he recalled, the late-model Mustangs "had a bubble canopy and six .50-caliber guns. Unfortunately, it was hard to modify the wing structure, so the outer two guns on either side had to share the same ammunition tray. This meant when you were halfway through shooting you only had two guns. It was sure good while it lasted!

"Both models could carry two 500-pound bombs or two 75-gallon drop tanks, which could be loaded with napalm. In May of 1945 our P-51s were modified with 'zero-rail' rocket racks and controls so we could carry 10 five-inch rockets in addition to the other stores.

"The C and D models had an 85-gallon fuel tank behind the pilot's seat. In order to keep the balance under control the wing was mounted a little further to the rear on the fuselage, which made the plane a little touchy on the brakes when landing with the tank empty. With these changes, the P-51 could do a 4½-hour mission carrying bombs or a 6½-hour mission carrying drop tanks. This would allow us to work 440 to 600 miles from our home base. I have seen eight planes come in from a 4½-hour mission with all of them showing empty with their tails down. They had maybe 20 minutes worth of fuel left.

"Another modification to the fighters I never heard of anywhere else was an automatic radio compass. The maps were so confusing, the visibility often poor and the road network so insignificant that it was hard to find your way home. We depended on the 25-watt homing beacons at each base to find our way home."[1]

Home for Bedient's 76th Fighter Squadron changed in late January with a move to the new base at Laohwangping. A convoy of trucks departed Tsingchen on January 21, and the pilots flew their Mustangs to Laohwangping on the twenty-third. Although thousands of coolie laborers were still building taxiways and other facilities on the base, its location, eighty miles east of Tsingchen, placed the P-51s closer to Japanese-held target areas from Hengyang to Liuchow. Furthermore, Laohwangping did not have large rivers or roads nearby to aid a possible enemy ground advance. Another pilot in the squadron, Lt. Joel Beezley, described the new base:

"At Laohwangping we had it pretty good, considering everything. We had British-style tents, with a double top, and they were quite comfortable. We had an electric generator pulled by a jeep motor and as long as five gallons of gas lasted, we had lights and radio until about 9:30 P.M. Our tents had wood floors with a wainscoting up about three feet. We made a stove out of an empty gas barrel and kept warm. For an icebox, we dug a hole about three feet deep under our floor, equipped with a trapdoor, and made a container out of metal portions of .50-caliber ammo containers. The moisture in the ground under the tent, which was in an old rice paddy, kept food and water cool. We sodded the lawn around our tent, built a picket fence around the area, and painted it white. We hung our steel helmets up and made flower pots out of them.

"Ben S. Lyen and Lewis H. Carpenter were my tentmates. We got along marvelously. We got some big clay pots and made a brew of peach brandy, using peaches, yeast, sugar and water. It turned out pretty good after you strained out all the junk."[2]

Unfortunately for the men who served in China late in the war, living conditions on the forward bases actually got more primitive as time went on and the older air bases fell into Japanese hands. During the first months of 1945, Lieutenant Beezley and the rest of the pilots at Laohwangping had plenty of time to fix up their tents while waiting for good flying weather to arrive with the spring.

One bit of excitement broke the monotony at Laohwangping when the technical supply building caught on fire and burned to the ground on February 18. Most of the men were at the mess hall when the fire broke out. By the time they arrived on the scene, ammunition was exploding and the building was engulfed in flames. Fortunately, some fragmentation bombs stored there did not explode, but despite the men's best efforts to save them, most of the squadron's tools, spare parts, guns, and radios were destroyed. That evening, their CO, Maj. L. V. Teeter, called the men together and thanked them for doing what they could. The mechanics managed to cobble together enough tools to keep the planes operational, and soon a planeload of tools arrived from Chihkiang, compliments of the 75th Squadron, to tide them over until new tools could be sent from Luliang.

For the 118th Tac Recon Squadron at Chengkung, February and March were lost months. Aside from a makeshift ground school and some practice flights, the only excitement in February was a visit by three major league baseball stars on a USO (United Service Organizations) tour: Paul Waner of the Yankees, Luke Sewell of the St. Louis Browns, and Dixie Walker of the Brooklyn Dodgers. The next month Lt. John Egan, who went down on the Hong Kong mission in January 16, returned to the squadron. On March 12 during a training mission, Lt. Roy Christenson died in a flying accident. Softball, volleyball, and basketball leagues helped keep the men busy, as did weekly lectures on the war situation presented by Capt. Robert Burke, the squadron's intelligence officer. Finally, in April, the 118th moved up to Laohwangping and joined the 76th Squadron.

★ ★ ★ ★

The 74th Fighter Squadron spent nearly two months cooped up at Luliang with little to do except run occasional weather recon missions. In mid-February, Lt. Col. Pappy Herbst received his orders to go to the States, and command of the squadron passed on to Maj. Phil Chapman. At the time, Chapman was in Karachi on a ferry mission, but the Arkansan ace returned to the squadron late in the month and assumed command.

About that time, an advance party was sent to Tushan, approximately three hundred miles east of Luliang, to oversee completion of a new airstrip there. A member of that party, Lt. Al Griffy, described Tushan: "It was carved out of a mountain top and looked like a bowling alley, with as much as 10- to 15-foot walls on the sides of the runway. The coolies finally got all those walls down."[3]

When the base was ready, late in March, the 74th Squadron moved to Tushan. Although the base lacked permanent housing and the men had to live in tents, the move put the squadron's Mustangs much closer to potential targets in the Hsiang River valley. It also allowed them to resume operations against China's seaport cities of Canton and Hong Kong. Major Chapman chose to lead the first Hong Kong mission from Tushan. Sadly, it would also be his last.

At 11:00 A.M. on March 28, Major Chapman and his wingman, 1/Lt. Wade Terry, took off from Tushan under clear skies. Chapman planned to lead twelve P-51s south on the long haul to Hong Kong, where they would strafe the familiar target of Kai Tak Airdrome. Fifteen Mustangs of the 76th Squadron flew from Laohwangping and met them over Tushan's field. The big formation then headed for the coast.

Before long, the 74th was down to nine Mustangs. Lieutenant Terry was unable to get his drop tanks to feed and turned back, as did Lt. William Dunn, who had hit a coolie on the runway while taking off and damaged one of his tanks. A third pilot, Lieutenant Harrison, developed engine trouble a little later.

The weather thickened as the Mustangs neared the coast. At Sanshui, the 76th split off and made for two other familiar targets, White Cloud and Tien Ho airdromes, in Canton. Major L. V. Teeter led his flight to White Cloud and shot up vehicles and men after he determined the field was nearly empty of aircraft. The Mustangs then proceeded to a satellite field and made three passes, damaging several parked Ki-44 Tojos. The other strafing flight found several dummy aircraft and one Ki-43 Oscar at Tien Ho. Lieutenant Chuck Breingan strafed the Ki-43 and was credited with damaging it. No serious ground fire was evident at Canton, and all of the 76th's Mustangs returned safely to Laohwangping without a single bullet hole in any of them.

It was a different story for the 74th. The cloud ceiling was down to fifteen hundred feet or less when Major Chapman and his nine Mustangs arrived over Hong Kong. He left two Mustangs above for top cover and led the other seven straight in from the northwest for a strafing pass over Kai Tak's runway. There were not many targets on the field, just a couple of aircraft parked here and there. Revetments were empty, and a junk pile on the edge of the field appeared to contain several discarded fuselages.

Chapman encountered little ground fire as he crossed the field. He spotted a big Kawasaki H6K "Mavis" flying boat moored in the harbor off the end of the runway, turned slightly to bring his guns to bear, and set it ablaze with a long burst of fire. A pilot in the second flight, Lt. John Branz, made a similar pass and destroyed a single-engine Aichi E13A "Jake" float plane. Four other pilots—Lts. Tony Cole, John Conn, Stanley J. Chmielewski, and Albert H. Sims—each shot up planes on the field.

The Mustangs regrouped south of the field, and Chapman decided to make another pass. This time, the Japanese gunners were ready for them. Intense ground fire bracketed the Mustangs from positions at the northwest corner of the field and on the adjacent docks. Lieutenants Chmielewski and Sims both were shot down and killed. Major Chapman's Mustang was badly hit, and he lost about five feet off the left wing. Chapman called to Capt. Barney Fudge to take over as leader and nursed his damaged fighter into the clouds. The six remaining Mustangs strafed shipping in the harbor and then turned north for the long flight back to Tushan.

Rather than attempt to reach Tushan, Chapman set out for Changting, a small field to the northeast in Fukien Province that remained in the hands of the Chinese. It was about 250 miles to Changting, but Chapman's Mustang still flew well enough to get there. He knew the damaged wing would be a problem when he slowed the plane to landing speed, so when he reached Changting, he circled and let the Mustang's speed bleed off to test the plane's low-speed characteristics. Sure enough, the left wing stalled. Perhaps the stall was more violent than Chapman expected. The plane whipped into a spin and dropped straight to the ground with him still in the cockpit. He was killed instantly.

When confirmation of Chapman's death reached Tushan, Capt. Floyd Finberg, the 74th's operations officer, was named the new squadron commander. Captain Finberg, a veteran of the 74th's guerrilla operations, had 16.5 ground kills to his credit and one confirmed aerial victory scored on December 27, 1944. He had led the second Shanghai strike in January, and he would lead many more missions before the war's end. His assignment as squadron commander, however, would end abruptly in June when he ran afoul of a visiting general over a curfew violation.

★ ★ ★ ★

As far as the Japanese were concerned, the Ichi-Go offensive ended successfully on February 8, 1945, with the capture of the last section of the Hankow-Canton railroad line and the airfields at Kanchow and Suichuan. They now held a land link all the way from Indo-China to the seaports of northern China. The corridor contained railroad lines, roads, and long stretches of navigable rivers, but the Japanese were unable to make full use of their prize. In fact, during daylight hours, the Japanese along the corridor came under continual attack by units of the Fourteenth Air Force.

After the U.S. squadrons withdrew from the guerrilla bases, the 75th Fighter Squadron at Chihkiang was the closest 23rd Fighter Group unit to enemy positions at Hankow and in the Hsiang River valley. The 75th shared space at Chihkiang with one B-25 squadron of the Chinese-American Composite Wing and the four squadrons of the 5th Fighter Group, CACW. About 150 miles north of Kweilin, Chihkiang became the focal point for operations against Japanese lines of communication and transportation.

Despite an eleven-day stretch of bad weather, the 75th flew twenty-five combat missions totaling two hundred sorties during January 1945. All but five of these missions were against ground targets. February was much the same, with twenty-one missions flown in the eleven days of good weather. Primary targets were road and railroad bridges in the Hsiang River valley. Using their Mustangs as dive-bombers, pilots of the 75th knocked out seven bridges. Their only loss occurred on February 25, when 1/Lt. Harold T. Byrd hit a tree while strafing and tore one of the horizontal stabilizers off his P-51C. The Mustang crashed and burned, killing Lieutenant Byrd, who had only been flying with the squadron since late December.

March 1945 brought better flying weather at Chihkiang, and the 75th took advantage of it. The squadron was assigned a specific area of responsibility along the railroad line between Chananyi, just north of Tungting Lake, and Hankow. Most missions were contained in this area, with the goal of keeping at least one railroad bridge out of commission at all times. While doing so, the pilots noticed very few trains along the tracks. Nevertheless, a flight led by Lt. Russell Fleming caught a train north of Puchi on March 25 and thoroughly wrecked it. The Mustangs blew out the engine's boiler on their first pass, stopping the train. Then they proceeded to shoot up twenty-five boxcars and seventeen flatcars before exhausting their ammunition and returning to base.

Three days later, on March 28, the 75th got exciting orders. Major Clyde Slocumb was to take a detachment—all of his pilots and aircraft, plus fifty enlisted men—to Changting for a series of missions against Japanese targets on the eastern coast of China.

Changting, the last remaining guerrilla air base, was located about eighty miles east of Kanchow. It was barely big enough to use as a staging base, but after the larger bases at Suichuan and Kanchow fell, an effort was made to stockpile gas and ammunition there. Changting's small contingent of permanent American personnel was completely cut off from the rest of China and extremely vulnerable to capture by the Japanese. So they were very glad for the company when aircraft began bringing in men and supplies on the twenty-eighth, the same day Major Chapman of the 74th crashed there. First, a flight of four Mustangs escorted seven C-46 transport planes in from Chihkiang. Later in the day, Col. Ed Rector, the 23rd Fighter Group's CO, led a formation of twenty-one Mustangs to Changting. Flying with them was a B-25 carrying Col. Clay Claassen, commander of the 68th Composite Wing. Offensive operations began first thing the next morning.

The first order of business March 29 was to figure out how close Japanese forces were to Changting. An offensive recon mission left at 8:30 A.M. to scout the roads west of the base. Later in the day, separate missions hit airfields at Amoy Island and Swatow on the coast. Captain Eugene McGuire, a former 76th Fighter Squadron pilot on his second tour in China, was shot up by ground fire on his second pass over Amoy. He managed to reach the mainland before bailing out, and he later walked back to rejoin the 75th. Captain Stan Kelley destroyed one Oscar and damaged three others on the ground at Kilok Airdrome, Swatow. On the last mission of the day, Colonel

Rector led a two-plane recon of Quemoy Island and shot up a building he spotted there.

The first big mission from Changting occurred the next day, March 30. Colonel Rector led twelve Mustangs off at 8:10 A.M. in clear weather. They were headed for Hangchow, a city south of Shanghai, to strafe airfields and railroad yards. Lieutenant Weldon Riley had engine trouble en route to the target and turned back. His plane went down, however, and he had to make the long trek home on foot. The Mustangs carried drop tanks, which they jettisoned just prior to reaching the city.

The attack on the airfield was disappointing. The men saw only one real airplane and a handful of dummies, but Lt. Gordon Berven did receive credit for damaging a single-engine plane that he shot up in a revetment. The Mustang pilots found better targets at the railroad yard. Their gunfire burst the boilers of seven steam engines and tore up a number of railroad cars. When the canopy of Lt. James ("Mouse") Carter's P-51 was hit by ground fire, he received a flesh wound in the face, but he continued his attack and completed the mission.

Meanwhile, another twelve P-51s led by Lieutenant Fleming bombed and strafed facilities at Kanchow Airfield and then returned to Chihkiang. Two more small missions on March 31 and another on April 1 moved six more P-51s back to Chihkiang, including one flown by Colonel Rector.

Later on April 1, Lt. John Rosenbaum led four Mustangs from Chihkiang back to Changting, while escorting five C-46s that were bringing in more fuel and supplies. Then Colonel Rector returned to Changting with a flight of six more Mustangs from the 75th after a detour to Hengyang for a look around. Also arriving at Changting that day were twenty-five Mustangs from the 76th Fighter Squadron, led by Maj. L. V. Teeter. Something big was brewing, no "April fooling" about it.

★ ★ ★ ★

It was supposed to be foggy at Changting when the sun rose on the morning of April 2, 1945. That is what the pilots had been told during the previous night's mission briefing. Then they went to bed in their tents, expecting to have to take off the next morning in zero-zero conditions in their heavily loaded Mustangs. The planes needed to carry all the fuel they could because their targets were the airfields at Shanghai, some five hundred miles to the northeast. Intelligence reports estimated the Japanese had nearly one hundred aircraft at Shanghai. The Mustang pilots did not find that many, but there would be enough targets to make the mission worthwhile.

A beautiful sight greeted the pilots when they arose that Saturday morning. A thick coat of dew covered everything, including their

Mustangs, but the air was clear with an eight-thousand-foot ceiling. Takeoff runs began at 5:20 A.M., with Col. Ed Rector leading the way. After forty minutes, all thirty-two Mustangs were airborne from the narrow strip at Changting. Before long, however, the flights began to thin out as, one by one, seven Mustangs turned back. Then the attackers encountered thick haze near Kienow, and it stayed with them all the way to the target area, making for a long and tedious flight.

Visibility improved somewhat near Shanghai, and the Mustangs dropped their tanks as they neared their target areas. One of Colonel Rector's tanks failed to release, but he chose to make the attack anyway. The Mustangs in his flight were assigned to hit Kiangwan Airdrome. He led five P-51s from the 75th down across the field, but they found only one Oscar, which Rector damaged in its revetment.

The second flight was down to just two Mustangs, flown by Maj. Clyde Slocumb and Lt. Gordon Berven of the 75th. As they prepared to make their run, they spotted a Betty bomber in the landing pattern. They hoped to shoot it out of the sky, but the plane was nearly on the runway before they got in range. Slocumb fired first and apparently hit the bomber, but it landed under control. Then Lieutenant Berven opened fire on it, and the plane ground-looped and crashed.

Both Mustangs were hit by ground fire on the pass. Lieutenant Berven pulled up and headed for home, but Major Slocumb pulled around to make a second pass. This time he was hit in the wing by a forty-millimeter shell, which set the plane on fire. He nursed the plane to five hundred feet altitude and then bailed out about four miles away from the field. Luck was with Slocumb; he was rescued by friendly Chinese who helped him elude the Japanese and return to his squadron a month later.

While all this was going on, Colonel Rector was busy trying to shake off his hung-up belly tank. While doing this, he spotted a twin-engine Japanese training plane ahead of him that was flying toward the auxiliary field at Woosung. Pulling in right behind it, he opened fire and saw the plane blow up and fall to the ground. He swept ahead in the direction of Tachang Airdrome, where he expected to find better hunting.

Major L. V. Teeter of the 76th led the attack on Tachang, where about twenty aircraft were parked. One of the six pilots in his assault flight was Lt. Jerome P. Ellis, who had just joined the squadron and was on his first combat mission. He wrote the following account of the action later that night:

"Today we raided Shanghai and had a lot of fun, though I was pretty scared. I damaged one plane, got a 75 mm gun and strafed a bus. My element leader [Lt. B. C. Hawk] claimed three, and I saw him get one. I was so busy keeping on his wing, though, that I didn't look around too much. There was flak, but no aerial opposition. We made five passes, which was too many for me. . . . The deal took six hours, and my fanny hurts."[4]

One of the other pilots in Teeter's flight was Capt. Bernard A. Dyrland, who set fire to a twin-engine bomber on a taxi strip at midfield and then shot up a radio station on the edge of the base. Another veteran of the early days in China, having flown a tour with the 16th Fighter Squadron in 1942–43, Dyrland now was back for more action.

In all, Teeter's pilots accounted for five aircraft destroyed at Tachang. Colonel Rector added one more to the count when he shot up an Oscar and it caught fire on the airfield's north side.

Four more Mustangs from the 76th, led by Lt. Joseph D. Murray, attacked Hungjao Airdrome and destroyed three of the four aircraft spotted there. The planes were parked in a row along a runway and made easy targets. Then the Mustangs turned south toward the rendezvous area and strafed seven barges on a river before heading for home. During the Hungjao attack, Murray reported having seen a P-51 passing over the base southbound at 150 feet and trailing black smoke. This may have been Maj. Slocumb's airplane, or it could have been one of the three from the 75th that were shot down while attacking Lunghwa Airdrome.

The Lunghwa attack was led by the last active 75th Fighter Squadron ace, Capt. Pappy Parham. Flying with him in the assault flight were 1/Lt. Jack Quinn and 2/Lt. Don King. As they made their first pass from the south, Parham spotted an Oscar taxiing toward him on the runway. He opened fire and hit it in the fuselage, setting the plane on fire. Another Oscar parked nearby got the same treatment, and then Parham pulled up and turned to make a pass from north to south. This time he spotted a parachute coming down and called it in to his flight. Parham then fired at a flying boat moored in the river nearby.

Parham made a third pass and damaged another Oscar in a revetment, but then Lieutenant Quinn called that he had been hit. Parham spotted some antiaircraft batteries firing at Quinn and dived down to strafe them, but on this pass, his own Mustang was hit hard in the nose. He, like Slocumb and then Quinn, cleared the area and bailed out. Lieutenant King was separated from Parham after the second pass, and then he also was shot down. Amazingly enough, all four pilots returned to fly again in the 75th. In fact, Slocumb and Parham met up en route to Chihkiang and returned together on May 5.

While Parham's flight of three was strafing at Lunghwa, Capt. Eugene Harper and 1/Lt. Ed Bollen of the 75th provided top cover.

The two pilots spotted a Ki-44 Tojo circling the airfield at two thousand feet, and Harper led the attack on it. He got in a snap shot from thirty degrees deflection, but the Tojo pulled away from him. Harper took another shot from dead astern. The Tojo pilot tried to turn away, but his action gave Bollen a good deflection shot and he made the most of it. Three bursts hit the Tojo before Bollen got too close and had to pull up in a zoom. He looked back to see the Tojo's left wing break off from the fuselage and the plane go down in a spin. The pilot bailed out and descended in his chute, which apparently was the one Parham saw.

Lieutenant Bollen and Colonel Rector each were credited with a confirmed aerial victory on the April 2 mission. These kills were the last of the war for the 23rd Fighter Group. It is interesting [and fitting!] to note that one of them belonged to the man who also got the 23rd's first confirmed victory on July 4, 1942. That pilot was Ed Rector.

★ ★ ★ ★

The Shanghai mission was the last big strike for the task force at Changting. The 76th Fighter Squadron refueled its Mustangs and flew back to Laohwangping the next day, detouring over the airfields at Kanchow and Kweilin to shoot up targets of opportunity. The 75th also sent half of its Mustangs back to Chihkiang on April 3, with Colonel Rector leading one flight. The remaining Mustangs flew only a few more local missions from Changting before they, too, were pulled back to Chihkiang.

Changting had proven too far removed from its source of supplies to remain operational. Moreover, the Japanese were just eighty miles away at Kanchow and could choose to take the base at any time. Even worse, all gas and ammunition had to be flown in, and the nearest friendly air base was Chihkiang, which had problems of its own.

On April 10, 1945, Japanese ground forces in the Hsiang River valley launched what would be their last offensive of the war in China. Their primary target was the air base at Chihkiang. Taking the base not only would deny its use to the Fourteenth Air Force's bombers and fighters that had been deviling the Japanese for months, it would also provide a stepping-stone toward the key city of Kweiyang, capital of Kweichow Province. An estimated twenty-five thousand frontline troops, drawn from at least six Japanese divisions, were committed to the effort. They moved west and north in a three-pronged attack centered at Paoching, and within only a few days, Chihkiang was seriously threatened.

On April 11, the remaining Mustangs of the 75th Fighter Squadron at Changting were withdrawn to Chihkiang, where they immediately joined the massive effort to save the base. For once, the

Chinese Army put up a determined and effective defense, and the flying units coordinated closely with it to provide pinpoint close air support. Units of the Chinese-American Composite Wing flew the bulk of these missions, but the 75th at Chihkiang and the 76th at Laohwangping also contributed many hours of dangerous low-level bombing and strafing to the effort. In fact, on April 15 at Luchai, the 76th lost two pilots—Capt. Richard Johnson and Lt. Jerome Eisenman—on the same bridge-busting mission.

A week later, the 118th Tac Recon Squadron ended its long layoff at Chengkung and was sent to join the 76th at Laohwangping. One of the pilots who made the move was Lt. Russell E. ("Rusty") Packard. He had been assigned to the squadron back in January but missed the action at Suichuan. After three months, he had yet to fire the guns of a Mustang on a combat mission. In his diary, Rusty Packard recorded the following details of the trip:

"April 7, 1945—Well, we are on our way. Left Kunming at 0800 and arrived at Chanyi at 1600 [4:00 P.M.] by train. Have tents to sleep in tonight and a cot to sleep on.

"April 8, 1945—One hell of a night last night. I almost froze to death. Had four blankets but it wasn't enough. May leave tonight at 1800 and be on our way to a good fight. A 39-hour ride to Kweiyang, 60 miles from our destination.

"April 13, 1945—Friday the 13th. Last night we arrived at Laohwangping, our destination. A five-day convoy trip that was really one hell of a ride. We got into Kweiyang the morning of the 11th and stayed until the morning of the 12th. From there to here it took about 10 hours, but the trip itself wasn't too bad. 'Lightning' [the squadron's mascot dog] was right with us and didn't get sick at all. He did piss twice in the truck, but that is considered good for him. Our living quarters here are boarded tents, which are *ding-hao* [Chinese for 'OK'] setups. Had a two-ball alert last night, but nothing happened. Also heard that President Roosevelt died, which is very bad news at a time like this. Sure hope Truman does a good job now. Our planes should be here tomorrow and then we should start operating. I hope.

"May 2, 1945—Got my fourth mission today. This is the first time I ever fired my guns or dropped bombs. Dropped parafrags. Lots of fun."[5]

Rusty Packard would not fly his next combat mission until June 15. His record was typical of pilots who served in China at the end of the war. He was on combat status for nearly eight months but only managed to enter twelve combat missions in his logbook between January and August. Then combat ceased.

Packard and other pilots had so little opportunity to fly because of gas supply problems. Stocks got so low at Chihkiang that, to avoid losing its planes in case Chihkiang fell to the Japanese, the 75th was evacuated 190 miles west to Tsingchen. At Laohwangping, supplies dwindled to the point that the Mustangs often stopped at Tsingchen to fill up with gas before returning from a mission. Before long, the well began to run dry at Tsingchen also. The month of May passed with the squadrons flying just a few strikes in the Paoching region.

Besides the move to Laohwangping, the only excitement in the 118th came on the first of May, when Capt. Oran Watts finally completed his long tour with the squadron and left for home. Lieutenant Colonel Charles Simpson was the next squadron commander. He would only serve in the squadron for about six weeks before being transferred to the 68th Composite Wing's headquarters. During his command, however, the 118th's action did pick up because fuel supplies were replenished at Laohwangping and Tushan early in June.

★ ★ ★ ★

The gasoline put the 118th, 76th, and 74th squadrons back in action at a crucial time. The Chinese defenders had held at Chihkiang and were beginning to push the Japanese back. Meanwhile, the Japanese also were withdrawing from the Nanning area down south toward Canton. After all their efforts expended during the Ichi-Go campaign, the Japanese now were unable to hold on to the captured Chinese territories. They were expecting an American landing on the eastern coast of China at any time and knew that the invasion of the Japanese home islands could not be far off, either. They could no longer afford to tie up large numbers of ground forces in central China; they were needed closer to home.

The Mustangs of the 23rd Fighter Group hit the retreating Japanese hard during June. Now, in addition to strafing and conventional bombing, the P-51s were equipped to fire rockets and drop napalm firebombs. The city and former American air base at Liuchow became a prime target.

Captain Ray Crowell of the 118th had good reason to remember the mission of June 3, 1945. That day, the 76th and 118th flew together, meeting forty B-25s over Ishan and escorting them to the target before going down to strafe. According to Crowell, "It was my last mission. I was on photo recon to observe bomb damage in the Liuchow area of the B-25s. I had a P-51 with an oblique camera, so you had to stand aside and take an oblique shot.

"We got down to Liuchow, and the B-25s were just above the broken clouds. They made a run, but I couldn't get a picture of it. I was below the clouds, so I couldn't see the bombs coming through.

"They did several runs, and on the next one I stayed up above the clouds and a little behind and watched the bomb bay doors open. The minute the bombs went, I dived full power under the clouds and took the pictures. The only thing was, I caught hell when I got back and the film was developed, because every bomb landed in the river. Not one bomb hit dry land. They were none too happy about that.

"On that same mission, after the photo part of it was over, there was one anti-aircraft gun down there that I made a pass at. I had napalm on, because after the run I was going to work the place over. There was a gun pit there, and just as luck would have it the napalm hit in front of the pit and slid right across it. People running out of the pit were all burning.

"Another incident happened on that flight. I don't think there were any enemy aircraft in the area, but somebody yelled, 'Break right!' Well, my God, every airplane in the area broke right. There was no identification given. But without identification, when somebody hollers 'Break,' you break."[6]

The men of the 76th Fighter Squadron also remembered well the June 3 mission, because they lost their longtime commanding officer, Lt. Col. L. V. Teeter. After one flight of B-25s finished their runs, they radioed the all-clear so that Teeter could lead his flight of Mustangs down to strafe gun positions on the airfield.

Pilot Joel Beezley recalled what happened after that. He wrote, "I was leader of the second element of Col. Teeter's flight. When we went in for our strafing run, we went from southwest to northeast and flew through a dense cloud of black smoke that I suppose the bombers caused by setting fire to ammo and fuel dumps of the Japs. Colonel Teeter went down and through the smoke. Then his wingman and I followed with my wingman after me. When we came out the other side of that big column of smoke, there were only three of us. After circling and calling for Col. Teeter for a long time, we decided that he had gone down, and I led the flight home."[7]

Lieutenant Colonel Teeter was never seen again. Major David T. Whiddon, operations officer, was named temporary CO of the 76th and later became permanent commander when Teeter did not return. During a mission to Liuchow on June 17, Major Whiddon's Mustang was hit under the cockpit by a twenty-millimeter slug. He was wounded by flying fragments but managed to fly home to Laohwangping and land safely.

The 118th and 74th squadrons also received new commanders in June. When Lieutenant Colonel Simpson went to the 68th Composite Wing, Capt. Marvin Lubner took his place as commander of the 118th. Lubner had just arrived in China, but he was no stranger to the country, having served in the 76th Fighter Squadron during 1942–43. An ace, Lubner had six confirmed victories and three probables to his credit. The 118th's pilots learned immediately that they had an aggressive officer in command whose combat experience and ace status easily offset the fact that he still wore captain's bars on his shoulder.

Major Floyd Finberg turned over command of the 74th to Maj. Bruce C. Downs on June 10, though Finberg remained in the squadron. Downs, from Wichita, Kansas, had just arrived in China, but he had previous combat experience. He served in the RAF's No. 121 Eagle Squadron in England during 1942 and later flew for seven months with the RAF on the island of Malta in the Mediterranean Sea.[8] Along with Slocumb of the 75th, Whiddon of the 76th, and Lubner of the 118th, Downs would remain in command through the end of the war.

Meanwhile, the heavy pace of missions took their toll, as Mustangs roamed from Hengyang to Liuchow seeking targets. The 76th was hit hardest by far, losing nine Mustangs during June and July. Three pilots, including Lieutenant Colonel Teeter, were killed, but the rest bailed out and returned safely to the squadron.

First Lieutenant Ed Lawman had a particularly close brush with death when his plane went down on June 19. He wrote the following account:

"I left Laohwangping leading two flights of four Mustangs on a dive-bombing and offensive recon mission to the Kweilin area. After having dropped our bombs on a rail bridge a short distance north of Kweilin, my second flight broke off to recon another sector while I took my flight northeast along the road and railroad. I was on the deck with my wingman slightly behind and above me and with the second element flying cover about 3,000 feet above.

"Approximately 10 miles northeast of Chuanhsien I came abruptly upon four 40 mm anti-aircraft positions in a rail cut. They had not been previously reported, and I had little time to get in a burst before I was past them. The rest of the flight circled wide, and I racked it in and came around for a better pass. The guns were ready both times, although I noticed only three bursts the first time over.

"Coming in for the second pass I sprayed the whole area and concentrated particularly on one gun and crew which I could see very well. After passing over I took evasive action and was not hit until I started to turn in again. This time at least one 40 mm shell hit the nose of the plane and got the engine and coolant.

"When I got hit I pulled up off the deck and almost immediately caught fire, since the coolant tank had been punctured. The momentum of my dive took me back up perhaps 1,000 feet, and I lost power. I crawled over the side—after a prayer. I was swept back into the stabilizer and knocked unconscious. My hand had been on the ripcord ring, and I guess the impact caused it to be pulled. I came to on the ground not 50 feet from my burning plane. I was in some sort of shock. I tried to gather up the chute so I could not be found easily. I could not, as I realized I had been burned and had two cracked ribs, an extremely swollen leg, and cuts. An hour later as I tried to escape the area, I stopped by a pool of water to try to throw some on my face. I looked up to find three men with coolie hats, cross belts of ammo, and rifles. I started repeating 'Megwa Figisee'—phonetics my own—which is 'American pilot,' and I was relieved that they indicated they were friendlies."[9]

Two days later, Lt. William H. Quimby Jr. of the 76th was hit on a low-level recon mission near Tunganhsien. He wrote the following in his report of the incident.

"It was on my first strafing run that I noticed machine gun opposition coming from both sides of the road. There were several puffs of flak on both sides of me. We thought it uncanny the way they could judge our height. The machine guns, however, did the damage. I could see the tracers going into my engine and as I pulled up to evade the fire my power cut out dead.

"I was struck immediately by the realization that I must bail out because the rough terrain and the curving road would not permit a belly landing. My altitude was approximately 200 feet, though I never took time to glance at the altimeter. Quickly I pulled the lever to jettison the canopy, and with it gone flames were sucked up from the engine into the cockpit. I cursed the rushing air as I frantically tried to stretch my way out over the left side of the plane. I had placed my hands on each side of the cockpit and was pushing desperately up and out, away from the flames. Unfortunately, I had forgotten to release my safety belt. Resuming a normal sitting position, I reduced the pressure of my body on the safety belt and was able to release it.

"All of this maneuvering took but a few seconds and again I pushed out into space. Suddenly I was suspended upside down in midair. I was moving at such a rate of speed that it was difficult to bring my hand over to my chest, against the air, to pull the rip cord. With a quick yank of the cord, my chute opened at once and had just jerked me right side up in breaking my descent when I landed."[10]

As Lawman and so many others before him, Quimby was contacted by friendly Chinese and escorted safely out of enemy territory. Lawman walked in at Laohwangping on July 3. It took Quimby four attempts to cross Japanese lines, and he did not return until mid-August.

★ ★ ★ ★

By mid-July 1945, the 75th Fighter Squadron had been idle at Tsingchen for nearly two months, and the inactivity was beginning to wear down the squadron's morale. Spirits were lifted a little with an awards ceremony in June. Among other medals, Lieutenant Colonel Slocumb was given an oak leaf cluster to his Distinguished Flying Cross in recognition of having completed 150 combat missions. Three missions in early July also helped, but then on July 13 came the word everyone had been waiting for: The squadron was moving to Liuchow.

The Chinese Twenty-ninth Army had recaptured Liuchow and its air base from the Japanese at the end of June. Ever since, work crews had been busy preparing the airfield to go back into action. The 75th was the logical choice to move in first, because it was well rested and its former base at Tsingchen had been farthest away from the front lines. Transport planes carried most of the 75th's ground personnel to their new base. There they found engineers still involved in the dangerous work of clearing mines and booby traps from the field. Work was interrupted every so often when a mine was exploded. Danger areas were posted, and everyone moved around cautiously, keeping to known, clear paths. The men slept on cots in an abandoned building and ate Army one-in-ten rations until a permanent tent area and mess facilities were established.

Flight operations began on July 17. The Mustangs mostly ranged to the east to strafe river and railroad traffic between Kukong and Sanshui. On July 27, Capt. Skip Stanfield led a particularly successful strike in which twelve river vessels were burned. Two days later he was leading again when the Mustangs caught a troop train in a gorge near Kukong and shot it to pieces. By the end of the month, the 75th had flown thirty-nine missions, and morale was sky-high.

The Japanese in China were now in full retreat. Kweilin was recaptured late in July, and the 23rd considered moving some of the squadrons back into their old bases. Many months of heavy air attacks had taken their toll, however; the facilities were in shambles. Soon the group decided instead to concentrate all of the 23rd Fighter Group at Liuchow. The squadrons continued to fly missions from Tushan and Laohwangping as preparations for their next move were being made.

On July 27, the group suffered its last combat fatality. A flight of four P-51s of the 76th Fighter Squadron, led by Capt. Bill Evans, encountered heavy twenty-millimeter ground fire during a dive-bombing attack on a railroad bridge near Tajunghsiang. Lieutenant William R. Brokaw's Mustang was hit as he pulled up from his second bomb run. His plane rolled over on its back and then nosed down, dived straight into the ground, and exploded. Brokaw did not have a chance to bail out. Brokaw, who hailed from Clearwater, Florida, had done a great deal of work on developing the 76th's rocket installations on its Mustangs and was greatly missed by his fellow pilots.

The course of the war moved faster than anyone expected. On August 6 and August 9, B-29s dropped atomic bombs on the Japanese cities of Hiroshima and Nagasaki. Within days, the Japanese entered into peace talks. In China, the 23rd Fighter Group continued to fly missions, though operations were limited by bad weather. Then on August 11, the Fourteenth Air Force ordered all squadrons to stand down from combat operations. Everyone hoped and prayed that the Japanese would accept peace terms. Bull sessions about the men's plans for after the war took on a new edge of reality.

Finally, on August 15, 1945, China time, the Japanese accepted an unconditional surrender. After three full years in combat and with 594 confirmed aerial victories, the 23rd Fighter Group's long war in China was over.

★ ★ ★ ★

Whatever hopes the men of the 23rd Fighter Group had for going home immediately after the armistice proved unrealistic. That good fortune only went to pilots who had completed their combat tours and some high-point ground personnel. Moving plans went forward, and by the end of the month, everyone had moved to Liuchow. For the first time ever, all squadrons plus the headquarters of the group were stationed on the same base. Immediately after the armistice was signed, the squadrons resumed flying missions. Now, however, they were strictly reconnaissance flights to keep an eye on the Japanese troop locations. Occasionally, the Mustang pilots got an assignment to drop leaflets over areas that remained occupied by the Japanese.

But if anyone had any doubt that the war really was over, they got their proof on August 29. That day, Capt. Bill Lillie and Lt. Chuck Breingan of the 76th Fighter Squadron were sent out to recon the West River, Canton, and Hong Kong. When they got to Canton, Lieutenant Breingan noticed trouble with his fuel tanks; he would not have enough gas to get home. Rather than risk going down out in the boondocks, Breingan elected to land his Mustang at Tien Ho Airdrome in Canton and try to refuel there.

The Japanese still occupied Tien Ho, and Breingan had no idea what sort of reception they would give him. After landing, he jumped down from his Mustang, which he called "Big Dog," and looked around for someone who could help him. He found a lieutenant who could speak English and was relieved when the officer was not hostile to him. The lieutenant left for a few minutes and returned with a major and an interpreter in tow.

The major ordered a ground crew to service "Big Dog," and Breingan spent a couple of hours nosing around the base while the work was being done. He took pictures of aircraft and installations on Tien Ho, but the Japanese personnel would not allow him to take pictures of them. Once the work was finished, Breingan cranked up his Mustang and flew back to Liuchow to tell his interesting tale. He had met his former enemies face-to-face, and they had shown him the respect that aviators have reserved for each other ever since man first took flight.

The 23rd Fighter Group remained at Liuchow until mid-October 1945, when its men and planes moved to the east coast city of Hangchow. Ironically, the air base at Hangchow was the same one that General Chennault had used to set up his first Chinese flight school when he went to work for Chiang Kai-shek in 1937. Most of the flying now consisted of ferry flights, as the United States was funneling combat aircraft to the Chinese Nationalist Air Force as fast as possible. These planes would be needed to help fight off the Communist uprising that was expected to begin as soon as the Japanese cleared out of China.

Finally, on December 4, 1945, the men of the 23rd Fighter Group boarded a train for Shanghai and began the first leg of their journey home. When they arrived in that great port city, they were assigned to quarters in the Embankment Building, a prewar apartment building. Six days later they marched down to the docks and boarded the USS *Alderamin*, a 14,257-ton auxiliary cargo ship built in 1943. The ship pulled out of Shanghai on the afternoon of December 11, 1945, and set off on the 6,600-mile trip to the United States.

Unfortunately, the *Alderamin* was not a speedboat. Its top speed was just six knots, and to make matters worse, it tended to roll in open seas. When a storm hit on December 17, the rolling became downright alarming and stayed that way for two days. Christmas passed, as did New Year's Day 1946.

Slow as it was, the *Alderamin* delivered its cargo safely. At 9:45 P.M. on January 3, 1946, the ship landed at Tacoma, Washington. A few people were waiting on the dock to greet the ship, and from the deck, the men could see the lights of the city on the hills above. They were kept aboard the ship for a day, and on January 5, they were transferred to Fort Lewis, just south of the city, to process out of the service. Captain Lee K. Chadwick, historical officer of the 75th Fighter Squadron, recorded the event: "Three and a half years of slash and thrust back and forth across China became just a chapter, albeit a colorful one, in the archives of the greatest war in history."

★ ★ ★ ★

The shark-faced fighter planes that patrolled the skies over China during World War II are long gone now, and the veterans who served in the 23rd Fighter Group are well into retirement age. But even in the 1990s, their accomplishments still stand as prime examples of the courage, sacrifice, and ingenuity it takes to win a war.

No single U.S. fighter group in World War II performed more varied missions, had more relative success, and was more central to the war effort in its theater of operations than the 23rd. In fact, for

its first year in existence, the 23rd carried on the war in China virtually by itself.

It seemed the 23rd never had enough of anything. Never enough
pilots, never enough planes. Never enough gasoline, never enough
ammunition. Sometimes, not even enough air bases. Then in 1944,
just as the situation was beginning to improve, the Japanese
launched a massive ground campaign that nearly broke the back of
the Allied defense of Free China.

The 23rd Fighter Group fought through every hardship, every
shortage, every setback. Its pilots learned to shoot down enemy aircraft, and they did so with deadly efficiency. By the end of the war,
they had tallied 594 aerial victories and destroyed nearly 400 more
Japanese aircraft on the ground. Thus, the 23rd placed fifth among
all USAAF fighter groups that flew in the war. In the process, forty-
one pilots of the 23rd achieved the coveted—though unofficial—title
of "ace" by shooting down five or more enemy aircraft. They also
learned to drop bombs in a dive and to skip them off the water into
their targets. They learned to destroy targets on the ground by strafing them with their machine guns and blasting them with rockets.

The ground personnel of the 23rd were hardly less heroic. Besides
suffering through enemy bombing raids and patching up battered
fighters that should have been scrapped, they developed techniques
and personal flexibility that enabled them to pack up their work and
move it hundreds of miles away to a different airfield on a moment's
notice.

And through it all the men kept smiling. They were at the far end
of the longest and most tenuous supply line in the world, but they
did not let it bother them. They were in China to win the war, and
win they did.

After the war, many of the 23rd's personnel went on to have distinguished military and civilian careers. An accounting of the men in
later life would turn up success stories in virtually every field of
human endeavor—four-star generals, college presidents, physicians,
business tycoons, artists. You name it, and someone from the 23rd
has done it.

The unit itself carried on after the war as well. The 23rd was reactivated in 1947 and has continued to serve off and on throughout the
years. As of early 1994, the 23rd is a composite wing stationed at
Pope Air Force Base, North Carolina.

Every year, the World War II veterans of the 23rd Fighter Group
gather for a reunion. The turnout thins a little at each gathering, but
usually more than one hundred guys show up. For a few days they
can peel back fifty years of bark and return to the core of their lives,
the pivotal days they shared in China. The bar opens early and stays
open late, with no money changing hands. Voices rise in laughter as

old stories are retold. Hands swoop and dive when the pilots describe air battles of long ago.

In October 1991, when the reunion took place at Fort Walton Beach, Florida, the men of the 23rd got a special treat. On a warm afternoon they stood on the field at Eglin Air Force Base and watched two menacing-looking jet aircraft performing aerobatics in the sky above. Eventually, the two jets landed and began to taxi toward the crowd. As they drew closer, it was clear to see that the dark green A-10 Thunderbolts were sporting a familiar decoration on their noses: a leering shark's mouth and eye.

These two fighter-bombers were assigned to the present-day 23rd. And they were combat veterans, too. For earlier that year when U.S. military forces had joined the fighting in the Persian Gulf, the 23rd went back into action as a key unit in Operations Desert Shield and Desert Storm.

During Desert Storm, the A-10s of the 23rd Tactical Fighter Wing's flew more than twenty-seven hundred combat sorties over Kuwait and Iraq. They were credited with destroying hundreds of Iraqi tanks, artillery pieces, armored personnel carriers, and other targets. And the 23rd only lost two aircraft during the entire campaign. It was a performance fully worthy of the Shark tradition established by the 23rd Fighter Group in the dangerous skies over China more than fifty years ago.

Roster of Commanders

23RD FIGHTER GROUP COMMANDERS

Col. Robert L. Scott	July 4, 1942
Lt. Col. Bruce K. Holloway	Jan. 9, 1943
Lt. Col. Norval C. Bonawitz	Sept. 16, 1943
Col. David L. ("Tex") Hill	Nov. 4, 1943
Lt. Col. Philip C. Loofbourrow	Oct. 15, 1944
Col. Edward F. Rector	Dec. 12, 1944
Lt. Col. Clyde B. Slocumb	December 1945 until decommissioning

16TH FIGHTER SQUADRON COMMANDERS

1/Lt. Harry B. ("Hal") Young	April 30, 1941 (in United States)
Maj. George W. Hazlett	Sept. 14, 1942
Maj. Harry M. Pike	Jan. 27, 1943 (POW Sept. 15, 1943)[1]
Capt. Robert L. Liles	July 2, 1943, through transfer to 51st Fighter Group

74TH FIGHTER SQUADRON COMMANDERS

Maj. Frank Schiel Jr.	July 4, 1942 (KIFA Dec. 5, 1942)[2]
Maj. Albert J. ("Ajax") Baumler	Dec. 11, 1942
Capt. John D. Lombard	Feb. 18, 1943 (KIFA June 30, 1943)
Maj. Norval C. Bonawitz	July 7, 1943
Capt. William R. Crooks	September 1943
Capt. Paul N. Bell	Oct. 11, 1943
Capt. G. Eugene Lundy	Dec. 5, 1943
Maj. Arthur W. Cruikshank Jr.	May 17, 1944
Capt. John C. ("Pappy") Herbst	June 30, 1944
Maj. Philip G. Chapman	Feb. 16, 1945 (KIA March 28, 1945)[3]
Capt. Floyd Finberg	March 29, 1945
Maj. Bruce C. Downs	June 10, 1945, until end of war

75TH FIGHTER SQUADRON COMMANDERS

Maj. David L. ("Tex") Hill	July 4, 1942
Maj. John R. Alison	Dec. 5, 1942
Maj. Edmund R. Goss	May 10, 1943 (date approximate)
Maj. Elmer W. ("Rich") Richardson	Oct. 9, 1943
Maj. Philip C. Loofbourrow	March 1944

Maj. Donald L. Quigley   June 1944 (POW August 1944)
Maj. A. T. House Jr.   Aug. 15, 1944 (date approximate)
Maj. Clyde R. Slocumb   Nov. 9, 1944, until end of war
Capt. Eugene Harper   April 3 until May 5, 1945 (acting)

76TH FIGHTER SQUADRON COMMANDERS

Maj. Edward F. Rector   July 4, 1942
Maj. Bruce K. Holloway   Dec. 5, 1942
Capt. Grant M. Mahony   Jan. 2, 1943
Capt. Robert Costello   June 9, 1943
Capt. James M. ("Willie") Williams   Oct. 24, 1943
Capt. John S. Stewart   Dec. 1, 1943
Maj. Charles E. Griffith   May 17, 1944 (KIFA Dec. 18, 1944)
Maj. L. V. Teeter   Dec. 19, 1944 (KIA June 3, 1945)
Maj. David T. Whiddon   June 4, 1945, until end of war

118TH TACTICAL RECONNAISSANCE SQUADRON COMMANDERS

Maj. Edward O. McComas   Sept. 29, 1943 (in United States)
Capt. Oran S. Watts   Jan. 10, 1945 (date approximate)
Lt. Col. Charles C. Simpson   May 1, 1945
Capt. Marvin Lubner   June 10, 1945, until end of war

449TH FIGHTER SQUADRON COMMANDERS

Capt. Sam Palmer   August 1943
Capt. Lewden M. Enslen   Sept. 17, 1943, until transfer to 51st
                                              Fighter Group

1. POW = prisoner of war

2. KIFA = killed in flying accident

3. KIA = killed in action

Roster of Personnel Who Died in Overseas Service

HEADQUARTERS

Pvt. Marshall F. F. Brown July 3, 1942 K in accident aligning guns; Kunming, China; P-40B[1]

16TH FIGHTER SQUADRON

Sgt. John A. Sabat Feb. 3, 1942 Died on march to Camp Darley, Australia

1/Lt. George A. Chipman March 31, 1942 KIFA; Karachi, India; P-40E[2]

2/Lt. Edward J. LaCour May 20, 1942 KIFA; Karachi; P-40E

2/Lt. Richard C. Gee Aug. 26, 1942 KIFA landing accident; Peishiyi, China; P-40E

2/Lt. Walter E. Lacy Nov. 2, 1942 KIA; Kweilin, China; P-40E-1 41-36401[3]

1/Lt. Robert H. Mooney Dec. 26, 1942 KIA; Yunnanyi, China; P-40E

1/Lt. L. F. ("Chip") Myers Jan. 12, 1943 KIFA; en route to Yunnanyi; P-40

2/Lt. George V. Pyles Jan. 16, 1943 KIA; Yunnanyi; P-40

1/Lt. William W. Druwing May 6, 1943 KIFA; near Kunming; P-40K

1/Lt. Chester D. Griffin May 19, 1943 KIFA burned in takeoff accident May 18; Yunnanyi; P-40K

1/Lt. Robert ("Ace") Dersch Aug. 31, 1943 KIFA in bad wx; en route to Yunnanyi; P-40K[4]

(Seventeen others in squadron killed while assigned to 51st Fighter Group.)

Following service in China:

Maj. George W. Hazlett Aug. 6, 1943 KIFA; Landhi, India; AT-16

1/Lt. Llewelyn H. Couch 1943 KIFA ATC flight; Africa

Maj. Robert E. Smith June 22, 1944 KIA w/367th Fighter Group, Ninth Air Force; Cherbourg, France; P-38

74TH FIGHTER SQUADRON

2/Lt. Joseph L. Mikeworth Aug. 21, 1942 KIFA on test flight; Lake Kunming; P-40B #40

1/Lt. T. V. Skelly Aug. 26, 1942 KIFA landing accident, hit Lt. Gee of 16th; Peishiyi; P-40

Maj. Frank Shiel Jr. Dec. 5, 1942 KIFA in bad wx; near Yunnanyi; F-4

Capt. Raymond W. Lucia	March 19, 1943	KIA ground fire; near Mangshih; P-40
1/Lt. Robert E. Atkinson	March 29, 1943	KIA strafing; Chefang; P-40
1/Lt. David W. Mitchell	April 8, 1943	KIFA engine fire; New Delhi
Staff Sgt. Allen C. Eskridge	April 26, 1943	K enemy bombing raid; Yunnanyi
Sgt. Raymond A. Lynch	April 26, 1943	K enemy bombing raid; Yunnanyi
Sgt. Forest R. Shoemaker	April 26, 1943	K enemy bombing raid; Yunnanyi
Pvt. Oscar J. Brown	April 26, 1943	K enemy bombing raid; Yunnanyi
Pvt. Frederick D. Hall	April 26, 1943	K enemy bombing raid; Yunnanyi
Staff Sgt. Harold L. Harwell	April 28, 1943	K enemy bombing raid; Kunming
Maj. John D. Lombard	June 30, 1943	KIFA in bad wx; near Tungting Lake; P-40K #48
2/Lt. George R. Barnes	July 24, 1943	KIA dogfight; Kweilin; P-40
Capt. Truman O. Jeffreys	Aug. 20, 1943	KIA dogfight: Kweilin; P-40K
Lt. Mao, Y. K. (CAF)	Aug. 20, 1943	KIA dogfight; Kweilin; P-40
1/Lt. Altheus B. Jarmon	Dec. 10, 1943	K hit by fragmentation bomb; Hengyang, China
Capt. Harlyn S. Vidovich	Jan. 26, 1944	KIFA ferry flight; Kunming-Kweilin; P-40N-15 42-106270
1/Lt. Lawrence W. Smith	Jan. 26, 1944	KIFA ferry flight; Kunming-Kweilin; P-40N-15 42-106285
Maj. Barry E. Melloan	June 15, 1944	KIA strafing; Chuchow; P-40N
1/Lt. Thomas H. Aston	June 29, 1944	KIFA hit mountain; Hengyang; P-40N-5 42-105157
1/Lt. Richard D. Mullineaux	July 23, 1944	KIA ground attack; Changsha; P-40N-5 42-104923
2/Lt. Thomas H. Upchurch	Oct. 10, 1944	KIFA hit mountain (location unknown); P-40N 43-22786
Lt. Harold V. Robbins	Nov. 7, 1944	KIFA in bad wx (location, plane unknown)
Lt. Norman S. Firestone	Nov. 11, 1944	KIA hit by AA; Hengyang; P-51C-11 44-10810
1/Lt. John F. Evans	Nov. 25, 1944	KIA hit by AA; Anking; P-51C-11 43-25219
1/Lt. Manchester B. Watson	Dec. 3, 1944	KIA harbor sweep; Wuhu; P-51C 44-10794
Lt. Richard Fitzgerald	Dec. 23, 1944	KIA hit by AA; Tien Ho Airdrome, Canton; P-51C 43-24963
Capt. Paul J. Reis	Dec. 25, 1944	KIA; Nanking; P-51C
Capt. Robert E. Brown	Dec. 27, 1944	KIA; Canton; P-51
2/Lt. Wiley E. Hawkins	Jan. 15, 1945	KIA strafing boat; Kiukiang; P-51
F.O. Billy G. Seago	Jan. 20, 1945	KIA strafing; Shanghai; P-51C 43-25288
1/Lt. Nick Gazibara	Jan. 23, 1945	KIFA on takeoff; Kanchow; P-51
Maj. Philip G. Chapman	March 28, 1945	KIA hit strafing Canton airfields; crash at Changting; P-51C 44-11055
2/Lt. Stanley J. Chmielewski	March 28, 1945	KIA strafing; Hong Kong; P-51C 44-11110

2/Lt. Albert H. Sims	March 28, 1945	KIA strafing; Hong Kong; P-51C 43-24977
2/Lt. Ralph McMasters	March 29, 1945	KIFA in bad wx; Kweiyang; P-51
Lt. —— Berven	July 17, 1945	KIA hit by AA; Kweilin; P-51
2/Lt. John A. Oparowski	July 18, 1945	KIA hit by AA; Hsinganhsien; P-51
2/Lt. Walter A. Cunningham	Oct. 7, 1945	KIFA; x-country Liuchow-Peishiyi; P-51

Others unconfirmed:

Technical Sgt. George E. Maage	April 26, 1943	wounded in enemy bombing raid; Yunnanyi
Lt. C. D. Garrett	July 6, 1944	MIA strafing; near Changsha; P-40N-5 42-105009[5]
1/Lt. Clyde C. Vaughan	(not known)	listed KIA in *Guerrilla One* (Kissick)
2/Lt. Sam G. Armstrong	(not known)	listed KIA in *Guerrilla One* (Kissick)

75TH FIGHTER SQUADRON

John E. Petach Jr. (civilian)	July 10, 1942	KIA hit strafing; Nanchang; P-40E
Arnold W. Shamblin (civilian)	July 10, 1942	KIA hit strafing; Nanchang; P-40E
2/Lt. Lee N. Minor	Aug. 5, 1942	KIA dogfight; Leiyang; P-40
1/Lt. Henry P. Elias	Sept. 2, 1942	KIA shot in parachute; Nanchang; P-40E
2/Lt. Martin S. Cluck	Sept. 23, 1942	KIFA; Kunming; Ryan trainer
Capt. Phillip B. O'Connell	Oct. 28, 1942	KIA; Victoria Harbor, Hong Kong; P-40E
Lt. William T. Gross	Feb. 11, 1943	KIA strafing troops; Nan Sang bridge; P-40K-1
Capt. Burrall Barnum	April 1, 1943	KIA dogfight; Lingling; P-40K-1 41-5567
Lt. Fu Chung Ching (CAF)	April 9, 1943	KIFA; Lingling
Pvt. Donald Goldsmith	April 28, 1943	KIA enemy bombing raid; Kunming
Pvt. Robert E. Graham	April 28, 1943	KIA enemy bombing raid; Kunming
Pvt. Charles R. Tompkins	April 28, 1943	KIA enemy bombing raid; Kunming
Capt. John F. Hampshire	May 2, 1943	KIA dogfight; Changsha; P-40K-1
Lt. W. S. Epperson	July 30, 1943	KIA dogfight; Hengyang; P-40
Lt. Robert Maxent	Sept. 5, 1943	KIFA takeoff; Chanyi; P-40
Lt. Wang, T. M. (CAF)	Oct. 1, 1943	KIFA engine trouble; en route to Haiphong; P-40
Lt. Chen, P. J. (CAF)	Oct. 1, 1943	KIA dogfight; Haiphong; P-40
Lt. Robert E. Beauchamp	Dec. 10, 1943	KIA dogfight; Hengyang; P-40K-5 42-9885
2/Lt. John A. Beaty	Dec. 12, 1943	KIA dogfight; Hengyang; P-40K-1 42-45730
Lt. Joseph E. Oswald	April 19, 1944	KIFA; Hengyang-Kweilin; P-40K-1 42-45903
1/Lt. Marvin E. Balderson	May 26, 1944	KIA crash landing; Changsha; P-40N-5 42-105249

Lt. Warren Smedley	May 26, 1944	KIA strafing; Kingmen; P-40N-5 42-105002
Lt. Thomas J. Noonan	June 13, 1944	KIFA landing; Hengyang; P-40K-1 42-65727
Lt. Francis H. Armstrong	June 26, 1944	KIA dogfight; Kweilin; P-40N-5 42-105276
1/Lt. James C. Vurgaropulos	June 29, 1944	KIA strafing; Changsha; P-40N-5 42-104941
Lt. Robert G. Koran	June 29, 1944	KIA hit by AA; Tsaoshih; P-40N-5 42-105159
1/Lt. James E. Folmar	Aug. 17, 1944	KIA strafing; Chunglupu; P-40N-5 42-104921
1/Lt. Robert P. Miller	Nov. 11, 1944	KIA dogfight; Hengyang; P-51C-11 43-25229
Capt. Sam Dance	Dec. 9, 1944	KIA hit by AA; Hengyang; P-51C-10 43-25197
1/Lt. Robert M. Bellman	Dec. 7, 1944	KIA frags explode on landing; Chihkiang; P-51C-10 43-25027
1/Lt. Harold T. Byrd	Feb. 25, 1945	KIA hit tree strafing; Kaitow; P-51C-10 43-25029
1/Lt. Jesse Gray	Spring 1945	K in jeep accident; Luliang
Staff Sgt. Anthony Lombardo	Sept. 1945	K by accidental gunshot; Liuchow

Others unconfirmed:

1/Lt. Buddie C. Baldwin	Aug. 16, 1944	MIA; Changsha area; P-40N-5 42-105273
2/Lt. William W. Smith	Aug. 19, 1944	MIA; Changsha area; P40N-15 42-106264
—— Haughney	Listed by 75th Fighter Squadron veterans, 1957
—— Lapp	Listed by 75th Fighter Squadron veterans, 1957

76TH FIGHTER SQUADRON

2/Lt. Leon C. Allen	July 21, 1942	KIFA flight test; Kunming; P-40
1/Lt. Patrick H. Daniels	Nov. 24, 1942	KIA bombing; Canton; P-40
F.O. A. W. Henry	June 17, 1943	KIA strafing; Yumatien; P-40
Capt. Howard H. Krippner	Aug. 27, 1943	KIA strafing; Sitang; P-40
1/Lt. Bruce G. Boylan	Dec. 29, 1943	KIFA on takeoff; Suichuan; P-51A
2/Lt. Walter C. Washer	Jan. 18, 1944	KIFA; Kunming-Kweilin; P-40N 42-106994
Maj. Lee P. Manbeck	Feb. 10, 1944	KIA dogfight; Kiukiang; P-51A
Lt. William A. Butler	Feb. 12, 1944	KIA intercept; Suichuan; P-51A
Lt. Henry R. Farris	April 29, 1944	KIFA hit roller on takeoff; Suichuan; P-51
Lt. Lewis M. Holcomb	Aug. 6, 1944	KIA dive-bombing; Hengyang; P-51B-7 43-6875

l/Lt. William D. McLennon	Aug. 30, 1944	KIA dogfight; Kiyang; P-51B-10 43-7084
Lt. Henry Leisses	Oct. 4, 1944	KIA shot down; near Wuchow; P-51B-2 43-12395
Lt. Rex B. Shull	Oct. 4, 1944	KIA shot down; near Wuchow; P-51B-15 42-106966
Lt. E. E. Smith	Oct. 6, 1944	KIA shot down; near Wuchow; P-40N-15 42-106206
Lt. A. J. Newsome	Oct. 30, 1944	KIFA in bad wx; Liuchow-Luliang; P-40N-20 43-23616
Lt. Frank P. Policarpo	Oct. 30, 1944	KIFA in bad wx; Liuchow-Luliang; P-40N-20 43-23657
Lt. R. P. Torango	Oct. 30, 1944	KIFA in bad wx; Liuchow-Luliang; P-40N-1 42-104619
Lt. John P. Houck	Nov. 23, 1944	KIA strafing; Tanchuk; P-51C-10 43-25176
Lt. Robert J. Raymond	Nov. 25, 1944	MIA bailout; Hohshih; P-51C-11 44-10814
Lt. Col. Charles E. Griffith	Dec. 18, 1944	KIFA stunting; Luliang; P-51B 43-7097
Lt. —— Hewitt	Dec. 18, 1944	KIFA stunting; Luliang; P-51C 43-24978
Sgt. Allen A. Sheider	Feb. 24, 1945	K truck crash; Chanyi-Laohwangping
Lt. —— Edwards	Feb. 26, 1945	KIA dive-bombing; Tien Ho Airdrome; P-51K-1 44-11426
Capt. Richard Johnson	April 15, 1945	KIA dive-bombing; Luchai; P-51K-1 44-11442
Lt. Jerome F. Eisenman	April 15, 1945	KIA dive-bombing Luchai; P-51D-5 44-11274
Lt. Col. L. V. Teeter	June 3, 1945	KIA strafing; Liuchow; P-51
Lt. —— Steinhardt	June 20, 1945	KIA recon; location unknown; P-51C 43-25231
Lt. William R. Brokaw	July 27, 1945	KIA hit by AA; Tanjunghsian RR bridge; P-51K-5 44-11574
1/Lt. John W. Van Voorhis	Sept. 16, 1945	KIFA recon; Hankow; P-51

Others unconfirmed:

Lt. W. O'Dell	Oct. 4, 1944	MIA bailout; near Wuchow; P-51B-2 43-12364
Lt. E. E. Bell	Oct. 21, 1944	MIA; location unknown; P-40N-20 43-23464
Maj. Fleming	Oct. 29, 1944	M; cross-country; P-51B 43-7116
Lt. E. R. Bowman	Oct. 29, 1944	M; cross-country; P-51C 4324986

Killed following service in China:

| Lt. Col. Grant M. Mahoney | Jan. 3, 1945 | KIA w/Fifth AF; Philippine Is. |
| Maj. Kenneth E. George | 1944–45 | KIFA ferry mission; India |

118TH TACTICAL RECONNAISSANCE SQUADRON

2/Lt. Edward J. Vanacek	April 3, 1944	KIFA; Chakulia, India; P-40
1/Lt. Warren J. Christenson	June 12, 1944	KIFA; lost over Hump; P-40N
Technical Sgt. John E. McKinney	July 12, 1944	Died at Kweilin of natural causes
Capt. Robert E. Gee	Aug. 6, 1944	KIFA in bad wx; cross-country; P-40N
Lt. Robert G. O'Brien	Aug. 6, 1944	KIFA in bad wx; cross-country; P-40N
2/Lt. Ernest W. Swanson	Aug. 6, 1944	KIFA in bad wx; cross-country; P-40N
Lt. W. F. Lovett	Sept. 15, 1944	KIFA; Liuchow; P-51C-6 42-103418
1/Lt. Henry E. Miehe	Nov. 7, 1944	KIFA bad wx; cross-country; P-51C-6 42-103421
Lt. Herbert N. White	Nov. 7, 1944	KIFA bad wx; cross-country; P-40N 43-22779
Capt. Samuel R. Bowen	Nov. 20, 1944	KIA hit by AA; Kiukiang; P-51C-6 42-103610
Lt. Carlton Covey	Dec. 21, 1944	KIA skip bombing; Canton; P-51
Lt. Robert E. Boernke	Dec. 23, 1944	KIA parachute didn't open; 100 miles east of Suichuan; P-51
Lt. Bryan L. Kethley	Dec. 24, 1944	KIA wing blown off; Hong Kong; P-51
Lt. Elmer L. Chancellor	Dec. 26, 1944	KIA skip bombing; Anking; P-51
Maj. David A. Houck	Jan. 15, 1945	K hit by AA but died in captivity; Kowloon; P-51
1/Lt. Roy H. Christenson	March 12, 1945	KIFA; near Chengkung; P-51

Others unconfirmed:

Lt. John H. Six	Sept.–Oct. 1944	listed as "deceased" in 23rd Fighter Group's records

449TH FIGHTER SQUADRON

1/Lt. George J. Enssler	Aug. 31, 1943	KIA strafing; Yochow; P-38
Lt. Ivan Rockwell	Sept. 12, 1943	KIA dive-bombing; Hong Kong; P-38

(Plus more later with 51st Fighter Group)

1. K = killed
2. KIFA = killed in flying accident
3. KIA = killed in action
4. wx = weather
5. MIA = missing in action
6. M = missing

Roster of Fighter Aces

Name[1]	Units	Score[2]	Notes
Lt. Col. John C. Herbst	76th, 74th	18-1-3	
Lt. Col. Charles H. Older	AVG, HQ	18-0-0	
Col. David L. Hill	AVG, 75th, HQ	14.75-1-5	
Lt. Col. Edward O. McComas118th	118th	14-1-1	
Col. Bruce K. Holloway	76th, HQ	13-4-0	
Capt. John F. Hampshire	75th	13-3-0	
Col. Robert L. Scott	HQ	10-5-3	
Maj. John S. Stewart	76th	9-4-2	
Maj. Albert J. Baumler	75th, 74th	9-2-0	(inc. 4.5-2-0 Spain)
Maj. Arthur W. Cruikshank Jr.	74th	8-6-0	
Capt. James W. Little	75th	8-0-0	(inc. 1-0-0 Korea)
Maj. Elmer F. Richardson	AVG, 75th, HQ	8-0-0	
Col. Edward F. Rector	76th, HQ	7.75-1-2	
Maj. John D. Lombard	16th, 74th	7-1-0	
Maj. Philip G. Chapman	74th	7-0-0	(KIA March 28, 1945)
Capt. Joseph H. Griffin	75th	7-0-0	(inc. 4-0-0 ETO[3])
Maj. Grant Mahony	76th	6-3-1	(inc. 4-3-1 17 PS & 1-0-1 1st ACG.)
Maj. John G. Bright	AVG, 75th	6-3-0	(inc. 1-0-0 14th FG)
Maj. Marvin W. Lubner	76th, 118th	6-3-0	
Capt. Lee O. Gregg	449th	6-2-1	(inc. 5-2-1 51st FG)
Capt. James M. Williams	76th	6-2-1	
Maj. Edmund R. Goss	16th, 75th	6-2-0	
Lt. Col. John R. Alison	16th, 75th, HQ	6-1-0	
Capt. Charles H. DuBois	76th	6-0-0	
Maj. Robert L. Liles	16th	5-5-2	(inc. 1-2-1 51st FG)
Capt. Stephen J. Bonner	76th	5-5-1	
Maj. Donald L. Quigley	75th	5-3-5	(POW August 1944)
Capt. William Grosvenor Jr.	75th	5-3-3	
Capt. Lynn F. Jones	74th	5-3-1	
Capt. Dallas A. Clinger	16th, 74th	5-3-0	
Capt. Matthew M. Gordon	75th	5-3-0	
Capt. Roger C. Pryor	75th	5-3-0	
Capt. Forrest F. Parham	75th	5-2-5	
Capt. Robert B. Schultz	449th	5-1-1	(incl. 5-0-1 51st FG)
Capt. Donald S. Lopez	75th	5-0-5	
1/Lt. John W. Bolyard	74th	5-0-1	
Capt. Oran S. Watts	118th	5-0-1	
1/Lt. Russell D. Williams	118th	5-0-1	

Attached

Maj. Witold A. Urbanowicz	75th	20-0-0	(inc. 17-0-0 w/ RAF; Polish AF)
B/Gen. Clinton D. ("Casey") Vincent	68th CW	6-4-1	(all with 23rd)
1/Lt. Tsang Hsi-Lan	75th	6-0-1	(inc. 5-0-1 3rd FG, CACW)

AVG aces who served two weeks after disbandment, July 1942

Robert H. Neale	13-6-0	
James H. Howard	8.33-1-2	(inc. 6-1-2 ETO)
Charles R. Bond	7-3-1	
C. Joseph Rosbert	6-0-0	
J. Richard Rossi	6-0-0	
Robert H. Smith	5-1-0	

----

1.   Ranks listed are the highest each pilot held while flying with the 23rd Fighter Group.

2.   Air-to-air credits only

3.   European theater of operations

Aircraft Camouflage and Markings

The original aircraft assigned to the 74th, 75th, and 76th fighter squadrons were the P-40s that the American Volunteer Group handed over when it disbanded July 4, 1942. The majority of these were Curtiss Tomahawk models, export versions of the P-40B, and the rest were P-40Es.

The Tomahawks retained the RAF camouflage scheme they had worn in service with the AVG, dark "earth" and dark green shadow shading on the upper surfaces and "sky," a pale greenish blue, underneath. The ex-AVG P-40Es were in standard USAAF camouflage of olive drab over neutral gray. One exception to the scheme was in the 16th Fighter Squadron. From India, its pilots brought P-40Es that were delivered in RAF desert colors of dark earth and "middlestone" on the top surfaces and neutral gray underneath.

P-40Ks were delivered to all squadrons of the 23rd Fighter Group beginning in the fall of 1942. They came in all three of the top-surface color schemes described above, although desert colors on P-40Ks were rare. P-40Ms began to arrive in mid-1943, and P-40Ns followed soon thereafter. These two models were usually painted olive drab over neutral gray. Some top surfaces also were mottled around the edges with medium green, which was slightly darker than olive drab.

North American P-51A Mustangs for the 76th Fighter Squadron arrived in late 1943 and were followed by P-51Bs in the spring of 1944. All of these aircraft were painted dark olive drab over neutral gray, as were the P-38Gs that equipped the 449th Fighter Squadron when it arrived in China.

In the summer of 1944, P-51Bs and Cs began to arrive in natural metal. These aircraft, and the unpainted P-51Ds and Ks that followed, eventually equipped all squadrons of the 23rd Fighter Group.

Numbering

The 23rd Fighter Group, and later the entire Fourteenth Air Force, used an integrated numbering system to identify its aircraft by squadron. This system was phased in while the ex-AVG P-40s were replaced in late 1942 and early 1943, because most of these planes carried their AVG numbers throughout their service life.

From July 1942 through early 1945, the numbers were assigned as follows:

Headquarters: 1–10

16th Fighter Squadron: 11–40 (changed to 350–400 in

October 1943)

74th Fighter Squadron: 11–50

76th Fighter Squadron: 100–149

75th Fighter Squadron: 150–199

118th Tactical Reconnaissance Squadron: 550–600

(beginning in June 1944)

449th Fighter Squadron: none; from October 1943,

300–349

In 1945 the Fourteenth Air Force reassigned the 23rd's squadron numbers to accommodate additional units. They became

74th Fighter Squadron: 1–40

75th Fighter Squadron: 40–80 (applied on the nose)

76th Fighter Squadron: 100–140

118th Tac Recon Squadron: 150–199

Squadron Markings

When the 23rd Fighter Group was formed in July 1942, its most distinctive insignia was, of course, the shark mouth and eye applied to all P-40s. These varied from one plane to the next. Also, most AVG fighters retained their group's crest—a tiger jumping through a Chinese insignia with a shredded Japanese flag in its paws—on the fuselage. Another common practice throughout the units in China for most of the war was to paint out the aircraft's serial number, which was applied on the vertical tail surfaces at the factory.

There were other specific markings. The three permanent squadrons were assigned colors based on the old AVG system. These colors were displayed in a narrow band running around the fuselage just forward of the tail group: 74th, red; 75th, white; 76th blue. In addition, all three of these squadrons painted over the national insignia on both sides of the fuselage with the aircraft's number in white.

During the spring and summer of 1943, the 75th Fighter Squadron also applied its squadron insignia, a flying shark, on the fins of its P-40s. This practice remained in effect until early fall 1943, when the aircraft numbers were moved to the fins on all fighters in the three squadrons. At this time, the 75th and 76th began applying their squadron colors to the fighters' propeller spinners. The 74th continued to use its red fuselage band on previously assigned aircraft, but it did not apply it to all new P-40Ns that began to arrive later in the year.

Again, the 16th Fighter Squadron was different. Its P-40s retained the national insignia on the fuselage, with the aircraft's number applied forward of that. Later, a squadron patch depicting the wall of China with wings and a shark's mouth was added to the fuselage, and a white star on a blue disk was painted on the hubcaps of the P-40s' wheels.

The 449th's P-38s did not display any squadron markings during their temporary assignment to the 23rd Fighter Group during 1943.

The 76th Fighter Squadron applied shark mouths and eyes to its P-51As when they arrived in late 1943, and the squadron's first P-51Bs also got the shark-mouth treatment. The shape of the P-51's nose was not particularly suited to this design, and it was dropped in the summer of 1944.

Information on the markings of the P-40Ns flown by the 118th Tac Recon Squadron during the summer of 1944 is very slim, but it is possible that most of them did not carry shark mouths. The 118th led the group, however, in applying distinctive markings to the natural metal P-51s that began arriving later in 1944. The squadron devised a distinctive black lightning bolt with yellow trim that ran nearly the length of the fuselage, with smaller versions around the wing and tail tips, and a black band around the propeller spinner.

The 75th Fighter Squadron followed suit by painting the entire tail of its natural metal P-51s black and adding a black stripe around the rear of the fuselage. The 76th applied a large black Indian head in profile to the vertical tails of its P-51s in recognition of its call sign, "Pontiac." Last to use distinctive markings on its Mustangs was the 74th, which painted the entire nose black from the cockpit forward. Some 74th Mustangs also carried the squadron insignia, a flying gorilla, on their fuselages.

Individual Markings

Most pilots and crew chiefs added nicknames to the airplanes assigned to them. On P-40s, they were usually applied on the cowling panel between the exhaust stacks and the top of the shark mouth, though some were painted above the exhausts. Crew names and kill markings also were common, and these were applied near the cockpit on the port side of the fuselage.

Kill markings varied quite a bit in design and application. Some squadrons used a plain red-sun-on-white-field flag versus the rising sun naval ensign to distinguish between confirmed aerial victories over fighters and bombers. Late in the war, the 74th allowed kill flags for ground victories, which made for some impressive scoreboards on its Mustangs. Some pilots even stenciled on profiles of trucks, boats, trains, and other ground targets destroyed.

In the 75th Fighter Squadron during 1942 and 1943, the commanders' P-40s were identified by double white stripes around the fuselage. It is not known if this practice continued later in the war or if the other squadrons used a similar system. However, at least one commander of the 76th, Maj. Grant Mahony, carried two distinct white stripes horizontally around the vertical tail of his aircraft, P-40K number 111. During 1945, the commander and vice commander of the group flew P-51s that carried red, white, and blue bands around the rear of the fuselage.

Distinctive nose art on the fighters of the 23rd Fighter Group, especially early in the war, was rare. However, the P-40's rounded rudder made a tempting canvas for a few aspiring artists who painted cartoons, nudes, and other subjects on them. These were most prevalent in the 16th and 74th squadrons. A good example is the "Holdin' My Own" cartoon on the P-40s flown by Capt. Dallas Clinger; it depicted a toddler in a cowboy outfit urinating on the rising sun. Some P-38s of the 449th Fighter Squadron did have nose art, such as the golden eagle on Lt. Bob Schultz's plane.

During 1945, many Mustangs of the 76th Fighter Squadron were decorated with cartoons on their fuselages forward of the national insignia. These were painted by Capt. Bill Lillie, a flight leader who also happened to be a talented artist.

Chinese Place Names

In 1958, the Chinese government adopted a new phonetic system for romanizing Chinese language sounds. That system, called "pinyin," replaced the traditional spelling of place names created by the British colonial postal service during the nineteenth century and still used by Americans in China during World War II. For the purposes of consistency and familiarity, this book uses the traditional spellings for place names in the 1940s. The chart below provides the pinyin spelling of many geographic locations mentioned in the book. However, some American air bases such as Chihkiang, Laowhangpin, and Suichuan were named for tiny nearby villages that do not appear on contemporary maps.

Traditional	Pinyin
Amoy	Xiamen
Canton	Guangzhou
Changsha	Changsha
Changteh	Changde
Changting	Changting
Chanyi	Zhanyi
Chekiang Province	Zhejiang Province
Chengtu	Chengdu
Chenhsien	Chenzhou
Chungking	Chongqing
Foochow	Fuzhou
Formosa	Taiwan
Fukien Province	Fujian Province
Hainan Is.	Hainan Is.
Hangchow	Hanzhou
Hankow	Wuhan
Hengshan	Hengshan
Hengyang	Hengyang
Hsiang River	Xiang Jiang
Hsiangteh	Xiangyin
Hunan Province	Hunan Province
Kanchow	Ganzhou
Kiangsi Province	Jiangxi Province
Kingmen	Jingmen
Kiukiang	Jiujiang
Kunming	Kunming
Kwangsi Province	Guangxi Autonomous Region
Kwangtung Province	Guangdong Province

Kweichow Province	Guizhou Province
Kweilin	Guilin
Kweiyang	Guiyang
Lingling	Lingling
Lishui	Lishui
Liuchow	Liuzhou
Lungling	Longling
Mengtze	Mengzi
Nanchang	Nanchang
Nanking	Nanjing
Pakhoi	Beihai
Paoshan	Baoshan
Peiping (or Peking)	Beijing
Poyang Lake	Boyang Hu
Puchi	Puqi
Shasi	Shashi
Shanghai	Shanghai
Tali Lake	Dali Hu
Tengchung	Tengchong
Tien Chih Lake	Dian Chi Hu
Tungting Lake	Dongting Hu
Tushan	Dushan
West River	Xijiang
Yangtze	Changjiang
Yochow	Yueyang
Yunnan Province	Yunnan Province

Chapter Notes

CHAPTER 1. DESPERATE DAYS

1. Daniel Ford, *Flying Tigers* (Washington, D.C.: Smithsonian Institution Press, 1991), pp. 365–6.

2. Frank J. Olynyk, *AVG & USAAF (China-Burma-India Theater) Credits for Destruction of Enemy Aircraft in Air-to-Air Combat, World War II* (Aurora, Ohio: Self-published, 1986), pp. 8–9.

3. Arthur W. Waite, letter to author, June 30, 1987.

4. Larry M. Pistole, *The Pictorial History of the Flying Tigers* (Orange, Va.: Moss Publications, 1981), p. 215.

5. Robert L. Scott, *God Is My Co-Pilot* (New York: Charles Scribner's Sons, 1943), p. 116.

6. Robert M. Smith, *With Chennault in China* (Blue Ridge Summit, Pa.: Tab Books, Inc., 1984), pp. 92–106.

7. Col. Robert L. Scott, interview with U.S. Army Air Force, S-2 Division, Washington, D.C., February 15, 1943.

CHAPTER 2. CHINA AIR TASK FORCE

1. David L. Hill, telephone interview with author, April 26, 1993.

2. *The Record, 11th Bombardment Squadron (M)* (Nashville, Tenn.: Harris Press Inc.), p. 36.

3. George R. Barnes, letter to author, April 16, 1984.

4. Tom Britton, "51st Insignia and Early History—Homer's Volunteer Group," *AAHS Journal* 25, no. 3 (Fall 1980): 240.

5. Barnes, letter.

6. Richard C. Lee, tape recording to author, November 1981.

7. Robert L. Liles, interview with author, October 12, 1991.

8. Ibid.

9. George F. Aldridge, letter to author, March 12, 1987.

10. Liles, interview.

11. Ford, *Flying Tigers*, p. 222.

12. Ibid., pp. 370–1.

13. Hill, interview.

CHAPTER 3. HENGYANG IN THE CROSSHAIRS

1. Richard Ward, *Sharkmouth, 1916–1945* (New York: Arco Publishing Co. Inc., 1970), pp. 3–4.

2. Ray Wagner, *American Combat Planes* (Garden City, N.Y.: Doubleday & Company Inc., 1968), p. 210.

3. George D. Mackie, letter to author, October 14, 1986.

4. Japanese Monograph no. 76, *Air Operations in the China Area, July 1937–August 1945* (Tokyo: Headquarters, USAFFE and Eighth U.S. Army, 1956), p. 109.

5. Ibid., p. 110.

6. Col. Raymond F. Tolliver and Trevor J. Constable, *Fighter Aces* (New York: The Macmillan Co., 1965), p. 73.

7. William M. Harris, letter to author, October 11, 1983.

8. 75th Fighter Squadron unit history, microfilm roll A0755, Maxwell Air Force Base (AFB), Ala., Air Force Historical Research Agency, July 1942.

9. Ibid.

10. 23rd Fighter Group unit history, microfilm roll B0091, Maxwell AFB, Ala., Air Force Historical Research Agency, July 1942.

11. Hill, interview.

12. Diary of Bruce K. Holloway, July 30, 1942. Gen. Bruce K. Holloway collection.

13. 16th Fighter Squadron unit history, microfilm roll A0723, Maxwell AFB, Ala., Air Force Historical Research Agency, July 1942.

14. 75th Fighter Squadron unit history, July 1942.

15. Scott, *God Is My Co-Pilot*, pp. 167–73.

16. Liles, interview.

CHAPTER 4. THE SCHOOL SQUADRON

1. Liles, interview.

2. Hill, interview.

3. Liles, interview.

4. 74th Fighter Squadron unit history, microfilm roll A0754, Maxwell AFB, Ala., Air Force Historical Research Agency, September 1942.

5. William B. Hawkins, videotape to author, 1987.

6. Lester C. Pagliuso, letter to author, July 14, 1992.

7. John M. Andrade, *U.S. Military Aircraft Designations and Serials Since 1909* (Leicester: Midland Counties Publications, 1979), pp. 99–100.

8. Holloway, diary, December 5, 1942.

9. 74th Fighter Squadron public relations form. Luther Kissick collection.

10. Hawkins, videotape.

CHAPTER 5. BRANCHING OUT

1. Lee, tape recording.

2. Bruce K. Holloway, "The P-40," *Aerospace Historian* 25, no. 3 (Fall 1978): 139.

3. Holloway, diary, September 22, 1942.

4. Ibid.

5. Ibid.

6. Ibid., September 25–27, 1942.

CHAPTER 6. DUEL IN THE EAST

1. Louis L. Snyder, *The War: A Concise History 1939–1945* (New York: Simon & Schuster, 1960), pp. 220–1.

2. Scott, *God Is My Co-Pilot*, p. 221.

3. Hill, interview.

4. Scott, *God Is My Co-Pilot*, p. 222.

5. Ibid., pp. 229–30.

6. *The Record, 11th Bomb Squadron (M)* (Nashville: Harris Press Inc., no date), p. 41.

7. Ibid.

8. A discrepancy exists between group and 76th Squadron's histories over the location of DuBois in combat. He may have been on an intercept mission at Mengtze that occurred the same day.

9. Hill, interview.

10. Jack R. Best, tape recording to author, November 1991.

11. 16th Fighter Squadron unit history, October 1942.

12. 75th Fighter Squadron unit history, November 1942.

13. Holloway, diary, November 24, 1942.

14. Glenn E. McClure, *Fire and Fall Back* (San Antonio: Barnes Press, 1975), pp. 53–57.

15. Holloway, diary, November 27, 1942.

16. Hill, interview.

CHAPTER 7. THE FIRST WINTER

1. Harris, letter.

2. Robert A. O'Neill, letter to author, January 9, 1985.

3. Holloway, diary.

4. Ibid.

5. Scott, *God Is My Co-Pilot*, p. 263.

6. Liles, interview.

7. Best, tape recording.

8. O'Neill, letter.

9. Holloway, diary, January 9, 1943.

10. Robert L. Scott, *The Day I Owned the Sky* (New York: Bantam Books, 1988), pp. 95–104.

11. Diary of William N. Reed, August 17, 1943. Jo Anna Athey collection.

12. Hill, interview.
13. 76th Fighter Squadron unit history, March 1943.
14. Holloway, diary, February 2, 1943.

CHAPTER 8. FIGHTING ON TWO FRONTS

1. 16th Fighter Squadron unit history, March 1943; 26th Fighter Squadron unit history, microfilm A0729, Maxwell AFB, Ala., Air Force Historical Research Agency, March 1943; "Daring Air Rescue Behind Enemy Lines," *Ex-CBI Roundup* (September 1951): 7; Holloway, diary, March 30, 1943.

2. Vernon J. Henderson, unpublished memoir, pp. 10–16.

3. 75th Fighter Squadron unit history, April 1943; Holloway, diary, April 24, 1943; Milt Miller, "To Hoax or Not to Hoax," *Jing Bao Journal* (August–September 1992) 39–40.

4. 74th Fighter Squadron unit history, April 1943.

5. Hawkins, videotape.

6. Lee, tape recording.

7. Robert T. Smith, letter to author, April 2, 1992.

8. McClure, *Fire and Fall Back*, p. 87.

9. James L. Lee, letter to author, February 1986.

10. Holloway, diary, April 26, 1943.

11. Ibid., April 28, 1943.

12. 23rd Fighter Group History, April 1943.

13. Robert F. Barnes, telephone interview with author, September 25, 1992.

14. Hollis M. Blackstone, letter to author, December 30, 1986.

15. Wayne G. Johnson, ed., *Chennault's Flying Tigers, 1941–1945* (Dallas: Taylor Publishing Co., 1982): p.157–8.

CHAPTER 9. THRUST AND PARRY

1. Yasuo Izawa, "Japan's Red Eagles, Part Two," *Air Classics* 8, no. 10 (August 1972): 66.

2. Holloway, diary, May 15, 1943.

3. John S. Stewart, telephone interview with author, February 2, 1993; Holloway, diary, June 20, 1943.

4. Japanese Monograph no. 76, *Air Operations in the China Area*, p. 126.

5. Hawkins, videotape.

6. Ibid.

CHAPTER 10. BUILDUP

1. Holloway, diary, July 20, 1943.

2. Hawkins, videotape.

3. Holloway, diary, July 24, 1943.

4. Ibid., July 29, 1943.

CHAPTER 11. SUMMER OFFENSIVE

1. Harvey G. Elling, letter to author, March 1984.

2. Ibid.

3. James M. Williams, letter to author, February 17, 1992.

4. Hawkins, videotape.

5. Holloway, diary, September 9, 1943.

6. William B. Evans, letter to author, November 12, 1984.

7. 75th Fighter Squadron unit history, September 1943.

8. Japanese Monograph no. 76, *Air Operations in the China Area*, pp. 137–8.

CHAPTER 12. RAID ON SHINCHIKU

1. Williams, letter.

2. Richard J. Templeton, letter to author, February 26, 1993.

3. Robert L. Milks, letter to author, January 19, 1988.

4. Hill, interview.

5. Ibid.

6. Malcolm Rosholt, *Flight in the China Air Space, 1910–1950* (Rosholt, Wisc.: Rosholt House, 1984), p. 165.

7. Hill, interview.

CHAPTER 13. DEFENDING THE RICE BOWL

1. 76th Fighter Squadron unit history, December 1943.

2. Hill, interview.

3. Diary of Charles E. Cook Jr., December 10, 1943. Col. Charles E. Cook Jr. collection.

4. Christopher Shores and Clive Williams, *Aces High* (London: Neville Spearman Ltd., 1966), p. 285.

5. Donald S. Lopez, interview with author, 1978.

6. 76th Fighter Squadron unit history, January 1943.

CHAPTER 14. QUIET BEFORE THE STORM

1. Stephen J. Bonner Jr., letter to author, February 8, 1993.

2. Vernon J. Kramer, letter to author, January 15, 1993.

3. Cook, diary, February 19, 1943.

4. John W. Wheeler, letter to author, October 17, 1988.

5. Cook, diary, February 19, 1944.

6. 76th Fighter Squadron unit history, March 1944.

7. Dr. Jones C. Laughlin, squadron medical history in the 75th Fighter Squadron unit history, April 1944.

CHAPTER 15. ICHI-GO

1. F. F. Liu, *A Military History of Modern China* (Princeton: Princeton University Press, 1956), p. 219.

2. Hill, interview.

3. William T. Watt, letter to author, November 24, 1991.

4. Oswin H. Elker, letter to author, June 30, 1991.

5. Philip C. Loofbourrow, letter to author, May 7, 1986.

6. Hill, interview.

7. Wilbur H. Morrison, *Point of No Return* (New York: Playboy Paperbacks, 1979), pp. 72–80.

8. Cook, diary, June 16, 1944.

9. Robert S. Peterson, letter to author, December 26, 1992.

10. Hill, interview.

11. Ronald M. Phillips, letter to author, October 10, 1980.

CHAPTER 16. FIRE AND FALL BACK

1. Hill, interview.

2. Cook, diary, June 27–July 5, 1944.

3. George H. Greene, letter to author, January 22, 1992.

4. Charles E. Cook Jr., letter to author, November. 24, 1992.

5. Donald L. Quigley, letter to author, November 22, 1991.

6. Mervin E. Beard, letter to author, July 15, 1991.

7. McClure, *Fire and Fall Back*, p. 191.

8. Watt, letter.

9. Hill, interview.

10. Louis W. Weber, letter to author, October 25, 1986.

11. Peterson, letter.

CHAPTER 17. GUERRILLA OPERATIONS

1. Cook, letter.

2. Bernard Fudge, letter to author, February 2, 1987.

3. H. L. Kirkpatrick, letter to author, August 20, 1986.

4. Greene, letter.

5. Hill, interview.

6. Beard, letter.

7. Diary of Robert P. Miller, June 4–November 9, 1944. Robert M. Fay collection.

8. Berthold H. Peterson, letter to author, January 18, 1992.

9. McClure, *Fire and Fall Back*, pp. 210–11.

10. Edward F. Rector, interview with author, October 13, 1991.

CHAPTER 18. THE LAST WITHDRAWAL

1. Wheeler, letter.

2. Milt Miller, "Malfunction," *Jing Bao Journal* (June–July 1991): 16.

3. 118th Tactical Reconnaissance Squadron unit history, microfilm A0917, Maxwell AFB, Ala., Air Force Historical Research Agency, December 1944.

4. Art Goodworth, letter to his parents, December 25, 1944. Art Goodworth letter collection.

5. John C. Conn, letter to author, January 7, 1992.

6. Raymond A. Crowell, tape recording to author, April 1992.

7. Glenn J. Geyer, letter to author, January 9, 1992.

CHAPTER 19. FINAL VICTORY

1. Harold A. Bedient, letter to author, August 10, 1989.

2. Joel E. Beezley, letter to author, January 19, 1992.

3. Alfred F. Griffy, letter to author, October 30, 1991.

4. Diary of Jerome P. Ellis, April 2, 1945. Jerome P. Ellis collection.

5. Diary of Russell E. Packard, April 7–May 2, 1945. Russell E. Packard collection.

6. Crowell, tape recording.

7. Beezley, letter.

8. Vern Haugland, *The Eagle Squadrons* (New York: Ziff-Davis Flying Books, 1979), p. 127.

9. Ed H. Lawman Jr., letter to author, December 10, 1991.

10. William H. Quimby, letter to author, September 14, 1993.

Bibliography

BOOKS

Andrade, John M. *U.S. Military Aircraft Designations and Serials Since 1909*. Leicester, U.K.: Midland Counties Publications, 1979.

Buchanan, A. Russell. *The United States and World War II*. New York: Harper Torchbooks, 1964.

Byrd, Martha. *Chennault: Giving Wings to the Tiger*. Tuscaloosa: The University of Alabama Press, 1987.

Chivers, Sydney P. *Flying Tigers*. Canoga Park, Calif.: Challenge Publications Inc., no date.

Christy, Joe, and Jeff Ethell. *P-40 Hawks at War*. New York: Charles Scribner's Sons, 1980.

Cohen, Stan. *Destination: Tokyo*. Missoula, Mont.: Pictorial Histories Publishing Co., 1983.

Cornelius, Wanda, and Thayne Short. *Ding Hao: America's Air War in China, 1937–1945*. Gretna, La.: Pelican Publishing Co. Inc., 1980.

Ethell, Jeffrey. *Mustang: A Documentary History*. New York: Jane's Publishing Inc., 1981.

Ford, Daniel. *Flying Tigers*. Washington, D.C.: Smithsonian Institution Press, 1991.

Harmon, Tom. *Pilots Also Pray*. New York: Thomas Y. Crowell Co., 1944.

Haugland, Vern. *The Eagle Squadrons*. New York: Ziff-Davis Flying Books, 1979.

Heiferman, Ron. *Flying Tigers: Chennault in China*. New York: Ballantine Books Inc., 1971.

Hess, William N. *Fighting Mustang: The Chronicle of the P-51*. Garden City, N.Y.: Doubleday & Co. Inc., 1970.

Japanese Monograph no. 76. *Air Operations in the China Area, July 1937–August 1945*. Tokyo: Headquarters, USAFFE and Eighth U.S. Army, 1956.

Johnson, Wayne G., ed. *Chennault's Flying Tigers, 1941–1945*. Dallas: Taylor Publishing Co., 1982.

—— (ed.) *Chennault's Flying Tigers, 1941–1945*. Vol. II. Dallas: Taylor Publishing Co., 1983.

Kaplan, Frederic M., Julain M. Sobin, and Arne J. de Keijzer. *The China Guidebook*. Boston: Houghton Mifflin Co., 1986.

Kissick, Luther C. Jr. *Guerrilla One*. Manhattan, Kans.: Sunflower University Press, 1983.

Little, Wallace H. *Tiger Sharks!* Memphis: Castle Books, no date.

Liu, F. F. *A Military History of Modern China*. Princeton: Princeton University Press, 1956.

Lopez, Donald S. *Into the Teeth of the Tiger*. New York: Bantam Books, 1986.

McClure, Glenn E. *Fire and Fall Back*. San Antonio: Barnes Press, 1975.

McDowell, Ernest R. *The P-40 Kittyhawk*. New York: Arco Publishing Co., 1968.

Morrison, Wilbur H. *Point of No Return*. New York: Playboy Paperbacks, 1979.

Olynyk, Frank J. *AVG & USAAF (China-Burma-India Theater) Credits for Destruction of Enemy Aircraft in Air-to-Air Combat, World War II*. Aurora, Ohio: Self-published, 1986.

Pistole, Larry M. *The Pictorial History of the Flying Tigers*. Orange, Va.: Moss Publications, 1981.

The Record, 11th Bombardment Squadron (M). Nashville: Harris Press Inc., no date.

Rosholt, Malcolm. *Days of the Ching Pao*. Amherst, Wisc.: Palmer Publications Inc., 1978.

————. *Claire L. Chennault: A Tribute*. Rosholt, Wisc.: Flying Tigers of the 14th Air Force Association, 1983.

————. *Flight in the China Air Space, 1910–1950*. Rosholt, Wisc.: Rosholt House, 1984.

Rust, Kenn C., and Stephen Muth. *Fourteenth Air Force Story*. Temple City, Calif.: Historical Aviation Album, 1977.

Schultz, Duane. *The Maverick War: Chennault and the Flying Tigers*. New York: St. Martin's Press, 1987.

Scott, Robert L. *God Is My Co-Pilot*. New York: Charles Scribner's Sons, 1943.

————. *The Day I Owned the Sky*. New York: Bantam Books, 1988.

Shores, Christopher, and Clive Williams. *Aces High*. London: Neville Spearman Ltd., 1966.

Smith, Robert M. *With Chennault in China*. Blue Ridge Summit, Pa.: Tab Books, Inc., 1984.

Snyder, Louis L. *The War: A Concise History 1939–1945*. New York: Simon & Schuster, 1960.

Szuscikiewicz, Paul. *Flying Tigers*. New York: Gallery Books, 1990.

Taylor, John W. R. *Combat Aircraft of the World from 1909 to the Present*. New York: G. P. Putnam's Sons, 1969.

Thorpe, Donald W. *Japanese Army Air Force Camouflage and Markings, World War II*. Fallbrook, Calif.: Aero Publishers Inc., 1968.

Tolliver, Col. Raymond F., and Trevor J. Constable. *Fighter Aces*. New York: The Macmillan Co., 1965.

Tuchman, Barbara W. *Stilwell and the American Experience in China, 1911–45*. New York: The Macmillan Company, 1971.

Wagner, Ray. *American Combat Planes*. Garden City, N.Y.: Doubleday & Company Inc., 1968.

Ward, Richard. *Sharkmouth, 1916–1945*. New York: Arco Publishing Co. Inc., 1970.

UNPUBLISHED UNIT HISTORIES

23rd Fighter Group headquarters. Microfilm roll B0091, frames 0682–end. Maxwell Air Force Base, Ala., Air Force Historical Research Agency, undated.

16th Fighter Squadron. Microfilm roll A0723, frames 0222–1778. Maxwell Air Force Base, Ala., Air Force Historical Research Agency, undated.

26th Fighter Squadron. Microfilm roll A0728, frame 1443. Maxwell Air Force Base, Ala., Air Force Historical Research Agency, undated.

74th Fighter Squadron. Microfilm roll A0754, frames 1181–end. Maxwell Air Force Base, Ala., Air Force Historical Research Agency, undated.

75th Fighter Squadron. Microfilm roll A0755, all frames. Maxwell Air Force Base, Ala., Air Force Historical Research Agency, undated.

76th Fighter Squadron. Microfilm roll A0756, all frames. Maxwell Air Force Base, Ala., Air Force Historical Research Agency, undated.

118th Tactical Reconnaissance Squadron. Microfilm roll A0917, frames 0377–1991. Maxwell Air Force Base, Ala., Air Force Historical Research Agency, undated.

PERIODICALS

Bauer, Daniel. "Legend of the China Skies." *Air Classics* 24, no. 10 (October 1988): 14–23, 67–73.

————"Legend of the China Skies." *Air Classics* 24, no. 11 (November 1988): 16–22, 60–67.

Britton, Tom. "51st Insignia and Early History—Homer's Volunteer Group." *AAHS Journal* 25, no. 3 (Fall 1980): 240.

"Daring Air Rescue Behind Enemy Lines." *Ex-CBI Roundup* (September 1951): 7.

Farmer, James H. "Hollywood's Flying Tiger." *Wings* 9, no. 4 (August 1979): 26–34, 49.

Holloway, Bruce K. "The P-40." *Aerospace Historian* 25, no. 3 (fall 1978): 139–40.

Izawa, Yasuo. "Japan's Red Eagles, Part Two." *Air Classics* 8, no. 10 (August 1972): 66.

Miller, Milt. "Malfunction." *Jing Bao Journal* (June–July 1991): 16.

————. "One-Man Air Force." *Air Classics* 16, no. 9 (September 1980): 62–67.

————"To Hoax or Not to Hoax." *Jing Bao Journal* (August–September 1992): 39–40.

Minnich, Mike. "Tiger in the Sky: The Saga of the AVG." *Air Enthusiast Quarterly*, no. 4 (Winter 1977): 113–29.

Index

About the Author

CARL MOLESWORTH is an Air Force veteran and the editor of the *Pacific Builder & Engineer* magazine. He is the author of *Wing to Wing*, a history of the Chinese–American Composite Wing, and coauthor of *Gabby*, an autobiography of renowned fighter ace Francis S. Gabreski. He lives near Mount Vernon, Washington.